D0983547

THE LIBERAL POLITICS OF JOHN LOCKE

THE
LIBERAL POLITICS
OF
JOHN LOCKE

BY

M. SELIGER

FREDERICK A. PRAEGER, *Publishers*

New York · Washington

BOOKS THAT MATTER

*Published in the United States of America in 1969
by Frederick A. Praeger, Inc., Publishers
111 Fourth Avenue, New York, N.Y. 10003*

© *1968, in England, by George Allen & Unwin Ltd., London, England*

All rights reserved

Library of Congress Catalog Card Number : 69-11606

Printed in Great Britain

TO EVA, MY WIFE

ACKNOWLEDGEMENTS

I owe a special debt of gratitude to the two outstanding English Locke scholars, Mr. Peter Laslett of Trinity College, Cambridge, and Mr. Maurice Cranston of the London School of Economics and Political Science. On reading the first chapters in the autumn of 1962, they urged me to write a full-scale study of Lockeian politics, instead of confining myself to a few select issues for comparison with what I had already written and published on French liberal thought. Mr. Laslett has read the first draft, comprising then half of the book in its present shape, and commented on it as well as on part of the last but one draft. Discussions and correspondence with him have always been stimulating, sometimes they have revealed disagreement, but have never failed to be conducive to the improvement of the book. I owe Peter Laslett a debt which can never be repaid. I am likewise indebted to Maurice Cranston for his comments on the first draft, his continuous advice and unflagging encouragement when it was most needed.

My appreciation is extended to Mr. John Plamenatz of Nuffield College, Oxford, for his discerning comments on the first draft; to Sir Isaiah Berlin for reading the draft and discussing Locke with me on several occasions; to Professors John W. Yolton of York University, Canada, and Hans Aarsleff of Princeton for favouring me with detailed comments on issues connected with Locke's conception of natural law; to Professor Raymond Polin of the Sorbonne for a lively exchange of views in Jerusalem. It goes without saying that none of the aforementioned friends and colleagues bears any responsibility for the views I have seen fit to advance. Indeed, the fact that I present my views often in contradistinction to other interpretations seems to me to call for a somewhat unusual acknowledgement. Since it is hardly avoidable that the recording of disagreement with other scholars should outweigh that of agreement, I should like to stress that wrestling with interpretations which I found unacceptable has on a number of occasions made me aware of problems which otherwise might have escaped my notice. I feel particularly indebted in this respect to the fascinating expositions of Professor Leo Strauss.

My students who participated in the Locke seminar of 1963-4 have been helpful in that their reactions have sometimes indicated where my theses were in need of further elaboration. I probably owe not only thanks but an apology to friends and colleagues here and abroad, who on the slightest provocation have had to endure detailed expositions on any matter related to Locke, providing me

ACKNOWLEDGEMENTS

thus with opportunities of testing the consistency of conclusions by a knowledgeable audience.

Drs. K. M. Baker and S. Applebaum have amended the English of the first drafts; Sidra Esrachi has dealt with two particularly difficult chapters; Max Nurok, the Dublin-born scholar of classics and philosophy, an Israeli diplomat who carries on editing as a hobby, has checked on and improved these efforts. In all stages, but especially in the final preparation of the manuscript for the printer, my wife has rendered invaluable help. This is only one, and not the most important, reason for dedicating the book to her.

I should also like to thank my assistants Miss Raphaela Bilski and Mr. Michael Freeden for checking the typescript and the references to the Lockeian text, as well as for otherwise helpful suggestions. Mr. Freeden did the final checking and assisted in reading the proofs.

Chapter II, the last section of Chapter IX and Chapter X contain in revised form material previously published in two articles: 'Natural Law and the Foundations of Politics,' *Journal of the History of Ideas*, July-September 1963 and 'Locke's Theory of Revolutionary Action,' *The Western Political Quarterly*, September 1963. I am grateful to the Editors of both journals for having accepted these articles with the foreknowledge that they were going to form part of this book.

My thanks for financial assistance go to the English chapter of the Friends of the Hebrew University. Their generosity has enabled me to spend a year in England. They have extended further support which together with the assistance afforded by my University have made it possible to see the venture through to its completion.

Last not least, I want to thank my daughters Daniela and Yael for their patience with an all too often preoccupied father.

Jerusalem, 1967   M.S.

CONTENTS

ACKNOWLEDGEMENTS   *page* 9

I. INTRODUCTORY   17
   1. Liberal Theory and Practice   17
     A. Non-Democratic Minimal Government   18
     B. The Inner Unity of the Liberal Outlook   21
   2. The Strands of Political Philosophy   26
     A. Facts   26
     B. 'Oughts'   28
   3. The Approach to Locke   31
     A. Contradictions and Historical Conditions 32
     B. The Test of Consistency   36

PART ONE: METAPOLITICS AND POLITICS   43

II. NATURAL LAW   45
   1. Rational Politics and Ethical Pluralism   45
   2. Knowability   49
     A. Unequal Knowledge: 49
       a. Equality and Inequality, 49
       b. The Many and the Few, 53
     B. Scriptural Evidence: 56
       a. Supposed Deviations, 56
       b. Overt Biblical Criticism, 58
     C. Self-Preservation and Traditional Values   62
   3. Applicability   66
     A. Natural Law and Consent   66
     B. Moral Deterioration and Positive Law   71
     C. Individual and Collective Consent   75

III. THE NATURAL AND THE POLITICAL CONDITION   82
   1. The Hypothetical State of Nature   83
     A. Man's Perpetual Status   83
     B. Empirical and Historical Verification   85
     C. Social and Political Existence   88
   2. The State of Nature, the State of War and Political Society   91
     A. The Relationship in Principle   91

Contents

B. The Application: 94
    a. Uniform Tenor of Argumentation, 94
    b. Absence of Governmentless States and Stages of Socio-Economic Development, 96
3. The State of Nature in Political Society   101
A. The Cause – Arbitrary Rule   101
B. The Consequence: War between Political Society and Arbitrary Rulers   103

IV. THE EXTREMITIES OF THE POLITICAL CONDITION   107

1. The Dissolution of Government and the Dissolution of Society – Connections   107
2. The Dissolution of Society   109
A. The Moral and Practical Limits of Dissolution through Foreign Conquest   109
B. Colonial Conquest and Slavery: 114
    a. Explicit Exception to the Interdict of Annexation, 114
    b. Implicit Limitation of the Universal Applicability of Slavery, 118
3. Dissolution of Government from Within   124
A. The Survival of Society   124
B. Democratic Interregnum   127
4. Power   130
A. The Concept   131
B. Might and Right   135

PART TWO: METAPOLITICS AND HISTORY   139

V. PROPERTY RELATIONS   141

1. Limitation of Appropriation   141
A. Portents of Capitalism in Retrospective   141
B. The Natural Limitations: 144
    a. Validity and Effectiveness, 144
    b. The Effect: Moderate Possessions, 149
2. The Introduction of Money   153
A. The Causal Nexus   153
B. Ends and Means   157

Contents

3. Consent in Property Relations   159
   A. Contractual Interdependence   160
   B. Consent as the Function of Freedom   163
4. Political and Economic Power   165
   A. The Inclusion of the Economic in the Political Sphere: 165
      a. The Right of Property – A Natural Right among Others, 165
      b. Law and Freedom, 167
   B. The Supremacy of the Sphere of Politics: 170
      a. Moral Superiority, 170
      b. Purposes of Governmental Interference, 172
      c. Assurances of Governmental Limitation of Distress, 176

VI. THE ORIGINAL OF PROPERTY   180
1. The Primeval Community of Things – Grotius and Pufendorf   180
   A. Positive and Negative Community   180
   B. Conditions for Negative Community   184
2. The Primacy of Private Property: The Rational Argument   187
   A. The Universal Common for Private Appropriation: 188
      a. God's Gifts and Men's Claims, 188
      b. Usage Requires Individual Appropriation, 190
   B. Private and Collective Ownership: 194
      a. The Unity of Natural Law Ethics, 194
      b. Liberalism Divorced from Socialism, 198
3. Confirmation of the Primacy of Private Property   203
   A. The Bible   203
   B. Philosophy   206

VII. THE FOUNDATION OF POLITICAL SOCIETY   209
1. Paternal and Political Authority   210
   A. Paternal and Parental Power   210
   B. Father and Monarch: 213
      a. The Right over Life and Death, 213
      b. Legislative Authority, 214
      c. Household and Commonwealth, 216

CONTENTS

2. Incorporation by Tacit Consent   219
   A. Natural and Contractual Foundations: 219
      a. *Ius Paternum* and *Consensus Populi*, 219
      b. Voluntariness and Naturalness, 221
      c. The Terms of the Compact, 223
   B. Historical Incorporation – Inevitability and Choice   226
3. Reason and History   230
   A. Precedent   230
   B. Rational Politics and Common Law Tenets   233

VIII. ONE-MAN RULE IN HISTORICAL PERSPECTIVE   238
   1. Prerequisites for Continuity   238
   A. Predispositions and Environment   238
   B. The Ruler's Quality   241
   2. Absolute Monarchy and Arbitrary Rule   244
   A. Arbitrary Power and the Form of Government   244
   B. The Legitimacy of Absolute Monarchy   247
   3. Royal Absolutism and Filmerism   250
   A. Lawful Kingship, Tyranny and Usurpation   251
   B. The Use of Traditionalist Views and the Abuse of
      Filmer   254
SYNOPSIS   256

PART THREE: THE ACCEPTABLE REGIME   265

IX. INDIVIDUAL CONSENT   267
   1. Acceptance and Rejection of Membership   268
   A. Reaffirmation: 268
      a. The Indirect Evidence for Acceptance, 268
      b. The Separability of Property and Political Rights
        and Obligations, 271
      c. The Dispensability of an Express Declaration, 274
   B. Emigration: 278
      a. The Restriction, 278
      b. The Evidence to the Contrary, 280
   2. Suffrage and Citizenship   283
   A. Suffrage for the Propertied: 283
      a. The Thesis, 284
      b. The Application, 287
   B. Citizenship for the Propertyless   290

Contents

X. POPULAR CONSENT – A THEORY OF REVOLUTIONARY
ACTION   294
  1. The Nature of the People's Judgement   294
    A. Disapproval of Wrongs Inflicted by Rulers   294
    B. The Adequacy of Locke's Theory of Consent: 297
      a. Dissent and Consent, 297
      b. Acts and Attitudes, 300
  2. The Majority's Power and Its Use   302
    A. The Majority Principle and the Greater Force 303
    B. The Improvidence of the Majority: 306
      a. Support of Arbitrary Rulers and Conquerors, 306
      b. The Will of the Majority: Its Indifference and Forbearance, 307
  3. The Frequency of Revolt   311
    A. 'Many Revolutions'   312
    B. Rebellion and Rightful Resistance   315
  4. Towards a Modern Conception of Revolution   320

XI. EXECUTIVE AND LEGISLATURE   324
  1. Sovereignty   325
  2. Subordination and Balance of Powers   328
    A. The Balance of Power and the Balance between the Branches of Government   328
    B. The Executive's Share in Legislation   331
    C. Locke – Montesquieu – Madison   335
  3. The Executive's Prerogatives *vis-à-vis* the Legislature   339
    A. Adjournment and Dissolution   340
    B. The Reform of the Franchise: 343
      a. The Pragmatic Justification, 343
      b. The Incongruous Argument, 345

XII. AUTHORITARIAN REPRESENTATION AND CONSTITUTIONALISM   350
  1. Confrontations   350
    A. Executive, Legislators and Revolt   350
    B. Just and Unjust Prerogative   353
    C. Limitation by Consent and Trust   356

CONTENTS

2. Specific Conditions and Limitations 359
 A. Emergency Conditions 359
 B. Direct Legal Limitation 362
 C. Indirect Legal Limitation 364
3. The Godlike 'Representer' 367

BIBLIOGRAPHY 373

CHAPTER I

INTRODUCTORY

T HE following attempt to re-assess Locke's political teachings grew out of increasing doubts as to the adequacy of prevailing opinions concerning what is, or is not, part of the historical tradition of liberal thought. The reasons for these doubts, and the bearing they have on a more comprehensive presentation of Lockeian politics than has so far been available, demand some prefatory explanation.

I. LIBERAL THEORY AND PRACTICE

As a recent writer has accurately remarked, criticism of liberalism from Right and Left has blurred the differences between early modern liberal thought and that of its continuators.[1] Yet, in arguing that early liberalism laid the foundation for the progressive devaluation of politics, the same writer himself enlarged upon a major theme in the long-prevailing assessment of liberalism. That assessment corresponds for the most part to what English idealist philosophers eventually found unacceptable in the liberal thought of the eighteenth and nineteenth centuries. The influence of German idealism, and especially of Hegel, easily accounts for the fact that early liberal theories have been criticized from the Right and from the Left, and even by liberals like T. H. Green, for an overemphasis upon individual liberty and a corresponding neglect of the positive aspects of community. Building upon this common foundation, conservative criticism has censured early modern liberal thought for 'mechanistic' conceptions which obscure, as it were, the naturalness of political organization. It has been held that its exaggerated belief in reason leaves little room for the appraisal of irrational motivation, for 'the cake of custom' and historical experience in general. The liberal state has been painted as a predominately artificial contrivance devised for men's convenience, in which 'minimal' or 'negative' government would have been more than enough. Liberal government has been regarded as weak govern-

[1] S. S. Wolin, *Politics and Vision* (London, 1960), 293, and Chs. VIII and IX in general.

17

ment by definition, the main purpose of the division of political authority being to protect individual liberty and especially to guarantee uninhibited acquisitiveness. At first sight, this evaluation of liberalism would seem to be borne out by Locke's theory of the social compact, his appeal to reason over and above history, his division of political authority and his view of private property as the epitome of the individual rights consecrated by the law of nature, which is the law of reason and of God.

A. Non-Democratic Minimal Government

Liberalism does not identify a minimal state with weak government. To think so is to impute to it a serious fallacy. Clearly, to function effectively as the instrument of the socially and economically successful minority of society, a government can hardly be allowed to be weak. In the first place, specific political arrangements must be maintained, if the less fortunate members of society, who for the better part of history have been in the majority, are to be prevented from determining the composition of governmental bodies. Otherwise government interference with the aims and policies of privileged minorities would be legally possible. In fact, it is for this very reason that liberals, too, have for centuries denied the masses formal participation in politics. Moreover, early liberals, such as Locke, may have thought it easier than their successors in the second half of the nineteenth century to perpetuate political arrangements to that effect. They were no less aware than later liberals of the authoritarian and elitist character of the political arrangements by which limited political participation is tenable.

It has not escaped notice, of course, that in practice liberal politics has generally been associated with anything but weak and unoppressive government. The moral indignation and hatred that Marx, Engels and Lenin nursed against 'bourgeois society' stemmed from the realization that its 'action-committee', the state, lacked neither the will nor the means to assert its authority. The state could not have been supposed to guarantee the exploitation of the majority without a considerable show of force. Nor could it otherwise help to generate the final outburst of revolutionary zeal which signals the complete polarization of bourgeois society. Marx and Engels largely underplayed the fact that so far the bourgeois 'action-committee' had kept the masses economically as well as politically under-privileged mostly by withholding the suffrage from them or manipulating it to their disadvantage. And while the deprecation of universal suffrage as a fundamental hallmark of political democracy has survived Marx and Engels, for example in the conception of Schumpeter,[2] neither Marxists nor non-Marxists have failed to realize that political non-interference in the objectives of some people almost invariably means political interference in the interests of others. Statesmen who were keen on freedom of trade nevertheless 'had to interfere with interferences'[3]; and this applies also to the policy of governmental non-intervention in socio-economic issues such as working hours or wages. The authoritarian character of interference with interferences is particularly obvious wherever the freedom of organization is directly or indirectly obstructed by law.

Colonial expansion, too, contradicts the fiction that liberal government must necessarily be weak. The historical fallacy of associating the practice of liberal rule with 'minimalness' or 'negativeness' has already been recognized. It has even been acknowledged that, on the plane of theory, 'realism and liberalism can very well go together'.[4] It is seldom realized, however, to what extent strong and high-handed government has been sustained by liberal theory.

When Robert Michels broke new ground with his theory of 'democracy and the iron law of oligarchy', he recognized that liberal ideology did not base its aspirations upon the masses and that, for the liberals, the masses were no more than a necessary evil.[5] Yet the fact that liberalism had become committed to universal suffrage caused Michels to adopt a course of argument which presupposed an original liberal commitment to democracy. In the light of this erroneous assumption, he assessed the attempts of liberals at a conciliation with monarchic autocracy.[6] Instead of confronting liberal and democratic principles in historical perspective, he confused them retrospectively. He failed to see that, for the greater part of its history, the liberal tradition had been opposed to general suffrage, and hence to democracy, and that it was also on this ground

---

[2] J. A. Schumpeter, *Capitalism, Socialism and Democracy* (1942. Harper Torchbooks, 1962), 244, 276.

[3] Cp. C. J. Friedrich, *Constitutional Government and Democracy* (rev. ed., New York, 1950), 25.

[4] Cp. G. Sartori, *Democratic Theory* (Detroit, 1962), 40. See also F. Neumann, *The Democratic and the Authoritarian State* (Glencoe, 1957), 22, and Wolin, *op. cit.*, 312.

[5] R. Michels, *Political Parties* (Dover Books, 1959), 7.

[6] *Ibid.*, 9-10.

that it had in the past come to terms with the autocratic prerogatives of monarchs. Had this been taken into account by Michels and those who followed him, they might not have been satisfied with a realistic juxtaposition of democratic ideology and modern democratic practice. They might have become aware of the attempts, which culminated in the political theory of John Stuart Mill, to reconcile democratic theory with the elitism which non-democratic liberal theory had all along put forth in the form of both an assertion of ethico-political norms and the different capabilities of men. As it is, a renowned political sociologist still regards as something of a revelation the mere suggestion that the liberal tradition lacked a popular base and that in essence it is '*perhaps* an elitist tradition'.[7] Conversely, even when Locke's theory is credited with having anticipated almost all the tenets of the English idealists, this is not seen as detracting from Locke's supposedly democratic outlook, and his concessions to executive prerogatives are roundly asserted to be in accord with democratic principles.[8]

As for the general historical significance of both democratic and non-democratic liberal ideas, there is certainly something to be said in favour of considering them in terms of the progressive devaluation of politics and its autonomy.[9] But if all liberal thought had sought to assign an inferior status to politics, liberal theory might still reflect the awareness of irrefutable demands of politics in its own right and not merely for as long as it has not become what it is destined to be. It is trite to observe that ends require appropriate means as much as the available means restrict the realization of ends, even if the appraisal of available means does not (as common sense suggests that it should) circumscribe the conception of ends in the first place. In any case, political means are needed to reduce the status and prestige of politics as well as to keep it restrained. Much as liberalism has proceeded from premises which have served anarchism and, in the long run has tended to deprive politics either of its autonomy or of its prestige as the predominant means in the implementation of human values, it has remained aware of the continued importance of the political system.

Liberalism is characterized not by serious consideration of the

---

[7] S. M. Lipset, *Political Man* (New York, 1960), 97, quoting A. A. Rogow, 'The Revolt Against Social Equality,' *Dissent* IV (1957), 370. The italics are mine.

[8] Thus W. Kendall, 'John Locke and the Doctrine of Majority-Rule,' *Illinois Studies in the Social Sciences*, Vol. XXVI, 2, 1941.

[9] Cp. Wolin, *op. cit.*, 286 f.

dispensability of the state but by the contrary emphasis on constitutionalism, that is, the insistence on political guarantees for the maintenance of individual liberties. Only as a combination of a particular philosophy of values with an elaborate theory of political organization is the liberal tradition a specific product of the political tradition of the West, and indeed only one of the West's political traditions. The appearance of one or another liberal tenet in it does not make a system of thought part of the liberal tradition.[10] If ideological pluralism were accepted as a generally applicable rule, the recognition that non-liberal systems contain liberal tenets might be paralleled by the view that liberal systems exhibit illiberal elements. Even so, and especially in view of the prevailing image of liberalism which does not fit observed liberal practice, the essential question is whether such deviations are only occasional aberrations or not. If no consistently justified concessions to authoritarianism and extra-legal practice exist in representative liberal theory, it must be pronounced invariably at cross-purposes with liberal practice. This conclusion has been avoided only because the questions which lead to it have been left unasked and where they have been hinted at, no attempt has been made to follow up their implications. To imply by default, or to assume more or less inadvertently, that liberal practice and theory are incompatible is to assume either the intellectual inadequacy or the dishonesty of liberal thought. It means to assume that liberal political philosophy has constantly misunderstood, or turned a blind eye on, the nature and requirements of political power.

B. The Inner Unity of the Liberal Outlook

Misapprehensions about liberal theory are largely the result of endeavours to cope with the urgent political problems of our century. Just as in these endeavours liberalism has often been indiscriminately associated with democracy, it has also been over-sharply set apart from it.

Mosca, Pareto and Michels, each of them moved by different ideological purposes, were concerned to show that in practice democratic institutions fail to live up to the idea they claim to implement.

---

[10] This is obscured in F. Watkins, *The Political Tradition of the West, A Study in the Development of Modern Liberalism* (Cambridge, Mass., 1948) and to some extent also in G. de Ruggiero's classic, *The History of European Liberalism*, translated by R. S. Collingwood (Beacon Press, 1959. First published Oxford, 1927).

Yet democratic theory itself has been seen to contain ideas which justify totalitarian dictatorship as the means towards the ultimate realization of radical egalitarian democracy. Liberal theory has been pronounced intrinsically different in this respect. Lord Lindsay has traced to Rousseau the 'totalitarian' conception of sovereignty, taken up by the French Revolution, and contrasted it with the Anglo-Saxon conception and realization of the natural rights theory.[11] To Bertrand de Jouvenel the phrase 'la démocratie totalitaire' denotes that stage in the 'natural history' of power in which the democratic extension of liberty leads to an unprecedented governmental supremacy; when the defence of individual liberty against a government acting in the name of all becomes illusory, if not a sin. Rather than prevent the eventual degradation of politics and liberty under dictatorship, democratic principles are found capable of promoting it.[12] J. L. Talmon[13] has modernized and refined the reaction of Burke and the French theocrats to the French Revolution and to the Enlightenment which begat it. The totalitarian practice of the Left, he argues, emanates from the very nature of the ideologically determined patterns of behaviour attendant upon, or engendering, the ideal of radical democracy. The totalitarian practice of the Jacobins, as well as of the Bolsheviks appears, therefore, due to the paradoxes in the political messianism of the Left, as if the requirements of conquering and maintaining political power had never predominated over ideology. Thus, where totalitarianism is concerned, ideology and theory, i.e. the consciousness of what ought to be done and what actually is done, are given more than their due. Liberal ideology and theory are given less than their due exactly because an idealized version is read back into the historical tradition of liberal thought. Its realistic concern with political power as the means of safeguarding ideals remains unconsidered or, to use the language of psychoanalysis, is being suppressed under the weight of upholding liberalism as the antidote against totalitarianism. Only radical egalitarianism would reflect a paradox of freedom on the philosophical level; only egalitarian ideology would seem to acknowledge that one might have to resort to extra-legal coercion in order finally to reduce coercion and increase freedom.

---

[11] A. D. Lindsay, *The Modern Democratic State*, Vol. I (London, 5th impr., 1951; 1st ed., 1943), 115 f.

[12] B. de Jouvenel, *Du Pouvoir* (rev. ed., Genève, 1947), 313 f.

[13] J. L. Talmon, *The Origins of Totalitarian Democracy* (London, 1952).

According to this view, doctrinairism is the monopoly of leftist messianism while liberal thought is by definition empiricist.[14] It is admitted, however, that the liberal's reliance on eternal reason gives way to empiricist and pragmatic arguments only when he is in power; he has to reject the claims made in the name of reason if they are made by the politically underprivileged.[15] All this means overlooking the fact that liberal philosophy has from its modern beginnings adopted a doctrinaire attitude in the derivation of the liberty of man from the command of the law of nature and of reason, but has conditioned the enjoyment of liberty on the different abilities of men to live by reason. The qualification of the general principle is clearly grounded on empirical fact. Liberal thought has therefore not turned empiricist only the moment liberals got into power. It is also said that 'the liberals of the early nineteenth century attack the very notion of emergency and preventive action'. It is stated, on the other hand, that 'illiberal measures . . . were applied by Guizot against democracy on behalf of liberal values and on the unshakable assumption that democracy means social revolution'.[16] Yet the political doctrine and philosophy of history of both Mme de Staël and Guizot expressly allowed for the unconstitutional breakthrough, guided by the enlightened few, as well as for the representation of the aspirations of a century by a great man.[17] If these are also corollaries of democratic radicalism, democratic theory must in this respect too be considered as a continuation of liberal theory, to say nothing of the inner unity of liberalism as a philosophy of values and a strategy of politics. One cannot define liberal political philosophy as empiricist and yet consider it at cross-purposes with liberal politics. If a political philosophy requires that fundamental tenets have to be gainsaid in the practice that goes with its realization, it is not empiricist but opportunist.

Liberalism has become an intellectual and political force by confronting an established theory and practice of government with a new vision and definite doctrine of politics. (Or is it not a political vision which guides the attempt to set limits to political power?) However unchiliastic (because less optimistic than often assumed),

---

[14] Cp. Talmon, *op. cit.*, 20, on Mme de Staël and Benjamin Constant.

[15] J. L. Talmon, *Political Messianism* (London, 1960), 325.

[16] *Ibid.*, 320; 328–9.

[17] See my 'Napoleonic Authoritarianism in French Liberal Thought,' in A. Fuks and I. Halperin (ed.), *Scripta Hierosolymitana*, vol. VII (Jerusalem, 1961), esp. 260 f., 276 f. and 288, note 114.

however curbed by anxiety[18] or egotistic circumspection, liberal doctrines and aspirations grew out of dissatisfaction with an existing political order and demanded its change. Representative liberal thinkers judged the changes they advocated as fundamental ones, even if they considered them only as an amelioration of the existing regime.[19] They knew that the powers that be will resist moderate changes more than radical ones, because it is more difficult to justify the preservation of an existing order in the face of moderate demands. Almost from its inception, modern liberalism had, therefore, justified revolt and adopted a doctrinaire attitude to decisive issues. Democratic revolutionism and doctrinairism merely amplify, although they also complicate, the revolutionism and doctrinairism of their liberal predecessors.

The implication that liberalism denies in theory what it accepts in practice seems no longer self-contradictory and unhistorical as soon as a distinction is drawn between etatist and non-etatist liberalism. To the extent that in this way the practice of continental and Anglo-Saxon liberalism may be set apart,[20] the question is still whether this holds good also for the theoretical and ideological foundations which are at the root of modern liberal systems of thought. Aside altogether from the fact that Hobbes' absolutism rests on rationalistic, individualistic and contractual foundations upon which Locke elaborated, there is the generally accepted view of the widespread influence of the *Second Treatise* beyond the shores of Britain, and especially in France and America. Indeed, it was only after ascertaining the co-existence in French liberal thought of authoritarian and extra-constitutional notions with the more common liberal elitist preoccupations[21] that I asked myself how much of this, if anything at all, could be found in the *Second Treatise*.

As a detailed examination will show, Locke's concessions to authoritarian leadership and extra-legal action are fundamental to his political theory. They counterbalance his allowances for the principle of popular participation in politics. In fact, with the single

---

[18] Cp. Wolin, *op. cit.*, 293–4, 315 f.

[19] M. Cowling, *Mill and Liberalism* (Cambridge, 1963), 157, overstates the case in denying any difference in this respect between liberalism and other doctrines.

[20] Cp. M. Cranston, *Freedom, A New Analysis* (London, 1953), 69 f., 83 f. See also Lindsay, *op. cit.*, 126. Ruggiero, *op. cit.*, 12, 347 f., saw an antithetical development of liberalism in eighteenth-century England and France giving way to a synthesis in the nineteenth century.

[21] See the essay mentioned in note 17.

exception of the right to revolt, these allowances are not genuinely democratic. The distinction between liberal and democratic principles, constitutional and extra-constitutional forms of action, is of special importance here. For democratic radicalism, but hardly ever liberalism, is usually saddled with the quandary of professing constitutionalism on the one hand and of allowing its suspension on the other, as a means of instituting, improving or guaranteeing constitutionalism. Logically and historically, such an attitude tallies with liberal opposition to democracy as much as it reflects the contradictions in which impatient advocates of egalitarian radicalism have become entangled.

Inasmuch as every author has an axe to grind, I can perhaps make it plausible that there is no reason why a scholarly vested interest or an ideological one should have predetermined the outcome of my inquiry. In the first place, the correction of a partial image of past liberal thought gains considerable weight from, but does not depend upon, proof that Locke's theory is at variance with this image. There remains the positive attitude of the *philosophes* towards the founding lawgiver, their attempts to come to terms with enlightened absolutism and the evaluation of Napoleonic authoritarianism on this basis by French liberals of the Restoration. Nor are similar trends absent in the Anglo-Saxon domain. But even if nothing similar were detectable in Locke, it would still be interesting to learn how certain arguments in the *Treatises* fit in with the mainstream of Locke's exposition and how that exposition, supposing it were really free of any deviations from a partial or purified version of liberal theory, was made compatible by him with the eminently practical purposes for which the *Treatises* were written and published. For their superiority over the *Leviathan* is quite rightly seen in their containing 'just that ingredient which Leviathan lacked – policy'.[22] Lastly, the adoption of a liberal empiricism as the safeguard against the authoritarian, totalitarian and terroristic backwash of political messianism, does not depend upon what liberal thought in the past has really been like. Each generation forges its ideological tools according to its needs, even if it does no more than shift the emphases of its predecessors. Nothing is gained, however, but something possibly lost, by a misconception of ideological antecedents. Inasmuch as the past holds any lesson for the future, and both can be discussed freely, it is not streamlining but the recognition of complexity which is of value. So

[22] P. Laslett (ed.), John Locke, *Two Treatises of Government* (Cambridge, 1961), 91.

long as the pursuit of truth has any relevance for politics, responsible scholarship may hope to contribute to the clarification of basic ideological issues by elucidating the components of a political tradition. The correct assessment of ‡he complexity of liberal thought is not a matter of gleefully exposing its seamy side but of accounting more fully for its stature as a political theory. Indirectly, it is also a matter of correctly assessing the nature of traditional political philosophy.

2. THE STRANDS OF POLITICAL PHILOSOPHY

A. Facts

The implication that there is an inadvertent or wilful rift in liberal thought between its ideals and the hard facts of politics amounts to an indirect confirmation of the criticism which in our days is so often levelled against traditional political philosophy in general. Many proponents of an empirical science of politics deprecate traditional political philosophy as a source of relevant knowledge because they hold that normative and empirical theory can cohabit in the same system only at the cost of gaining pertinent knowledge about the real world.

When reverence for reality is extended to the teachings of political philosophers, it is recognized that they have been quite heavily engaged upon the description and analysis of actual situations. But they are still found guilty of having made 'no clear separation . . . between hypotheses of political science and the demands of political philosophy'.[23] Still, Lasswell's and Kaplan's apposite references to the works of political philosophers do not indicate that they have found it particularly difficult to sort out statements of fact and empirical hypotheses. Of course, political philosophers have erred in their assessment of facts, but so have scientists. A good many modern political scientists simply proceed upon the assumption that nothing about the real world can be learnt from political philosophers because preoccupation with valuations leads almost invariably astray in the description and analysis of facts. To my knowledge,

[23] H. D. Lasswell and A. Kaplan, *Power and Society* (Third Printing, New Haven, 1957), 118. Out of the vast literature on the subject and apart from the authors specifically referred to in the remainder of this chapter, I should like to mention W. G. Runciman, *Social Science and Political Theory* (Cambridge, 1963), and express my fundamental agreement with his succinct appraisal of the mutual involvement of the sociological and philosophical study of politics.

nothing of the kind has ever been demonstrated with regard to one of the classics of political philosophy, let alone all of them. There are good reasons why such an attempt has not been made. It would entail more than quoting textual evidence out of context; and it would require the presupposition that until quite recently, the segment of the public graced with intellectual curiosity has been either confused about, or unwilling to learn something about the real facts of politics. How else could one explain why since its inception, purportedly unrealistic political philosophy has been taken seriously by a considerable number of people who were neither fools nor knaves? Understandably, the assumption has been evaded.

But blame for the calumny of the teachings of political philosophers does not attach to modern empiricists alone, nor even mainly to them. Quite apart from requiting disregard of political philosophy with disregard of empirical theory, those concerned with political philosophy have rarely troubled to identify its empirical components, let alone enlarged upon them for their own sake. More often than not, they have also neglected the interdependence of the various strands of a political philosophy when it comes to the evaluation of prescriptive theory itself. It is the distinguishing feature of traditional political philosophy that it designates specific modes of possible or desirable organization for the realization of what ought to be done. These provide the decisive criteria for the exact meaning of philosophical statements concerning liberty, authority, consent and the like. Hegel, for example, was serious in seeing freedom progressively realized. But what he said on the organization of the state reveals that his conception of the political representation of individual wills is neither democratic nor liberal, since the individual liberty of citizens counts for little, if anything, in the authorization of political decisions.

Moreover, the prescriptive parts of political philosophy cannot be adequately judged in isolation from its analytical insights. Prescriptive theory has the object of determining actual conduct. All political philosophers have therefore apportioned political functions according to the lessons drawn from the observed conduct of various categories of men and to the empirically inferred requirements of efficient political organization. In this way traditional political philosophy has at least adumbrated models of systematic theorizing. Its mark is discernible in modern empirical theories, although contemporary theorists are often unaware of this. If their awareness were

27

greater, less would be done all over again. At any rate, we have to pay attention to the descriptive analysis that goes with prescriptive theory, if we wish to assess the tension in a system of thought between the 'is' and the 'ought', and the sensibleness of the measures suggested to bridge the gap between them. Modern political science cannot evade the tensions which in their criticism of existing forms of organization and current maxims, political philosophers have created.

B. 'Oughts'

When analysing and comparing observable behaviour and the ideals according to which the agents justify it, empirical theory uses criteria of logic and scientific utility with which political reality – comprising both action and ideology – obviously fails to comply. Having a practical purpose, empirical theory is not content with stating the discrepancy. Mostly, the result is not to stipulate the substitution – as distinct from the supplementation – of ideology or deontology by science. As an outstanding empirical theorist frankly admits: 'Ideologies serve a variety of needs . . . that transcend the need of pedants for scientific cogency.'[24] If so, it must also be recognized that scientific theory transcends reality. It creates a tension between itself and at least some of the determining factors of the 'is', in that it reveals discrepancies between what is actually done, or can be done, and the principles which in the real world are said to account for these doings. But since it is also concerned with suggesting how to come to terms with these discrepancies, it makes proposals for the proper working of a particular political regime. Granted for the sake of argument that it is possible to do this on the basis of an ethically neutral theory, it is impossible to do so without resorting to an 'ought'.

Not all norms are ethical ones. As Sartori says, 'using the form *ought* does not automatically place us in the sphere of ethics'.[25] But it does not follow that we must set all political norms apart from ethical ones. The distinction between the private and the public spheres does not require us to call political norms the values we pursue in society and ethical norms the values pertaining to our inner integrity. Though not identical in all respects, social and individual values, and hence political and ethical values, are com-

[24] R. A. Dahl, *A Preface to Democratic Theory* (Chicago, 1956), 30–1.
[25] Cp. Sartori, *op. cit.*, 180, and for the views criticized see *ibid.*, 180–2.

parable and interdependent to a considerable extent. Within the public and the private sphere, we can distinguish, broadly speaking, between two kinds of 'ought'. A purely functional 'ought' bridges the gap between any kind of ends and the means necessary for their implementation. If ethically neutral, and yet containing a preference, the 'ought' is one not merely of expediency but also of efficiency. To attain a certain goal, only certain means may be used, and some of them are more effective than others. Functional, too, in the sense of both expediency and efficiency, is the ethico-political 'ought' which is conceived in the light of non-relativistic ethics: the demands of justice being what they necessarily are, men ought to be under definite obligations, have certain rights and adhere to, or devise, specific institutional arrangements. Each ethico-political 'ought' is a functional one, but not *vice versa*.

Empirical theory, so long as it wishes to be practically helpful, intends to bridge the gap between itself and the reality on which it theorizes by a merely functional 'ought'. Its proponents, however, do not always feel inhibited from declaring that the results of ethically neutral theory are essential for the maintenance of quite definite operative ideals which for the most part they openly embrace. Some even admit to having engaged upon their empirical pursuits out of concern with the viability of these ideals.[26] The same transpires when more dogmatic empiricists resort to a *ruse de guerre* and camouflage their preferences for ideologically determined forms of the political process by asserting that they do no more than advise anyone who happens to prefer one model to others to comply with what the preferred model requires.[27]

One probably does not go far wrong in stating that, particularly in America, the aspirations towards scientific political theory originate also from a moral judgement. Commitment to democracy has bred disgust with the ideological embroidery which hides those facts that give the lie to democratic principles. The initially ethical protest of non-ethical theory has gained its full momentum in view of the iniquities committed in the name of ethico-political truths, which communism, unlike fascism, partly shares with democracy. It is characteristic of the pervasiveness of scientism in modern social

[26] Thus Lipset in the work quoted in note 7.

[27] For criticism of the failure to articulate the criteria of their commitments and the tendency of such studies towards affirming the *status quo*, see C. Bay, 'Politics and Pseudopolitics: A Critical Evaluation of Some Behavioral Literature,' *The American Political Science Review*, LIX (March, 1965), 39–51.

thought that Marxism, for its part, has dressed up its ethical motives and aims as scientific laws. On both sides, then, ostensibly value-free theory hides ideological commitments and ethical aims more or less successfully. Modern empirical theory, inspired by Max Weber, does not put forth, like Marxism, an ultimately true, or at least representative, structure of observable phenomena, but it cannot help implying such a structure in its attempts at theoretical integration.[28] It has also come to realize that, even if it were desirable, it is obviously beyond its power to put ideology to death, and that indifference would be fatally short-sighted. Science would only contribute to the abuses of ideology if it were to pronounce as equally valuable everything available in the ideological market. The student of political behaviour would then supply the know-how for the realization of any ideological purposes, and more often than not, for that of the less engaging ones. As Bertrand de Jouvenel has pointed out, it is not the lessons drawn from weak political behaviour, such as voting, that may be 'nefariously suggestive', but the picture of politics which is likely to emerge from the analysis of political behaviours inspired by strong passions.[29]

Modern political science can lay claim to important factual and logical insights, but it cannot disclaim its visible positing of functional norms nor its implicit alliance with ethico-political ones. Nor can it maintain that the closer it comes to the ideal of value-free theorizing, the more does it safeguard politics against abuse in the service of ideology. If a political theory does not for these reasons forfeit its claim to usefulness, then traditional political philosophy must not be *a priori* disqualified as a source of relevant knowledge. To say this is not to justify political philosophy as an alternative to modern political science. On the contrary, the student of political philosophy who pays attention to the composite character of the classics of the past, will be less tempted to ignore modern empirical findings. He will also be in a better position to meet the challenge which arises from the present antagonism to ethico-political prescriptions. This is not so much a matter of prospecting for anticipations of modern empirical insights in classical political philosophy, as for elucidating the inner connection between the various layers of

---

[28] Cp. B. de Jouvenel, *The Pure Theory of Politics* (Cambridge, 1963), 30-2 and for the at the moment most advanced example, see D. Easton, *A Framework for Political Analysis* (Englewood Cliffs, NJ, 1965).

[29] Jouvenel, *op. cit.*, 37.

traditional political philosophy in particular, and of political thinking in general: the analysis of observed facts, the induction of empirical principles of behaviour, the deduction or stipulation of ethico-political concepts and of the ways and means of political organization. For these are the strands of political thinking, which takes its cue from political life as it actually is. To accept that these strands of thinking explain each other is not to assert that in any given system of thought they are always consistent in themselves or without friction in their relation to each other. Locke's theory would seem to be an outstanding example.

3. THE APPROACH TO LOCKE

During the last two decades there has been a steady increase in the number of works on Locke's thought, although full-scale monographs on his political theory have remained surprisingly few in number. Hitherto unpublished material, such as his *Essays on the Law of Nature*, have been made available by Wolfgang von Leyden.[30] Maurice Cranston has written an admirable biography and aptly appraised the development and achievements of Locke's thought. Finally, Peter Laslett has placed all those interested in Locke in his debt by providing the first critical edition of the *Treatises of Government*. In the introduction, Laslett has not only suggested a convincing theory as to the time and circumstances in which the *Treatises* were written. Apart from supplying a critical apparatus and a running commentary on the sections of the work, he has, in a relatively short chapter, explicated and related to each other the major tenets of Locke's political theory and indicated problems of interpretation largely ignored by other scholars. Indeed, despite the continuous interest in Locke's political theory, some strands in Locke's argumentation have been left unconnected and others almost completely disregarded. Although significant advances have been made in the understanding of Lockeian politics, this criticism applies even to the few books dealing exclusively with Locke's political theory – the pioneer study of Willimore Kendall, the works of J. W. Gough, Richard Cox and Raymond Polin. Though, again, important insights have been added in some of the countless references to Locke

[30] The particulars of the works mentioned in these passages will be given when the specific views of their authors are referred to. Meanwhile, P. Abrams has also published the early *Two Tracts on Government*.

in books on politics and, of course, in special articles, the gaps have not been filled. This goes for interpretations as stimulating and as controversial as those of Leo Strauss and C. B. Macpherson, as well as for those inspired by Strauss' hypotheses of interpretation – such as the writings of Richard Cox and Robert A. Goldwin.

A. Contradictions and Historical Conditions

No one denies that Locke was preoccupied with politics as the means to safeguarding a set of values later labelled 'liberal'. But he is widely held to be contradictory, either in a cunning or a superficial way. Since not everything in his philosophical thought is borne out in his political writings, and *vice versa* and since the composition of the *Treatises* was occasioned by political exigencies, it is often assumed that he was less systematic (because more pragmatic) in writing the *Treatises* than in his philosophical works. Hence the view that the phraseology of the *Treatises* does not bear too close a scrutiny and that contradictions need to be explained by reference to the conditions of his time.[31] Yet whether or not a text deserves close scrutiny can only be established after the closest scrutiny has been applied. The fact that a man of the intellectual stature of Locke wrote a *pièce de circonstance* – albeit taking his time in doing so and going to great pains over the editing and re-editing of the text, as Laslett has shown – is by itself no indication, and still less proof, that the *Treatises* are a non-philosophical work, or that the threads of its argumentation are inconsistent in themselves and in their relation to each other. After all, a book on politics can be both philosophical and an *oeuvre de circonstance*. There is no necessary contradiction between writing a book under the pressure of political demands and providing an answer to their challenge as a political philosopher. This is the way almost all the classics of political philosophy were composed.

What appears to the interpreter as contradictory in a political thinker's work – as, for instance, the advocacy at one and the same time of executive prerogatives and parliamentary supremacy – cannot always be fully explained by prevailing conditions and practices. Established practices are almost invariably a matter of controversy amongst contemporaries, who may endorse or reject existing conditions consistently or inconsistently, and with varying

[31] J. W. Gough, *John Locke's Political Philosophy* (Oxford, repr. 1956), 35 and *passim*; J. Plamenatz, *Man and Society* (London, 1963), 2 vols., I, 211 f.

degrees of awareness of the conflicts between existing practices. In short, it bears repeating that historical conditions need as much explanation as they provide one. Locke's political theory and his patent commitment to the cause of the Whigs explain each other to a considerable extent. They do not explain each other entirely. Locke did not merely say what the Whigs wanted to be said, if for no other reason than that not all the Whigs always said and wanted the same things; nor did the same people say and want the same things at different times. Whatever one cares to make of the difference between the ideological and organizational coherence of the Whigs (or of any other groups of the time) and that characteristic of a modern party, in Locke's time as in ours a theorist's party affiliation is in itself no indication of either the consistency or the quality of his theory. This elementary truth is often forgotten in the discussion of Locke.

All this is not meant to deny, but rather to affirm, that an unhistorical attitude is at the root of much of the talk about Locke's inconsistency or ambiguity. Lockeian *formulae* are often read on the supposition that they had the same meaning for Locke as they acquired later on, and which historically they helped to bring about. Since not everything Locke said can be squared with the meaning later generations have associated with his *formulae*, the resulting contradictions or ambiguities are often of the interpreters' rather than of the philosopher's making. This is especially true of interpreters who, while far from depicting Locke as a muddled pragmatist, yet attribute to him fundamental contradictions. Whether it is assumed that Locke's views reflect the inner conflicts in the outlook of his class or that he veiled his true intentions by contradictions,[32] it is held to be more or less self-evident which opinions were at the time considered to be irreconcilable, or should be so considered now, and which were unsafe to utter. Especially when the view of Locke's esotericism is advanced, no allowance is made for the fact that new and controversial opinions are often tolerated simply because established authorities do not care to persecute them or do not dare to do so, if such opinions are protected by powerful groups. Mainly on the basis of stipulating an unbridgeable gulf between a naturalistic and a religiously-founded conception of morals and politics, Leo Strauss finds that Locke expressed his

[32] C. B. Macpherson, *The Political Theory of Possessive Individualism* (Oxford, 1962), Ch. V, and L. Strauss, *Natural Right and History* (Chicago, sec. impr., 1957), Ch. V, B.

inclination towards a purely Hobbesian conception in one set of statements which is irreconcilable with Locke's more frequently stated views. According to the esoteric method the inoffensive views must be cancelled; they are intended to mislead the censor and protect the writer.

Sophistication in this approach reaches impressing heights. Some relevant problems of interpretation are raised and the tension between theory and practice is illustrated, although from too narrow an angle. Furthermore, considering the assumption that esotericism pervades Locke's metapolitics, it stands to reason that he did not wish to discredit his political doctrine by offending religious sensibilities and therefore refrained from purely secular and naturalistic interpretations of the origin of power, the rights of men and of political society in general. He certainly attenuated the naturalistic character of his teachings by references to the Scriptures. But it is by no means certain that these were deliberately inexact and hence intentionally misleading, for Locke was not always careful even in his own cross-references.[33] Moreover, we cannot dismiss the overwhelming evidence which shows that Locke's own sensibilities were engaged in his attempts to reconcile his concessions to hedonistic naturalism with an enlightened belief in Christianity. In the first place, the contradictions which are singled out to prove the existence of a concealed teaching are for the most part no contradictions at all. Secondly, Strauss fails to maintain his thesis consistently. Perhaps the contradictions on the interpreter's part have the same aim as the contradictions which he sets out to reveal in what he interprets, namely, to conceal an esoteric teaching.[34] Whether or not it can fairly be said that Strauss camouflages a critical attitude towards the American tradition, or that he does not wish us to accept his opinions on the relationship between pagan natural law and the Bible at their face-value (and if so, it is certainly a highly individual presumption that such a teaching is so shocking that it must be con-

---

[33] Cp. Sec. 94, which refers for further discussion only to 'the following part of this discourse,' whereas the matter had also been dealt with in Secs. 74-5. I have used Laslett's edition of *Locke's Two Treatises of Government*. When only the section is indicated the quotation is from the *Second Treatise*. In speaking in the text of the *Treatise*, I always mean the *Second Treatise*. Quotations from and references to the *First Treatise* are prefixed by I, e.g. I, 25. I have rendered the quotations into modern English and substituted my italics for those of the Laslett edition.

[34] Cp. S. Rothman, 'The Revival of Classical Political Philosophy,' *The American Political Science Review*, LVI (1962), 347-8, and R. J. McShea, 'Leo Strauss on Machiavelli,' *The Western Political Quarterly* (December, 1963), 782-97.

cealed), one thing seems to be certain. In the West, with the possible exception of propagating communism at a University, things have not come to such a pass that philosophies of any kind must be hidden behind a contradictory interpretation of the contradictions attributed to a thinker of another time. To do so, is to risk that none but the orally initiated will know what is at stake and at the same time jeopardize scholarly probity in the pursuit of the history of ideas. Unless this, too, is part of the overall intent, one's feelings about the need for esotericism in one's own time and country are no excuse for arbitrary assumptions as to what was commanded in this respect in another time and place, and still less for failing to account for the audacities which admittedly were uttered in a straightforward manner.

The thesis that Locke must be interpreted in terms of esotericism is not only questionable on the ground that too much is explained away. It is invalidated because his unveiled justification of the right of revolt is left unexplained. Strauss and his followers are far from denying that the right of revolt is one of the central elements of Locke's political teaching. As Cox emphasizes, civil and external war are, according to Locke, the closest reproduction to be found in political society of the inconveniences which make that society necessary; war and revolution thus illustrate the nature of the philosophically-based argument about the naturalistic origin of society.[35] Must it not be asked, then, what the concealment of a radical political teaching amounts to if revolution is openly advocated, and in a way which gives the whole philosophical show away for all to see? To say that Locke concealed his authorship of the *Treatises* because he was haunted by the spectre of Algernon Sidney, who paid with his life for the advocacy of the lawfulness of deposing kings,[36] is a convincing inference. But it disproves rather than proves that Locke engaged in esoteric writing. Under the cover of anonymity he made plain that to countenance resistance to the iniquities of arbitrary rule is 'presently the voice of faction and rebellion' (Sec. 93); moreover, he gave such prominence to the rightfulness of revolt that it is easily the most belaboured single issue of the *Treatises*. If he felt safe in doing so by concealing his authorship, it is altogether improbable that for presenting the philosophical argument he should have sought the additional security of hiding his true

[35] R. H. Cox, *Locke on War and Peace* (Oxford, 1960), 185, 72.
[36] *Ibid.*, 15.

intentions behind contradictions. Clearly, the question which needs answering is whether the philosophical foundation of an argument was more offensive than its most poignant practical conclusion. Those who argue the case for Locke's esotericism do not broach this question at all. On this score alone, their case becomes tenuous, if it does not entirely go by default. For no considered view of the character of the man, or of his times and personal experiences, allows one to assume that he regarded the right of revolt as less opposed to traditional views (and therefore less dangerous to advocate) than allowances for hedonistic principles or for the accumulation of property, to say nothing of the threadbare opinions which the neurotically cautious Locke is said to have veiled by contradictions: the coerciveness of political society, the priority of the self-preservation of the commonwealth over that of the individual, the notion of sovereignty, and the lawlessness of inter-state relations.[37]

Indeed, Locke's justification of the right of revolt has been taken so much for granted that its significance has never been adequately realized. Even Laslett, who has shown that the *Treatises* were written to justify a possibly revolutionary solution of the Exclusionist controversy (1679-81), does not think that his discovery calls for far-reaching revisions of interpretation.[38] Admittedly, it does not greatly matter for the understanding of the inner unity of his political theory, whether Locke published the *Treatises* to vindicate a revolution which had taken place, or wrote them at Shaftesbury's instigation to justify a revolution yet to be made should other means fail. What matters is that the nature and pervasiveness of his revolutionism should be correctly understood. This will also help to resolve apparent contraditions or ambiguities.

B. The Test of Consistency

To reveal a thinker's ambiguities and contradictions is one part of the interpreter's task. The other is to account for them in the attempt to understand the thinker's system as a whole. What at first sight might appear contradictory in a political theory may reflect the different aspects under which the theorist views reality, and the corresponding awareness of the frictions in reality itself. As Polin has pointed out, it would be wrong to credit Locke with a subtle approach to reality at the cost of condemning him for incoherence,

[37] Cox, *op. cit.*, 118, 121, 109-11 and 113 and 167 f. respectively.
[38] Laslett, *op. cit.*, X.

and to identify his complexity with equivocation because his intentions defy easy classification.[39] One must allow that a political thinker's claim to consistency does not rest mainly on his success in dissolving in thought the contradictoriness of phenomena, and in suggesting ways and means of fully eliminating these tensions in practice. He has first of all to recognize their nature. It is understandable that political philosophers should have excelled more in their ability to expose contradictions in existing conditions and especially the inconsistencies in the systems of their colleagues and predecessors than in making plain that which in their own appraisals remains tentative or contradictory.

Theorizing with a view to improving established habits of thought and performance would be impossible, if it were incumbent upon a theorist to remain silent, until he had envisaged and provided against all conceivable difficulties. The things which he leaves unsettled, are often those that he has been unable to explore sufficiently and that he believes he may safely leave unconsidered for the moment. Often he is not aware of either their existence or importance. Hence, no shocking insight or solution necessarily lurks behind *lacunae* or passages which might, by the interpreter's standards, appear ambiguous or even contradictory. Moreover, the requirements of logic and of political persuasion have so far never been fully compatible, and earlier generations might have entertained different notions of logic in the demonstration of political matters, not fully sharing our own concern with the need of explicit elaboration and adjustment of principles and assumptions.[40] The interpreter's task remains, however, to find out whether tensions in a system of thought do not indicate the different perspectives from which a fact or an idea have been, and possibly still might be, viewed; whether, within the framework of the thinker's own terms of reference and in consideration of how things are actually done, these *manières de voir* do not supplement rather than contradict each other. An historical approach recommends itself in which criteria of logic and of the viability of specific insights are not bartered away in exchange for,

---

[39] Cp. R. Polin, *La Politique Morale de John Locke* (Paris, 1960), 27, 48, 304–5.

[40] Cp. Macpherson, *op. cit.*, 5. I agree with Macpherson on the necessity of making explicit 'imperfectly stated' assumptions rather than what he calls 'unstated assumptions' (194; 7–8), especially since the latter are identified as the outlook of class and time in the manner of the sweeping generalizations of Mannheim's sociology of knowledge and its Marxist source of inspiration.

but are made instrumental in, an understanding of a system of thought on its own terms and those of its time.

Any kind of theory subsumes phenomena under specific categories and establishes general rules, listing qualifications as to their applicability. The discourse usually reflects these aspects of the process of ratiocination. Take, for instance, a writer who concludes from certain facts and premises that we ought to accept the principles of equality and of the superiority of the legislature over the executive. In establishing both principles he is liable to speak of them as admitting no exception and to preclude any subsequent acknowledgement of inequality and of executive prerogatives. If these are nevertheless allowed, and a similar course is followed as regards other issues, it is reasonable to infer that the writer's discourse, like most political discourse, proceeds by reducing the validity of what is held to be generally true or desirable in the light of what is regarded as practically possible. Even if it is not expressly announced as the writer's procedure, his following the course of reducing propositions must be inferred if what appears to be in contradiction with one set of principles links up with another set of principles to which the discourse leads. No writer can say everything at once. Each argument needs to be developed if it is to be intelligible and to cover the cases to which it is relevant. Thus one definition or maxim becomes counterbalanced by others, until fundamental propositions become enlarged or restricted, and are given their operational meaning in view of observed modes of behaviour and of the requirements of concerted action. Thus statements concerning the appositeness of certain forms of social and political action indicate the exact meaning of the general principles of the theory. With varying degrees of explicitness, all traditional systems of political thought reflect this interplay between analysis and the establishment of rules of observed and prescribed behaviour. If no political philosophy can be properly explained by fastening upon general statements and discounting their subsequent qualifications, least of all one like that of Locke which was so obviously preoccupied with endorsing a quite specific conception of the political process.

To be sure, one often wishes that he had been more explicit in linking up arguments. Yet we must keep in mind that, where we we crave for greater explicitness, Locke and his contemporaries might not have felt any need for it. If the importance of a political philosophy is gauged by the extent to which it converts 'paradoxes into platitudes or *vice versa*',[41] one should not expect all that is commonplace to be enlarged upon but rather that which has become controversial in otherwise accepted standards and is consequently thought to be crucial. Thus Locke made the most of his differences with Filmer and very little, if anything, of how far he agreed with him. At the same time, he overstressed conformity with other absolutist theories to isolate Filmerism and present as 'platitudes' opinions which were still 'paradoxes'. As propaganda and as a political philosophy, the *Treatises* aim less at a full-scale rejection of traditional values and institutions than at showing that they require government by consent. They may be regarded as an attempt at perfecting a platform which would not only fortify partisans in their convictions but also appeal to the greater part of national opinion, an objective which in the course of time the *Treatises* achieved. As philosopher, keen observer, and efficient practitioner of politics, Locke could not expect uncritical acceptance of his views and indulgence for incoherence. In the *Preface* to the *Treatises* he therefore admonished his readers that exceptions to his views should proceed from being 'conscientiously scrupulous in the point' and 'that cavilling here and there, at some expression, or little incident of my discourse, is not an answer to my book'. Interpreters ought not, without weighty proof to the contrary, dismiss what is implied in this entreaty, namely the author's assurance that he had made his points with a view to inviting careful scrutiny, indulgence being asked for no more than an occasional slip of expression. My study of Locke has convinced me that he was guilty of more than an occasional lapse into inaccurate language. In a few instances he creates a baffling contradiction in making a sudden statement which runs counter the whole trend of his argument; he also does not always demonstrate what he has promised to, nor abide strictly by his conceptual distinctions or make those which the nature of his opinions calls for; and, as I have already said, he does not always establish the proper connections between his arguments where such might be expected. Nevertheless, his discourse is not nearly as muddled or as superficially transparent as is frequently asserted. I have come to the conclusion that, for the most part, he made his points carefully so that they add up to a fundamentally coherent and practicable theory. To show this means suggesting what his statements amount to when

[41] I. Berlin, 'Does Political Theory Still Exist?' In P. Laslett and W. G. Runciman, *Philosophy, Politics and Society* (sec. ser., Oxford, 1962), I.

considered in the light of political experience and in the context of the demonstrable interrelatedness of the layers of his argument. This demands also establishing connexions, thinking matters through and developing implications where Locke felt no need for doing so. To go in this way beyond Locke is not to step out of his system but to explicate it by considering also its potentialities.

I have, therefore, undertaken to ask whether his examples from history can be regarded as constituting the empirical illustration and validation of his theory of incorporation by compact; whether the notion of consent, thereby implied, is consistently upheld when it comes to the political participation of the majority; whether anything can be made of his attack on paternalism and patriarchalism on the one hand, and of his far-reaching concessions to them on the other; whether the justification of one-man rule in the beginnings, and the allowances for executive prerogatives in the regime acceptable to him are compatible with his violent outbursts against royal absolutism. This means also an inquiry into how much of all this is covered by the metapolitical foundations of Lockeian politics. To test the inner consistency of Locke's political theory I have not only dealt with the contradictions signalled by other scholars. I have also raised questions of compatibility which have so far hardly been asked. They are not answered in terms of the development of Locke's thought. I am concerned only with the meaning of his mature political thought as expressed in the *Treatises*. The answers rely on detailed analyses of the text. I have rather quoted from, than referred the reader to it, for different readings of the text have been suggested by interpreters as regards almost all the major topics of Locke's teaching.

The extent to which the layers of Locke's argumentation confirm each other is best revealed, because most severely tested, by dealing separately with his metapolitics in the first part of this book; with his attitude towards historical precedents in the second; and in the third part with the nature of the regime which he was ready to endorse. It will thus become clear in each part that Locke's metapolitical foundations are conceived to justify the basic forms of political action which experience has taught to be practicable and commendable. Conversely, it will become evident that, for him, historical experience demonstrates how the same metapolitical principles remain applicable in the course of political development. To explore the political theory of Locke in the manner outlined, it is necessary to focus attention upon topics which have not so far been duly considered. Although for this reason a good deal of space had to be allotted to their interpretation, care has been taken to determine their intrinsic relevance for the proper understanding of Locke's political theory as a whole.

The dictates of academic integrity apart, the components of Locke's theory must each be given its due weight if the general purpose of the book is to be achieved: the correction of the prevailing image of the liberal tradition. What implications the resulting view of Locke's politics hold in this respect, and wherein lies the continued relevance of his empirical insights, is indicated by the nature of our analysis. Indeed, to the extent that the primary purpose of presenting the inner coherence and unity of the Lockeian argument has been achieved, I believe that I have clarified the lines on which one might attempt a comprehensive reassessment of the liberal tradition, as well as an evaluation of what is still vital in it.

PART ONE

METAPOLITICS
AND POLITICS

CHAPTER II

NATURAL LAW

I. RATIONAL POLITICS AND ETHICAL PLURALISM

LOCKE was the first to elaborate modern liberalism in a comprehensive and influential system of thought, and it still reflects fully the recognition of men's obligation to abide by a 'higher law' than that devised by humans. The belief that politics can and must be guided by the injunctions of reason contained in a 'law of nature', has been persistently maintained by philosophers and jurists during decisive phases of the development of political thought. The inner consistency of Locke's natural law doctrine lies in its vindication of a specific conception of the political process, and of popular participation in it, which is held to be in accord with reason and with the different abilities of men to ascertain and apply its universal precepts.

In his conception of natural law, theorems of utility coexist with traditional norms of perfection and virtue.[1] Already in his time, this aroused suspicion of Hobbism.[2] Today, Leo Strauss and his disciples are convinced that Locke surreptitiously followed Hobbes –

---

[1] Cp. H. R. F. Bourne, *The Life of John Locke*, 2 vols. (London, 1867), II, 64; L. Stephen, *English Thought in the Eighteenth Century*, 2 vols. (3rd ed., London, 1902), II, 135–41; S. P. Lamprecht, *The Moral and Political Philosophy of John Locke* (New York, 1918), 9, 30, 39, 81 f.; C. E. Vaughan, *Studies in the History of Political Philosophy Before and After Rousseau*, 2 vols. (new ed., Manchester, 1939), I, 140, 170, 181; W. Kendall, 'John Locke and the Doctrine of Majority-Rule,' *Illinois Studies in the Social Sciences*, XXVI, 2 (1941), 68 f.; W. Simon, 'John Locke: Philosophy and Political Theory,' *American Political Science Review*, XLV (1951), 386–8 f.; J. W. Gough, *John Locke's Political Philosophy* (repr., Oxford, 1956), 19 f., 22, 114; R. I. Aaron, *John Locke* (2nd ed., Oxford, 1955), 256 f.; Polin, *op. cit.*, 53 f., 81 f., 113 f., 119–20, 126; H. Moulds, 'John Locke's Four Freedoms in a New Light,' *Ethics*, LXXI, 2 (1961), 122–3; R. Singh, 'John Locke and the Theory of Natural Law,' *Political Studies* (June 1961), 114.

[2] Thus the third Earl of Shaftesbury, who considered Locke as his 'friend and foster-father,' in his private letters. See J. Aronson, 'Shaftesbury on Locke,' *The American Political Science Review* (Dec. 1959), 1103, and Lamprecht, *op. cit.*, 96, note. Cp. V. Cousin, *Philosophie de Locke* (Paris, 1829; 4th ed., 1861), 54, 57, on Newton who apologized after having been corrected by Locke. According to von Leyden, John Locke, *Essays on the Law of Nature* (Oxford, 1954), 76, Tyrrell repeatedly urged Locke to publish his essays on natural law and remove the suspicion of Hobbism.

intimating, by way of contradictions, that he regarded as ineffective the hierarchy of ends to which the teaching of traditional natural law, pagan and Christian, stands committed.[3] In its extremity, the thesis is untenable. Quite apart from exceptions to the interpretations of the Lockeian text, objections against the assumption of the irreconcilability of utilitarian and absolute norms suggest themselves.

In the first place, in political theories, ends and means are not unequivocally determined by the judgement passed on utilitarian and absolute norms. Different ethical premises are not invariably accompanied by different conceptions of human nature, or of the requirements of political organization. Hobbes appears to have denied what Plato had affirmed and traditional natural law theorists had continued to maintain, namely, that absolute norms of virtue ought to have precedence over the rationalized dictates of mere self-preservation and convenience. Yet Plato and Hobbes agreed in their sceptical view of human nature. According to Plato, ordinary men cannot become really virtuous; while, for Hobbes, virtue by itself appears to have little, if any, relevance for men. The two philosophers were sufficiently at one in their scepticism for both to advocate the imposition of rational standards of political behaviour by authoritarian rule. In this respect, Plato, Machiavelli and Hobbes were as much in accord as they differed from Aristotle and Locke. Yet in their conception of ethics, Plato and Aristotle had not less

---

[3] This is the thesis of Leo Strauss, *Natural Right and History* (2nd impr. Chicago, 1957), 203-4, 209, 212, 217, 219-22, 226-8, and 'Locke's Doctrine of Natural Law,' *The American Political Science Review*, LII (1958), 490, 492, 493, 496, 500, where Strauss defends his case against von Leyden, *op. cit.*, 60, 65 f., 71-80, 77 f., and his 'John Locke and Natural Law,' *Philosophy*, XXI (1956), 26. Von Leyden explains contradictions as a change of mind not affecting Locke's faith in a traditional natural law. Likewise, J. W. Yolton, 'Locke and the Law of Nature,' *The Philosophical Review*, LXVII (1958), 477 f., whose re-appraisal differs in some respects from von Leyden's views and is directed against Strauss' interpretation. Cox, *op. cit.*, and R. A. Goldwin, 'John Locke,' in L. Strauss and J. Cropsey (eds.), *History of Political Philosophy* (Chicago, 1963) follows Strauss, though they do not refer to him in the many instances where they merely enlarge upon his interpretations. Among earlier commentators, Stephen, *op. cit.*, 136-7, declared Locke's theory of the compact as almost identical with the utilitarian *formula* and regretted Locke's inability to free himself from the vestiges of the metaphysical method. According to A. P. Brogan, 'John Locke and Utilitarianism,' *Ethics*, LXIX, 2 (1959), 82 f., 86, 90-1, 97 f., Locke's *Essay Concerning Human Understanding* and his political writings, unlike the earlier *Essays on the Law of Nature* and the later *Reasonableness of Christianity* (97-9), consistently explain voluntary action in the vein of Hobbes and the utilitarians of the eighteenth century.

in common than had Machiavelli and Hobbes. The correspondence in systems of thought between moral contents and the forms of political action and organization, though an indispensable criterion of evaluation,[4] shows itself to be highly equivocal. This relationship is made even more complex by the fact that conflicting moral and political maxims have often been derived from identical theological and metaphysical premises, just as similar moral and political maxims have been based upon divergent theological and metaphysical premises.[5] Secondly, whether or not it is philosophically admissible to assume that utilitarian and traditional ethical values are mutually exclusive, their incompatibility has seldom been fully maintained in theories concerned with the political realization of values. This might even be said of Hobbes.[6] In J. S. Mill's humane utilitarianism, the eventually assured harmony of individual interests is explicitly associated with the imperative of human perfectibility and dignity. Traditional natural law theories had subjected considerations of convenience and individual happiness to absolute norms of perfection. In their purity, however, such norms were to serve only for passing judgement. For purposes of civil action, they had to be diluted by conventional right.[7] Plato did not stipulate that the best state could come about, or even function, with a total disregard for conventional motives and rules of conduct. The greater part of the city, from which a measure of consent is also to be obtained, cannot shake off its utilitarian standards. In fact, it must live by them to enable the guardians to fulfil their function. The Platonic division of labour depends upon the effectiveness as much of the lower-rated as of the higher-rated motives and norms of behaviour.

Thirdly, although post-Lockeian utilitarianism and idealism dispensed more and more with the notion of natural law, they preserved, with varying emphasis, the belief that political life cannot be ordered without reference to rational standards. As Green said, so far as the institutions of civil life are

[4] Cp. N. Rotenstreich, 'Rule by Majority or by Principles,' *Social Research*, XXII, 4 (1954), 411–27.

[5] Cp. J. W. Yolton, *John Locke and the Way of Ideas* (Oxford, 1956), vi, 13 and *passim* on the relationship between Locke's epistemology and the theological discussion of his time. See also Yolton's introduction to his edition of Locke's *An Essay Concerning Human Understanding*, 2 vols. (Everyman's Library, London-New York, 1961), I, ix–x.

[6] For a discussion of the major modern interpretations, see K. C. Brown (ed.), *Hobbes Studies* (Oxford, 1965).

[7] Cp. Strauss, *op. cit.*, 146, 152–3, 165.

'giving reality to these capacities of will and reason and enabling them to be really exercised . . . they may be said to correspond to the "law of nature" . . . according to the only sense in which that phrase can be intelligibly used.'[8]

In utilitarian theories, while men's desires and interests alone constitute the criterion of eventual harmony, they still require the mediation of reason for the attainment of the greatest possible happiness of all. In other words, dictates of reason are reverted to as a means to restrict human arbitrariness, irrespective of whether human motives and ends are predicated on men's personal desires and interests or are subjected to an objective teleological order. In both instances, dictates of reason have the identical function of effecting justice through a rational reconciliation of interests. What such dictates enjoin may differ according to the motivational and teleological nature of the underlying ethics. But there is also a fundamental correspondence. Both utilitarian and idealist political theories agree – though on different grounds – on the necessity of political organization and its major practical purposes; nor do they differ so very much about what men must and must not do to maintain it.

Given the fundamental agreement between utilitarian and traditional ethics on the central function of dictates of reason, their role in Locke's system need not be affected even if he had really wished to insinuate that natural law in the Christian sense cannot be known by mortals, and hence does not exist for them. Such an intimation need not amount to more than that reason is unassisted by revelation. Mortals may still know a law of nature which is nothing but a law of reason. This would be true, of course, even if this law were one merely of hedonistic self-preservation. Yet we can also infer from Strauss' own interpretation that, in what they enjoin, the fundamental dictates of reason in Locke's doctrine and in traditional natural law theory correspond in conclusive points.[9]

Finally, whatever side one takes in the controversy over the question whether the strands of Locke's writings are consistent with

[8] T. H. Green, *Lectures on the Principles of Political Obligation* (new impr., London, 1959), sec. 7.
[9] See below, 57 f. and 62.

each other,[10] one has to take into account that the mature Locke refrained from a full exposition and logical examination of the concept of natural law in his philosophical *Essay*.[11] There, natural law is scarcely mentioned. The opposite is true of his political *Treatises*, where he related to natural law each of the major rules of social conduct and political organization. He nevertheless stated in the *Second Treatise*, which contains his fully developed political doctrine, that it is 'besides my present purpose, to enter here into the particulars of the law of nature' (Sec. 12). Since he never did, he obviously thought that his natural law concept needed no further epistemological elaboration to serve as the moral foundation of his political theory,[12] in other words, that no radically new conception was required. Indeed, the justification of the competitive diffusion of political authority recommended in the *Second Treatise* reveals itself as grounded on a natural law teaching, which, like that of his early *Essays on the Law of Nature*, assumes the subjection of theorems of utility to traditional norms together with a considerable degree of compatibility between them. Hobbes' emphasis of egoistic self-preservation was not lost upon Locke, but he tried to accommodate individualistic ethics within the framework of traditional natural law.

2. KNOWABILITY

A. Unequal Knowledge

a. *Equality and Inequality*
Traditionally, natural law had been held to obligate all men, though

---

[10] Polin, *op. cit.*, esp. 97, 115, and Singh, *loc. cit.*, 108, note, argue in favour of the unity underlying all Locke's works. So does Strauss for his different interpretative purpose. M. Cranston, *John Locke, A Biography* (London, 1957), 208, stresses the non-philosophical character of the *Treatises*. Likewise, Laslett, *op. cit.*, 80, who, however, admits that this may be overstating the case (89). Similarly Lamprecht, *op. cit.*, 80. In fact, to argue like G. Parry, 'Individuality, Politics and the Critique of Paternalism in John Locke,' *Political Studies*, XII, No. 2 (1964), 167, that Locke's epistemology and politics remain at odds, is to discount that, on quite important points, the arguments in the *Essay* and the *Treatises* bear each other out. (See for instance below 59, 69, 137, 206 f, 257.) I sympathize with the suggestion of H. Aarsleff, 'Leibniz on Locke on Language,' *American Philosophical Quarterly*, I, 3 (1964), 12, and note 39, that the *Essay* and the *Treatises* are not disparate, and that 'they are not, of course, systematically similar treatments of different subjects, but both deal with our "conduct"'.

[11] On this point, and the logical criticism to which Locke's natural law concept is open, see von Leyden, *op. cit.*, 59, 73 f., 75-7, 80. For criticism, see also his 'John Locke and Natural Law,' 27, 30, 34; Vaughan, *op. cit.*, 158; Kendall, *op. cit.*, 76, 81; J. W. Yolton, 'Locke and the Law of Nature,' 487-8; and Laslett, *op. cit.*, 81.

[12] Cp. von Leyden, *op. cit.*, 80 f.; and Polin, *op. cit.*, 77, 118.

they were not supposed to have an equal knowledge of it. The direct appeal of ordinary men to that law had, therefore, usually been confined to prayer, or, at the limit, to passive resistance. Locke went further by advocating direct interference of the mass of ordinary men with the powers that be, though he confined it to revolt.[13] His concessions to egalitarian principles did not lead him to abandon altogether the unegalitarian grounds of his predecessors.

Men, as 'creatures of the same species and rank promiscuously born to all the same advantages of nature, and the use of the same faculties, *should* also be equal one amongst another'.[14] Locke would not have said 'should' if he had not recognized the actual inequality of capacities.[15] Equality is, above all, a moral postulate, concerning duties as much as rights.[16] Men's natural equality is, as 'the judicious Hooker' shows, 'the foundation of that *obligation* to mutual love' upon which are built 'the *duties* they [men] owe one another', and whence are derived 'the great maxims of justice and charity' (Sec. 5). This the law of nature, which is reason, 'teaches all mankind, *who will but consult it* . . .' (Sec. 6). Not all mankind does what it is capable of doing, nor do men, born to use the same faculties, invariably or equally make use of reason, and hence of their physical endowments. Even when he is emphasizing the idyllic aspects of the state of nature, that is of human nature, Locke deals extensively with the right to punish offenders so 'that all men may be restrained from invading others' rights' (Sec. 7), and with the right to secure reparations. [17] There is no doubt about the divinely ordained precedence of 'the industrious and rational' over 'the quarrelsome and contentious' (Sec. 34). In acknowledgement of the fact of differential rationality – or irrationality – he directs the absolute imperative inherent in natural equality not against any kind of subordination but against that only which 'may authorize us to

[13] For detailed demonstration, see Chapters IX and X.

[14] Sec. 4. Cp. I, 67.

[15] Cp. Laslett, *op. cit.*, 287. He refers to additional evidence for Locke's recognition of the inequality of capacities, but does not suggest how this is to be reconciled with his assertion that the *Second Treatise* contains nothing to support a theory of differential rationality (96). Likewise Polin, *op. cit.*, 91, 253-4, 273, who concedes Locke's acknowledgement and justification of inequality and denies that he distinguished among classes according to rationality and income (40-1, note 5).

[16] Kendall, *op. cit.*, 68, 76, 79 f., 105 f., 113, has exposed the misapprehension that Locke stressed rights rather than duties. But Kendall tilts the Lockeian balance in his attempt to turn him into a collectivist. Incidentally, even Vaughan, *op. cit.*, 138, was aware that Locke's natural law, 'this accommodating oracle' (140), also enjoins duties.

[17] Secs. 8-12.

destroy one another, as if we were made for one another's uses, as the inferior ranks of creatures are for ours'.[18] Only in respect of 'an absolute, arbitrary power one man has over another, to take away his life, whenever he pleases ... nature ... has made no such distinction between one man and another' (Sec. 172).

Natural equality so conceived is not inconsistent with different personal status and possessions. To consider in the state of nature 'every man his equal', means that, as the 'absolute lord of his own person and possessions', he is 'equal to the greatest ...' (Sec. 123). Indeed, anxious to prevent any misunderstanding of his statements on natural equality in the *Second Treatise*, Locke stressed: 'Though I have said above, Chapter II, that all men by nature are equal, I cannot be supposed to understand all sorts of equality', (Sec. 54). It is compatible with natural equality that

'age or virtue may give men a just precedence: excellency of parts and merit may place others above the common level: birth may subject some, and alliance or benefits others, to pay an observance to those to whom nature, gratitude or other respects may have made it due.'

Nature having provided the same advantages to all, has provided at the same time for the differential use of these advantages and does not, therefore, justify 'all sorts of equality'. Nothing Locke had said before – or after – contradicts that 'the equality, which all men are in, in respect of jurisdiction or dominion one over another, . . . was the equality I there [in Chapter II] spoke of, as proper to the business in hand . . .'

We may say, then, that the postulate of equal natural rights is turned into, though not displaced by, the postulate of unequal rights and capacities, to justify the differentiation of property,[19] though not of property alone. Of course, Locke thus read back into the state of nature, that is, ascribed to human nature, assumptions – not *the* assumptions – about equality prevailing at the time. Yet it does not follow, as Macpherson further argues, that Locke was unconscious of the implications of his assumptions about equality, and of an unresolved dualism between them, especially if the supporting argument is that Locke started with an initial postulate of unqualified equality. This is sufficiently disproved by Locke's own

[18] Sec. 6. Cp. I, 25–8.
[19] Macpherson, *op. cit.*, 231–2.

testimony which we have just considered. It does not countenance any attempt to isolate parts of normative statements on natural equality and pass them off for factual statements about an initial equalitarian stage, nor to dismiss offhand as abstract and unrelated to the issue of equality Locke's distinction between the rational and depraved. It is likewise unfounded that Locke's distinction between 'the industrious and rational' on one side and 'the quarrelsome and contentious', on the other is unrelated to class differentiation, since Locke does not mean, as Macpherson asserts,[20] that industrious appropriation is untarnished by covetousness so long as possessions are small. Locke speaks about the '*covetousness* of the quarrelsome and contentious' (Sec. 34) in clear reference to the very beginnings of property, and when he mentions 'each man's small property', he speaks, therefore, not of the absence of controversies, trespasses, and offenders but of 'few controversies . . . few trespasses, and few offenders' (Sec. 107). Locke did not entertain a conception of an original society as comprised of undifferentiated beings. Consequently he had no need to displace it by a 'more marked bourgeois' conception of differential rights and rationality.[21]

It is legitimate to take exception on logical and moral grounds to Locke's notion of equality which amounts to the view that 'all men have equal rights; but not to all things', as Burke later put it. Yet it is uncalled for to stigmatize Locke's stand as conflicting and ambiguous in comparison with the Aristotelian conception of equality, and from a Marxist point of view at that. Macpherson offends (as Marxists are wont to do) against Marx's own judgement. Marx appraised the equal right of all to receive rewards proportionate to their labour not as the egalitarian foundation of property, but as 'a right of inequality in its content, like every right'.[22] 'Right', as he explains, 'by its very nature can only consist in the application of an equal standard'. If such a standard of measurement is applied to unequal performances, 'this equal right is an unequal right for unequal labour'. To avoid this and yet recognize 'unequal individual endowment and thus productive capacity as natural privileges . . . right instead of being equal would have to be unequal'. The compelling logic of this reasoning underlies both the Aristotelian and

---

[20] *Ibid.*, 237.

[21] Macpherson, *op. cit.*, 243, 245.

[22] *Critique of the Gotha Program* in Karl Marx, *Selected Works* (2 vols.), ed. V. Adoratsky (London, Martin Lawrence Ltd), 564–6.

the Lockeian notion of equality. Indeed, since, according to Marx, men 'would not be different individuals if they were not unequal', Marx's crossing beyond, no less than Locke's remaining within, 'the narrow horizon of bourgeois right' invites questions of logical and moral consistency.

b. *The Many and the Few*

If natural equality is modified by different capacities, natural law cannot be known equally by all men. All men have some knowledge of it, but not everybody is, or can be, 'a studier of that law' (Sec. 12), 'the greater part' not being 'strict observers of equity and justice' (Sec. 123). The appeal to heaven, however, is open to all men although it is a matter not merely of will but of right. 'He that appeals to heaven, must be sure he has right on his side; and a right too that is worth the trouble and cost of the appeal . . .', for he is accountable – like the divine-right monarch, we may add, in conducting government – to 'a tribunal, that cannot be deceived . . .' (Sec. 176). Are, then, the masses of ordinary and morally rather unreliable men supposed to know when they have right on their side? Locke's statements provide a positive answer but admit also of doubts. His sceptical statements relate, however, less to the possibility of knowing than of implementing natural law. I shall therefore deal first with the knowability and then with the applicability of natural law.

Locke clearly assumed that ordinary men are not incapable of knowing when they have right, and hence reason, on their side. Natural law is plain – even plainer than positive law – to rational creatures.[23] The possession of reason, which is the condition for freedom of action within the boundaries of natural or any other proper law, is granted to all men.[24] All are therefore by nature free and rational, inasmuch as 'age that brings one, brings with it the other too'.[25] Despite the clear language of these sections it has been maintained that Locke never meant to say that natural law can be known by all men. In support of this claim, Cox quotes as follows: '. . . we are born free as we are born rational, not that we have actually the exercise of either.'[26] He simply omits the subsequent passage: 'age that brings one, brings with it the other too.' Locke

[23] Secs. 12 and 124. Similarly, Secs. 6 and 11.
[24] Secs. 57, 58, 60, 63, 98.
[25] Sec. 61. Cp. Secs. 56–60, and 170.
[26] Cox, *op. cit.*, 80, note 7.

leaves no doubt that the impossibility to exercise freedom and rationality is confined to 'the imperfect state of childhood', to 'ignorant nonage, till reason shall take its place' (Sec. 58). No devious self-contradiction was intended by Locke's qualification of the ability to exercise freedom and reason. He merely wished to show 'how natural freedom and subjection to parents may consist together . . .' (Sec. 61). Indeed, Cox shifts his grounds in the direction of contradictions. He claims that from the middle of the *Treatise* onwards Locke reverted from affirmative to negating statements on the knowability of natural law as well as on the state of nature.[27] Although most of the sections which I have referred to so far occur in the first half of the *Treatise*, three appear in the second.[28] They affirm like the others the rationality of men and their capability of knowing the law of nature. There is as little of a break or reversal here as in respect of the inequality of men's moral and physical capacities. And both arguments are compatible. The propositions 'all men are rational' and 'all men are not equally rational' are not in conflict.

To know natural law properly is the concern of those who, by nature and occupation, are more rational than others. This does not entail that the less rational have no choice but to follow their betters blindly. Ordinary people are surely thought capable of distinguishing between true and false interpreters of natural law, if it is argued that 'so plain was it writ in the hearts of all mankind' that its precepts are reflected in deep-set convictions.[29] This is likewise affirmed by the voice of the Scriptures – which 'is the voice of reason confirmed by inspiration' (Sec. 31). The *Treatises* thus point to faith and tradition as consistent with natural law,[30] and as supporting avenues for its knowledge. Locke nowhere disputes the lowly-born the capacity of a rational life. The view to the contrary is often based on a famous

[27] Cox, *ibid.*, 37–8, 77, 79. See below, 94, as regards the state of nature.

[28] Secs. 124, 170, 176.

[29] Sec. 11. Locke here, as in Sec. 56 and I, 86, seems to contradict his denial of innate ideas in the *Essay*. Though important as regards the relationship between his philosophy and political theory, it is not relevant to the question of the knowability of natural law whether, as Laslett, *op. cit.*, 223, 292, points out (especially in Sections 11 and 56 where he spoke of 'the dictates of the law of reason which God had implanted in him [Adam]'), Locke resorted to the naive form of belief in innate knowledge or remained consistent in considering innateness in terms of the disposition to attain knowledge through one's natural faculties. On this distinction, see Yolton, *John Locke and the Way of Ideas*, and 'Locke and the Law of Nature,' 480 f.

[30] Brogan, *loc. cit.*, 87, and Wolin, *op. cit.*, 334–6, maintain the contrary.

passage in *The Reasonableness of Christianity*.[31] It denies the greater part of mankind the comprehension of the 'superfine distinctions of the schools', yet not of 'plain propositions, and a short reasoning about things familiar to their minds, and nearly allied to their daily experience'. Claiming supernatural sanctions as necessary to ensure compliance with rationalistic ethics, Locke recommended simple articles of faith and 'plain commands', since 'the greatest part cannot know, and therefore they must believe'.[32] The ultimate sanctions and truths of religion on which practical morality is based are beyond the ken of the masses. But this does not mean they are devoid of all rationality. They do not grasp the niceties of theological and philosophical discourse; only the things 'nearly allied to their daily experience' are open to plain men's 'short reasoning'.[33]

Locke could not very well argue that political experience is excluded from ordinary men's judgement of daily experience if he placed within the compass of their 'short reasoning' the right to decide which of their betters to support in case of revolt. Whether in their decision they might be right was our initial question. So far the answer is that the common man is held capable by Locke of having a knowledge of right and wrong so as not to be forced to follow his betters without any discernment. When Locke says, 'talk . . . hinders not men, from feeling' (Sec. 94), he does not at all mean, as a follower of Strauss will have it, that arguments have no influence on the people's feeling, that 'the natural forces are unaffected by doctrines'.[34] On the contrary, the question, for Locke, is which talk does and which does not agree with men's feeling. He answers:

'But whatever flatterers may talk to amuse people's *understandings*, it hinders not men, from feeling: and when they *perceive*, that any man, in what station soever, is out of the bounds of the civil society . . . and that they have no appeal on earth against any harm they may

[31] Thus Macpherson, *op. cit.*, 224. For Strauss and Cox, see below, 58.

[32] Cp. Macpherson, *ibid.*, 225, and the quotations from *The Reasonableness* there.

[33] Macpherson equates 'superfine distinctions' with reason as such (cp. I. Berlin, 'Hobbes, Locke and Professor Macpherson,' *The Political Quarterly*, XXXV, 4 (1964), 465). He bans 'short reasoning' from the confines of reason, and confuses a rational life with a fully rational life. Macpherson says, first, that for Locke 'the labouring class are in too low a position to be capable of a rational life' (*op. cit.*, 224), and then that the labourers are incapable of leading 'a fully rational life' (226, 232, 238 f.).

[34] Goldwin, *op. cit.*, 463, who makes the assertions discussed in the text, quotes from Sec. 94, irrespective of the context and by quoting from Secs. 224, 225 contradicts his own assertion.

receive from him,' they will 'take care as soon as they can, to have that safety and security in civil society, for which it was first instituted . . .' (Sec. 94).

Talk, to be influential, must have some relation to what the people see and feel, i.e., to observed facts. Their understanding and perception – not only their feeling – cannot be befuddled for long by the talk or doctrines of the flatterers of oppressive rulers, for the people are capable of appreciating the ruler's 'goodness and virtue . . . his uprightness and wisdom', and of differentiating between good rulers and 'successors of another stamp'. Ordinary men are clearly believed to be not incapable of passing political judgement according to the standards of natural law.

B. Scriptural Evidence

a. Supposed Deviations

To corroborate that specific rules of conduct are commanded by natural law and are knowable by men, Locke fell back on the evidence of the Scriptures. He did so in respect of the very foundation of his doctrine of political rights and obligations: his theory of the natural right of men to inflict capital punishment. What is 'writ in the hearts of all mankind' teaches '*all reasonable things*' that a man may do for his and mankind's preservation against 'a criminal, who having renounced reason, . . . has . . . declared war against all mankind' (Sec. 11). The self-evident character of the injunctions of the law of nature and of God is illustrated by Cain, who 'was so fully convinced' of what his punishment must be that 'he cries out, every one that findeth me, shall slay me'.

According to Leo Strauss and his disciples, this and similar passages are a manoeuvre to insinuate that men are in no condition to know the law of nature, and that the people would not know the means of its implementation.[35] Because Locke put together *Genesis*, X, 2 and IV, 14 in reversed order and did not quote them in full, he stands accused of misusing biblical evidence for the sake of contradicting it.[36] But it is easy to see that, though technically guilty of the first, he is not guilty of the second charge.

[35] Thus Strauss, *op. cit.*, 225, and Goldwin, *op. cit.*, 444. Similarly Cox, *op. cit.*, 89, 93. For examples of Strauss' references to Locke's text which actually go against Strauss' own interpretations, see Yolton, 'Locke and the Law of Nature,' 485 f. Cox, *op. cit.*, 35 f., 52 f., 75 f., 85 f., 111, 117, is particularly intent on showing as premeditated the inexactness of Locke's references to biblical and other accepted authorities.
[36] Cox, *op. cit.*, 54–6, following Strauss, *op. cit.*, 223, note 84.

His omission of the passage of Genesis, IX, 6: 'for in the image of God made He man,' proves nothing. He had already rendered its crucial part in paraphrase: 'men being all the workmanship of one omnipotent, and infinitely wise maker' (Sec. 6). Further the passage in question, according to which all men – including murderers – are created by God, does not, as Strauss asserts, provide a different foundation for the right to kill murderers than the one Locke gave in likening a murderer to '*things* noxious' (Sec. 8), or 'wild savage beasts' (Sec. 11). He derived from biblical evidence the right of men to use the inferior ranks of creatures – 'all the species of *irrational* animals' (I, 27) – by destroying them.[37] Insisting, with the traditional philosophers, on reason as the distinguishing property of man, he could identify 'a criminal . . . having renounced reason' as having lost his godlike image, as 'one of those wild savage beasts, with whom men can have no society nor security' (Sec. 11). No contradiction of the Bible is thus involved in concluding that 'upon this is grounded the great law of nature, "who so sheddeth man's blood, by man shall his blood be shed",' i.e. the law of nature which gives men the right to inflict capital punishment.

The Bible is also not contravened by the omission of the divine prohibition against the slaying of Cain.[38] Here again he had already a few pages earlier acknowledged the basis of the divine interdict to slay Cain. Men 'are his property, whose workmanship they are, made to last during his, not one another's pleasure' (Sec. 6). Having said this, Locke need not expressly put on record his acceptance of God's authority to commute the death penalty into another punishment. No more was at issue, after all, than an authority which flows from the legitimacy of imposing the sentence in the first place. If anything can be read into Locke's words, it might be his considering Cain's self-condemnation as an exception. After having referred to Cain in Section 11, he says in Section 13 'that he who was so unjust as to do his brother an injury, will scarce be so just as to condemn himself for it'. The exception does not affect the rule; the criminal deserves punishment, whether he asks for it or not.

Locke's reliance on biblical evidence thus renders it difficult to use it for the purpose of invalidating his affirmations of the knowability of natural law and of its affinity with the traditional law of nature. Strauss feels therefore bound to explain that, in addition to Locke's

[37] I, 25–8, 86–7, 92.
[38] The assertion is made by Cox, *loc. cit.*

wish to protect himself against persecution, concessions to scriptural principles pervade the *Treatises* because they embody the non-philosophical presentation of Locke's political doctrine. Such a presentation, Strauss says, accords with the view expressed in *The Reasonableness of Christianity*, that the majority of men cannot know but must believe, and are therefore best left to be instructed in the precepts of the Gospel.[39] Yet this line of argument implies that reliance on the Scriptures makes possible a political mass education that does not defeat the purpose of the *Treatises*, which in Strauss' opinion is to persuade the more rational minority to believe in and practice uninhibited hedonistic self-preservation. Only if the role of the majority were defined as passive, could one perhaps say that their instruction in scriptural principles is no impediment to their betters. But according to Strauss, Locke thought that the majority were a better guarantor of individual self-preservation than monarchic and oligarchic rulers; and that the right of the majority to check their betters did not hinder, but was conducive to, the excercise of the right of the minority to lead the way towards the self-preservation and mundane happiness of all.[40] Strauss thus contradicts, or at least implies the irrelevance, for civic purposes, of his central thesis that the esoteric intention of the *Treatises* proceeds from the irreconcilability of a natural law of hedonistic self-preservation with the natural law which agrees with scriptural principles.

b. *Overt Biblical Criticism*

Locke's natural law does not comprise only what is vouchsafed by the Scriptures. Although he did not care to enlarge upon this whenever the occasion offered itself, this is no proof of an esoteric intention of divorcing his natural law from Scripture. He made no secret of the occasional need of biblical criticism. Just as the authentic message of Scripture 'is the voice of reason confirmed by inspiration' (Sec. 31), the words of Scripture, though for the most part they confirm reason, must not contradict it. The relationship between reason and revelation is not exactly the same as between reason and Scripture.

'To warp the sacred rule of the word of God . . .' is characteristic of 'those, who embrace not truths, because *reason and revelation* offer them; but espouse tenets and parties, for ends different

---

[39] Strauss, *op. cit.*, 221. Similarly, Cox, *op. cit.*, 69.
[40] Strauss, *op. cit.*, 232–4.

from truth . . .' (I, 60). Whatever is referable to God's will is consistent with reason. 'Whatsoever providence orders, *or* the law of nature directs, *or* positive revelation declares, may be said to be by God's appointment...' (I, 16). Locke speaks of 'Scripture *or* reason' (I, 4) as the vehicle of truth, for he admits that Scripture occasionally gives rise to misunderstandings because of the imperfections of language.[41] In most instances our comparison of 'parallel places of Scripture . . . [will] make us know, how they may be best understood . . .' (I, 36). Yet at times we encounter 'so doubtful and obscure a place of Scripture' that nothing much can be done about it; thus it 'can be but an ill proof, being as doubtful as the thing to be proved by it, especially when there is nothing else in Scripture *or* reason to be found, that favours or supports it'.[42] To fall back on the rules of reason is not to doubt but to ascertain God's truth.

'God, I believe, speaks differently from men, because he speaks with more truth, more certainty: but when he vouchsafes to speak to men, I do not think, he speaks differently from them, in crossing the rules of language in use amongst them. This would not be to condescend to their capacities, when he humbles himself to speak to them, but to lose his design in speaking, what thus spoken, they could not understand' (I, 46).

Thus, where scriptural language is obscure, we are entitled to doubt whether the words reported 'must be understood literally to have been spoken' (I, 86). In stipulating that the Scriptures may occasionally offend against the rules of consistent speech, but never God himself, Locke openly secured reason against being subjected to the literal meaning of each biblical passage.

With biblical criticism carried to such lengths, it is gratuitous to prove its existence mainly by inverting the literal meaning of Locke's words. He was only too well aware that even in a political discourse 'it may perhaps be censured as an impertinent criticism . . . to find fault with words and names that have obtained in the world' (Sec. 52). Yet he insisted that 'it may not be amiss to offer new ones . . .' – such as 'parental' instead of 'paternal' authority – by consulting 'reason or revelation', and also 'the style of the Old and New Tes-

---

[41] Cp. Lamprecht, *op. cit.*, 2. The *Treatises* reflect the argument set forth at length in the *Essay*, Book III, especially ix–xi. On the importance of the issue of language in the *Essay*, as well as on Boyle's preoccupation with the subject and Locke's admiration for Boyle, see Aarsleff, *loc. cit.*, 12 f.

[42] I, 112. Cp. *Essay*, III, ix, 22–3.

tament'. He rejected the method of diluting 'some harsh or corrosive liquor . . . that the scattered parts may go down with less feeling, and cause less aversion' (I, 7) and castigated Filmer who through offending against 'propriety of speech' leaves matters of fundamental importance 'like the philosopher's stone in politics, out of the reach of anyone to discover from his writings'.[43] Since the methodological criticism was part of the substantive criticism of orthodox opinions and institutions, Locke foresaw the attack of the zealous Christians who 'charge atheism on those who will not without examining, submit to their doctrines, and blindly swallow their nonsense' (I, 154). Anticipating the stance of the Enlightenment, which took much inspiration from him, he frankly questioned the title of the Christian nations alone to represent 'the civillest nations . . .' (I, 141). We find 'in holy writ children sacrificed by their parents and this amongst the people of God themselves' (I, 58). Locke may be said to have relied here on Scripture when he maintained that 'God judged not of this by our A[uthor]'s [i.e. Filmer's] rule, nor allowed of the authority of practice against his righteous law'. He invoked, however, the same law against practices which were not condemned in Scripture.[44]

It is undeniable that Locke deviated from the Scriptures,[45] or went far beyond them in his derivations of individual rights, not to mention, as Strauss correctly insists, his elaborate rules of government. The *tour de force* of connecting the belief in reason with the belief in Christianity had become more marked in Locke than it was in pre-seventeenth century doctrines of natural law. Reason had ceased to be the handmaid of theology. Still, Locke's assumption is that any rift between scriptural principles and dictates of reason is purely fortuitous; there is none whatsoever between God's righteous law and reason. The law of God and nature is a law of reason. This entails, however, that the obligations of 'the laws of God and nature', which represent the obligations conducive to sociability, are 'so great, and so strong, in the case of promises, that Omnipotency itself can be tied by them. Grants, promises and oaths are bonds

[43] I, 109. According to Cox, *op. cit.*, 31, Locke's intention was to indicate that he was practising this kind of writing himself, the interpretational pre-supposition being that in esoteric writing you mean the opposite of what you are saying.

[44] Thus his denial of 'a sole or peculiar right' of the first-born, in I, 93, 97, 101-3.

[45] Cp. Lamprecht, *op. cit.*, 2 f. Yolton, 'Locke and the Law of Nature,' *loc. cit.*, 484 f., and Polin, *op. cit.*, 102 f., 117. On the significance of Locke's epistemology in this respect and its influence, see Yolton, *John Locke and the Way of Ideas*, Chs. III and V.

that hold the Almighty' (Sec. 195). God is bound by reason. This is not to limit his will, because his will is reason supreme. In its entirety, Locke's natural law requires the universe to be understood rationally; it has, therefore, to bear comparison with empirical facts.[46] It contains the affirmation of the ultimate truths of revealed religion together with – to use Strauss' apposite formulation – 'the partial law of nature which is limited to what "political happiness" – a "good of mankind in this world" – evidently requires'.[47] As such it guides the people's judgement whether or not to support attempts 'to amend the acknowledged faults, in the frame they have been accustomed to', whether it be 'any original defects, or adventitious ones introduced by time, or corruption . . .' (Sec. 223). Locke's awareness of the necessity of political change according to unassailable standards of rationality entails a critical attitude to history. Sacred history is no exception.

At the limit, Locke's 'political' law of nature could reflect the rational order of this world even if there had been no revelation.[48] The ascent from sense data through discursive reasoning, or by direct inference or intuition through the 'light of nature', is the preferable way of gaining knowledge about standards of action. It is not the only one.[49] There is revelation, and it does not contradict reason. Although the minor imperfections in the transmission of

[46] Cp. Laslett, *op. cit.*, 87.

[47] Cp. Strauss, *op. cit.*, 213-4. According to Strauss, however, the final definition of Locke's natural law must take into account that, on Locke's premises, a natural law in the proper sense must be known to be given by God and conform in all its parts to the New Testament (204 f., 214-19, 233).

[48] According to Polin, *op. cit.*, 123, note 1, this is part of the modification in the *Treatises* of the relation between reason and natural law, though reference to God is not thereby precluded. Cp. Lamprecht, *op. cit.*, 11-12. In fact, in the *Essay* (I, iii, 6), too, Locke said in one instance that the existence of God and obedience to him are 'so congruous to the light of reason' that a great part of mankind 'give testimony to the law of nature'; while in the other instance (I, iii, 13) he defended the view 'that there is a law knowable by the light of nature, i.e. without the help of positive revelation'. On Locke's adumbration of this position in the early *Essays*, and the affinity there with Culverwell and Grotius, see Leyden, *op. cit.*, 52 f.

[49] On intuition as Locke's ideal of knowledge, and the identification of reason with what is known as well as with the act of knowing, see Aaron, *op. cit.*, 222 f. On Locke's prevarications and confusion of issues in this respect, see von Leyden, *Essays*, 59; and 'John Locke and Natural Law', *loc. cit.*, 28-9. See also Lamprecht, *op. cit.*, 85; Cranston, *op. cit.*, 65; and Yolton, *loc. cit.*, 482. On alternative or conjunctive ways of knowing, and on the relation between reason and revelation, see Aaron, *op. cit.*, 253, 264-6, 296 f., 305; Yolton, 'Locke and the Law of Nature', 481-3, 486, 489, 491; Polin, *op. cit.*, 3 f., 25, 40 f., 55 f., 68, 91, 117, 121; Simon, *op. cit.*, 389 f.; Gough, *op. cit.*, 11 f., 17; and Laslett, *op. cit.*, 87-8, 92 f.

God's will through the Scriptures force us to test and supplement them through reason, they supply enough plain and divinely-sanctioned knowledge for ordinary men to know when they have right on their side. Scripture illustrates also that in their daily experience men are moved by deeply-rooted convictions and feelings of right and wrong, reflecting precepts of natural law. This law, even when Locke expounds it without reference to Scripture, is not merely a law of convenient or hedonist self-preservation.

C. Self-Preservation and Traditional Values

'The first and fundamental natural law, . . . is the preservation of the society, and (as far as will consist with the public good) of every person in it.'[50] An almost unlimited number of derivations can be made from this law. It might seem that Locke had saved the compatibility of his natural law with the traditional one only at the price of framing the first natural law in the most general way, so as to leave the widest latitude for its application to particular cases. But such an objection applies to any natural law doctrine, for in each the determination of particular rules is a matter of derivation from general principles. In awareness of the unequal powers of understanding, all natural law doctrines entrust an elite with responsibility, remaining all the while cognizant of the discrepancy between the observed management of private and public affairs on the one hand and the precepts of natural law on the other. Locke proposed to reduce this discrepancy. He did not set about it by detracting from the moral claims of traditional natural law.

His first and fundamental natural law ties the preservation of the individual to that of society, in accord with the traditional limitations of individual and collective self-preservation by which a proper civil society is distinguishable from a happy-go-lucky gang of robbers.[51] The distinction meets the requirement of consistent speech and action if one prefers life in civil society, although one is aware that it might be more conducive to temporal happiness to live like a robber than to live in a civil society. In making the traditional distinction Locke shows his concern not with happiness but with true, namely, virtuous, happiness.[52]

---

[50] Sec. 134. Cp. 16, 123, 128, 129, 149, 159, 168, 220.

[51] Secs. 176, 177, 228.

[52] I have commented on the distinction in the terms used by Strauss, *op. cit.*, 229, who in this case too contradicts his thesis of Locke's concern with a purely hedonistic

Locke derived from the individual right of self-preservation that political guarantee against the necessarily defective implementation of natural law, in the exercise of which every man has an equal share: the right of revolt. The right of self-preservation itself is justified by the moral imperative of natural equality. In accord with the Scriptures, it forbids that subordination which 'may authorize us to destroy one another . . .' (Sec. 6), and entails the right to resist the degradation of 'the inferior ranks of creatures'. To exist only for another's use is the ultimate evil, not only because this may lead to violent death, but because it is not necessarily better than death. Hence the right to resist the offender – whether he is a common murderer, a thief, a robber or an arbitrary ruler, for 'the injury and the crime is equal, whether committed by the wearer of a crown, or some petty villain' (Sec. 176).

Locke stressed that to grant 'every man . . . a right to punish the offender, and be executioner of the law of nature' (Sec. 8), 'will seem a very strange doctrine to some men' (Sec. 9). This theory of punishment is 'strange' inasmuch as it supports a novel doctrine of political rights. There is nothing new or strange in maintaining that reason forbids us to kill our fellow-men, while it allows us to kill the killer – or would-be killer. This is not opposed to earlier natural law teachings and their concern with excellence, virtue and love, nor to the practice of the world.[53] Perhaps by implying a parallel between the relations among men and among nations, Locke played a trick on naïve readers,[54] although he had forewarned them by insisting on the 'strangeness' of his doctrine. Locke could legitimately rely on the Bible for the right to kill in war or inflict capital punishment on a criminal; for equating 'the injury and the crime' whether perpetrated by individuals or nations; he could again cite the Bible when he effaced the distinction between the appeal to heaven and the appeal to arms: the second is nothing

law of self-preservation. On Locke's explicit distinction between happiness and true happiness, see in Lord Peter King, *The Life of John Locke with Extracts from his Correspondence, Journals and Common Place Books* (London, 1829), 304, and the *Essay*, III, xxi, 50–2, 56–7. Cp. Aaron, *op. cit.*, 257, on the affinity between Locke's hedonism with the Christian hedonism of Gassendi, and as not deriving from Hobbes' materialistic brand. See also, Fox Bourne, *op. cit.*, II, 90 f.; Lamprecht, *op. cit.*, 90 f.; von Leyden, *op. cit.*, 71 f.; and Polin, *op. cit.*, 21–4, 49 f.

[53] Goldwin, *op. cit.*, 439, 441, suggests that these are the novelties. See also Cox, *op. cit.*, 159.

[54] Strauss, *op. cit.*, 214–15.

but the realization of the first. Jephta was 'forced to appeal to heaven . . . and then prosecuting, and relying on his appeal, he leads out his army to battle' (Sec. 21). The novelty – or the trick – lies in stretching the right of an armed appeal to be used by one people against another, so that the governed may use this right against their own rulers. That 'God in heaven is judge' when 'there is no judicature on earth' entails that '*every man is judge for himself*, . . . whether *another* has put himself into a state of war with him, and whether he should appeal to the supreme judge, as Jephta did'.[55] Through paralleling external and internal relations any contradiction is removed between the traditional Christian view which restricted the appeal to heaven of the governed to mere prayer, and the justification of active resistance derived from natural law.[56] Locke's doctrine of punishment is novel in that it derives the right of revolt, as well as the magistrate's right to inflict the death penalty, the decisive hallmark of political authority,[57] from a right which every individual has and never irretrievably surrenders to any government.

Yet in thus providing the basis for the justification of government by consent, he did not oppose Hobbes' conclusions while accepting the substance of his natural law of mere self-preservation.[58] True, 'the right of my freedom' to resist and, if need be, to kill anyone who is about to enslave me 'is the only security of my preservation' (Sec. 17). But this right is, as we have seen, derived from the moral imperative of natural equality and serves, therefore, as the ultimate safeguard against the greatest iniquity, which is tyranny. Tyranny – like the incursions of thieves and robbers – does not consist merely in the threat to life and possessions. These are insecure 'against the violence and oppression of this absolute ruler' (Sec. 93), not because, under him, laws, judges and the restraint of violence between subjects are lacking, but because the security which the arbitrary ruler provides does not emanate 'from a true love of mankind and society, and such a charity as we owe all one to another . . . .' Not mere self-preservation, but security against 'the *unjust* will of another' (Sec. 13), is at stake. 'When all cannot be preserved,

---

[55] Sec. 241; cp. Sec. 176.
[56] I. Bode, 'Ursprung und Begriff der parlamentarischen Opposition,' *Sozialwissenschaftliche Studien*, Heft 3 (Stuttgart, 1962), 32 f., who maintains the opposite, misreads Locke.
[57] See below, 213 f.
[58] As Strauss, *op. cit.*, 231, argues.

the safety of the *innocent* is to be preferred' (Sec. 16). Only 'so far as calm reason and *conscience* dictates' may 'every man . . . by the right he has to preserve mankind in general, . . . restrain, or where it is necessary, destroy things noxious to them . . .' (Sec. 8). 'And any other person who finds it *just*, may also join with him that is injured' (Sec. 10). The right of self-preservation, exercised in accord with the judgement of individual conscience is a unifying factor, because it must be guided, if it is to be right, by the principles of justice. Individual conscience, when so guided abides by the rule of 'reason and common equity, which is that measure God has set to the actions of men, for their mutual security' (Sec. 8).[59]

Equity is the measure and means of security. Security is also the condition for equity. Neither material interest nor self-preservation replaces or determines virtue. Only, as self-preservation is the physical condition for the attainment of virtue, it is also part of the hierarchy of ends. The right to one's life is not just a naturalistic imperative. Natural law constitutes distinctions between human beings, matter and the lower creatures. It permits men, for the sake of their self-preservation, to use the lower creatures to the point of destroying them. But it forbids men to degrade other men to 'the inferior rank of creatures'. Since innate natural rights are so visibly tied up by Locke with the immutable principles of equity and justice, innate natural right does not oust innate natural duty, yet neither is there a 'sleight of hand' by which the right of the innocent to be preserved becomes a duty rather than a right.[60] Locke's awareness that there are no rights without corresponding duties is made clear from the outset in his agreement with Hooker.[61]

Indeed, the generally accepted distinction between the traditional and the new natural law doctrines might merit some re-examination. At any rate, it is easily carried too far. Duties create spheres of right, inasmuch as clearly defined duties limit arbitrariness and hence mutual interferences in human relations. In classical and mediaeval natural law, the hierarchy of ends and duties corresponds largely to the hierarchical order of society. Over and above what applies to all men, there are special duties of life commensurate

---

[59] Strauss, *op. cit.*, 222–3, goes against the textual evidence when he maintains that the judgement of individual conscience is detached from that of God and ends by opposing conscience and human beings.

[60] The first evaluation is by Strauss, *op. cit.*, 226–7, and the second by Kendall, *op. cit.*, 79.

[61] See above, 50.

with the special functions of corporate groups. Special duties actually entail privileges which accrue through the group to its members. With Locke, the reverse is true. The group derives its special standing from the personal attributes of the members who compose it. Broadly speaking, the difference between pre- and post-Hobbesian natural law seems to be this: in the former, duties implicitly constitute rights; in the latter, individual rights explicitly entail duties. Locke may, therefore, be said to have paved the way – prepared by Hobbes – to a new kind of conscience and consciousness. Even so, I think it mistaken to define the new conscience as 'one that would be an internalized expression of externalized rules,' as opposed to 'the externalized expression of internal convictions'.[62] Traditional natural law, no less than that of Locke, identifies the judgement of individual conscience with observing 'the eternal rule' which is external to men inasmuch as it is not made by them.

3. APPLICABILITY

A. Natural Law and Consent

I have so far concentrated on Locke's positive statements on the knowability of natural law. Even when taken by themselves, they do not admit the conclusion that he regarded the people as the proponent of 'the legitimacy and infallibility of reason itself', and still less that everybody is authorized to set himself up as an interpreter of natural law, with the consequence that the existence of the state would become impossible.[63] While Locke justified the collective appeal of the ruled against their rulers, he did not transfer infallibility from the rulers to the ruled. In fact, he made statements which raise the question as to whether the reliance on natural law amounts after all to any more than an arbitrary rationalization of conveniences, the ultimate justification of which lies in that it is consented to. He cast serious doubt, if not on the knowability of immutable natural laws, then on their applicability.

He pointed out 'that self-love will make men partial to themselves and their friends . . . that ill nature, passion and revenge will carry them too far' (Sec. 13). He stressed 'the variety of opinions,

---

[62] Wolin, *op. cit.*, 338.
[63] Polin, *op. cit.*, 235, and Vaughan, *op. cit.*, 168–70, respectively. Vaughan does not see that the revolutionary judgement is a collective one and that what he said on the prevalence of the wise few (178) is Locke's own view.

and contrariety of interests' (Sec. 98) and the natural tendency of men to invade each others' rights. He concluded: 'there wants an established, settled, known law, received and allowed by common consent to be the standard of right and wrong . . .'[64] It does not follow, however, that for purposes of civic action, Locke granted men unlimited competence to change natural law by agreement.[65]

If men are completely divided by the contrariety of interests and opinions and by partiality, consent to anything is out of the question. This much was already recognized by Hobbes. He distinguished between passions which make for strife and passions which incline to peace, whence the possibility that 'reason suggests convenient articles of peace, upon which men may be drawn to agreement'.[66] In exchange for the benefits of political society Hobbesian men agree on articles of peace by which they renounce once and for all the right to dissent from established authority through concerted action. According to Locke, the capacity to reach informed agreement goes further, so that ordinary men can be trusted to retain the right of agreeing to dissent collectively from their rulers – and in accord with natural law at that. Even if Locke thought men might be more interested in agreeing to deviations from natural law than in heeding it, he did not think the heeding impossible, let alone concede men the right, as distinct from the capacity, to change natural law by consent. The mature Locke stood by his earlier views that 'utility is not the basis of the law or the ground of obligation, but the consequence of obedience to it'.[67] What is moral, is in the end useful; but not all that is useful is moral. He may in later years have become even more aware of the discrepancy between a commonly-agreed interest and natural law, between rationality exercised for expediency's sake and that guided by the objective standards of natural law. The validity of the law of nature remained for him independent of consent.

In his *Essays on the Law of Nature*, he had rejected the hypothesis that universal consent could be proof of the existence of natural

[64] Sec. 124. Lamprecht, *op. cit.*, 135, note; Vaughan, *op. cit.*, 171; and Gough, *op. cit.*, 34, who refers to R. Niebuhr, *The Children of Light and the Children of Darkness* (1945), 25, are evidently somewhat rash in maintaining that Locke thought public and private interests easily reconcilable.

[65] Kendall, *op. cit.*, 82, 85, 108, suggests this conclusion and Strauss implies it. See above, 58. Stephen, *op. cit.*, 133–4, had already maintained that the compact is more important than natural law.

[66] *Leviathan*, ch. 13.

[67] *Essays*, 215.

law.[68] In the *Second Treatise*, he omitted any direct reference to this hypothesis. Instead, he emphasized that, although by 'the law of nature . . . common to them all . . . mankind are one community . . . the corruption, and viciousness of degenerate men . . .' compels them to 'separate from this great and natural community, and by positive agreements combine into smaller and divided associations' (Sec. 128). This implies that if natural law were fully observed by all men, they would live in one world-community and thus be united by universal consent; which is not to say that all that is universally agreed is, for that reason, in accord with natural law.[69] Locke's theory of labour and property in general, and particularly his moral disparagement of the introduction of money by universal consent, are striking cases in point.[70] Likewise, the existence of positive agreements on which divided associations are founded proves no more than the impossibility of universal consent, and not that natural law does not exist or is dependent on consent. As stated in the *First Treatise*, widely-accepted customs, such as primogeniture, do not confirm the existence of 'a natural or divine right of primogeniture, to both estate and power . . .' (I, 91). Similarly, though the right of children to succeed to the possessions of their parents is 'common practice, . . . we cannot say, that it is the common consent of mankind' (I, 88), which establishes this right. It is not decisive that such a consent 'has never been asked, nor actually given'. Even 'if common tacit consent has established it, it would make but a positive and not natural right . . .' When Locke admitted that 'where the practice is universal, it is reasonable to think the cause is natural', he admitted no more than that God's laws and men's convictions (as expressed in positive laws) often do coincide. Yet such coincidence is not the rule, as Locke's attitude to primogeniture shows. Similarly, the father's right to inherit from his son who dies without issue stands, 'whatever the municipal laws of some countries, may absurdly direct otherwise' (I, 90).

Just as universal consent does not necessarily indicate what natural law enjoins, consent in society does not necessarily testify to the observance of natural law. Starting from the premise that men's

[68] *Ibid.*, 42 and 106 f.
[69] As Locke said in the *Essay*, I, iii, 6: 'several moral rules may receive from mankind a very general approbation, without either knowing or admitting the true ground of morality . . .'
[70] Cp. C. H. Monson, 'Locke and His Interpreters,' *Political Studies*, VI (1958), 126–7, and below, 157.

failings cause their separation into distinct communities although by the law of nature 'mankind are one community', it would have been self-defeating to maintain as a rule without exception that, the greater the number of people who consent to something, the greater the observance of natural law. This is true only in the hypothetical case when the whole of mankind are inclined to live peacefully in one world-community. In political society the legislature makes laws by consent but has only as much competence as the law of nature gave man for his own preservation and that of the rest of mankind.[71] That consent remains subject to natural law does not derogate from its being the rightful instrument for the realization of that law in society. Rather, consent must remain subject to natural law, because the right of individuals to consent to particularizations of natural law emanates from that law. 'Men being, . . . by nature, all free, equal and independent, no one can be put out of this estate, and subjected to the political power of another, without his own consent' (Sec. 95). Only by consent may men turn natural into political freedom, that is, limit their freedom so as to ensure both an optimal observance of natural law and an optimal enjoyment of the rights it bestows upon individuals.

Men may err by consent as otherwise. But consent is still the bulwark against men's arbitrary dependence on each other and on their rulers. On this basis Locke combined the rejection of universal consent as the indicator of ultimate truths, and of majority consent as a fool-proof approximation to these truths, with the distinctive feature of his natural law doctrine: the authority of the ruled to consent to – or rather dissent from – their rulers' particularizations of natural law.

A traditional natural law theorist like Thomas Aquinas was well aware of deviations from natural law – manifest in unjust or tyrannical laws – which are the result of the rule of men by men. But on the strength of Pauline teachings, he still found the imprint of the eternal rule in such laws. They retain the quality of law because their objective, to assure obedience, is as such wholesome and necessary.[72] Notwithstanding his distinction between moral and legal obligations,[73] and despite his eloquent condemnation of tyranny, he agreed to the limitation and deposition of rulers

---

[71] Sec. 135.
[72] *Summa Theologica*, qu. 93; qu. 92, art. 4; qu. 95, art. 2.
[73] *Ibid.*, qu. 100.

only where legal provisions or customs to that effect were established. He rejected tyrannicide and active extra-legal resistance on the part of an aggregate of private citizens.[74] This conclusion was accepted by Hobbes, who identified right and law in public matters, although one might well ask how consistent he was in doing so.

Locke was at one with Aquinas in distinguishing between moral and legal norms. But unlike both his predecessors he maintained the right of private citizens to join together in extra-legal resistance. In this instance, at least, he was more consistent than either Aquinas or Hobbes, and especially more than the latter, from whom he took the emphasis upon the principle of self-preservation. For Hobbes prudence does not require more than securing the right to evade military service, imprisonment and giving testimony against blood-relations.[75] These are all rather futile safeguards against the political insecurity of individuals. Locke went further: Besides recommending the institutionalization of consent, and thereby the sharing of political power, he advised prudence against putting a practically irrevocable trust into the hands of any government and insisted on the right of concerted resistance against the government's breaches of natural law. The authority to apply natural law and judge the appositeness of its application is made a matter of competition between governmental agencies and between them and the people.

'Thus the law of nature stands as an eternal rule to all men, legislators as well as others. The rules that they make for other men's actions, must, as well as their own and other men's actions, be comformable to the law of nature, i.e. to the will of God, . . . and . . . no human sanction can be good, or valid against it' (Sec. 135).

This obligation stands, whether the legislature is 'placed in one or more'. So does the right of revolt.

In principle, one might thus regard consent as subject to natural law, and competitive consent as most conducive to its proper realization. One may nevertheless think that, while men are capable of knowing that law, in practice they have become more and more incapable of heeding it.

---

[74] *De Regimine Principum*, ch. VI. There are, however, many affinities between Locke and Aquinas which would repay a close analysis.
[75] *Leviathan*, ch. xxi.

B. Moral Deterioration and Positive Law

Considering Locke's insistence on human frailty and baseness, one is led to ask whether human sanctions, granted they were once good and valid according to the eternal rule, will not increasingly deviate from it, and by competitive consent at that. The wider sharing of political power, i.e. the placing of its several parts into different hands, is the product of historical experience and development.[76] This development would seem to indicate a departure from men's allegiance to natural law. For how can positive laws still reflect the obligations of natural law, and these obligations even become 'drawn closer' if with the vanishing of the 'golden age' of 'the infancies of commonwealths,' governors have become worse and subjects more vicious?[77] The moral deterioration of subjects certainly necessitates more legislation, and the deterioration of governors requires a diffusion of power. The degeneration of both governors and subjects could hardly be propitious for an increased correspondence of legislation with natural law, and so the condition for any correspondence would seem to become less favourable as history went on. If it could be said that according to Locke moral regression is an uninterrupted process, it would follow that what counted in the end were his negative views concerning men's capacity to be guided by natural law. However, his positive and negative views supplement rather than supplant one another.

In the first place, Locke's positive and negative statements on men's capacity to know and apply natural law are predicated on what is permanent in human nature. Accordingly, the evolutionary argument of moral deterioration does not denote a unilinear process, whether we proceed on the assumption that Locke means by 'the state of nature' a pre-political stage of historical development or merely uses the notion as an expository device. On the first reading, the state of nature is superseded by the 'golden age' of early and minimal government. It is a stage of harmonious simplicity and an advance beyond the inconveniences, fears and dangers of the state of nature.[78] It follows that the observance of natural law in the infancy of governments was greater not only than in more developed stages, but also than prior to the institution of government. Retrogression also follows a previous ascent from a worse to a

[76] Secs. 94, 107.
[77] Secs. 135, 111, 110, respectively.
[78] Secs. 13, 37, 92, 101, 123, 124, 126, 127, etc.

better situation if we understand the notion of a pre-political state of nature as an extrapolation and identify the beginnings of society with the near-political stage of family organization. On this reading, too, Locke did not only accuse subsequent ages of having perverted the excellent government of the 'golden age',[79] but he also pointed to a contrast between it and the previous condition of insecurity. Thus, whether we interpret Locke's state of nature as a previous non-political or politically inferior condition, the observance of equity and justice is greater when government exists than when it does not, and development does not simply proceed from better to worse. On no account can we say that his admission of retrogression ought to have led Locke to Paine's conclusion that government is evil and unnecessary.[80] Since according to both Locke and Paine moral defects are not the consequence but the cause of the institution of government, Locke was the more consistent of the two in making it plain that government provides the means to cope with moral deterioration. This is only a first indication of a more level-headed and frank acknowledgement of the function and merits of government activity than that still too often associated with liberalism.

Governors, rather than government as such, also became the cause of deficiencies, because the social and economic development achieved by the rule of good and wise princes offers unworthy successors an increased temptation to abuse power for their private interests.[81] The misuse of governmental authority does not discredit its positive function but induces men to make provisions against its abuse. Although the observance of equity and justice has decreased after the golden age of early government, governors and subjects have become worse but not incorrigible. Under bad government on the one hand and under the strain of social and economic differentiation on the other, men remain what they are by nature – that is, as they are depicted in 'the state of nature'. It is true that bad rulers had often succeeded good rulers, but this does not mean that the opposite could not happen.[82] Hence, like the institution of legislative activity, the intensification and the enlargement of political competitiveness are intended as the means

[79] Cp. Lamprecht, *op. cit.*, 127, note.
[80] As Vaughan, *op. cit.*, 161–2, maintains. Polin, *op. cit.*, 34, note 5, asserts that the idea of progress is not implied in Locke's conception of change.
[81] Secs. 42, 94, 107, 111, 162, 166.
[82] See below, 272 f.

to increase the observance of equity and justice. No contradiction of men's ability to keep on applying natural law is therefore involved in the assumption that a tolerable degree of equity and justice must, and can, be ensured when the ceaseless obligations of natural law 'in many cases are drawn closer, and have by human laws known penalties annexed to them, to enforce their observation' (Sec. 135).

The thesis of the continuous applicability of natural law is not affected by the conviction that rules of conduct which are sanctioned by human law, although they become thereby more effective, are not for that reason alone also more in harmony with natural law. A great many of 'the municipal laws of countries' reflect the 'fancies and intricate contrivances of men, following contrary and hidden interests put into words'. What is thus put into words is not right, since positive laws 'are only so far right, as they are founded on the law of nature, by which they are to be regulated and interpreted'.[83] While Locke again insists that men flout natural law by consented laws, although they have no right to do so, he had no intention of implying that a correct adaption of consented laws to natural law is impossible. Since the possibility to conceive law 'in its true notion' (Sec. 57), is the prerequisite of the obligation to honour laws, the denial of such a possibility would have amounted to preaching anarchy. This was quite beside Locke's purpose. For, 'where there is no law, there is no freedom' (Sec. 57). But although 'no man in civil society can be exempted from the laws of it' (Sec. 94), there is also no freedom where obedience to positive laws is mandatory, whether they are just or unjust.[84]

That Locke did not intend to decry the belief in the applicability of natural laws by a sleight of hand is finally confirmed by his alignment of the gist of his sceptical and optimistic statements in the following instances. He said:

'There wants an established, settled, known law, received and allowed by common consent to be the standard of right and wrong . . . For though the law of nature be plain and intelligible to all rational

---

[83] Sec. 12. Cp. 135 and I, 90, 92, and *Essays*, 118–19, 188–9. See also above, 68.

[84] Sec. 93. Kendall, *op. cit.*, 76, sees an absolute obligation to obey the law of the commonwealth as following from Locke's conception of natural law. Kendall confuses the law of the commonwealth with 'good laws' (80–1), just as he confuses absolute moral obligations with ' "rigid" constitutions' or ' "principles" of jurisprudence'. On Locke's understanding of 'constitutions', see below, 136 and 235 f.

creatures; yet men being biassed by their interest, as well as ignorant for want of study of it, are not apt to allow of it as a law binding to them in the application of it to their particular cases' (Sec. 124).

What is stated here is neither different from traditional natural law teaching nor self-contradictory. The argument is simply that, considering men as they are, natural law cannot be applied to particular cases without the intermediacy of government and positive law. Because this is due to the bias and ignorance of men, but not of all men, positive law may still reflect natural law through the prevalence of those who are neither ignorant nor biassed. Thus Locke spoke first of what is plain 'to all rational creatures' and not of what is plain to all men. But when he spoke of bias and ignorance, he referred simply to 'men' and not to 'all rational creatures'. If this appears to be hair-splitting exegesis, it is confirmed by Locke's acknowledgement of the differential capacities of men. What is more, in the very section which is adduced by some interpreters to prove that according to Locke natural law is of no avail, he made it clear that because natural law is 'unwritten, and so nowhere to be found but in the minds of men, they who through passion or interest shall mis-cite, or misapply it, cannot so easily be convinced of their mistake where there is no established judge' (Sec. 136). Evidently, not all men are misled by passions and interests. Otherwise nobody would be left to try and convince anybody. And what is not easy is clearly not impossible. This applies, according to Locke, where there is no established judge, and much more, where there is one.

In an attempt to attribute the opposite intention to him, Strauss and Cox leave out the part of Sec. 136 which we have just quoted[85] and rely exclusively on the other part, which says that natural law 'serves not, as it ought, to determine the rights, and fence the properties of those that live under it, *especially* where every one is judge, interpreter, and executioner of it too, and that in his own case'. The 'especially', however, is a qualification which establishes the connexion with the foregoing part of the section. It also indicates the limitation of Locke's distinction between the state of nature – where everybody is judge, interpreter and executioner of natural law – and political society – where there is one established judge.

[85] Strauss, *op. cit.*, 225–6, and Cox, *op. cit.*, 80–1.

There is, then, a clear foundation for the interpretation that men as men, and ordinary men at that, may know natural law, and that the correspondence between natural and positive law is possible and increasingly so under government by consent.

C. *Individual and Collective Consent*

Since both individual and majority consent are sanctioned by natural law, the question arises how Locke related individual to collective judgement, individual to collective consent. My treatment of the topic is determined by the fact that for Locke the pressing issue was to secure the recognition of majority rights,[86] and that in *The Treatises* he revealed little awareness of the logical difficulties involved in the relationship between individual and collective consent.[87]

Even when Locke is most severely taken to task as 'the prince of individualists' whose individualism serves to destroy but not to build again, some allowance is made for the historical conditions in which he pleaded for individual will, energy and initiative.[88] The doctrine of individual rights had been fiercely attacked by Filmer after having been forcefully – too forcefully perhaps – highlighted by Hobbes, although he had blessed the contracting-away of individual rights to the *Leviathan* and found government by consent objectionable. Locke militated against both the meta-political principles and the political techniques which, he thought, curtailed the well-being and dignity of the individual more than the preservation of political society warrants. Rather than let himself be carried away by his insistence on individual rights, his main endeavour was to make political society secure against the political triumph of the fully desocialized individual of Hobbes, i.e., the tyrant.[89] He sought to achieve this by a pragmatic alternation in emphasis on individual and social claims, on private and

---

[86] Cp. Kendall, *op. cit.*, 103, who, nevertheless, argues that the nature of Locke's views commits him to the disregard of minority rights. In his, on the whole, well-taken exceptions to Kendall's interpretation, Gough's own criticism of Locke is not always commensurate with his rejection (*op. cit.*, 41–2) of the unhistorical attitude of finding theories wanting in the light of the experiences of the nineteenth and twentieth centuries.

[87] Cp. Gough, *op. cit.*, 43. For an extended philosophical evaluation of Locke's views on the relationship between the individual and the community, see Polin, *op. cit.* Ch. IV.

[88] Cp. Vaughan, *op. cit.*, 156, 220, 200–1.

[89] Cp. Polin, *op. cit.*, 138.

public interests, rather than by any systematic correlation between them. In other words, assuming that the principles of individuality and sociability both flow from reason,[90] Locke ruled out, in principle, any incompatibility between individuality and sociability because he admitted none between the precepts of natural law.

'Virtuous actions themselves do not clash' and 'the duties of life are not at variance with one another.'[91] If natural law were fully observed, men would live in a world-wide community, because the mutual adjustment of individual claims would be no problem. Problems arise, not because of the content of natural laws, but because of men's incapability to apply them faultlessly.[92] Since, however, there is no unbridgeable gulf between natural law and men's capacity to live by it, and their division of interests is no unsurmountable barrier to agreement, the claims of individual wills can be assumed to converge in a rightful public will. The assumption is the more feasible as individual rights entail individual duties towards other men and individual conscience is a unifying factor. On these premises, a proper collective judgement can be regarded as the composite of individual judgements, which do not clash with each other nor with the standards of natural law.

Actually, clashes do happen in both respects. But, unlike Rousseau, Locke did not set apart the 'will of all' from 'the general will', the wrong will of a self-interested aggregate of subjects from the right will of the citizens who think and act as the corporate sovereign body.[93] He did not distinguish between the whole as the sum total of individuals and the whole as the embodiment of the 'general will'. Mankind, like society or any group, always meant for Locke the sum of the individuals who compose it.[94] For him, the coexistence of centrifugal and centripetal tendencies in human nature was no impediment to, but the basis of, establishing an area of common interest as the natural concomitant of any

[90] Cp. Polin, op. cit., 138, 162 f., and Simon, loc. cit., 392.

[91] Essays, 212.

[92] This distinction is disregarded by Kendall in all the instances which he adduces to demonstrate the incompatibility of the contents that Locke ascribed to natural law. See op. cit., 76 f., 81 f.

[93] Du Contrat Social, Livre II, Ch. III.

[94] See below, 170, 188–9 and 204. Locke's views in this respect reveal the affinity between his normative individualism and 'methodological individualism' (for this term see K. Popper, The Open Society and Its Enemies [Princeton, 1950], 284), as applied in J. M. Buchanan and G. Tullock, The Calculus of Consent : Logical Foundations of Constitutional Democracy (Ann Arbor, 1962).

viable association, and not only of a particular one.[95] From the empirically incontestable assumption that without some measure of consent no form of society is imaginable, he proceeded to the postulate of government by consent. This means the confluence of individual decisions in majority decisions as well as the subjection of the first to the second.

On account of the subjection of individual wills to a public will Locke is charged with 'collectivism', once because he is held to have been a democrat and then because he was not a democrat. That he was no democrat would not seem to matter if collectivism is characterized by lack of concern with minorities. A ruling minority might suppress other minorities either with the tacit, i.e. non-democratic, or the express, i.e., democratic, consent of the majority. In other words, collectivism does not simply inhere in the method of decision but foremostly in its contents.

A decision or policy is collectivist if it leaves little room for private interests to be distinguished from public ones. Empirically, no modern state is either purely individualist or purely collectivist, fully liberal or fully totalitarian.[96] But the mere over-ruling of a minority by a majority is no proof that a majority decision – or, for that matter, the decision of an autocrat or a minority – is collectivist. A decision in favour of freedom of thought and expression is individualistic, whether imposed by the will of one, a few or the many. To hold the government committed to the protection of individual freedom does not, therefore, by itself provide the logical grounds for government by consent, but the responsibility of the rulers to the ruled becomes mandatory in relation to the observed fact that governors are less likely to tamper with the freedom of their subjects where legislative power is vested in elected bodies than where it is not.[97] Consent is a function of individual freedom, because it is endangered by the transgressions of individuals no less than by arbitrary government. Thus, although the method of making decisions, or of authorizing others to make them, does not determine whether the decisions increase or curb freedom, the method bears on the content of decisions

---

[95] As asserted by Kendall, *op. cit.*, 92–3.
[96] Cp. B. Akzin, 'Analysis of State and Law Structure,' in *Law, State and International Legal Order : Essays in Honor of Hans Kelsen* (University of Tennessee Press, 1964), 17, note 3.
[97] Cp. Plamenatz, *op. cit.*, 235 and *passim*. On Plamenatz's criticism of Locke's notion of consent, see below, 298 f.

inasmuch as some procedures are more conducive than others to the protection of individual freedom.

Free multilateral consent on the basis of general or of restricted suffrage, has shown itself rather more of a bastion against the engulfment of private interests by the public interest than an instrument for it. Perhaps one can make the individual the centre of the world, base public on private interests, and yet assert the unqualified subjection of the individual to a society ruled by consented government.[98] It remains a confusion of issues to assume a decision to be more collectivist the greater the number of those who make or countenance it. To call Locke an authoritarian who outdid Rousseau as a collectivist, invalidates itself not so much by turning Locke into a democrat as by abstracting from the content of the decisions and concentrating solely on the method of making them – and then confusing them.[99] No less misleading is the argument that the assertion of the supremacy of political society over each individual is collectivist when this supremacy is wielded by the few to protect the realization of their individuality in the unhampered accumulation of property at the expense of the individuality of the many.[100] To call this order collectivist has no foundation other than the purpose of turning the tables on liberalism. Much as we may condemn such an order, it is still individualist in its aim and methods insofar as individual competion remains the basis of property and politics. This was undoubtedly Locke's conception. It went together with the conviction that once consent is recognized as the necessary legitimation of governmental action, the means are provided, both morally justifiable and practically efficient, for a viable adjustment of public and private aims. For Locke, the adjustment is never complete because natural law is never fully realized.

True, he did not see the principle of individual consent affected by the overruling of individual wills through the will of the majority. Fighting for the recognition of the principle of majority decision on a non-democratic basis, he evidently had less reason than latter-day critics (not necessarily opponents) of democracy to be troubled by the problem of the majorization of minorities, although

[98] Cp. Strauss, *op. cit.*, 232, 248; and Macpherson, *op. cit.*, 255.

[99] Thus Kendall, *op. cit.*, 113, 118.

[100] Macpherson, *op. cit.*, 255-6, who, in substance, enlarges on the criticism of Vaughan (*op. cit.*, 194) that Locke's individualism enslaves the poor and the weak.

he was aware of the possible acquiescence of majorities as well as of minorities in tyranny.[101] But considerable concern with these problems has not lead to a denial of Locke's conclusion that 'the consent of every individual . . . is next impossible ever to be had . . .' (Sec. 98). Nor have modern preoccupations caused liberal democrats to reject the view that, so far as the empowerment of government and the making of decisions in representative bodies is concerned, 'the act of the majority passes for the act of the whole . . .' (Sec. 96). Although more and more deprived of its halo, majority decision is still acceptable as the best approximation to the principle of 'that which acts any community, being only the consent of the individuals of it'. For Locke as for us, the consent of a majority stands *in lieu* of the consent of all, but is to all intents and purposes an aggregate of individual decisions. None but the individuals themselves can cast their vote or join in revolutionary action in order to express either consent or dissent. Decisions in these matters are properly called 'individual' so long as pressures and counter-pressures allow a reasonable margin of choice. Whether the purpose of a majority decision is to put the good of society above that of each individual or to further the interests of the majority at the expense of the minority, individual rights are exercised to a greater extent than when a minority decides either for the public good or for the promotion of its own interests at the cost of those of the majority. The premise of individual consent is undoubtedly given wider application in the first than in the second instance. What Locke had in mind was surely this still valid central core of the majority principle, anchored in individualist premises.

Locke's natural law theory has been appropriately defined as a doctrine of 'natural political virtue'.[102] In it rights reflect individual wants and needs yet correspond to duties of dignity and virtue. It guarantees the exercise of individual wills by requiring consent as the means for the unison of wills. It gives everybody a share, though not an equal one in the formation of a public will, which entails both the self-imposed and other-imposed restriction of individual wills. This interplay of self-willed and other-willed decisions entails the overruling of individual wills by reference to absolute norms and considerations of expediency. But the ethically

---

[101] See below, 113, 306 f.
[102] Laslett, *op. cit.*, 108.

THE LIBERAL POLITICS OF JOHN LOCKE

and practically justifiable method of making decisions does not guarantee the making of ethically right decisions. As Locke does not believe in the ability of ordinary men or even the more rational ones to apply natural law faultlessly, it is doubly out of place to suggest[103] that Locke – or for that matter any sensible person who defends the majority principle – need to be saved from the accusation of ethical relativism.

Of course, one can say that the belief in the right of the majority to impose its will is compatible with the belief in objective moral standards, if the proposition 'the majority wills always that which is right' is the corollary of the proposition 'right is that which the majority wills'.[104] Apart from having nothing to do with Locke's views, this leads to a *reductio ad absurdum*, as far as a reasonably realistic view of the human condition is concerned. First, Locke does not mean to say that the majority's will is always right, nor that what it wills must be right to obligate all, but that what it wills obligates all. Secondly, it is not against common sense to stipulate that there is no ethical right to make intentionally unethical decisions. This is different from making the ethical rightness of the content of decisions the condition for having the right to make decisions. Such a proposition is self-defeating. If we say that only those have the right to make decisions who can be supposed to make only right decisions, we make infallibility the condition for having an ethical right to make decisions. Nobody could have this right since no single person, or body of persons, is infallible. If, with Locke, one embraces the moral imperative of natural equality, the procedure of majority decisions recommends itself because it is morally superior to obligate all by virtue of what most approve than by what one or a few approve, not to mention that generally political decisions affect the majority more, and certainly no less, than the minority. If one exempts, like Locke, neither the few nor the many from failure to arrive at ethically right decisions, but thinks the few less fallible than the many, one way to ensure the optimal application of absolute ethical norms by ethically justifiable and practically efficient procedures, is the distribution of power which he had in mind.

By placing political authority in more than one hand, the fallibility of the prince is offset by his obligation to collaborate with

<hr>

[103] Kendall, *op. cit.*, 134.
[104] Kendall, *op. cit.*, 117–18, 133.

an elective and a hereditary body of legislators. The fallibility of the two collective bodies is checked in exceptional cases by prerogative, and the fallibility of legislators and princes is checked by the right of revolt. This extension of the authority to compete over the realization of natural law beyond the constitutional framework presupposes the validity of natural law and the possibility of applying it in all conditions of human existence. That is why Locke's distinction between the state of nature, the state of war and political society cannot exclude relatedness between them, or in effect their co-existence.

CHAPTER III

THE NATURAL AND THE POLITICAL CONDITION

IF the idea of the state of nature were not a hypothesis about what men are by nature and to what extent they are capable of knowing and applying natural law, and if the state of nature and political society were meant to denote different forms of human existence, Locke's theory would be thoroughly contradictory. If the state of nature were an ideal condition from which anything like war-like tensions is excluded, natural law could be fully observed in it but then the necessity for political society would be inexplicable. The same would hold if the state of nature were identical with the state of war. So long as the war of all against all is the order of the day, it is difficult to account for an agreement to submit to a Hobbesian superior, and still more so for the readiness to live by laws 'received and allowed by common consent', except by presupposing a change for the better in human nature in the state of nature. But then the state of nature is not an unmitigated state of war. If neither the state of nature nor political society had anything in common with the state of war, each would be an ideal realization of natural law. But then again, political society would be superfluous, or if for some unexplained reason it were preferable to the state of nature, revolution would have no place in it.

In one way or another, each of the inconsistencies just mentioned has been laid at Locke's door. He can be acquitted of all of them if we do not fasten upon isolated statements but seek to relate them, and if we make allowance not so much for muddled thinking but for the occasional nominalistic inflation of the term 'the state of nature'. Comprehension is sought above all for what Locke in *An Essay Concerning Human Understanding* himself exposed as the source of misunderstanding: the imperfection of words.

I shall try to show that when Locke was speaking of 'the state of nature' he did not vacillate between describing an ideal situation and its opposite, nor did he associate with it the supposition of a governmentless phase of development which invariably precedes political society. Interpretations like these, I suggest, do not take into consideration all the contexts in which the notion of the state of nature is used by Locke or to which it must be related; the purposes for which the concept was devised; and what he said about the actual way in which political society emerges. Locke's 'state of nature' is a hypothesis or interpretative device designed to illustrate the fundamental traits and rights of men *qua* men by abstracting from political organization. At the same time it denotes not so much one, but several, real situations: that which obtains between states as well as that in which individuals of a political society and entire political societies are apt to find themselves.

I. THE HYPOTHETICAL STATE OF NATURE

A. Man's Perpetual Status

The state of nature excludes political organization by definition. Men are free to act 'without asking leave, or depending upon the will of any other man . . . all the power and jurisdiction is reciprocal . . . without subordination or subjection . . .' (Sec. 4). When everybody is judge and executioner of the law of nature and no man more than another, rights are assumed to exist but not political society.[1] This is the hypothesis which denotes the background against which government must be understood; it abstracts from, in order to determine, the political obligations that men can reasonably impose upon one another.[2] No initial historical situation is meant, but merely that which underlies and coexists with all historical situations. For in the same context, i.e. right at the beginning of the chapter 'Of the State of Nature', Locke wishes to consider not the state all men have once been in, but 'what state all men *are* naturally in' (Sec. 4). This is 'a state of perfect freedom . . . a state also of equality . . .' 'Man being born . . . with a title to perfect freedom, and an uncontrolled enjoyment of all the rights and privileges of the law of nature . . .' (Sec. 87), this is the condition given with which the

[1] Barker, *Social Contract*, xxiv, and Lamprecht, *op. cit.*, 131, 133, fail to see the distinction.

[2] Cp. Strauss, *op. cit.*, 231, and Laslett, *op. cit.*, 99, 114 f. Strauss (230) and Laslett (69, 108) however assume also – like Lamprecht, *op. cit.*, 130, 138, 140, and Cox, *op. cit.*, 79, 104 – the historicity of Locke's state of nature. Laslett qualifies this view, and according to Strauss the question becomes finally irrelevant in Locke's exposition. Gough, *op. cit.*, 29, is not sure whether Locke's intention was historical. F. Pollock, 'Locke's Theory of State,' *Proceedings of the British Academy* (1903-4), 241, and Kendall, *op. cit.*, 75, abide by the view that the idea of the state of nature is an expository device.

subsistence of political society has to be reconciled and on which its management by consent rests. 'Men being . . . by nature, all free, equal and independent, no one can be put out of this estate, and subjected to the political power of another, without his own consent' (Sec. 95). The state of nature denotes the perpetual personal status of man as a free being. This is not controverted by statements to the effect that all who do not 'join and unite into a community . . . are left as they were in the liberty of the state of nature' or 'that all men are naturally in that state, and remain so, till by their own consents they make themselves members of some political society' (Sec. 15).

Speaking at times of the state of nature as of something which was antecedent to and separate from political society, Locke succumbed to a manner of speech which had by then become rather common in natural law theories. But like Hobbes, he did not abide by what this usage of the term implies, namely, that people by their consent make themselves members of a political society out of a pre-political state.

To begin with, Locke regarded it as one and the same whether men 'are so united into one society' when 'any number of men, in the state of nature, enter into society to make one people, . . . or else when any one joins himself to, and incorporates with any government already made' (Sec. 89). Government and the state of nature are coexistent in time. Moreover, right from the beginning new political societies were the result of secession from existing commonwealths 'from whence sprang all that number of petty commonwealths *in the beginning of ages* . . .' (Sec. 115). From the very beginning of history there had been a way of creating political societies other than by incorporation out of a state of nature. It is in no sense curious that, to cite instances of free incorporation, Locke alluded to secession from one society to another, rather than confine his references to the passage from a pristine state of nature to political society.[3] If incorporation by consent is a principle of general application, it must be immaterial whether men were born under a government or not. If proper government rests on consent, people must not be bound by whatever government they happen to live under. Locke rejects, therefore, that even on the supposition 'that *all* men being born under government, some or other' none of them 'should ever be free, and at liberty to unite together, and begin a new one . . .' (Sec. 113). It is a mistake to think 'that by

---

[3] Cox, *op. cit.*, 42, finds that Locke ought to have done so.

being born under any government, we . . . have no more any title or pretence to the freedom of the state of nature . . .' (Sec. 116). Since man's natural liberty may be re-enacted in opposition to existing governments and legal procedures, the right to incorporate freely is not limited to what otherwise would appear to be its logical prerequisite, viz. a state of nature as a stage of development which precedes political societies.

In point of fact, the existence of such a stage is ruled out by Locke's answer to the usual objections against the reality of the state of nature and by his historical examples of incorporation by consent. To say that these examples were not decisive for Locke, because he was ready to accept the hypothetical character of a prepolitical state of nature,[4] is characteristic of the widespread identification of a liberal with a largely unhistorical approach. It is to disregard that Locke ostensibly resorted to these examples for the historical, i.e., empirical, verification of the two intimately connected ideas of the state of nature and of incorporation into political society.[5]

B. Empirical and Historical Verification

Locke's provisional rejoinder to the objection 'Where are, or ever were, there any men in such a state of nature?' refers first to 'all princes and rulers of independent governments' and then to two ordinary men who meet in a 'Desert Island' or 'in the woods of America'.[6] The relationships between the two categories of individuals reflect 'the state of nature between men' and prove that 'the world never was, *nor ever will be*, without numbers of men in that state' (Sec. 14).

Although these relationships are placed outside political society, each of the persons involved belongs to a political society. This is immediately obvious as regards princes. It holds good also for the second example. 'The promises and bargains for truck, etc. . . .

[4] Ch. Bastide, *John Locke, ses théories politiques et leur influence en Angleterre* (Paris, 1907).

[5] On incorporation, see below, 226 f.

[6] Sec. 14. Cp. Secs. 183, 184. Hobbes had already answered the question by referring to princes without considering the state of nature as a primeval condition. He was followed in this by Pufendorf, who, like Locke, differed from Hobbes in the evaluation of the natural condition as a state of war. Cp. I. Fetscher, 'Der gesellschaftliche "Naturzustand" und das Menschenbild bei Hobbes, Pufendorf, Cumberland und Rousseau,' *Schmollers Jahrbuch für Gesetzgebung, Verwaltung und Volkswirtschaft*, LXXX (1960), 647, 658 f.

between a Swiss and an Indian, in the woods of America, are binding to them, though they are perfectly in a state of nature, *in reference to one another*. For truth and keeping of faith belongs to men as men and not as members of society' (Sec. 14). It follows, first, that both princes and ordinary men are under moral obligations, although princes and commonwealths have no common superior and ordinary men may conduct business in no-man's land. Nor, indeed, are princes necessarily in a state of war because they are in a state of nature with each other. They may be in league with each other and bound by promises and compacts.[7] Secondly, Locke speaks of a Swiss and an Indian as perfectly in a state of nature 'in reference to one another'. This implies that they are not in such a state in reference to the political societies to which they otherwise belong. Locke undoubtedly supposed that the Swiss originated from a political society. The same applies also to the Indian, as we shall presently show. Thus, inasmuch as the two examples prove the existence of a state of nature, it is coeval with the existence of political society, and does not comprise a considerable number of men, who are, except 'in reference to one another', members of political societies. With respect to a considerable number of men, as in the historical or otherwise empirical examples, the 'plain instances' of 'the uniting together of several men free and independent one of another' (Sec. 102) likewise do not illustrate a transition from a pre-political state of nature to political society.

Locke does not concern himself with the antecedents of the union in Rome and Venice. He offers as a conjecture on the part of Josephus Acosta, that in America, 'which is still a pattern of the first ages in Asia and Europe' (Sec. 108), 'there was no government at all' (Sec. 102). Locke quotes that 'these men . . . for a long time had neither kings nor commonwealths, but lived in troops' but he also quotes that to live thus is to live like 'many other *nations*, which have no *certain* kings, but as occasion is offered in peace or war, they choose their captains as they please'. The interpretation of sacred history reveals the same pattern. Uncertainty as to what followed the confusion of Babel exists merely in so far as 'we know not *who* were

---

[7] Sec. 14 does, therefore, not identify the state of nature with the state of war, but allows, like the other sections of Chapter II, for the possibility of war in the state of nature. His acceptance of the possibly peaceful coexistence of states explains perhaps why Locke did not argue that the multiplication of small states brings men nearer to the war-like state of nature. This was the view of Pufendorf and Rousseau. See Fetscher, *loc. cit.*, 657, 665.

their governors, nor what their form of government, but only that they were divided into little *independent societies*, speaking different languages' (I, 144). The instances of the 'multitude of little kings' in the West Indies, of the 'kings . . . out of Homer' and those 'out of Scripture', were adduced by Locke to contradict Filmer on both absolute monarchy and the derivation of kingship from Adam's fatherhood. They conform, however, with the examples otherwise adduced inasmuch as pristine societies are not conceived to have been without governors, without judges or generals such as more or less recurrent exigencies required.[8] The examples, drawn from contemporary America, from the Bible and Homer, illustrate the beginnings in terms of an initial stage of political society. As described by him, these societies do not conform with the definition of a state of nature, which is without government.[9] We can also not evaluate them as a stage between a governmentless state of nature and political society,[10] once we take into consideration that Locke did not attempt to prove the historicity of a governmentless state.

If Locke had supposed that primitive men lived in unorganized hordes, it would, indeed, have been strange to ascribe to them characteristics produced by political training.[11] But the point he wished to make in referring to men that 'lived in troops' is that 'by consent [they] were all equal, till by the same consent they set rulers over themselves' (Sec. 102). This they did intermittently as an independent community. A condition is described which conforms roughly with the picture of primitive societies given by modern anthropologists and which answers to Locke's own definition of a commonwealth. A commonwealth is an 'independent community' (Sec. 133) and primitive societies are 'independent societies'. Their form of government corresponds to a mixture between his 'perfect democracy' and 'elective monarchy' (Sec. 132). Temporarily, they have not only generals and judges, but also kings.

The empirical and historical verification of the state of nature leaves

---

[8] I, 153, 158, 130–1. Cp. Sec. 109.

[9] Thus Lamprecht, *op. cit.*, 127, against Stephen, *op. cit.*, II, 137. Polin, *op. cit.*, 36, appears to revert to Stephen's position. Similarly Strauss, *op. cit.*, 230, who suggests that an elite of English colonists in America rather than the wild Indians, or, better still, highly civilized men after the breakdown of their society, would be the proper examples of men living in an actual state of nature. But Locke did not give these examples. And those he did cite do not satisfy the terms of definition of a governmentless condition, nor does English colonization, which was subject to royal charters.

[10] As Laslett, *op. cit.*, 357–8, 380, suggests.

[11] Vaughan, *op. cit.*, 158, and Lamprecht, *op. cit.*, 132, respectively.

a governmentless condition as a hypothesis. Further corroboration provides his explanation of incorporation in terms of the unavoidable and barely perceptible transformation of paternal into monarchic rule. More will be said about this in Chapter VII. Here it suffices to indicate that he deals with the family in an Aristotelian fashion. It is the first and fundamental condition of human existence and bears the traits of political rule. A family with grown-up children is already a political society, because 'without some government it would be hard for them to live together . . .' (Sec. 74). He did not imply the gradual appearance, in individuals living separately, of the inclination to live together, as distinct from the passing of families from a less to a more defined form of political organization. On this basis he made the general statement that 'government is hardly to be avoided amongst men that live together'.[12] He did not conceive of men living otherwise.

C. Social and Political Existence

Even taken by themselves, the statements which convey the impression as if the state of nature were a condition preceding political society do not refer to a non-social form of existence. Commentators hardly differ on this point.[13] Locke's belief in the knowability and applicability of natural law rests on the conception of man as a natural social being. Yet the belief in the validity of natural law is not predicated on an ideal state of nature either; it does not presuppose ideal human beings.

The state of nature is 'a state of peace, good will, mutual assistance, and preservation' (Sec. 19), inasmuch as men are predisposed and in necessity of living together. It is likewise a state that reveals the disruptive tendencies of human nature, manifested by the transgressors of natural law, who slight and break 'the tie, which is to secure them from injury and violence . . .' (Sec. 8). On the one

[12] Sec. 105. Polin, *op. cit.*, 98, wrongly asserts that this assumption is explicitly stated only in the early *Essays*. Cp. *ibid.*, 118–9. The assumption shows once more that Locke was likely to deviate from Hooker when he quoted him approvingly. For Hooker, as Locke quotes him in Sec. 74, speaks about the possibility 'in nature, considered by itself' of the absence of 'any public regiment'.

[13] The exception is Gierke who wrongly juxtaposes natural law and 'social law' apart from identifying the state of nature with a historical condition. (O. Gierke, *Natural Law and the Theory of Society*, ed. by E. Barker, 101, 292). Plamenatz, *op. cit.*, 220, retains a position close to that of Gierke when he charges Locke with ignoring that only as 'creatures formed and disciplined by society, . . . men come to have rights and obligations'.

hand, therefore, in emphasizing – in Chapter II of the *Treatise* – the idyllic side of the state of nature, Locke did not overlook the necessity of self-defence. On the other hand, the right to and the ability of individual self-preservation are inseparably bound up with the right and ability of social self-preservation.[14] As the recapitulatory Chapter XV has it, 'the end and measure' of the right 'to punish the breach of the law of nature in others . . . when in every man's hands in the state of nature', is 'the preservation of all of his society, that is, all mankind in general . . .' (Sec. 171). This right is not postulated to make non-political existence credible but to serve as the foundation of all political authority. Because of the necessity of socialized self-defence, one single world-wide community – 'his society, that is, all mankind' – is out of the question. The inevitableness of living a socially inclusive life on a scale smaller than that of a world-wide community and larger than that of the family is the inevitableness of political organization.

Locke readily admits that 'it is not at all to be wondered, that history gives us but a very little account of men, that lived *together* in the state of nature' (Sec. 101). If he pointed to the absence of records of the beginnings of political societies, it was not because he expected them to reveal anything different from what the 'plain instances of such a beginning . . . or at least . . . manifest footsteps of it' confirmed. For 'the inconveniences of that condition [the state of nature], and the love, and want of society no sooner brought *any number* of them together, but they presently united and incorporated, if they designed to continue together'. Locke never treated of the isolated existence of individuals, but always of people who lived together. He upheld the traditional view that men, as God has made them, are by 'necessity, convenience and inclination' driven into society, and fitted 'with understanding and language to continue and enjoy it'.[15] Since he likewise admitted the impossibility of men living together 'without some government', he could easily conform with the Pauline teaching and grant that 'God has certainly appointed government to restrain the partiality and violence of men' (Sec. 13). He could round off the chapter 'Of the State of Nature' by citing Hooker's emphasis of the natural inducements 'to seek

---

[14] Cp. the *loci* mentioned in Ch. II, note 50.
[15] Sec. 77. Cp. *Essays*, 156–7, and *Essay*, III, i, 1. The significance of Locke's endorsement of this view was recognized by Leibniz, who commented on the passage in the *Essay*: 'Je suis réjoui de vous voir éloigné du sentiment de M. Hobbes.' Quoted in Aarsleff, *loc. cit.*, 19.

communion and fellowship with others . . . in political societies' (Sec. 15).

The conclusion remains, then, that the notion of a pre-political state of nature reduces itself in Locke's exposition to a hypothesis about human nature in its social significance. Because the notion abstracts from political society, so as to evaluate its nature, the state of nature is logically prior to society, but is not confused with what is previous in history.[16] Because of the existence of government in them, primitive societies do not answer the terms of definition of the hypothesis. The real original condition is not graced merely by the unorganized presence of political power but by its essential minimum. Government is recognized as the vital prerequisite of social life. 'The status of the political' is therefore not deprecated, nor is any advance made towards the reification of society over and against the state.[17] The historically demonstrable beginnings of social life are the 'golden age' of early government, never a state of nature. But the state of nature denotes not only a hypothesis. The use of the same term for real situations has its justification in the extent to which the meanings correspond.

More than any other situation, Locke designates as a return of a state of nature the conflict between rulers and ruled, the conflict which results from arbitrary government.[18] But the state of nature is not a real situation in the sense of a total state of war. He did not paint two contradictory pictures of the state of nature, one peaceful and hypothetical and one warlike and real. The same concept comprises both the warlike and the peaceful aspect, when used as a hypothesis or when it denotes specific situations. As a hypothesis, the state of nature is different from real situations because it is non- and pre-political but in its other properties there is no difference. Its peacefulness – that of human nature – is always in danger of being disturbed by ineradicable warlike predispositions. This applies also to what is the nearest reflection of the hypothesis in reality, i.e. to the situation between members of political societies who meet in no-man's land and between states. Only if Locke calls a situation within a political society a state of nature, he identifies it

---

[16] According to Laslett, *op. cit.*, 99, Locke in this case is only 'somewhat less vulnerable than his predecessors'.

[17] Wolin, *op. cit.*, 306, accuses Locke of the deprecation of 'the status of the political' and Polin, *op. cit.*, 135-6, note, sees Locke distinguish between society and political society.

[18] Secs. 13, 17-18, 135, 137, 149, 164, 168, 173, 203, 205, 207, 231.

with a complete state of war. But this 'return' of the state of nature is a war between political society and its rulers. Thus neither the hypothetical state of nature nor that which denotes real situations inside and outside political societies is unrelated to the state of war. It remains to demonstrate that Locke related to each other, both in principle and existentially, the state of nature, the state of war and political society.

2. THE STATE OF NATURE, THE STATE OF WAR AND POLITICAL SOCIETY

A. The Relationship in Principle

'The plain difference between the state of nature, and the state of war, which however some men have confounded', consists in that they 'are as far distant, as a state of peace, good will, mutual assistance, and preservation, and a state of enmity, malice, violence, and mutual destruction are one from another' (Sec. 19). This definition is incomplete. In his characteristic way of making points against his adversaries – in this case Hobbes – Locke recovered his ground in the next sentence and introduced the link which connects the two states:

'Men living together according to reason, *without a common superior* on earth, with authority to judge between them, is properly the state of nature. But force, or a declared design of force upon the person of another, *where there is no common superior* on earth to appeal to for relief, is the state of war.'[19]

The state of nature and the state of war have in common the absence of a common superior. The remaining fundamental differences become also attenuated, because the absence of a common superior in both states does not set them rigorously apart from political society.

Men's relations in political society are not entirely unlike the relations in a hypothetical state of nature. There remains 'a liberty to follow my own will in all things, where the rule prescribes not' (Sec. 22). Insofar as the commands of the common superior do not apply to all things, the 'freedom of nature . . . to be under no other restraint but the law of nature' exists also in political society.

[19] Sec. 19. Cp. I, 131.

Wherever there is such freedom there lurks the danger of its abuse. That is why 'the want of such an appeal [i.e. to the common superior] gives a man the right of war even against an aggressor, though he be in society and a fellow subject' (Sec. 19). Locke concludes logically enough: 'Want of a common judge with authority, puts all men in a state of nature: Force without right, upon a man's person, makes a state of war, *both where there is, and is not, a common judge.*' The state of war and the state of nature intrude both into political society.

The conclusion which implies that the absence of a common judge does not set the state of nature and the state of war entirely apart from political society is reconcilable with the definition which regards the absence of a common judge as the common denominator of the state of war and the state of nature. The state of war is associated first with the absence of provisions for the office of a common judge – as in the hypothetical state of nature and in inter-state relations. It is then defined as a situation where, as in political society, the office exists, but where appeals to the common judge are of no avail. Thus, when 'hands appointed to adminster justice' fail to act in accordance with the purpose of law, which is 'to protect and redress the innocent, by an unbiassed application of it, to all who are under it; *wherever* that is not *bona fide* done, war is made upon the sufferers, who having no appeal on earth to right them, they are left to the only remedy in such cases, an appeal to heaven' (Sec. 20). The state of war occurs in political society not only when political authority is not operative or effective,[20] but whenever it is wrought immorally. What is political and non-political are comparable because a state of war exists wherever force is used without right, whether there is, or is not, a common judge. What is political and non-political remains distinguished because the concerted appeal to heaven is occasioned by and directed against government, whereas in the hypothetical state of nature everybody is judge between himself and others. Herein lies the most important practical difference: political society minimizes the use of force.

[20] As Goldwin, *op. cit.*, 457–8, asserts, who sees Locke juxtapose 'the natural powers and the natural state' to men's 'political powers and political state' (452) so that the state of nature is 'the home – and the only home – of the state of war' (442). For the sake of impugning Locke's consistency – as commanded by the presupposition of esotericism – Goldwin thus contradicts his apposite interpretation of the relatedness between the state of nature, the state of war and civil society (436–7) and ends up with the strange conclusion that the 'right to resist is not a political right, but a pre-political natural right' (462).

'Where no such appeal [to a common judge] is, *as in the state of nature*, for want of positive laws, and judges with authority to appeal to, *the state of war once begun, continues*, with a right to the innocent party, *to destroy* the other . . . until the aggressor offers peace' (Sec. 20). 'To avoid this state of war (wherein there is no appeal but to heaven and wherein *every the least difference is apt to end*, . . . is one great reason of men's putting themselves into society, and quitting the state of nature' (Sec. 21).

Political society prevents 'every the least difference' from ending in war; it prevents newly restored peace from giving again way to war on the least provocation. Political society does not exclude the state of war but 'the *continuance* of the state of war', i.e., its frequent renewal.

Locke's systematic summary confirms that he did not intend to separate completely between the state of nature – whether denoting a hypothesis or real situations– the state of war and political society,[21] nor to identify the first two states. The conclusion tallies with what we have ascertained in the preceding chapter, namely that his allowances for the imperfections of human nature – the state of war – and his insistence on men's sociable and peaceful propensities – the idyllic side of the state of nature – supplement but do not supplant the other. They illustrate the two fundamental tendencies which, socially and politically, make for either consensus or conflict, the two basic attitudes which constitute the poles between which political life oscillates.[22] Political society neither precludes warlike tensions nor is it ever fully dominated by them, because the fundamental traits of human nature, as exemplified by 'the state of nature', do not change. Indeed, no convincing case has been made out for a transition in Locke's exposition from one conception of human nature to another, or from one stage of the state of nature to another.

[21] To regard them morally and practically, but not physically, distinguished (Cp. Polin, *op. cit.*, 180-1), raises the question of the difference between 'physical' and 'practical'. The stipulation of a difference is the less defensible, if its aim is to leave room for the assumption of a historical non-political state of nature.

[22] S. M. Lipset, *Political Man*, has many important things to say on the polarity between conflict and agreement. But he ignores (23) that Locke and many others, right back to the Greek philosophers, had been theoretically aware of this polarity without, moreover, predicating it on a cleavage between state and society. On the last point blame does not attach to Lipset but to Locke's interpreters who have for long reified Locke's state of nature, even when they recognized it as expressing also a theory of human motivation. See above, notes 16 and 17, and Vaughan, *op. cit.*, 135 f.

So far I have based my conclusions concerning the state of nature mainly on what Chapters II and III of the *Second Treatise* establish on principle. It remains, then, to demonstrate that this is applied consistently throughout the *Treatise*.

B. The Application

a. Uniform Tenor of Argumentation

It has been almost generally recognized that Locke's notion of the state of nature serves the purpose of showing that men are rational enough not to require a Hobbesian sovereign, but too contentious to do without political society. This conclusion has for the most part been presented as the one clear thing in Locke's theory about the state of nature. More recently, this kind of argument has been dismissed on the ground that it imputes to him intellectual dishonesty and superficiality. Yet Locke is acquitted of this charge not by proving him consistent but by explaining why he had to be contradictory and had to advance two different conceptions of the state of nature and imply two stages of it. One explanation is that he was unaware of any contradiction because he accepted the assumptions of his times. To believe another – the esoteric – interpretation, which leaves him with somewhat diminished honesty but with increased intellectual cunning, the contradictions were intended to hide his true intention. The surprising feature of these interpretations is that scholars like Strauss and Macpherson should pronounce on Locke's consistency as if one had to assume either the peacefulness or the quarrelsomeness of human nature, or else contradict oneself. It is surely neither novel nor unfounded to evaluate human nature as both peaceful and quarrelsome in varying degrees.

Locke is said to have provided clues for presenting two versions of the state of nature, the negative supplanting the positive picture. But such clues do not exist. There is no divide in the middle of the *Treatise* to indicate the progressive and systematic alteration of the tenor of the statements concerning the state of nature.[23] Just as Locke made positive statements about the knowability of natural law after the middle of the *Treatise*,[24] he made several references to the negative aspects of the state of nature well before the middle. There

---

[23] Cox, *op. cit.*, 37–8, 77, 79, 182, makes these assertions in working out Strauss' thesis (*op. cit.*, 225, 230, 231). He is followed in this respect by Goldwin, *op. cit.*, 439, 452. See note 20.

[24] See above, 54.

is no change of tenor in these statements as is best shown in connection with Macpherson's interpretation. It is the most detailed in
this respect and differs from the aforementioned only insofar as the
distinction between the peaceful and the warlike state of nature is
said to have evaporated as early as Section 21.[25] But as we have seen,
Sections 19 and 20 not only establish the difference between the
state of nature, the state of war and political society but also clarify
what they have in common. This is ignored together with the implications in this respect of Section 14. And like Cox,[26] Macpherson
simply writes off as immaterial the direct qualifications in Chapters
II and III of the peaceful state of nature. There remains the question whether any discrepancy can be discerned between what Locke
said about the inconveniences of the state of nature in the context of
Sections 6-15 and what he wrote from Sections 123 onwards.[27]

No doubt, in Chapter II Locke had in mind a comparatively small
number of men who infringed the rights of others and disturbed the
natural state of peace, whereas it might appear as if in the second
part of the *Treatise* the majority of men were branded as malefac-
tors.[28] He says explicitly in Section 123 that the enjoyment by man of
his natural freedom 'is very uncertain, and constantly exposed to the
invasion of others . . . all being kings as much as he, every man his
equal, and *the greater part* no strict observers of equity and justice
. . . ' But 'the corruption, and viciousness of degenerate men' (Sec.
128) which make political society inescapable, are nevertheless not
those of the majority. Locke is quite consistent when he again
implies in Section 171 that those who 'threaten the sound and healthy'
are few in number, because he does not simply group under one
head criminals and the majority who are 'no *strict* observers of equity
and justice'. He distinguishes throughout between criminals who do
wrong and those who transgress equity and justice in punishing them.
The observance of equity and justice is precarious because, when the
victims of criminals are left to do the punishing, they themselves and
those who individually assist them are liable to do wrong. The
majority of men are not criminals but biassed. 'Men being partial to
themselves, passion and revenge is very apt to carry them too far,
and with too much heat, in their own cases; as well as negligence,

---

[25] Macpherson, *op. cit.*, 240, 300.
[26] Cox, *op. cit.*, 77, note 5, and 78, note 1.
[27] Since Section 123 is the second section after the middle of the *Treatise*, Cox's
argument, insofar as Macpherson's contention can be disproved – falls also away.
[28] Macpherson, *op. cit.*, 240.

and unconcernedness, to make them too remiss, in other men's' (Sec. 125). Men who cannot help being partial in their own cases, or too remiss when others are concerned, are not for that reason aggressors against others; men who are not aggressors do not for that reason alone qualify as judges, least of all in their own cases. This is the fairly reasonable and hardly contradictory position which Locke maintained in the earlier and later parts of the *Treatise*.

In the first part he also insisted that nobody had the right 'to use a criminal . . . according to the passionate heats, or boundless extravagance of his own will . . .' (Sec. 8). This exhortation is obviously not addressed to one who is himself a criminal. For what else could one expect than that one 'who was so unjust as to do his brother an injury, will scarce be so just as to condemn himself for it' (Sec. 13). 'The partiality and violence of men' (Sec. 13) serves here, as in the later part of the *Treatise*, to derive from the right of the individual the right of the community and its magistrates to punish offenders.[29] In stating that 'the inconveniences of the state of nature, . . . must certainly be great, where men may be judges in their own case', Locke clearly meant that most men could not be expected to be impartial judges in cases in which they themselves were directly involved. On this premise, which is identical in the earlier and the later part of the *Treatise*, he advanced the same conclusion in both parts, namely that men were 'willing to quit a condition, which however free, is full of fears and continual dangers' (Sec. 123); in other words, that 'civil government is the proper remedy for the inconveniences of the state of nature' (Sec. 13). Just as Locke does not change the tenor of his argument to explain the inevitableness of political society, so does he not present two contradictory pictures, nor even two different stages, of the state of nature to accentuate the motive of the protection of property as a major foundation of political existence.

b. *Absence of Governmentless States and Stages of Socio-Economic Development*

The assertion that Locke held men to have been initially equal in their rationality but then to have become so unequal that the majority lag permanently behind the minority,[30] provides the ground for concluding that, according to him, civil society was preceded by

[29] Secs. 9, 11, 12 and 128–30.
[30] Macpherson, *op. cit.*, 241, 245. For my confutation see also above, 51 f, and below, 149 f, 163 f.

two stages of the state of nature, 'one before, and one after, consent to money and unequal possessions'.[31] 'The market relations of a developed commercial economy', were thus placed in the state of nature. Macpherson, who attributes this view to Locke, says that it does not make sense historically, but is hypothetically intelligible if, with Locke, one associates with man's nature the propensity to accumulate.[32]

It is questionable whether an interpreter may evade in this way the criterion of historicity, i.e. of empirical fact.[33] He lays himself particularly open to the charge of trying to escape the consequences of his own use of historical categories if he speaks of two stages in the state of nature, and thus implies a temporal sequence. As far as hypothetical intelligibility is concerned, accumulation is compatible with a non-monetary pre-political stage; it need not lead beyond barter, and might be considered as the prerequisite of human subsistence. The decisive point, however, is that for Locke even a primitive economy involves political organization. If, as Macpherson says, Locke's reference to 'the equality of a simple poor way of living' is predicated on the pre-monetary stage, we must note that this way of living is associated with '*a frame of government*, as was not only . . . most obvious and simple, but also best suited to their present state and condition . . .' (Sec. 107). In considering a non-commercial economy already in need of government, he did also not assume – hypothetically or otherwise – that all the land had been appropriated before the institution of civil society.[34] 'Any fixed property in the ground' necessitates political organization, yet not necessarily *vice versa*.

'It was *commonly* without any fixed property in the ground they [the families] made use of, *till they incorporated*, settled themselves together, and built cities, and *then*, by consent, they came *in time*, to set out the bounds of their distinct territories, and agree on limits between them and their neighbours, and by laws within themselves, settled the properties of those of the same society' (Sec. 38).

Political organization preceded the building of cities and everything which otherwise, by any standard of common sense, characterizes

---

[31] Macpherson, *op. cit.*, 211.
[32] *Ibid.*, 217, 235–6.
[33] The problem is raised against Locke by Vaughan, *op. cit.*, 176–7, and Gough, *op. cit.*, 92, note.
[34] For Macpherson, *op. cit.*, 217, this is an essential prop of his thesis.

a fully commercial economy. Since only after incorporation into political society the limits are set between the properties of families and the territories of wider groupings, Locke could maintain also that the pre-sedentary stage does not lack political organization. The 'several *nations* of the Americans . . . are rich in land, . . . yet for want of improving it by labour', even 'a *king* of a large and fruitful territory' in America is worse off than 'a day labourer in England' (Sec. 41). No governmentless situation is assumed when no land at all is improved by labour, and therefore not individually appropriated. Locke said nothing of all the land being appropriated with the institution of states. Quite to the contrary, he tells us of non-sedentary people using the land which lies in common within the sedentary people's territory. Under Abraham the families wandered.

'with their flocks, and their herds . . . in a country where he was a stranger. Whence it is plain, that at least, a great part of the land lay in common; that the inhabitants valued it not, nor claimed property in any more than they made use of' (Sec. 38).

Locke did certainly not assume that the kingdom of Egypt – or the other kingdoms which Abraham had dealings with – were in the state of nature because not all their land was yet appropriated. He spoke, moreover, in obvious reference to his contemporary England, of 'commons, which remain so by compact' (Sec. 28).

To read into Locke two stages of economic development in the state of nature is thus as little permissible as to attribute to him a contradictory conception of human nature or two opposite pictures of the state of nature. The verisimilitude of either assertion is not improved by granting no more than 'a certain similarity' between that of the two disparate versions of the state of nature and that of its two stages.[35] For if the first stage is one of equality, it ought to be peaceful and pleasant. If the second stage is one of inequality, indeed of cut-throat capitalist competition, it ought to be warlike and unpleasant. But according to Macpherson, both the pleasant and the unpleasant version of the state of nature characterize its second stage of capitalist inequality. This, and the very distinction between such a stage and an initial one of equality, has no other foundation than the aim of showing Locke committed to the justification of unlimited property accumulation on the basis of

[35] *Ibid.*, 242.

typically bourgeois contradictions concerning the postulate of equality. According to these hidden assumptions – indeed so well hidden that no trace of them is detectable in the text – the second stage of the state of nature must present a developed capitalist market economy and be not entirely unpleasant. For what is entirely unpleasant or wrong in the state of nature is not justifiable by the law of nature and ought not, therefore, to be carried over into political society. In the final analysis, Macpherson rests his case on the strange assumption that Locke's comprehension of the class character of his society made him unaware of what political philosophy had dealt with since its inception, namely, the tension between the positive and negative aspects of human nature and between the principles of equality and inequality.

Locke's point of departure is a mixture of a perfect theoretical and normative state which is derived from a definition of perfect man, and of a state of war which reflects the fact that men are corrupted by their passions.[36] *In fine*, however, he fused the different aspects of human nature and of the human condition in one concept of the state of nature. Inasmuch as the state of nature reflects a normative device to indicate deficiences it certainly applies not only to primitive forms of government but also to complex ones, i.e., to all governments which do not yet comply with the normative definition of political society. But this does not attest that an inclusive concept of the state of nature is being used besides a semi-romantic one.[37] Rather, although he did not simply identify the state of nature with the state of war,[38] Locke used the concept of the state of nature also to include the state of war between a government and its society alongside other real situations of a more and a less peaceful character. He certainly considered the deficiencies of human nature to form part of his hypothetical state of nature. Correspondingly, political society has manifest advantages over a hypothetical non-political condition but is not conceived by Locke as being composed of people who always behave rationally or can aspire to an ideal state.[39]

Moreover, as already pointed out, the assumption of an ideal state of nature makes the derivation of political society inexplicable,

[36] Cp. Polin, *op. cit.*, 174–8, 180.
[37] Cp. Yolton, 'Locke and the Law of Nature,' *loc. cit.*, 496, 493.
[38] *Ibid.*, 494–5.
[39] Cp. Polin, *op. cit.*, 150. Yolton, *loc. cit.*, and Simon, *loc. cit.*, 398, imply the idealization.

whereas to derive political society from the state of war cannot but lead to Hobbesian conclusions.[40] What is more, if men's natural condition were that of the brutes of the forest for whom, since they are devoid of reason, natural law has no significance,[41] the emergence of societal life itself would become inexplicable. This applies, whether or not we identify the peaceful and warlike aspects of Locke's state of nature as corresponding to the biblical distinction between the state of innocence and the state after the Fall.[42] In either case it does not follow that to explain the possibility and the necessity of political society, it is necessary to interject a third condition: 'the fallen state of nature', which, unlike the state of war – the one 'model condition' – provides men with the knowledge of the other one, 'the ideal condition'.[43] Whether we consider Locke to have conceived the ideal model condition as circumscribed by the beginnings of political society – 'a benign political condition having all of the idealized marks of a political society and none of its drawbacks'[44] – or as presenting its aim of perfection, the ideal model condition cannot be identified with the hypothetical or normative state of nature, which is by definition governmentless. The third condition is the only one, if for no other reason than that model conditions do not correspond to any actual condition.

As a hypothesis and as defined through real situations, the state of nature circumscribes the normal human condition which fluctuates between its two model poles – a state of war and a state of peace – without ever fully coinciding with them. Since in each stage of Locke's argument we face the same realistic, though not over-complex conception of human nature, his theory of the state of nature fulfils quite adequately the purpose of showing that men are as capable of political organization as they stand in dire need of it. It is, however, meant to do more than that. Its specific purpose is to prove that men need, and are capable of providing, not only a remedy for the inconveniences of a state of nature, but a remedy as well for the inconveniences of government. The theory of the state of nature supplies the basis for resistance to arbitrary rule.[45] In the extensive discussion in different parts of the *Treatises* of

[40] Cp. Wolin, *op. cit.*, 306.
[41] Cox, *op. cit.*, 79, 104.
[42] Strauss, *op. cit.*, 215, rejects and Cox, *op. cit.*, 49, accepts the parallel.
[43] Wolin, *op. cit.*, 307, suggests this solution.
[44] *Ibid.*, 305.
[45] Cp. Lamprecht, *op. cit.*, 123, and Goldwin, *op. cit.*, 438.

the causes and consequences of revolt, the correlation so far established between the state of nature, the state of war and political society remains unchanged. No confusion occurs between the hypothesis of a governmentless state of nature and a real situation.

3. THE STATE OF NATURE IN POLITICAL SOCIETY

A. The Cause – Arbitrary Rule

The motive behind the derivation of the magistrate's authority to punish criminals from the individual's natural right of self-defence is to leave to the individuals the right to oppose the prince who perverts equity and justice. This is why right from the beginning Locke speaks of '*a* criminal' as responsible for the greatest inconveniences,[46] and stresses that it is all the same whether a man attempts to get another into his absolute power in the state of nature or 'in the state of society, would take away the freedom belonging to those of that society or commonwealth . . .' (Sec. 17). He 'must be . . . looked on as in a state of war'. Since 'absolute monarchs are but men, and if government is to be the remedy of those evils, which *necessarily* follow from men's being judges in their own cases', there is still room to query

'what kind of government that is, and how much better it is than the state of nature, where one man commanding a multitude, has the liberty to be judge in his own case, . . . without the least liberty to anyone to question or control those who execute his pleasure.'[47]

The need to defend this liberty against Hobbes and Filmer explains the idealizing overtones concerning the natural condition of man, and the no less overcharged denunciation of its perversion, such as recur later in Rousseau. The aim and the vehemence of these outbursts explain Locke's rhetorical question whether irresponsible government was really better than a state of nature. People may after all still be heard saying: No government is better than this government.

When Locke went out of his way to denounce what 'folly or craft began' and 'custom makes . . . sacred' (I, 58), he wished to strike at the Filmerian theories of absolute paternal monarchy. He pointed out the unnatural character of some of the customs of

[46] Secs. 8, 11.
[47] Sec. 13. Cp. Secs. 137, 225.

the ancient Israelites, the Romans and the Peruvians,[48] although he otherwise referred to them, or their like, as examples of the golden age of early government. We are invited to survey impartially 'the nations of the world' to find 'so much of their governments, religions, and manners brought in and continued amongst them by these means', i.e. by fashion established by craft and folly. We shall then

'have reason to think, that the woods and forests, where the irrational untaught inhabitants keep right by following nature, are fitter to give us rules, than cities and palaces, where those that call themselves civil and rational, go out of their way, by the authority of example.'[49]

When Locke permitted himself this angry outburst of enjoining men to learn from beasts rather than from their own traditions, he stood by his view that where government 'is the product only of force and violence, . . . men live together by no other rules but that of beasts . . .' (Sec. 1). Wherever such a form of government is concerned, government is not 'civil government'. When rulers behave arbitrarily they sink to the level of beasts, and if this happens, the ruled had better learn something from beasts, than let themselves be misled by that which had begun in craft and folly but has become sanctified by custom, and hence 'it will be thought impudence or madness, to contradict or question it' (I, 58). To justify the right to contradict and question the acts of rulers with 'but little reverence for the practices which are in use and credit amongst men', Locke pointed to the state of nature as a hypothetical antithesis to uncontrollable government.

For Hobbes, the unavoidable shortcomings of governmental protection do not constitute an intrusion of the state of nature and of war into political society, although they perpetuate men's mistrust of each other in political society.[50] For Locke, the members of political society are apt to find themselves in a state of war not only in relation to common thieves and robbers or to a foreign

---

[48] I, 56–8.
[49] I, 58. The 'irrational untaught' most probably refer not to primitive men but to beasts. Cf. I, 56 and II, 79. Locke's outburst is a very faint echo of the argument advanced by R. Cumberland, *De Legibus Naturae Disquisitio Philosophica* (1672), who had tried to refute Hobbes by demonstrating the social nature of animals, asking whether the situation of mankind is the worse for men being rational. Cp. Fetscher, *loc. cit.*, 666, 675; also on Rousseau's view of 'man-animal' as a non-social being (668, 675).
[50] *Leviathan*, Ch. 13.

conqueror,[51] but also in relation to their rulers, because society is never secure from the greatest inconvenience, arbitrary rule. Arbitrary rule is repeatedly defined as reintroducing the state of nature in the sense of a state of war.[52] For men always retain 'the right of war' (Sec. 19) against 'whoever introduces a state of war, and is aggressor in it' (Sec. 18). If they exercise this right against arbitrary rulers, a state of war comes to prevail but not a relapse into a governmentless state of nature. The existence of political society is the irremovable datum.

B. The Consequence: War Between Political Society and Arbitrary Rulers

In the second and third chapter of the *Treatise* Locke has spoken about the possibility of a state of war, whether there was or was not a common judge, and about the preferability of the state of nature to unjust government. This is worked out in Chapter VII in two stages: in Sections 87-9 and in Sections 90-4. Method and aim are unchanged. The state of nature is referred to as the theoretical point of reference to determine the purpose of civil society and the exclusion of non-civil government from it. In the first stage of the argument Locke defines political society by distinguishing between those who 'are in civil society one with another' and those who 'are still in the state of nature', the difference being whether one has or has not 'a common established law and judicature to appeal to . . .' (Sec. 87). The second stage of the argument culminates in the violent denunciation of absolute monarchy as being 'inconsistent with civil society' and therefore 'no form of *civil* government at all'.[53] Arbitrary absolute monarchy does not provide a proper judicature to appeal to and therefore confronts civil society with a non-civil government, though – or better, because – 'absolute monarchy, . . . by some men is counted the only government in the world . . .' A form of government is disqualified by declaring it incompatible with political society as defined in the first stage of the argument.

It is to be noted that the arbitrary ruler is denied a public standing in the second stage of the argument after it has been made clear in the first that any ruler's authority is delegated to him by the public,

[51] Secs. 18-19, 176, 182, 186, 207.
[52] See above, note 18.
[53] Sec. 90. See p. 245 f., where I show that Locke did not simply mean absolute monarchy, but arbitrary absolute monarchy.

that is to say, authority inheres first and foremost in political society. In Sections 87-9, the main purpose of distinguishing between the state of nature and political society is to show how '*the commonwealth* comes by a power to set down, what punishment shall belong to the several transgressions . . . committed amongst the members of that society', and that only where everyone relinquishes the 'executive power of the law of nature' and resigns it 'to the *public*, there and there only is a political, or civil society' (Sec. 89). Thus 'the *community* comes to be umpire' (Sec. 87), and 'men having authority *from the community*' make laws and execute them. The public or community is the creation of the individuals and holds the first place as the recipient of their authorization especially to legislate for them. Civil society is so defined as to permit the community to take its stand as a political entity against the agents which it has entrusted with the exercise of political authority. After having defined political society in this way, by reference to the terms of definition of the hypothetical state of nature, Locke moves on to show in Sections 90-4 that absolute monarchy does not afford civil society with a proper judge. Anyone having 'both legislative and executive power in himself alone' is actually in a state of nature 'with all under his dominion' (Sec. 91). This normative appraisal of a form of government gives occasion, as in Section 13, for comparing 'the ordinary state of nature' favourably with this sort of government but not for considering a society ruled by absolute monarchs as living in 'the ordinary state of nature'.

True, concluding the first stage of his argument, Locke speaks of 'men, *however associated*', who, having no power to which to appeal, 'are still in the state of nature' (Sec. 89). But according to him men cannot be associated in a community and at the same time be in the state of nature with one another. They can yet be associated and the state of nature obtain between them and their prince. It is this situation which is explicitly allied with the model definition of the state of nature:

'Wherever any persons are, who have not . . . an authority to appeal to, for the decision of any difference between them, there those persons are still in the state of nature. *And so is every absolute prince in respect of those who are under his dominion*' (Sec. 90).

The existence of arbitrary rule indicates the absence of *civil* government, not of government as such. No governmentless state of nature can be meant when Locke censures the nature of the relations between the people and princes 'however entitled' (Sec. 91) in 'this sort of government' (Sec. 92). He does not deny the existence of political relations between the prince and the people. 'In absolute monarchies indeed, as well as other governments of the world, the subjects have an appeal to the law . . .' (Sec. 93). All that is doubtful is not the continual existence of political society, but whether the absolute rulers' provisions for law and order are motivated by 'a true love of mankind and society'.

But when the people finally see through the intentions of a vicious prince, they consider him, like 'any man, in what station so ever,' to be 'out of the bounds of the civil society *which they are of'* (Sec. 94). When 'they have no appeal on earth against any harm they may receive from him, *they are apt to think themselves* in the state of nature, *in respect of him'* (Sec. 94), that is to say, not in respect of themselves. According to this manner of thinking one asks 'whether he [the irresponsible ruler] be not perfectly still in the state of nature, and so can be *no part or member of that civil society'*.

The relationship defined as a state of nature exists first of all as a state of mind beyond and in contradiction to the legal and even factually obtaining situation. After the people arrive at the conclusion that their association is endangered by an arbitrary ruler, the question becomes that of ensuring the continuance of their association in view of its purpose – the preservation of 'life, liberty and estate' (Sec. 87) – and the punishment of those offending against it by excluding them from their society. Not to recognize that such an offender is outside the bounds of their society is to admit that 'the state of nature and civil society are one and the same thing' (Sec. 94), and this is more than what even 'anyone so great a patron of anarchy' might be expected to affirm. Locke deals with the confusion of criteria of judgement. He identifies anarchy with that kind of argument – the absolutists' argument – according to which no appeal may be pursued against the harm wrought by a man who does as he likes because he happens to be the ruler. This Locke had rejected all along, declaring it to be worse than the state of nature. The point he wishes to make is that, if the ruler acts this way, the people might act against him and yet remain, unlike the ruler, in political society.

We must, however, ask the following question: If for Locke a state of nature without government is a hypothesis, how could he explicitly associate the state of war between the ruler and the ruled with the dissolution of government? For 'by actually putting himself into a state of war with his people, [the prince will] dissolve the government, and leave them to that defence, which belongs to every one in the state of nature' (Sec. 205). With this, Locke's argument has reached its third, and indeed in every respect, its final stage. First he has explained 'wherein political society itself consists' (Sec. 86). The explanation then serves him to declare arbitrary government to be inconsistent with civil society and to exclude the arbitrary ruler from it. The third stage of the argument, from Section 203 in Chapter XVIII to the end of the *Treatise*, deals with how the clash between ruler and ruled actually comes to pass, and what it implies. None of the implications contradicts the conclusions reached so far.

To show that society survives as an action-unit the dissolution of government from within and is not necessarily destroyed by the dissolution of government from without, means to investigate Locke's views on the extremities of the political condition when force is pitted against force within political society and between nations. The examination of Locke's views on this topic leads us to his limitation of the realization of natural law through consent, and in conclusion to attempt a systematic presentation of his conception of power.

CHAPTER IV

THE EXTREMITIES OF THE POLITICAL CONDITION

I. THE DISSOLUTION OF GOVERNMENT AND THE DISSOLUTION OF SOCIETY – CONNECTIONS

CHAPTER XIX of the *Second Treatise* continues the argument of the two preceding stages, the basis of the further argument being that, when the ruler places himself in a state of war with his people, government is dissolved. The dissolution of government means first of all that it forfeits its moral claim to obedience.[1] Actually, to dissolve the government, the people must still win a struggle. They conduct their war against the government by resorting to the right of defence possessed by every one in the state of nature but in so defending themselves, the people keep on maintaining political society. 'Civil society' is 'a state of peace, amongst those who are of it, from whom the state of war is excluded by the umpirage, which they have provided in their legislative . . .' (Sec. 212). By denying membership to the prince civil society is plunged into civil war with him and his supporters. But between the majority there reigns peace and in acting themselves as the legislature they provide the umpirage that characterizes civil society.

This conclusion has been overlooked, or its definite character has been doubted, because critics have failed to keep the hypothetical meaning of Locke's concept of the state of nature apart from its practical meaning, and have, therefore, read the first into his statements on revolution and identified it as a condition which is social but without government. His distinction between the dissolution of government and the dissolution of society is thus held to permit the assumption of the entire break-up of political society on the one hand and of the persistence of society on the other, i.e., the assumption of a relapse into a governmentless yet social condition.[2] Conversely when, more correctly, no distinction between

---

[1] Rousseau continued to use 'dissolution' in the same sense. Cp. *Du Contrat Social*, III, v. and especially with regard to tyranny, III, x.

[2] Lamprecht, *op. cit.*, 130, 147, and Polin, *op. cit.*, 36, especially note 3 to 135-6.

society and political society is seen to be involved, but nevertheless the consistency of Locke's distinction between the dissolution of government and the dissolution of society is questioned,[3] the interpretation of the state of nature as a social condition is jeopardized. If it is not clear whether or not the dissolution of government entails the dissolution of society, there can be no clarity as regards the social character of a governmentless state of nature. If you say that a social condition can exist independently of a political condition, you cannot question whether the dissolution of government leaves men in a social condition. Again, if society is for Locke inconceivable without some kind of government, the revolutionary dissolution of the government by the people cannot denote a governmentless situation. If Locke was consistent, we can, with Laslett, attribute to him the view that the dissolution of government does not cause the dissolution of society if the people take upon themselves to act as the legislature.[4] But the ability of the people to act as a legislature and thus to survive as a political society the disfunction and actual elimination of the existing government, must emerge not as one possibility among others, but as the possibility envisaged by Locke first and foremost, if not exclusively.

The people's patience, or the non-resistance of governors to the 'umpirage' of the people, or the fact that the governors' misdemeanour does not threaten the existence of the community, are alternatives to the dissolution of society,[5] but only inasmuch as the question of the dissolution of government does not arise at all in these cases. When the people are patient there is no revolt; when the governors do not threaten the existence of the community, there is no just cause for revolution. Arbitrary rule is the menace, not only the extreme case when a ruler endangers the physical existence of the community by betraying his country to the ruler of another. Of course, there is no clash between rulers and ruled, and society can be easily said to subsist, if the governors who are resisted by the people do not resist the revolutionary umpirage of

[3] Laslett, *op. cit.*, 114–15. Similarly already Vaughan, *op. cit.*, II, 148–9.

[4] For a solution of the difficulties that Laslett raises, he suggests also a guarded allowance for a lack of rigidity in Locke's distinction between the natural and the political condition. I think we can say more than that, as I have tried to demonstrate in Chapter III. I also think that proof of Locke's consistency as regards the distinction between the dissolution of government and of society does not, as Laslett suggests, require a manipulation of Locke's statements in the light of a sympathetic appraisal of the tenor of his doctrine.

[5] Laslett, *op. cit.*, 107–8.

the people. The *Treatises* make no distinction between a revolution which governors resist and one they do not. If Locke had evaluated the *Glorious Revolution* in the second sense, as modern historians are inclined to do, his revision of the *Treatises* for publication under the impact of that event would have revealed traces of this attitude.

To appraise properly whether Locke was consistent we must bear in mind that Locke made two distinctions: the distinction between the dissolution of government from within and from without, and the distinction between the dissolution of government and of society. The first distinction indicates two possibilities of the dissolution of government. Only one is immediately related to the dissolution of society: this is the dissolution of government from without. Only foreign conquest usually dissolves both government and society. Locke does not directly relate the dissolution of government from within to the combined dissolution of government and society from without; but he judges both by the same moral criteria and considers them not dissimilar in all their practical effects.

Arbitrariness from within 'produces effects very little different from foreign conquest' (Sec. 218). The injury is the same 'whether they [the people] are made slaves to any of their own, or a foreign nation' (Sec. 239). Locke passed an identical moral judgement to draw an identical conclusion: the right to resist aggression from without as well as at home. Such resistance is the consummation of the 'state of nature' between the rulers and the ruled. It does not dissolve society, but only a government that has brought about the 'state of nature' by the moral forfeiture of its claim to obedience. In this respect the dissolution of government from within and from without resemble each other, and through the second – conquest – become related to the dissolution of society. But the distinction between the dissolution of society and that of government is maintained by Locke, on the basis of the view that society without a government is inconceivable.

2. THE DISSOLUTION OF SOCIETY

A. The Moral and Practical Limits of Dissolution Through Foreign Conquest

Considering the relationship between arbitrariness from within and foreign conquest, it is of interest to note one reference to the

Norman conquest in Section 177. Locke denies the conqueror 'a title to absolute dominion' over 'those that conquered with him'. Among the conquerors, political relationships after the conquest are determined by the political relationship prior to, and during, the conquest. This kind of argument was made famous by Boullainvilliers in the eighteenth century.[6] Locke did not here imply an indirect justification of conquest. He anticipated Voltaire's ridiculing the whole argument by saying that 'if I, or anybody else, shall claim freedom, as derived from them [the Normans], it will be very hard to prove the contrary.' That in Locke's time there were hardly any defenders of unlimited monarchy who argued from conquest,[7] does not affect the significance of his argument. He was fully justified in placing it in the context of his polemic with the absolutists, for like the term 'property', he used the term 'conquest' in an extended and a restricted sense. In fact, the two meanings are less differentiated in the case of conquest than of property. In accord with the words epitomizing the tendency of the *Treatises*, i.e., that government is not 'the product only of force and violence' (Sec. 1), the chapter 'Of Conquest' opens with the rejection of conquest 'as one of the originals of government' (Sec. 175). The chapter 'Of Usurpation' begins with the words: 'As conquest may be called a foreign usurpation, so usurpation is a kind of domestic conquest' (Sec. 197). When Locke spoke of the many who had accepted conquest as an original of government, he meant, therefore, all those who opposed the principle of government by consent, those who have 'mistaken the force of arms, for the consent of the people' (Sec. 175). In this respect there is no difference between subjugation from within and from without, between domestic despotism and foreign conquest. Neither carries with it a moral right to exert authority. External conquest is evaluated, however, in the light of the moral criteria applicable to internal relations, so much so that, except for two sections,

[6] On the nature of this pseudo-historical controversy, begun by Hotman in the sixteenth century, see my 'The Idea of Conquest and Race-Thinking during the Restoration,' *The Review of Politics*, Vol. 22, 4 (1960), 545–67, and the literature there cited.

[7] Laslett, *op. cit.*, 402–3, follows J. G. A. Pocock, *The Ancient Constitution and the Feudal Law* (Cambridge, 1957), 53–4, 148–50, in accusing Locke of disregarding this fact. To Grotius and Hobbes, whom Laslett mentions as coming close to accepting conquest as the foundation of government, we may add Bodin. In his *Six Livres de la République*, Book IV, Ch. I, he referred to violence and consent as alternatives to the historical foundation of government.

Chapter XVI is devoted to the limitations of 'a conqueror in a lawful war' (Sec. 177). There is no need to waste words on whether 'robbers and pirates have a right of empire over whomsoever they have force enough to master' (Sec. 176). What requires clarification are the purposes which may be secured by force and without reliance on the criteria that otherwise render the demands of governors legitimate. These purposes are so limited that the dissolution of society through the dissolution of government from without is indefensible and does, therefore, not establish an irreversible fact.

The lawful conqueror is a ruler who defeats the 'unjust force, that is used against him' (Sec. 179). 'It is the brutal force the aggressor has used, that gives his adversary a right to take away his life . . .' (Sec. 182). The terms of lawful conquest are the terms by which individuals may rightfully defend themselves against thieves and robbers when the common superior is of no avail, or against the ruler who puts himself in a state of war with his society. Just as the attempts of the domestic ruler or of anybody else upon the lives and property of the citizens create a state of war, so the lawful conqueror becomes an aggressor the moment he engages in real conquest. In the same way as an over-severe punishment of crime is unjust, so the conqueror remains lawful so long as he behaves as the adversary of the aggressor; so long as he is not engaged in conquest but in warding it off. His business is solely to punish all those who are guilty of aggression and to secure reparations for 'the charges of the war' which he has not begun and for 'the damages he has sustained by the war'.[8]

The lawful conqueror achieves no right to political rule by force of arms. He only acquires 'an absolute power over the lives of those, who by an unjust war have forfeited them; but not over *the lives or fortunes* of those, who engaged not in the war, *nor over the posses-*

[8] Sec. 182. H. Arendt, *On Revolution* (London, 1963), 3, is thus mistaken in maintaining that the notion that aggression is wrong and war only justifiable in order to ward off aggression, first acquired theoretical significance after the First World War. In fact, if on the whole seventeenth-century thinkers dealt rather helplessly with the causes of war, it was because they confused the question 'Who began it?' with the question 'Who was to blame?' (Cp. G. Clark, *War and Society in the Seventeenth Century* (Cambridge, 1958), 7, 11, and *passim*). Moreover, Grotius had merely continued with the medieval distinction between just and unjust wars, but was among the few to envisage the regulation of war by a law of nations based on contract and justice, and on legal and moral restraints recognized by sovereign states. (Cp. F. H. Hinsley, *Power and the Pursuit of Peace*, (Cambridge, 1963), 23-4, 27, 29.

sions even of those, who were actually engaged in it.'[9] The possessions of the guilty who are liable to become slaves remain in the family, like the possessions of those who have neither participated in, nor condoned, the unjust war. 'The miscarriages of the father are no faults of the children' (Sec. 182), nor for that matter of the mother.[10] Even the right of the lawful conqueror to cover his losses must give way to the right of subsistence of those who are guiltless.[11] The final issue of lawful 'conquest' is then that it

'will scarce give him [the conqueror] a title to any country he shall conquer. For the damages of war can scarce amount to the value of any considerable tract of land, . . . where . . . none lies waste . . . The destruction of a year's product or two, . . . is the utmost spoil, that usually can be done' (Sec. 184).

Lawful conquest is no more than a temporary occupation to secure military objectives and indemnities for the costs and damages of war. Not only are the material consequences of the community's war-guilt restricted, and exclude the annexation of territory. The dominion over those who have forfeited their lives is a dominion over slaves and hence not proper political power. The lawful conqueror has no right to arrogate to himself the government over the vanquished even if he does not touch their possessions. Only where a legitimate government exists, i.e., 'a government made by their consent' (Sec. 191), must a person give up his possessions, 'if he disclaim the lawful government of the country he was born in . . .' (Sec. 191). Accordingly, 'those, who are subdued . . . retain a right to the possession of their ancestors, though they consent not freely to the government' (Sec. 192). Besides those who have not joined in the war

'the posterity even of those that did, . . . are free from any subjection to him [the conqueror], and if their former government be dissolved, they are at liberty to begin and erect another to themselves.'[12]

---

[9] Sec. 178. Cp. Secs. 179, 180, 185, 196.
[10] Secs. 181-3, 188, 189, 192-4.
[11] Secs. 182-3.
[12] Sec. 185. D. P. Gauthier, 'The Role of Inheritance in Locke's Political Theory,' *The Canadian Journal of Economics and Political Science*, XXXII (February, 1966), 43-4, blurs the interdependence in Locke of the right to consented government and the duty to consent to the government as the condition of enjoying the right of inheritance.

Any promises to accept the conqueror's government are void if made under duress. Even if all the male members of the country have participated in an unjust war or have abetted it, this may entail only the temporary loss of the community's independence. The guilt of the fathers no more annuls the right of their offspring to possess a government by their consent alone[13] than it permits the sequestration of their property.

The conversion of individual into collective war-guilt being restricted, the relations between states are not permitted to violate the principle of government by consent. Locke maintains the parallel between ordinary individual aggression and that of the ruler, be he a domestic or a foreign one; between the right of individuals and of states to secure punishment of infractions of natural law and compensation in proportion to the extent of the offence.[14] Yet only individuals, not communities, may forfeit their right of existence. To the extent that foreign conquest may rightly be followed by the dissolution of the conquered society, the posterity of the individuals who have forfeited their lives and those who have not, lose their separate political identity on the condition that they do not lose the right to live under consented government. It 'seldom happens, that the conquerors and conquered never incorporate into one people, under the same laws and freedom' (Sec. 178). If they are not so incorporated, that is, if they do not consent to belong to the conquering society, they retain the right to a political society of their own. 'Who doubts but the Grecian Christians descendants of the ancient possessors of that country may justly cast off the Turkish yoke which they have so long groaned under whenever they have a power to do it' (Sec. 192)? The lawful conqueror's assumption of rule over the unconsenting vanquished

He thus maintains that Locke could have allowed disobedience to a conqueror, who honours the property of the vanquished and rules over them by standing laws, only if the conqueror can be shown up as an usurper. Gauthier advances the startling suggestion that Locke could not regard a conqueror as an usurper because conquest destroys the community and hence its laws by reference to which alone the conqueror could be called a usurper. But according to Locke the dissolution from without of political society justifies revolt against the conqueror and 'conquest may be called a foreign usurpation' (Sec. 197). Surely, if a usurper is a man who has come to power by ways other than prescribed by the community and its laws, the same must be said of the conqueror who has destroyed the community which has sanctioned certain ways.

[13] Secs. 186–7, 189, 192–3.
[14] For the parallelism in Chapter XVI, see especially Secs. 176, 181–3, 186.

converts him into an aggressor. The subdued or their heirs may, therefore, on their part assume the role of the lawful conqueror and shake off his government.

The dissolution of society as the result of the dissolution of government from without does not, according to Locke, necessarily destroy the vanquished society to the extent that its resurrection becomes impossible. He could therefore very well postulate that society is not dissolved at all by the dissolution of government from within. Before we examine whether he contradicted himself on this point, we must consider at what cost lawful conquest remains enclosed within the limits of defensive action and equivalent to individual and collective resistance to government without consent. For this very notion of lawful conquest is used, or rather misused, by Locke to justify colonial conquest. Thus the boundaries are drawn within which alone the Lockeian realization of natural law through consent applies. His justification of colonial conquest and slavery reveals also the over-simplification inherent in the distinction between a just and an unjust war and the tenuousness of his theoretical attempts in the field of foreign relations.

B. Colonial Conquest and Slavery

a. Explicit Exception to the Interdict of Annexation

Locke rejected the lawfulness of annexing territories. Yet he complained in the same breath 'that where there . . . [is] more land, than the inhabitants possess, and make use of . . ., there conquerors take little care to possess themselves of the lands of the vanquished' (Sec. 184). He seems to have covered himself against the charge of inconsistency by insisting on the high value of cultivated as compared with uncultivated land. The damages of war are insignificant 'in any part of the world, where all the land is possessed, and none lies waste', and no war-damage, therefore, justifies any appropriation of land. Yet 'any one has liberty to make use of the waste'. He exonerates colonial conquest on similar terms as was done by Sir Thomas More.[15]

Locke's definitions of 'waste' render the concept conveniently flexible. *Vacui loci* are not merely places, which people 'find free

---

[15] Cp. *Utopia*, Book II, Ch. 5. As Laslett, *op. cit.*, 267, notes, Locke possessed the book. He used the word 'Eutopia' to designate the outcome of political 'fancy or interest' (I, 147).

and unpossessed' (Sec. 121) but 'tracts of ground . . ., which . . . lie waste, and are more than the people, who dwell on it, do, or can make use of . . .' (Sec. 45). Land is not used 'if either the grass of his enclosure rotted on the ground, or the fruit of his planting perished without gathering, and laying up . . .' (Sec. 38). Consequently, 'this part of the earth, *notwithstanding his enclosure*, was still to be looked on as waste, and might be the possession of any other'. Waste land is not simply unoccupied land. Nor is it merely land which is enclosed, i.e., appropriated, but not used. Land which is more than can be made use of is also land which is improperly used. The flexibility of the definition of waste land is ominous because of the grounds by which one side is allowed to decide what is more than the other side can make use of.

One economic-cum-political condition must be fulfilled to permit members of one nation to sequestrate land in another nation's territory. Nations who 'have consented to the use of money' are usually not possessors of waste land, and their territories are immune because they are parties to 'the leagues that have been made between several states and kingdoms, either expressly or tacitly disowning all claim and right to the land in the others' possession . . .' (Sec. 45). From such leagues the possessors of great tracts of waste land are excluded, 'the inhabitants thereof not having joined with the rest of mankind, in the consent of the use of their common money . .'. On these grounds, which, as we shall immediately see, are by no means conclusive, Locke suspended the rule which forbids a lawful conqueror to annex any territory of the vanquished.

He bestowed upon the developed states, the states amongst which 'the silver money of Europe' (Sec. 184) is current, the right to determine what was more land than the inhabitants of undeveloped areas could make use of. War between the planters and the natives is assumed by him as a matter of course.[16] The unavoidable implication is that the natives' resistance to the conquest of their waste territory turns them into aggressors and the Europeans into 'just conquerors' of the natives' 'waste'. Since on Locke's terms captives in a just war become slaves, the same fate may lie in store for any nation that does not use Europe's 'silver-money'.

There is, of course, a striking paradox between Locke, the codifier

[16] I, 130.

of the doctrines of self-government and trust – and Locke, the founder-member of the Board of Trade who dominated its early history and hence the elaboration of the principles of its colonial policy.[17] But the paradox is not between the theorist and the administrator. The justification of colonial conquest is part of Locke's liberal theory, as it was part of Grotius' theory.[18] Locke, the administrator of slave-owning colonies, who considered the slave raids of the Royal Africa Company as just wars[19] and spoke in the *Fundamental Constitutions of Carolina* of the freeman's 'absolute power over his negro slaves',[20] was not disowned by Locke, the mature liberal theorist.

The justification of colonial rule and of its adjunct, slavery, rests on purely secular grounds. The Romans had accorded slaves membership in religious corporations on an equal footing with freemen.[21] From the days of the apostles and for a long period after the time of Thomas Aquinas, slavery was not considered inconsistent with membership in the *res publica Christiana*. Locke's plea for religious toleration, a concomitant of his enlightened belief in Christianity, makes no practical difference in this respect. 'Religion ought to alter nothing in any man's civil state or right.'[22] A slave has the right to choose his religion whereby 'that civil dominion his master has over him' is not affected, and idolatry, ignorance and other shortcomings of 'the natives of that place' furnish no right to expel them or to ill-treat them.[23] To be a freeman in Carolina, to own estate and merely to live there, requires therefore no more by way of confession than to acknowledge '*a* God, and that God is publicly and solemnly worshipped'.[24] No other consideration

---

[17] Cp. P. Laslett, 'John Locke, the Great Recoinage and the Origins of the Board of Trade: 1695–1698,' *The William and Mary Quarterly*, 3rd ser., XVI, 3 (1957), 371–2. For a detailed account of Locke at the Board of Trade see also the biographies by Fox Bourne and Cranston.

[18] Cp. Hinsley, *op. cit.*, 165. On the issue of colonization, there had not been much development on a high theoretical level. (Cp. Laslett, *ibid.*, 374.) This may account for the tenuousness and arbitrariness of Locke's argumentation.

[19] Cp. Laslett, *Two Treatises*, 302–3, and Stephen, *op. cit.*, II, 139.

[20] *The Works of John Locke* (London, 1823), X vols., 175 on, article CX. Cp. also art. XXII–XXVI on 'leet-men' and 'leet-women'.

[21] Cp. I. Schulz, *Prinzipien des römischen Rechts* (Berlin, 1954), 147.

[22] *Fundam. Constitutions*, art. CVII.

[23] *Ibid.*, arts. CVIII and XCVI.

[24] Art. XCVI. The italics are mine. In accordance with the preferability of 'numbers of men . . . to largeness of dominions' (Sec. 42), the pragmatic purpose of toleration

remains for declaring colonial conquest lawful in contravention of the rule which forbids a lawful conqueror to annex any of the territory of the vanquished, than that nations who have considerable waste territories are for this reason (or any other) excluded from the leagues between those nations who have consented to the use of *common* money'. In fact, Locke did not accidentally speak of common money instead of simply money. Since anything durable may serve as money,[25] he had to admit that the American Indians used a kind of money. But 'the Wampompeke of the Americans' is of as little account to 'an European prince' as 'the silver money of Europe would have been formerly to an American'.[26] In other words, nations qualify for membership of leagues and for at least moral immunity from territorial inroads, not because they use money, but because their money is based on the silver standard and is common inasmuch as its exchange value is recognized far beyond their frontiers. It ensues likewise that European merchants who in accordance with their government's policy refuse to accept 'Wampompeke', thereby alone establish the right of territorial annexation, and with it that of the political and social subjugation of the inhabitants. It also follows, however, that if the non-use by the natives of common money justifies the establishment of colonial rule, perpetuation of that rule becomes disqualified with the introduction of common money. Locke did not draw the conclusion which follows from his own argument. As his comparison between the 'Wampompeke' and 'the silver money of Europe' shows, the latter was only 'formerly' of no account to the American. He took it, therefore, for granted that the introduction of common money was part of colonial rule. The purpose of 'the government of this province', i.e. Carolina, was that it be 'made most agreeable to the monarchy, under which we live, and of which this province is part'.[27] Locke did not carry his argument to the point where by reference to its own premises the

---

in the *Constitutions* is firstly to increase population and secondly that Jews, heathens and other 'dissenters from the purity of the Christian religion', who ought to be admitted and granted freedom of worship, should eventually be won over to Christianity. The latter consideration perhaps served to make such toleration, which Locke professed also on principle in his *Letters on Toleration*, more palatable to the clergy.

[25] Sec. 46.

[26] Sec. 184. 'Wampompeke' means the bead money of the Algonkin Indians. Cp. Laslett, *op. cit.*, 409.

[27] *Fundam. Const.*, Preamble, *Works*, 175.

exception to the interdict of territorial annexation could be demolished. He evidently did not wish to grant to the natives the rights which he otherwise accorded to the vanquished, namely, to be incorporated on an equal footing with the conquerors into one people or else to endeavour to recover their independence. Just as in the *Treatise* the right of revolt is implicitly ruled out for the original possessors of justly annexed 'waste' territories, and for their offspring, so the *Constitutions* deny the right to break away from the mother-country.[28] They deny the right to change the *Constitutions*, and thereby the right of revolt to the heirs of the lord proprietors and all strata of settlers. Since the right of revolt expresses the ultimate sovereignty of the people, we must conclude that in theory and practice Locke denied such sovereignty to both colonial peoples and the colonies established on their territory.[29]

Locke's justification of colonization is a flagrant and inane deviation from his condemnation of foreign conquest. Its ostensible weakness might attest by way of contrast the strength of his humane principles, if those were not similarly impugned in his justification of slavery.

b. *Implicit Limitation of the Universal Applicability of Slavery*

The justification of slavery in the *Treatises* is presented in terms of universal applicability. The *Constitutions* make it plain that religion does not affect the issue. And since, in Locke's time, slavery had practical significance only in relation to colonization, we may ask whether the universal justification of slavery does not serve him to cloak the discriminatory division of mankind openly admitted in respect of colonial conquest.

A slave has 'by his fault, forfeited his own life, by some act that deserves death' (Sec. 23). The act in question is participation in an unjust war. A man who has thus forfeited the right to live has no right to property, because he has lost the right to his liberty. His property does not become that of the conqueror; it reverts to his wife and children in order to make their liberty possible. That is why the person of the aggressor is less sacred than his property, not

---

[28] *Ibid.*

[29] Only within this limitation may we speculate like Laslett, 'The Great Recoinage', 395, whether Locke's stand on the affiliation of the Board of Trade with the 'federative' – instead of with the legislative – power may be taken to indicate something of the latter-day theory of self-government within the Commonwealth.

because property was more important to Locke than liberty.[30] The slave's physical capacity both to be free and to acquire property – the capacity to work – is overridden by moral forfeiture. Yet moral becomes actual forfeiture only if the participant in an unjust war is taken prisoner. Because 'the perfect condition of slavery . . . is nothing else, but the state of war continued, between a lawful conqueror, and a captive' (Sec. 24), 'we call slaves . . . captives taken in a just war' (Sec. 85). Slavery has its source in inter-state relations. The actual forfeiture of the right to live as a freeman, and accordingly the exercise of a legitimately unlimited right over a group of particular human beings, depends in the first place on the fortune of the individual warrior. It did not occur to Locke to ask by what moral right those who have forfeited their lives, but are not captured, evade slavery. Apart from purely individual luck, slavery also depends on the strength of armies and the fortunes of war in general. Although Locke admitted that victory did not always favour the right side,[31] and was generally aware that right and might do not necessarily coincide, he made no effort to distinguish between actual and rightful enslavement. In fact, only on the basis of confusing the two do his views on slavery accord with the practice of his time, and make some sense. For Locke does not put up a half-hearted defence of slavery, but unreservedly explains it as a generally applicable form of punishment which is exceptional only by being divorced from legal procedures.[32] But he certainly did not mean that prisoners taken in European wars became, or ought to have become, slaves, although he did not say so. On the strength of the justification to annex waste territories ouside Europe, we are left to infer that resistance to colonial conquest is unjust and that there is only a certain part of mankind to which slavery has by now become applicable.

[30] As Polin, *op. cit.*, 280–1, and similarly Vaughan, *op. cit.*, 168, argues. While Locke defended property in order to guarantee liberty, he did not defend property at the cost of liberty but as its realization. See below, 194 f., 2, and 272 f., on the separability of property and political obligations and rights.

Exception must also be taken to Polin's contention that Locke did not justify 'la maîtrise de maîtres' (*op. cit.*, 280). He did not pose the riddle of how the slaves' forefeiture of rights was possible without constituting the right of mastership but clearly said that 'slaves . . ., are by the right of nature subjected to the absolute dominion and arbitrary power of their masters' (Sec. 85). Moreover, the division of mankind as regards conquest implies that slavery is hereditary and possibly assumed to be so in virtue of natural predispositions.

[31] Secs. 177, 180.

[32] Cp. Polin, *op. cit.*, 280, against Aaron, *op. cit.*, 276.

By itself the distinction between a just and an unjust war amounts to the truism that just war is defensive and unjust war offensive, as if nothing were easier than to determine who originally provoked the war. Such a theory of conquest is curious and unsatisfactory, especially in view of the most familiar type of war, that in defence of national interests.[33] Locke hardly meant to outlaw military action before the enemy had chosen to strike. Yet on his terms, to forestall the enemy is, at least technically, to wage offensive war. It must also be considered that, although Locke indubitably exempted European nations from slavery, he cannot be assumed to have excluded territorial annexation from relations between them. According to him, only the consent of the inhabitants of a territory renders its annexation legitimate. If, as he certainly thought, in this case, too, tacit consent on the part of the majority is enough, peace treaties which confirm the annexation remain more precarious than ever, since tacit consent may, according to him, by right give way to active dissent. But if, in a spurious attempt to apply his principles for the management of internal affairs to external relations, he had wished to advocate a right of national self-determination in opposition to prevailing inter-state relations, other examples besides that of the Grecian Christians' right to throw off the conquerors' yoke might have suggested themselves to him. Although he took into account the possible involvement of the whole community in war in connection with the defence of property, he revealed no consideration for the fact that most of the individual participants in war possess neither the information nor the opportunity to decide whether the war in which they are called upon to serve is just or unjust. He nevertheless pronounced all combatants individually responsible for aggression and liable to pay for it with slavery. Is not the summary nature of all this the clearest indication that, as regards slavery, he had only colonial war or slave-raiding in mind? On the one hand, he went to great lengths to give detailed instances of the dissolution of government from within, of the moral forfeiture of the rulers' authority through oppression of the people. On the other, he made hasty generalizations and question-begging pronouncements about unjust war which justifies the moral forfeiture of the life of men and their personal enslavement. What strengthens the assumption that

[33] Cp. Vaughan, *op. cit.*, 155, 196. But as Locke allowed for the acceptance by consent of the conqueror's rule, Vaughan gratuitously argued against him that individuals may prefer foreign rule.

in this respect natural law was not meant by him to apply equally to all peoples, is the fact that Locke used the idea of slavery also in a sense in which it seems universally applicable.

The relationship between a despot and his subjects is analogous to that between master and slave, for both are beyond the pale of proper human relationships. As usual in philosophical discourse, slavery is the antithetical point of reference for the definition of liberty. For Locke, resistance to a foreign ruler or domestic despot is a defence of liberty inasmuch as it is to ward off the crime of political enslavement, just as resistance to a common criminal is a defence of life and liberty. In calling despotism slavery and the despot's subjects slaves,[34] Locke extended the literal meaning of slavery as we still do today, when 'slave' is 'not a label but a trope'.[35] Although, just as with regard to property and conquest the enlarged does not eliminate the specific meaning, in the case of slavery the two meanings stand in contrast to each other. In Locke's conception, slaves in the specific sense of the word have no rights because they ought to have none. Slaves in the extended sense of the word are deprived of rights which they ought to have and which they are entitled to secure or retrieve.

What stamps the arbitrary rulers' actions as crimes is sufficiently well defined by instances to make their comparison with ordinary criminals, as well as that of their respective victims, convincing. The analogy is upset particularly from the evaluative point of view, when slaves are no more the victims of the arbitrariness of others but of their own aggressiveness; when they are not the objects of criminal attempts but their perpetrators. There is also an obvious difference between the unfreedom of a slave and that of the victim of theft and robbery, or of despotism from within or without. The parallel between criminals and captives in a just war is also open to objection. Not all who are guilty, but captives alone bear the brunt of the moral forfeiture of life incurred by participation in an unjust war. The identification of captives with criminals becomes directly discriminatory when resistance to colonial conquest is presented as a clear-cut empirical example of an unjust war. The striking discrepancies especially in the evaluative connotations of slavery in the

[34] As early as in the *Preface* and the opening sections of the *Two Treatises*, Locke used this figure of speech and continued to do so, often in comparison with slavery in the specific sense as defined in Sections 23-4, 85.

[35] Cp. C. Geertz, 'Ideology as a Cultural System,' in D. E. Apter (ed.), *Ideology and Discontent* (Glencoe, 1964), 58.

literal and extended sense add considerably to the doubts whether the terms of definition of slavery were meant to apply universally or whether it was not simply a piece of cant to have posited that they were universal. Doubt becomes certainty when we realize that Locke's justification of slavery and of colonial conquest are in full harmony with the opinions and practices of his time and that in relation to these, the justification of slavery makes no sense except in connection with colonial conquest. It appears that the absence of an explicit distinction between nations concerning the issue of slavery as well as the absence of any attempt to link the justification of colonial conquest with the question of the applicability of natural law, reflect Locke's reluctance to acknowledge that in its entirety natural law is not equally applicable to the whole species of men.

Natural law admits of distinctions between men but does not cease to be universal, so long only as it indiscriminately justifies the differential status of the individuals of all nations according to their differential moral and physical capacities.

It is important to recognize his deviation from the prescriptively overburdened interdict of territorial conquest, and so from the universality of natural law. For this helps to establish a proper perspective for viewing Locke's not very well-founded theoretical ventures into foreign relations. 'The international state of nature' does not preclude peace and co-operation.[36] Although he discriminates against undeveloped nations in respect of 'civil dominion', natural law still applies inasmuch as there is no right to expel or mistreat the natives.[37] That Locke did not consider positive laws as binding between commonwealths is no reason to attribute to him the notion that amongst sovereign bodies there was no place for natural sociability, or that he failed to recognize the responsibility of his political society towards the world outside.[38] The justification of colonial conquest is set off against the fact that the relations between developed states are regulated by 'leagues' between them, acknowledging 'either expressly or tacitly' (Sec. 45) the inviolability of their territorial boundaries. Although not identical with the compact which constitutes a body politic, leagues between

---

[36] Cp. Laslett, *op. cit.*, 99, and similarly Polin, *op. cit.*, 177. Cox's assertion to the contrary rests, of course, on his elimination of the natural inclination to peace from Locke's conception of the state of nature.

[37] See above, 116.

[38] Cox, *op. cit.*, 138–9, and Gough, *op. cit.*, 72 respectively.

'*independent* communities',[39] like the relations between 'a Swiss and an Indian, in the woods of America', include all kinds of compacts, promises and bargains, i.e., transactions characteristic of sociability and of the abidance by natural law. Thus, whether or not we estimate Locke's moral code of international relations as internally consistent, we cannot deduce from his awareness of the precariousness of maintaining peace and justice in external relations, or from his defence of mercantilist policy, that he was committed to naked power-politics between nations.[40] Nor does the fact that he did not postulate a world-state[41] prove a preference for the actual over the desirable.

His principles do not point that way because they serve not only to contrast the desirable with the actual but to bridge the gulf between them. His principles are attuned to the necessity of separate civil societies. Because Locke's moral code of international relations is a replica of his internal code, it is at once too summarily prescriptive to provide much practical guidance and in contrast to the codes of internal politics does not go consistently beyond existing conditions. The external is in fact more a prop of the internal code than *vice versa*. Although it becomes specific in order to restrict the right of opposing foreign conquest, it actually serves Locke to undermine the existing opposition to the right of resistance to domestic oppressors. For that 'subjects, or foreigners attempting by force on the properties of any people, may be resisted with force, is agreed on all hands. But that magistrates doing the same thing, may be resisted, has of late been denied' (Sec. 231).

Apart from colonial conquest, internal and external relations are judged by the same criteria to permit the subsumption of all arbitrary action under conquest and of its victims as slaves. Locke could thus illustrate the better what the dissolution of government from within and dissolution from without have in common: They are the antitheses of liberty and therefore justify resistance. Since the right to resist foreign conquest was not doubted, Locke stressed that the injury of domestic conquest was the same and the effects were 'very little different' (Sec. 218). But not all the practical results are, or must be, identical when force without right is used from without or within. What makes them comparable is that the dis-

---

[39] Sec. 14. Locke's italics.
[40] The line of argument and the conclusions rejected here are advanced by Cox, *op. cit.*, 165, 169, 178–9.
[41] *Ibid.*, 190.

solution of society by foreign conquest is not irrevocable; they are different because the dissolution of government from within and subsequent civil war do not dissolve society even temporarily.

3. DISSOLUTION OF GOVERNMENT FROM WITHIN

A. The Survival of Society

'Conquerors' swords often cut up governments by the roots, and mangle societies to pieces, separating the subdued or scattered multitude from the protection of, and dependence on that society which ought to have preserved them from violence' (Sec. 211). This is 'the usual, and almost only way whereby this union is dissolved'. When society thus ceases to be 'one entire and independent body. . . every one [must] return to the state he was in before, with a liberty to shift for himself, and provide for his own safety as he thinks fit in some other society'. The vanquished do not return to a pre-societal state of nature. No more is meant than that they retain the right of refusing their consent to belong to the conqueror's society and to join another one, or, as we have seen, to try and restore the independence of their own society. Still, although Locke speaks of 'any calamity' (Sec. 121), he indicates only foreign conquest as the event which is apt to dissolve government in such a way as to free men from the allegiance to their society.[42] The reason is not merely that government is dissolved, but 'cut up . . . by the roots' (Sec. 211). This happens when the 'conquerors' swords . . . mangle societies to pieces'. The world is sufficiently informed about and averse to 'this way of dissolving of governments . . . and there wants not much argument to prove, that where the society is dissolved, the government cannot remain'. But a good deal of argument, indeed the greater part of a whole chapter, seemed necessary to Locke to prove what actually constitutes the dissolution of government. An elaborate exposition is required since it does not follow that, because government cannot remain when a society is dissolved, society cannot survive whenever the established government is dissolved.

The conclusion that society is dissolved only through foreign conquest and 'the delivery also of the people into the subjection of a foreign power, either by the prince, or by the legislative . . .'

---

[42] I cannot see how Strauss, *op. cit.*, 232, note 100, can rely on Sec. 121, or for that matter on any passage in Sec. 211, for an indication of the view that society can exist without government.

(Sec. 217), seems to be immediately confuted by statements to the contrary. When the executive neglects or abandons its charge of executing the laws 'this is demonstratively to reduce all to anarchy, ... the government visibly ceases, and the people become a confused multitude, without order or connexion' (Sec. 219). Or, the legislature 'is the soul that gives form, life, and unity to the commonwealth ... And therefore when the legislative is broken, or dissolved, dissolution and death follows' (Sec. 212). What difference can there be between the 'confused multitude', the 'dissolution and death' caused by the dissolution of government from within and the 'scattered multitude' produced by the swords of conquest that 'mangle societies to pieces'?

In the first place, anarchy and the *de facto* existence of government were not considered by Locke as mutually exclusive. He equated arbitrary government with anarchy. The state of nature and civil society are confounded if 'any one, by his own authority, avoid the force of the law ...' or 'by any pretence of superiority, plead exemption, thereby to licence his own, or the miscarriages of any of his dependents' (Sec. 94). Even 'a patron of anarchy' would not dispute that such a man 'can be no part or member of that civil society'. Secondly, Locke could go on presuming the existence of society even 'where there is no longer the administration of justice, ... nor any remaining power within the community to direct the force, or provide for the necessities of the public ...' (Sec. 219). After dissociating itself from the power so far responsible for directing its force, the community can still administer to its needs. Mindful of the fact that 'a government without laws, is, ... a mystery in politics, unconceivable to human capacity, and inconsistent with human society' (Sec. 219), he at once insisted on the people's right 'to provide for themselves, by erecting a new legislative ...' (Sec. 220). Indeed, if the demise of the old legislature were to destroy beyond repair 'the essence and union of the society consisting in having one will' (Sec. 212), neither the new nor the old legislature, unless it was composed of all members of society, could ever have come into being or could do so in the future. Locke was careful to assign to the legislature 'when once established by the majority, ... *the declaring*, and as it were *keeping* of that will'. The majority possesses a will before society possesses a legislature, or rather society possesses a will because it can act as the constituent authority. 'The constitution of the legislative is the first and fundamental act of *society*, whereby provision is made for the *continuation* of their union . . .' Having said all this there was nothing to prevent Locke from stipulating that when the keeper of their will was disqualified, the formulation and execution of the will of society became society's direct concern again.

It would however still be something of a 'mystery in politics' if Locke had supposed 'a confused multitude, without order or connexion' (Sec. 219) capable of realizing 'the native and original right' (Sec. 220) of erecting a new legislature. He assumed the reform of government by a disorganized society as little as he assumed a transition from an unorganized state of nature to political society. He conjured up the vision of a confused multitude to justify the prevention of its realization. A people will not without more ado permit itself to become totally enslaved and converted into an inchoate mass. 'The state of mankind is not so miserable that they are not capable of using this remedy', i.e. resistance to arbitrary rulers, 'till it be too late to look for any'. [43] In fact, to be able to assume the role of the constituent legislator, the people must not await the actual disappearance of the disqualified legislature.

'To tell people they may provide for themselves, by erecting a new legislative, when their old one is gone, is only to tell them they may expect relief, when . . . it is too late, and the evil is past cure. This is in effect no more than to bid them first be slaves, and then to take care of their liberty; . . . Men can never be secure from tyranny, if there be no means to escape it, till they are perfectly under it: And therefore it is, that they have not only a right to get out of it, but to prevent it' (Sec. 220).

Princes 'put themselves into a state of war with the people' and the people are 'absolved from any farther obedience . . .' when

'the legislators *endeavour* to take away, and destroy the property of the people, or to reduce them to slavery under arbitrary power . . . and either by ambition, fear, folly or corruption, *endeavour* to grasp themselves, or put into the hands of any other an absolute power over the lives, liberties, and estates of the people.'

And this 'in general, holds true also concerning the supreme executor' (Sec. 222).

[43] Sec. 220. Cp. Sec. 239.

B. Democratic Interregnum

In justifying revolt to prevent political enslavement and anarchy, Locke could not very well suppose the people to fight the rejected government as a dissolved society. It has been suggested that he supposed society existed and acted without government only in the moment of revolution, and that this moment coincided with the majority-decision by which the new legislature was created.[44] But if a governmentless situation is assumed to ensue the moment society has dissociated itself from its government, the continuance of a governmentless situation must be assumed as well. Usually a new legislature is not established at the beginning of a revolution but rather in its course, if not as the result of its victory. Revolution itself would then still be anarchy, since 'the anarchy is much alike to have no form of government at all' (Sec. 198). Locke identifies anarchy with arbitrary government in a metaphorical way but also as existing in reality where there are no 'settled methods' for 'the designation of the persons, who are to bear rule . . .' As, however, the right of designating rulers, together with the determination of 'the form of the government itself . . . had its establishment originally from the people', the right can revert to the people. Revolutionary action which lasts for some time can be distinguished from anarchy, since a governmentless situation which is irreconcilable with the existence of society, is avoided if the disqualified government is faced by a revolutionary government. It need not be the government issuing from the victory of revolution. Locke clearly provided for this possibility.

No relapse into an unorganized state of nature is envisaged when the rulers 'untie the knot, and expose the people anew to the state of war' (Sec. 227). When the people have recourse to 'a right to resume their original liberty' (Sec. 222) with the result that 'all former ties are cancelled, all other rights cease . . .' (Sec. 232), only those rights and ties are annulled, and that knot untied, which bind the people to a particular government. Locke had the people's capacity to act as a constituent legislature in mind when he said that 'they have, by a law antecedent and paramount to all positive laws of men, reserved that ultimate determination to themselves, which belongs to all mankind, where there lies no appeal on earth, viz. to judge whether they have just cause to make their appeal to heaven'

---

[44] Cp. Strauss, *op. cit.*, 232, note 100.

(Sec. 168). In executing their appeal, the people resume as a society the authority vested in the government because 'the power that every individual gave the *society*, when he entered into it, can never revert to the individuals again, as long as the *society* lasts, but will *always* remain in the *community*; because without this, there can be no community, no commonwealth . . .' (Sec. 243). Society which cannot exist without government lasts through a revolution because, when the rulers betray the people's trust 'they forfeit the power, the people had put into their hands . . . and *it devolves to the people*' (Sec. 222). Society survives the dissolution of its legislature; for while 'the legislative can never revert to the people whilst that *government* lasts: . . . upon the forfeiture of their rulers . . . *it reverts to the society*, and the people have a right *to act as supreme, and continue, the legislative in themselves*, or erect a new form, or under the old form place it in new hands, as they think good.'[45] During the revolution, society governs itself as a direct democracy whether to perpetuate the latter or to devise a new non-democratic form of government or to make personal changes in the old one. No room is left for a governmentless interlude between the dissolution of the old legislature and the erection of the new one.

Locke did not favour the permanent establishment of democracy. But its recognition as a legitimate and workable form of government[46] enabled him to justify his advocacy of the right of revolt and yet evade two pitfalls: one of going back on his distinction between the dissolution of government and that of society; the other of implying that a confused multitude was capable of carrying through a revolution and establish a new legislature. His equation of a revolutionary democratic *interregnum* with a return to the state of nature in the sense of a state of war, attests his evaluation of democracy as well as the good sense – apart from the consistency – of his correlation of the state of nature, the state of war and political society.

In revolution each individual resumes in political unison with

---

[45] Sec. 243. Wolin, *op. cit.*, 309, to make Locke appear as dealing 'another blow to the distinctive role of the political order', divests the passage in Sec. 243 of its clear literal meaning when he says that Locke conceives the revolutionary majority 'independently of political processes [sic!] and institutions'. Similarly Goldwin, *op. cit.*, 457, who interprets that 'the majority must rule, . . . when society is briefly without government', and thus attributes to Locke a distinction between ruling and governing, which accounts apparently for Goldwin's arbitrary definition of Locke's right of resistance as a 'prepolitical' right (462).

[46] Sec. 132.

others the rights which, in the state of nature, i.e. by nature, belong to every man. By appealing directly to natural law, men united by society act in revolution collectively as each may be supposed to act individually, or spuriously together with others, in a hypothetical state of nature. The comparison is adequate, because whether we desire, fear, or reject revolution, we acknowledge that it creates a highly abnormal and precarious political condition. Revolutionary action is perhaps less often than Locke thought directed against the ruler's infraction of positive laws than against objectionable ones duly promulgated. It is neither action under one common superior – for the discredited government will not be without support – nor is it provided for by positive laws. As likely as not, revolution involves infraction of positive laws otherwise just and is as little conducive to circumspect legislation as it is to the formal ascertainment of the will of the majority. Locke did not, in fact, require the people, as the intermediate constituent legislature, to engage in proper legislation or in the otherwise formal making of decisions. Since he allowed the people no other form of political consent then either tacit consent or revolutionary dissent,[47] their acquiescence or the lending of their armed and other support to leading rival groups, manifest their endorsement of simple yet fundamental decisions concerning resistance to the old legislature and the erection of a new one.

A revolutionary situation and the hypothetical state of nature both suffer from 'inconveniences' and uncertainties. The hypothetical state of nature, though its inconveniences give rise to the state of war, is also a theoretical alternative to the state of war, and to an unjustly managed political society. Yet the only practical alternative to this kind of society is the state of nature which obtains in society. The real state of nature circumscribes the situation in which society pits force with right against force without right to save itself from the ultimate evil, which is the anarchy of tyranny, i.e. that state of war in society in which the conflict between the victor and the victims remains unresolved. The relatedness between the state of nature, the state of war and political society is predicated on the extremities of the political condition but it illustrates a fundamental trait and problem of social life: the interdependence and perpetual tension between might and right.

[47] Cp. below, especially 223 f., 275 f. and 284 f.

THE LIBERAL POLITICS OF JOHN LOCKE

4. POWER

The adoption of the principle of consent does not absolve men from concern with coercion. A decision reached by consent may lessen the will to resist the decision and hence lessen the need to resort to coercion. Yet consent serves to justify the use of force by recognized authorities against the refractory who reject the principle of consent; against those who agree to the principle but not to a specific resolution; or even against those who agree to both, but nevertheless would not comply if there were no threat of coercion, or who have to be constrained before they will comply. While for Locke consent derived from natural law as the means of applying it in society, he reckoned with the use of force to carry out purely individual jurisdiction under the law of nature in a hypothetical state of nature. The same is true of the institutionalized jurisdiction in political society and the concerted jurisdiction of individuals in a state of war inside political society. Being aware that men are prone to deviate from that law through consent, entailed awareness that a deviation is the more likely to arise out of the necessity to allow for the use of force in human affairs. While Locke's political system is concerned with the balance of powers in the constitutional and extra-constitutional fields, his recognition of actualities did not lead him to confuse what is often done with what ought to be done;[48] nor did he inadvertently confuse what men may do with what they are able to do.[49] Our discussions so far and those to follow require some systematic examination of what the *Treatises* have to offer about his conception of power.

[48] Strauss, *op. cit.*, 232–3, 249 f., in a general way stresses the importance of the power aspect in the institutional sphere, Locke's identification of might and right being the underlying interpretative assumption. Goldwin, *op. cit.*, 441, consequently says that, for Locke, 'men must be acknowledged to have a *right* to do what they are unable not to do', and Cox, *op. cit.*, 67–8, 154 f., 165, 183, 193, ascribes to Locke a Machiavellian conception of political power, which identifies might with right. Polin, in his otherwise very valuable philosophical analysis of Locke's idea of power (*op. cit.*, Ch. V and especially 43 f., 63, 86, 197 f., 254) goes too far in the opposite direction when he asserts that Locke was not interested in Hobbesian models of a dynamic equilibrium and disequilibrium of human relations in physical terms (181). To say that he saw the problem arising out of the need of society for juridical solutions, less as 'une problème de fait ou de puissance' than as one of right and morals (188), is to construe an oversharp juxtaposition not only in respect of Locke.

[49] Thus M. Cranston, *Freedom, a New Analysis*, 24 f. But in his biography of Locke (*op. cit.*, 209–11), he implies the distinction.

A. The Concept

Locke used 'power', like other central concepts, in more than one sense. As is still common, 'power' for Locke denotes natural capacities or might; so do 'strength', 'force' and 'violence', especially if the intention is perjorative. But 'power' is also, if not usually, used synonymously with 'right' or 'authority', and occasionally it connotes also illegitimate authority. In spite of the twofold use, in the sense of might and right, Locke did not confuse the two senses, as distinct from fusing them in the designation of institutions like the executive, legislature or even a whole state.

In defining the object of the *Second Treatise* to find out 'another rise of government, another original of political power . . . than what Sir Robert F. has taught us', Locke rejected the view 'that all government in the world is the product only of force and violence' (Sec. 1). Political power is 'a *right* of making laws . . . and of employing the *force* of the community, in the execution of such laws . . .' (Sec. 3). Power here denotes the right to do certain things for all concerned as well as to enlist their help for getting some things done. Force is here given its place as a component of political power, as distinguished from being considered as its fount and identified with it.

When Locke spoke of 'the right, or power' of husband and wife necessary to the ends of conjugal society, 'viz. procreation and mutual support and assistance . . .' (Sec. 83), he used 'power' and 'right' synonymously. He did so in a context which assumes more directly than the definition of political power the congruence of moral rights and obligations and of these with physical capacities. The same usage is in evidence when the congruence of right and capacities is again more complex, as in the treatment of slavery. Slaves 'are by the right of nature subjected to the absolute dominion and arbitrary *power* of their masters' (Sec. 85) because by engaging in an unjust war a man has 'forfeited his own life, by some act that deserves death . . .' (Sec. 23). Yet the master 'to whom he has forfeited it, may (*when he has him in his power*) . . . make use of him . . .' While power denotes both right and physical capacity, as our previous discussion of slavery has shown, Locke's argument in this case implies much greater scope for the possible divergence of right and capacities than is attributable to the relationship between husband and wife. Nevertheless, in all the three instances discussed so far the use of the word 'power' reflects the intention of stressing not just the desirability but also the possibility of might being commensurate with right. Without belief in commensurability a political thinker would hardly waste many words on desirability.

The right to do something loses in significance the less one is able to do what one is entitled to. In the interpersonal sphere the coincidence of right and might is prevented when some do all they are able to do. Authority is then claimed irrespective of right, or in excess of a right which one justly possesses. To explain how the individuals manage to protect themselves against this, Locke speaks of the surrender to society of the 'two powers' which they possess by nature.[50] This is the basis of 'the original right and rise of both the legislative and executive power . . .' (Sec. 127). The exercise of personal powers in the sense of rights is entrusted to 'powers' in the sense of legitimate institutions. Since these are composed of fallible human beings and the subject's property is, therefore, liable to be invaded by 'the will and order of his monarch', the subject cannot be denied 'a liberty to judge of, or to defend his *right* . . .' (Sec. 91). This residuary right or liberty is the foundation of the people's 'supreme *power* to remove or alter the legislative . . .' (Sec. 149). Although a distinction is made between 'a power to deliver up their preservation' – a right nobody possesses – and 'the means of it', i.e., the force which is placed at the disposal of the 'power'-institutions, 'power' and 'right' are used synonymously also when Locke concluded that 'they will always have a *right* to preserve what they have not a *power* to part with'. The interchangeability in his usage of the words 'power' and 'right' points to the possible confluence of might and right without obscuring their possible divergence. Thus, although governmental powers exist to restrain those who are capable of exceeding their rights, government itself is apt to exceed its authority. Like individuals, the executive and the legislature, either separately or conjointly, are therefore also referred to as overstepping the bounds of rightful authority.[51] As the result of its excess, power is called despotic and then denotes force alone.

'Despotical power is an absolute, arbitrary power one man has over another, to take away his life, whenever he pleases' (Sec. 172). The same competence as in the case of masters and slaves is under discussion here. But slaves in the literal and in the metaphorical

---

[50] Cp. Secs. 128–30 and 143–8.
[51] Sec. 149, 212–22.

sense connote normatively opposed meanings. 'Arbitrary power' over slaves in the literal sense stands for an unobjectionable right. Over free men 'arbitrary power' is rejected as despotic and such 'power' does not earn a right. Lacking the foundation created by moral forfeiture of a person's life, the despotical power over another man's life 'is a power, which neither nature gives' . . . nor compact can convey'. But 'nature' does not prevent men from forfeiting their lives, and, as Locke likewise knew, permits the mobilization of enough superior force, or even consent, to establish and maintain despotic rule.[52] Prescriptively 'despotical power' is never political power and descriptively it means 'right' only as far as an usurped or illegitimately conveyed right is concerned. This usage implies that political authority, whether conveyed or usurped, is not rightful by merely being effective. A despot imitates 'beasts by making force . . . to be his rule of right . . .' (Sec. 172). His 'rule of right' is grounded on 'power without right' (Sec. 168). 'Power' denotes brute force when coercion becomes detached from morally justifiable authority. As compared with the power of the magistrate 'despotical [power] exceeds it' (Sec. 174), and yet for the most part it is the outgrowth of the first. Those 'who are in power' are the likeliest to rely on force alone 'by the pretence they have to *authority*, the temptation of *force* they have in their hands . . .' (Sec. 226).

It is evident that Locke's distinction between right and might and in effect his use of 'authority' imply the distinction between authority and power. 'Force without authority' (Sec. 155) means the same as 'power without right' (Sec. 168). 'Using force upon the people without authority, and contrary to the trust put in him, that does so . . .' (Sec. 155) annuls his authority. An authoritative opinion or command has recently been defined as possessing 'the potentiality of reasoned elaboration'; so that authority is 'a quality of communi- cation, rather than of persons', and the reasoning involved relates 'actions to opinions and beliefs to values'.[53] Locke's conception of 'trust' can evidently be taken to stand for 'communications which may be elaborated by reasoning'. He was aware that connivance of at least the few enabled despotic rulers to acquire and maintain authority as part of the means to exact obedience. He acknowledged by implication that even in that case communications were involved

---

[52] See below, 306 f.
[53] Cp. C. J. Friedrich, 'Authority, Reason and Discretion,' in *Authority* (ed. by Friedrich, *Nomos* I, Cambridge, Mass., 1958), 35–6.

which could be the object of reasoning. But in virtue of his normative approach as it underlies his use of the terms 'power' and 'authority', he rejected such reasoning and the authority grounded on it. For him expedient and moral rationality are not identical.[54] The quality of communication is not only to be judged by the effect of securing any government in office, but ultimately by reference to a generally valid set of values, embodied in the law of nature.

It was by no means unrealistic for Locke to associate 'authority' with rightfulness, and thus stress that it is not enough to define it by effectiveness. Quite often the effectiveness of unrightful authority is bound to recede before the conviction that there is a right to shake off 'a power, which force, and not right has set over any one . . .' (Sec. 196). The criteria of logic and of what is objectively just and right, or is mainly by unenforced consensus accepted as such, are at times overruled or falsified by operative values propagated and enforced by those in power. The criticism of operative values in the light of objective criteria – or at any rate of criteria set above operative values – can be refused publicity. This is not to eradicate criticism, as is evidenced by the amount of overt and covert coercion associated with fascist and communist dictatorships – as well as by their tardy ventures in liberalization. Power in the sense of force may be more effective than power in the sense of right. Neither is more effective than power as understood by Locke, that is in the sense of both right and force. The mutual involvement of normative and analytical criteria in Locke's own appraisal of reality,[55] which caused him to distinguish between the rightfulness of authority and its efficacy, yet relate them to each other, does not necessarily distort reality or lead to special pleading, as in his argument concerning colonial conquest and slavery. Rather, his use of the terms 'force' and 'strength', like his use of the term 'power', reflects a realistic awareness of the double-faced role of force in human affairs, both to maintain and subvert right.

[54] See above, 62 f., 67 f. and below, 158.

[55] Such an involvement is by no means rejected by Friedrich, but is rather ingeniously handled *inter alia* in his early *The New Belief in the Common Man* (Boston, 1942), and his latest *Man and His Government* (New York, 1963). Allowances are made also by a proponent of an empirical or behavioural theory like D. Easton, in his *The Political System* (repr. New York, 1959), 52, 224 f.

B. Might and Right

Like all other theorists of natural law, Locke recognized clearly that 'the law of nature would, as all other laws that concern men in this world, be in vain, if there were nobody that in the state of nature, had a power to execute that law . . .' (Sec. 7). The securing of right by natural law alone turns 'upon equal terms of *force* to maintain it, whether invaded by a single man, or many in combination' (Sec. 137). On these terms force and right are far from being commensurable. 'He that has right on his side, having ordinarily but his own single strength, has not force enough to defend himself from injuries . . .' (Sec. 136). Thus, although man 'in the ordinary state of nature, . . . has a liberty to judge of his right, and according to the best of his *power*, to maintain it' (Sec. 91), the best of the power of the individual is not good enough. 'In the state of nature there often wants power to back and support the sentence when right, and to give it due execution' (Sec. 126). The rightful master of a captive may use him '*when* he has him in his power' (Sec. 23). Likewise 'they who by any injustice offended, will seldom fail, *where they are able*, by force to make good their injustice' (Sec. 126). In fact, 'such resistance many times makes the punishment dangerous, and frequently destructive, to those who attempt it.' Hence man willingly 'engages his natural *force*' and parts with a good deal of his 'natural liberty' (Sec. 130), and men 'unite into societies, that they may have the united *strength* of the whole society to secure and defend their properties . . .' (Sec. 136). Force is the inevitable concomitant of the effective maintenance of right, but force is also liable to be abused when institutionalized in government for defensive and punitive purposes. Popular resistance, too, may overshoot its mark like the punishment of criminals in the 'state of nature'.[56] The use of the executive power 'to back and support the sentence when right' (Sec. 126), depends on judging the merit of the sentence and on the available force to carry it out. 'In all states and conditions the true remedy of force without authority, is to oppose force to it' (Sec. 155). The use of force, which in the extreme case leads to the infliction of death, is necessary to enforce right in all conditions because the possession of force invites its use in excess of right.

It might appear that in granting the masses the right to dissent by revolt from those who make and execute laws for them, Locke

---

[56] See above 95 f., and below, 310.

not so much provided an additional safeguard against the abuse of political power as he increased reliance on force in politics. True, authority is 'founded only in the constitutions and laws of the government' (Sec. 226), and 'the people . . . are absolved from obedience' only when they meet with 'illegal attempts' or 'unlawful violence' (Sec. 228). As to 'constitutions', in Locke's usage, they have neither exclusively nor predominantly a legal connotation, but refer above all to the principles of 'any just government'.[57] If a 'higher law' serves as the standard of positive law, the formal legality of governmental procedure is not enough to bestow sanctity on positive laws. Legal and constitutional provisions may be rightfully pushed aside and force relied upon, if properly promulgated laws are not necessarily in accord with natural law, but often reflect 'the fancies and intricate contrivances of men . . .' (Sec. 12). Even when there are 'good and equitable laws' which regulate relations among subjects, one has to consider that especially in certain forms of government the rulers 'will think themselves to have a distinct interest, from the rest of the community' (Sec. 138). Legality is, therefore, not the only criterion when Locke says that 'force is to be opposed to nothing, but to *unjust and unlawful* force' (Sec. 204). If it were, why not simply say 'unlawful' instead of prefixing 'unjust'? Still, in making the right of revolt the foundation of his political theory, Locke thought – by no means unreasonably – not to increase, but to curtail, reliance on force in politics.

He had no unbounded confidence in human nature and least of all in the masses. The common run of men discern only the grossest deviations from reasonableness and righteousness in the behaviour of their rulers and revolt only when oppression becomes extreme,[58] though the common run of men need not behave unreasonably when they revolt against their rulers. But even if the contrary were true, it would still apply that 'this doctrine of a power in the people of providing for their safety anew . . . is the best fence against rebellion . . .' (Sec. 226). Since 'rebellion' means here the abuse of their power by rulers[59] the right of revolt is designed to fulfil a preventive function, to place restraint on the inclination of rulers to violate just laws or make unjust ones. It is to serve as a deterrent against making force the rule of right.

[57] Cp. Sec. 230, and Laslett, *op. cit.*, 338.
[58] Secs. 223–5.
[59] See below, 316 f.

Neither his advocacy of the right of revolt nor anything else in his theory allows us to charge Locke with the intention of simply transferring the principle of the balance of power from foreign to domestic politics and viewing internal and external affairs in terms of naked power politics.[60]

He considered power as right and power as might to be fatefully linked, though in themselves opposed to each other. On this basis he viewed power under its substantive and relational aspects. These aspects defined in his *Essay* have been recently re-defined as 'a thing had, a substance possessed by some human beings and employed by them in an effort to control others', and as a relation or 'a bond between people simultaneously embracing . . . the ruler and the ruled'.[61] For Locke, the point is not solely that governors only 'make a part of that politic body' (I, 93), but that all human beings, not just some, possess and employ political power, that is, have the ability and the right to control by sanctions the decisions and actions of others. The *Treatises* make the substantive inseparable from the relational aspect.[62] They do so in the factual as well as the normative sense and without viewing power exclusively in a hierarchical perspective.[63] Men's capacities and rights form the substance realized in the relationship between rulers and ruled, a relationship of mutual control whose nature varies in accordance with the ways in which rights and capacities are and ought to be

[60] Cox, *op. cit.*, 107, 172, suggests that Locke had acknowledged the all-pervading primacy of foreign over domestic politics. By way of proof Cox quotes the last sentence of Sec. 107 with complete disregard of the textual context, which shows – like Secs. 108–10 (which he adduces for the same purpose) – that Locke confined the overriding importance of military affairs to a simple, harmonious bygone 'state and condition which stood more in need of defence against foreign invasions and injuries, than of multiplicity of laws'.

[61] Cp. C. J. Friedrich, *Constitutional Government and Democracy*, 23. For similar definitions of power see also H. D. Lasswell and A. Kaplan, *Power and Society*, 75f., and Easton, *op. cit.*, 143–4. Locke's words are:

'for who is it that does not see that powers belong only to agents and are attributes only of substances, and not of powers themselves?'

'For powers are relations, not agents; and that which has the power or not the power to operate is that alone which is or is not free, and not the power itself.' (*Essay*, II, xxi, 16, 19.)

Although, as Friedrich points out, this definition is only to be found in the *Essay*, the 'relational' concept is evidently applied in the *Treatises*.

[62] Cp. Polin, *op. cit.*, 197, note 1.

[63] Cp. T. Parsons, 'The Political Aspect of Social Structure and Process,' in D. Easton, *Varieties of Political Theory* (Englewood Cliffs, N.J., 1966), 76, 85, 92, against the predominantly hierarchical conception of authority and power.

used. The political process is, in Locke's conception, a dynamic configuration characterized by the continuous endeavour to maintain by constitutional means and, if necessary, to re-adjust by extra-constitutional means an equilibrium between powers *qua* rights and powers *qua* might. It is the concern with the equilibrium of powers in this twofold sense, which caused him to define the function of political society as 'to limit the power, and moderate the dominion of every part and member of the society' (Sec. 222).

The power-right configuration includes also property relations. The relationship between the political and the economic sphere in Locke's thought does, however, not conform with the views usually taken of the liberal outlook. Although this issue pertains very much to Lockeian metapolitics, it involves a good deal of confrontation with the facts of historical development and its evaluation. The treatment of this topic opens therefore the second part of our study as a transition from the consideration of metapolitical to that of historical foundations. It precedes the investigation of Locke's views of the origin of private property because with the latter topic the emphasis shifts more decisively towards historical foundations, or rather towards the validation of reason by the testimony of history.

PART TWO

METAPOLITICS
AND HISTORY

CHAPTER V

PROPERTY RELATIONS

1. LIMITATION OF APPROPRIATION

A. Portents of Capitalism in Retrospective

As a result of arbitrary rule and subsequent revolt against it, political society finds itself intermittently in the state of nature as a state of war. If Locke had maintained with regard to property relations that the limitations of one's capacities were the sole limits of one's rights, it would follow that a sphere of relentless warlike competition were part of political society. The economic sphere would be unrestrained by the principles on which political society otherwise rests. This conclusion underlies two modes of interpretation, which though different in some respects, consider untamed *laissez-faire* liberalism as part of Locke's system.

On the one hand, his theory of property is understood to demonstrate that politics serves economics.[1] Macpherson, who has undertaken the most detailed investigation of Locke's theory of property and labour, tries to prove that his civil society is totally subject to economic control. The wholesale transfer of individual rights to the state is consistent with this, because the state is run by men of property.[2] More widespread and, on the whole, less thorough is the interpretation that Locke kept economic and political issues apart to restrict the role of the state.[3] In conformity with the most persistently embraced opinions about classical liberalism, the function of Locke's state is regarded as confined to the protection of the specifically civic rights of individuals. This function of the state is of no practical importance to the masses, as interpreters like Vaughan, who is inspired by the Hegelian conception of 'civic' society, maintains. Macpherson propagates the same conclusion by

[1] Strauss, *op. cit.*, 235, 240, 245–6; J. Cropsey, 'On the Relation of Political Science and Economics,' *The American Political Science Review* (March, 1960), 11 f.; Cox, *op. cit.*, 181–2; Wolin, *op. cit.*, 291, 203, 208 f.; Goldwin, *op. cit.*, 453.

[2] Macpherson, *op. cit.*, 256.

[3] This is summarily attributed to Locke by Stephen, *op. cit.*, II, 140–2; F. Pollock, *op. cit.*, 243; Lamprecht, *op. cit.*, 135; Vaughan, *op. cit.*, 167 f., 172, 175, 181, 191, 194. Likewise Polin, *op. cit.*, 273–4, 281, 295, in an otherwise extended treatment of Locke's theory of property.

holding to the Marxist evaluation of 'bourgeois' society. According to all these interpretations, Locke thought that the introduction of money had justly obviated the natural limitations set to appropriation.[4] Irrespective of whether he is held to have considered this as a justifiable evasion of natural law or as conforming with it, he is said to have provided no principles for curbing economic power by politics for the sake of equity and justice, or rather, to have accepted the invalidation of such principles in the course of history. Some scholars have recognized, however, that his admission of the authority of government to regulate, and not merely protect, property leaves room for justifying the political limitation of exploitation.[5] So far no attempt has been made to demonstrate this conclusion as fully as Locke's views on property and their relation to the fundamental tenets of his political theory allow.

Locke evidently accepted the growth of inequality attendant upon the introduction of money. Yet he failed to wax enthusiastic about the emergence of large possessions and the rising 'spirit of capitalism'[6] in general. Nothing in the highly repetitive chapter 'Of

---

[4] Thus also Plamenatz, *op. cit.*, 220. Likewise Vaughan, *loc. cit.*, Gough, *op. cit.*, 79, who assert, however (Vaughan, *op. cit.*, 195, and Gough, *op. cit.*, 84), that, if Locke had realized the practical consequences, he would have abhorred them and refrained from placing political power in the hands of the property-owning minority.

[5] This has been summarily, if rather contradictorily, overstressed by Kendall, *op. cit.*, 69–72, 84; it is also asserted by L. T. Hobhouse, 'The Historical Evolution of Property in Fact and Ideas,' in C. Gore, *Property, Its Duties and Rights* (New ed., London, 1915), 27; P. Larkin, *Property in the Eighteenth Century, with Special Reference to England and Locke* (Dublin, 1930), 64 f.; Aaron, *op. cit.*, 280 f. Monson, *loc. cit.*, 124 f., defends this view against Strauss, and Laslett, *op. cit.*, 43–4, 103–5, 366, attacks both Strauss and Macpherson. M. Cherno, 'Locke on Property, A Re-Appraisal,' *Ethics*, LXVIII, 1 (1957), 52–4, accuses Locke of not facing the issue of government interference squarely, but gives him the benefit of the doubt as to his intentions. According to R. Schlatter, *Private Property : The History of an Idea* (London, 1951), 156, it was obvious to Locke that his views might serve 'to condemn much property that the middle class regarded as legitimate'. Yet Schlatter finds also that due to ambiguity and logical obscurity Locke's theory culminates in justifying even by law the inviolability of modern property rights (160).

[6] The use of the term 'the spirit of capitalism', insofar as Locke is concerned, is, in my view, justified if understood in the sense established by Max Weber and adopted by R. H. Tawney – i.e., as expressive of views which alleviate scruples about acquisitiveness and stimulate industry, thrift and the accumulation of wealth. Cp. M. Weber, 'Die Protestantische Ethik und der Geist des Kapitalismus,' *Archiv für Sozialwissenschaft und Sozialpolitik*, XX–XXI (1904-5) and R. H. Tawney, *Religion and the Rise of Capitalism* (New York, 1926). On Weber's thesis see the critical essay by H. Luethy, 'Once Again: Calvinism and Capitalism,' *Encounter*, XXII, I (Jan. 1964), 26–38, and the literature cited there. O. H. Taylor, 'Economics and Liberalism,' *Harvard Economic Studies*, XCVI (1955), 26–7 (this part of Taylor's book appeared in 1927 as a review

Property' recurs more often than the criticism of acquisition beyond one's needs. Nevertheless, this chapter is said to have no other aim than to show that the release of individual appropriation from any limitation is in accord with natural law.[7] Since, according to Locke, it was comparatively easy to comply with these limitations before the introduction of money, it would appear that he insisted on their binding force only to remove them the moment they were really needed. Must we, therefore, evaluate them as residual qualms about acquisitiveness, which constitute a characteristic contradiction in seventeenth century thought, or, what comes to very much the same thing, as *niaiseries* introduced to disguise a hedonistic approach?[8]

Once such an attitude towards textual evidence is admitted, one might as well turn the tables and argue that it is Locke's very justification of capitalist acquisitiveness which is a concession to contemporary opinion and practice. Opinions prevailing even prior to the seventeenth century were certainly not calculated to give substance to traditional misgivings concerning acquisitiveness. Thomas More's concealment of his onslaught on property behind 'Nowhere' and the fate of the Diggers are among the cases in point. It was surely not more dangerous to develop a novel theory of property which was unreservedly in accord with the more and more self-assured and wide-spread capitalist consciousness antedating the Reformation than to admit into the novel theory principles which rendered it irreconcilable with prevailing practice. Contrariwise, a critical attitude towards uninhibited acquisitiveness can just as well go along with utilitarian as with traditional principles. Either separately or conjointly, concern for the 'good life', the public good, and hedonistic self-preservation could lead, and in fact often has led, from apprehensions about capitalist acquisitiveness to its negation. Thus, Locke might have shown no more than apparent conformity with the spirit of capitalism. Instead of an esoteric or

---

article), has questioned whether the evidence of some late seventeenth-century Puritan divines and pamphleteers is sufficient to support Tawney's 'conception of the liberal movement as simply a progressive stripping off of legal and moral restraints upon the anti-social greed of individuals'. My conclusions about Locke would seem to confirm Taylor's objections.

[7] Macpherson, *op. cit.*, 197 f., 203 f., 208, 299.
[8] Macpherson, *op. cit.*, 220, 247, and Strauss, *op. cit.*, 247, respectively.

unconsciously contradictory defence he might have launched a camouflaged attack on capitalism, for example, by first stating the principles that prohibit accumulation beyond one's needs, and then overriding those prohibitions, to intimate what unlimited acquisitiveness really implies. As befitting a convert against his deeper convictions, and a very cautious man to boot, Locke might have compensated for leaving somewhat confused, yet nevertheless conspicuous, traces of his critical attitude by swimming vigorously with the current. The assumption of his contradictoriness, with or without the explanatory device of esotericism, thus works in two directions. Rather than continue cancelling out the 'anti-capitalistic' arguments by the 'pro-capitalistic' ones or *vice versa*, it is worth inquiring whether, on Locke's terms, these arguments really are irreconcilable. What has occasioned controversy is largely due to reading the history of liberalism backwards.

B. The Natural Limitations

a. *Validity and Effectiveness*

Most of the talk of Locke's contradictoriness stems from the failure to recognize that he had no need to overthrow the natural limitations on property acquisition in order to justify economic inequality. Having acknowledged that the postulate of natural equality is modified by men's unequal capacities, he quite logically placed unequal appropriation from the outset within the bounds of these limitations. He insisted that 'the same law of nature, that does . . . give us property, does also bound that property too' (Sec. 31). This is to counter the assumption that 'anyone may engross as much as he will'. One notes that the law of nature precludes not engrossing in general, but only unlimited engrossing.[9] Until the introduction of money, this was to be secured by three natural limitations.

Labour fixes the amount of property men have a right to, whether they gather the fruits of the earth or cultivate the land.[10] 'The measure of property, nature has well set, by the extent of men's labour, and the convenience of life: No man's labour could subdue, or appropriate all: nor could his enjoyment consume more than a small part' (Sec. 36). Just as man's ability to consume is limited,

---

[9] Hobhouse in Gore, *op. cit.*, 26, quotes the passage but ignores the qualification.
[10] Sec. 27 *passim*, and Sec. 32 *passim*.

there is a natural limit to his exertions. The first natural limitation of appropriation is inherent in the means through which the right of private property is established. This limitation did not ensure equality.[11] 'This measure did confine every man's possession, to a very moderate proportion . . .' Neither the capacity for nor the propensity to labour was equally distributed. In defending in the same context 'the industrious and rational' against 'the fancy or covetousness of the quarrelsome and contentious' (Sec. 34), Locke clearly presupposed differential industry as the cause of differential property. He inveighed against the covetous who would 'meddle with what was already improved by another's labour', desiring 'the benefit of another's pains, which he had no right to'. On the ground of unequal proficiency a right to the fruits of another's labour can, however, be created through contract. Master and servant have been obviously rendered unequal by their disparate capacities, to apply their labour profitably.[12] That the one is under the necessity to sell his service and the other is in the position to buy the service does not indicate that labour has ceased to be the measure of property. As I shall show later in greater detail, Locke conceived the wage-labour relationship as an exchange of labour and did not confine it to a particular stage of economic development. His acceptance of wage labour is, therefore, no proof that, for the sake of justifying capitalism, he transcended, or never seriously contemplated, the limitation of property by labour.[13] He also was neither indecisive about the continual validity of the labour limitation, nor did he think it valid only as long as plenty lasts.[14]

If, for Locke, labour was the origin of wealth, but had ceased to supply the title to property, it would have been contradictory to intimate at the same time that the industrious and rational work hard spontaneously and force the lazy and inconsiderate to work against their will.[15] As we have every reason to believe, he assumed the industrious and not the lazy to be the rich, and therefore took it for granted that labour always determines whatever income or property there is, and not only in agriculture.[16] 'Justice

[11] As Schlatter, *op. cit.*, 157, deduces.
[12] Secs. 24, 85.
[13] As Macpherson, *op. cit.*, 214-5, 220, 234, maintains.
[14] The first is assumed by Larkin, *op. cit.*, 66, and the second by Polin, *op. cit.*, 269, and Goldwin, *op. cit.*, 254.
[15] Strauss, *op. cit.*, 243, attributes both views to Locke.
[16] Larkin, *op. cit.*, 67, makes the restriction.

gives *every man* a title to the product of his honest industry, and the fair acquisitions of his ancestors descended to him.'[17] Notwithstanding the importance which Locke attached to the cultivation of land, the 'catalogue of things, that industry provided and made use of, about every loaf of bread' (Sec. 43) spans all kinds of economic activity, including commerce, and thus associates them all with labour. Apart from predominantly physical labour, all else that goes into the acquisition and management of possessions of any kind is, as it would seem, as a matter of course assumed to be the product of labour. Locke did not care to spell out the standards by which a mixed labour product should be distributed.[18] A pointer for their gradation might be contained in his distinction, later adopted by Adam Smith, between the 'natural, intrinsic value' (Sec. 43) of things, measured by their usefulness and quantity, and the marketable value of things, which is reflected in the value that men agree to put on gold and silver.[19] It seems safe to infer that Locke who justified the advantages of 'the industrious and rational' believed that the value of labour was determined by the extent of rationality required in different kinds of occupation. Social thought of his time did not oblige him to intimate more than that, or to improve upon well-established, and since then hardly advanced, ideas about this matter.

The justification of property through labour is in line with Locke's individualistic bent.[20] Reliance on his efforts enables the individual to accumulate what he can without any concern for others.[21] Yet precisely this insight, that the labour limitation is at best, to put it in Mill's terminology, a self-regarding one, must have moved him to supplement it by two additional and specifically other-regarding restrictions. The first requires appropriation only of as much as leaves 'enough, and as good . . . for others'.[22] This

---

[17] I, 42. Sec. 72. As H. Rashdall, 'The Philosophical Theory of Property,' in Gore, *op. cit.*, 44–5, and Plamenatz, *op. cit.*, 244 f., observe, Locke did not bother to bridge the gap between the right of bequest and the right to appropriate external objects by one's labour. The right of bequest is, however, explained by Locke as required for the propagation of the species (see below, 204). It serves also as the basis of safeguarding the rights of the vanquished (see above, 111 f.) and of demonstrating the acceptance of political obligation of one generation by another (see below, 268).

[18] Cp. Cherno, *loc. cit.*, 54.

[19] Sec. 37. Cp. Polin, *op. cit.*, 284–5.

[20] Cp. Kendall, *op. cit.*, 70, and below, 187 f.

[21] Cp. Macpherson, *op. cit.*, 221, 231–2; Strauss, *op. cit.*, 236; Plamenatz, *op. cit.*, 243.

[22] Sec. 27. Cp. Sec. 33.

is the sufficiency clause. It turns into an imperative that which was ensured when there was no 'want of room to plant in' (Sec. 36). Objective conditions made it 'impossible for any man ... to entrench upon the right of another, ... who would still have room, for as good, and as large a possession (after the other had taken out his) ...' According to the second other-regarding injunction, the spoilage prohibition, one ought not to appropriate more than 'one can make use of ... before it spoils; ... whatever is beyond this, is more than his share, and belongs to others' (Sec. 31). The two distinctly stated restrictions, which supplement the deficiency of the labour limitation, are inseparable. Because a man can procure more things by his labour than he is able to use before they spoil, the prohibition of spoilage renders effectiveness to the sufficiency clause.

Waste must be prevented, to leave sufficient for others. Locke's intention and words to this effect cannot be dismissed by objecting that the observance of non-spoilage in itself does not guarantee that enough is left over for others, except under the most unlikely conditions.[23] And, if charity is consideration for others, then Locke's words which I have quoted, do not substantiate the view that he was silent about the duties of charity in his thematic discussions of property.[24] Indeed, it is to make free of the notions of penury and plenty to deny Locke's prohibition of waste its character of a moral rule and it is unfounded to see the rule predicated on conditions which render it either unnecessary or ineffective, and hence never meant to be applied.[25]

The commands of charity, so it would seem to follow, were redundant in 'the first ages', for man had no need to impinge on the interests and needs of others when the population was sparse and nature's products were abundant. But in truth, we are told, by plenty Locke really meant penury, plenty being indistinguishable from penury if men have to work for a living, particularly if the natural materials they have to work with are almost useless. In this way the lack of any need to care for others is turned by these interpreters into the impossibility of so caring.[26] Even if plenty meant penury, it does not follow that men could not care for others but only that it was difficult to do so. For, while indeed the question whether

[23] Plamenatz, op. cit., 242, 247, concludes from these objections unto Locke's intentions irrespective of what Locke actually said.
[24] Strauss, op. cit., 248.
[25] Thus Cox, op. cit., 90, 92; Strauss, op. cit., 237; and Goldwin, op. cit., 446 f.
[26] Strauss, op. cit., 238; Goldwin, op. cit., 447.

there was penury or plenty may ultimately become irrelevant,[27] Locke's notions of them does not permit, as Strauss suggests,[28] to cancel out the clearly stated opinion that early man did not want more than he needed, i.e., that he had it in him to be considerate whether there was plenty or penury.

First, Locke nowhere says or implies that plenty relieves of the need for labour. 'Plenty' refers to the materials which nature places at man's disposal, the fruits of the earth and the earth itself.[29] 'The penury of his condition' (Sec. 32) consists not in the fact that man has to work but in that 'God and his reason commanded him to subdue the earth', i.e., that his efforts have to be directed to producing the fruits of the earth instead of merely collecting them. Secondly, the worthlessness of nature's provisions is not emphasized by Locke to stress the misery of the human condition, but rather to accentuate the value of labour[30] as the means to procure the conveniences of life which makes it possible to care also for others.

While 'his wants forced him to labour' (Sec. 35), labour enables man to increase his wants. Labour itself is not scarce. The opposite does not follow from anything Locke said, least of all from his comparison between the wretched Indians and the English of his time.[31] The comparison in Sections 37 and 41, serves to underline the enormous differences which the cultivation of land makes in the standard of living, and the incomparably higher results labour affords when employed not merely for gathering or primitive cultivation.

In the *Treatises*, scarcity or penury is a matter of objective conditions insofar only as they provide the challenge to be overcome by the subjective attitude of men towards their environment.[32] Without the labour of collecting men could not subsist even when they could rely exclusively on what nature supplies for immediate consumption. By labour men supplemented natural with human productivity to thwart the scarcity attendant upon the growth of

[27] Strauss, *op. cit.*, 237.

[28] *Ibid.*, 239, note 113.

[29] Secs. 28, 37.

[30] Secs. 36, 40–6. If in this way Locke did not altogether put labour and property beyond the divine malediction, he placed them at its margin (Polin, *op. cit.*, 262–3). He definitely did not, as Cox, *op. cit.*, 92, and Wolin, *op. cit.*, 319, assert, continue to consider labour as a curse.

[31] As Goldwin, *op. cit.*, 445, will have it.

[32] On the passage in the *Essays* which seems to contradict this; see below, 151–2.

population. On these grounds, Locke asserted with perfect consistency the validity and applicability of the injunction that one must avoid waste out of consideration for the right to subsistence of one's fellowmen. If the spoilage prohibition indicts the prodigal it does not exonerate the covetous.[33] The covetous can by no means be trusted to appropriate no more than can be used before spoilage. To insure the subsistence of all, the spoilage prohibition aims at the waster in any case and at the covetous when he causes waste. The spoilage limitation implies a rationalization of thrift. To avoid spoilage, hoarding up for future consumption or barter necessitates, amongst other elements of rational planning, the rationing of the use of goods. Thrift would seem to become subject to the other-regarding interdict of spoilage for the very reason that it serves 'capitalist' ends. But, both the prohibition of spoilage and the sufficiency clause, the precept to leave 'enough, and as *good* . . . for others', restrict but do not prevent the effects of men's different capacities and proclivities. Like the self-regarding labour limitation, the two other-regarding restrictions were never intended to secure full equality.

b. *The Effect: Moderate Possessions*

Egalitarianism was not realized 'in the first ages of the world,' when property limitations were fully observed. When one man was assured 'as good, and as large a possession' (Sec. 36) as the other, possessions were not equal; they were necessarily of a 'very *moderate* proportion . . .' The impossibility 'to entrench upon the right of another . . .' results from the lack of necessity in view of the boundless opportunities to plant 'in the then vast wilderness of the earth . . .' Objective conditions enable everybody to acquire property of the same moderate proportions but subjective factors make a difference. Only those are not prejudiced by the exertions of others 'who would use *the same industry*' (Sec. 37). Thus, '*the equality* of a simple poor way of living . . .' is not revealed in equal but in 'each man's *small* property' (Sec. 107).

Locke not only broke with the tradition which right up to him had assumed an original community of all things[34] as expressive of a state of full equality. His belief that, in the first ages, men did not wish for more than they could use does not require as its logical

---

[33] As Strauss, *op. cit.*, 237, asserts.
[34] See below, Ch. VI.

concomitant the equality of private properties in the pre-monetary stage.[35] The proscription against acquiring more than one needs or can use is no postulate of equal acquisition. What one man thinks that he needs and what he actually is able to make use of does not equally apply to other men. Likewise, the right to use what you need and the right to set aside for use that with which you mix your labour are not necessarily compatible.[36] The incompatibility enlarges the span of inequality since there is above all a difference between what you can use and what you need. The first turns out to be the decisive criterion, although Locke often applied it interchangeably with the second. He was undoubtedly aware that a farmer may be able to use another stretch of land and the cattle-breeder some extra head of cattle, although they do not need the surplus for mere subsistence. This, as is easily seen, is not prohibited by the three natural limitations, which Locke thought satisfactorily sustained in the pre-monetary stage.

Men may acquire 'as much as any one can make use of *to any advantage of life* before it spoils; so much he may by his labour fix a property in' (Sec. 31). Within the limits of his ability, one may gratify one's hankering after any advantage of life, and not merely rest satisfied with maintaining the level of bare subsistence. The ratio between need and property per family is not regarded as fixed, therefore, when Locke said that, 'as families increased, and industry enlarged their stocks, their possessions enlarged with the need of them' (Sec. 38). As he had already remarked, 'it is commonly in the father's power' to determine his son's inheritance 'with a more sparing or liberal hand . . .' (Sec. 72). Since moreover at every stage of development the use of one's own labour makes it possible to avail oneself by contract of the labour of others, inequality in securing the advantages of life is evidently assumed to have been from the outset far from negligible. Even in the period before land cultivation, the prohibition of spoilage did not narrow men down to securing no more than bare subsistence – nor prevent a good deal of lack of consideration for others. The spoilage prohibition – apart from rendering effectiveness – lends also elasticity to the injunction to leave enough and as good for others.

If a man gathered as many acorns or apples as he could, 'he was only to look that he used them before they spoiled; else he

---

[35] Macpherson, *op. cit.*, 204, makes this deduction.
[36] Cp. Plamenatz, *op. cit.*, 204.

took more than his share, and robbed others' (Sec. 46). The standard is not one of need, but of capacity of usage. Actually Locke is saying: provided you use all you can amass, you have done no wrong, for nobody is robbed when nothing spoils. But the less diligent might starve before it can be proved that a man had erred and amassed more than he could consume.[37] Further, people may be robbed, even if nothing does spoil. In a certain region at a given time, the subsistence of others is liable to be jeopardized if some people gather as much as they can use either for consumption or barter. It might be theoretically feasible, but for practical purposes almost impossible for those who fall behind to resort in time to other places where they are sure to find sufficient nourishment. Yet anyone of 'the first commoners of the world . . . , as . . . the Americans now', who gathered what he could, 'did no injury', so long as 'he wasted not the common stock; destroyed no part of the portion of goods that belonged to others, so long as nothing perished uselessly in his hands' (Sec. 46). The prohibition of spoilage would seem to provide against waste and destruction of either goods or land in respect of what is available in the whole world, and at any rate beyond the immediate territory of a community. But 'the first commoners of the world' lived like 'the Americans now' that is, they roamed the land under some government.[38] The other-regarding, though non-egalitarian spoilage prohibition could thus be considered as a practicable rule of conduct because it was enforceable within the framework of non-sedentary community life.

The interdict of spoilage is not meant to guarantee subsistence for all in the long run. His earlier views appear even to indicate that the prospects are in any case bleak,

'The inheritance of the whole of mankind is always one and the same, and it does not grow in proportion to the number of people born . . . And so, when any man snatches for himself as much as he can, he takes away from another man's heap the amount he adds to his own, and it is impossible for anyone to grow rich except at the expense of someone else.'[39]

Locke might have had in mind the scarcity of resources attendant upon the growth of population in the stage of gathering nature's

---

[37] Cp. Rashdall, in Gore, *op. cit.*, 44.
[38] See above, 86 f.
[39] *Essays*, 210-11. The italics in the following quotation are mine.

directly consumable products. He said that 'nature has provided a certain profusion of *goods* . . . in a predetermined quantity'. The enlargement of stocks and possessions together with the need of them, as maintained in the *Treatises*, would then not be ruled out in the earlier *Essays* where Locke said that 'whenever either the desire or the need of property increases among men, there is no extension, *then and there*, of the world's limits.' He might have meant that only as long as men gather the goods which nature produces directly for consumption and do not cultivate the land, the rule obtains that 'surely no gain falls to you which does not involve somebody else's loss'.[40] If we ought not to interpret these passages of the earlier *Essays* in the light of the *Treatises*, we must likewise reject those interpretations which rule out part of the argument in the *Treatises* by reference to the early *Essays*. If both cannot be related in the way I have suggested, we have simply to admit that Locke's views had changed. For in the *Treatises* we hear not only about 'the food and rayment, and other conveniences of life, the materials whereof he [God] had so plentifully provided . . .' (I, 41); we find also that when land cultivation supersedes gathering, uneven appropriation, permitted even under the spoilage prohibition, is no hindrance to securing merely 'enough, and as good' but more and better for all.

'The great design of God, increase and multiply' is fully compatible with a 'liberal allowance of the conveniences of life' (I, 41), except under absolute monarchies. The unused cultivable land in the world, although rendered scarce by wanton abuse wherever money is used, 'is yet more than mankind makes use of'.[41] And where it is made use of, one man's gain will not be another man's loss, for 'he who appropriates land to himself by his labour, does not lessen but increase the common stock of mankind' (Sec. 37). The cultivation of land raises the general subsistence level. The 'several nations of the Americans . . . who are rich in land, . . . yet for want of improving it by labour, have not one hundredth part of the conveniences we enjoy' (Sec. 41). Although Locke contrasted here the conveniences available where land is cultivated and where it is not, he surely also had the difference between extensive and intensive cultivation in mind when he supposed that even if the excessive appropriation of land by some men leaves not enough,

[40] *Ibid.*, 212–13.
[41] Sec. 45, Cp. 36, 42.

and poorer land for others, their subsistence is yet ensured on a higher level than before land was cultivated or had become scarce in a given territory.[42]

Locke considered the sufficiency injunction assured through the prohibition of spoilage before and after the cultivation of land, before and after the introduction of money. Pre-monetary America and post-monetary England are comparable also because whether there is money or not, waste and destruction are not caused by a man's appropriating more than others, 'the exceeding of *the bounds of his just property not lying in the largeness of his possession*, but the perishing of anything uselessly in it' (Sec. 46).

2. THE INTRODUCTION OF MONEY

Since the other-regarding limitations of non-spoilage and sufficiency which are added to the self-regarding limitation of labour are not intended to secure the equality of possessions, they need not be rescinded to justify inequality of possessions. Having thus removed the main ground for reading a head-long collision between anti-capitalistic and pro-capitalistic arguments into Locke, we must ask the question: exactly what changes did Locke assume to have taken place with the introduction of money?

The answer is twofold but simple. First, money facilitates the enlargement of possessions because it enables the circumvention of the non-spoilage clause. Secondly, it does not follow that the introduction of money endangers the subsistence of mankind; law and government are the means to ensure the function of the non-spoilage and sufficiency clauses. But the context in which this conclusion is implied contains the one instance where Locke seems to contradict what underlies the first part of our answer – namely that possessions never were equal.

A. The Causal Nexus

In the last but one section of the chapter 'Of Property' Locke suddenly says that

'men have agreed to *disproportionate and unequal* possession of the earth, they having by a tacit and voluntary consent found out a way, how a man may fairly possess more land than he himself can use the product of, by receiving in exchange for the overplus, gold and

[42] Cp. Strauss, *op. cit.*, 241; Macpherson, *op. cit.*, 212.

silver, . . . these metals not spoiling or decaying in the hands of the possessor' (Sec. 50).

This passage has been subject to so many corrections in the Christ's copy as to make part of it unintelligible except by comparison with other copies.[43] Locke meant perhaps to say 'disproportionately unequal possession' instead of 'disproportionate and unequal possession', the latter two coming in any case to the same thing. If so, the passage would signify that, after possessions had been unequal all along, men had eventually discovered a way to make the principle of inequality more practicable, that is, capable of further extension. This reading seems to be supported by the following sentence: 'This partage of things, in an inequality of private possessions, men have made *practicable* [more practicable or tenable?] out of the bounds of society, and without compact, only by putting a value on gold and silver and tacitly agreeing in the use of money.' I do not wish to insist on the appropriateness of thus revising the literal meaning of these passages but rather on the fact that taken literally, they contradict all else that Locke said on the subject.[44] Hence I feel justified in considering these passages which appear to make the inequality of possessions attendant upon the introduction of money, as an inadvertent deviation from the fully elaborated argument, and not, like all other interpreters, as a peg on which to hang it.

Apart from Section 50, Locke nowhere in the chapter 'Of Property' speaks of the equality of possessions. The words 'equal' and 'equally' appear only once each and relate to the equal right of acquiring property. What 'belonged equally to all her [nature's] children' (Sec. 29), is what was common before any appropriation took place. All men have an 'equal title' (Sec. 32) to this, inasmuch as everybody has the right by his labour to enclose land from the universal common without needing the consent of mankind and nobody can have a title to what is already appropriated. Locke maintains the right of everybody to acquire property; the issue of equal appropriation is not under discussion. Moreover, the statement which immediately precedes Section 50 is particularly instructive because it epitomizes all that was said before. 'Find out something that has the *use and value of money* amongst his neigh-

[43] Cp. Laslett, *op. cit.*, 320, 477.
[44] For the two other similarly drastic contradictions see below, 277 f. and 345 f.

bours, you shall see the same man will begin presently to *enlarge* his possessions' (Sec. 49). The enlarging of possessions does not depend upon money in the strictly technical sense of the word. Nuts and shells serve the same purpose as a piece of metal or 'a sparkling pebble or a diamond' (Sec. 46). The cardinal point is however that Locke consistently speaks of enlarging possessions and not of possessions becoming unequal. Obviously, the enlargement of possessions can be either the cause or the result of unequal possessions. According to Locke, different proportions of property are the consequence of different degrees of industry and the enlargement, not the creation, of unequal possessions is the result of the invention of money. 'As *different degrees of industry* were apt to give men possessions *in different proportions*, so this invention of money gave them the opportunity *to continue and enlarge them.*'[45]

Money makes a difference only regarding the degree to which possessions become enlargeable. Before there was real money and so long as there were enough vacant places, 'the possessions he could make himself upon the measures we have given, would not be *very* large . . .' (Sec. 36). Hence, Locke could 'boldly affirm, that the same rule of propriety, (viz.) that every man should have as much as he could make use of, would hold still in the world, . . . had not the invention of money, . . . introduced (by consent) *larger* possessions, and a right to them'. Again Locke does not imply that possessions had been once equal, but that they had been more equal because the equal opportunity for everybody to appropriate as much land as he could utilize had once not been foreclosed. Money gives wider scope to man to exercise according to his ability the title to what he can make use of, a right which by itself conforms even less to standards securing equality than the right to what a man needs.

The view expounded in the chapter 'Of Property' in all sections but one, namely that inequality of possessions reaches a turning point with the introduction of money, follows also from the causal relationship which Locke assumed between money and the desire for more than one needs. If there is no gainsaying that what a man can make use of is seldom the same as what he needs, the acquisition of more than he can utilize must surely be ascribed to his desire to possess more than he needs. It seems likewise clear that where

. .[45] Sec. 48. In Sec. 108, what makes the Indian Kingdoms in America 'a pattern of the first ages in Asia and Europe' is 'want of people and money [which] gave men no temptation to *enlarge* their possessions of land'.

money exists it kindles this desire, but that without such promptings men hardly would have invented money, or its equivalent in the first place. Indeed Locke's thoughts on this subject were those any sensible person would entertain.[46] Appropriation was not considerable and not to the prejudice of others,

'before the desire of having more than men needed, had altered the intrinsic value of things, which depends only on their usefulness to the life of man; *or* [men] had agreed, that a little piece of yellow metal, which would keep without wasting or decay, should be worth a great piece of flesh, or a whole heap of corn' (Sec. 37).

By using 'or' instead of 'and' Locke cannot have meant that agreement to the use of money is the alternative to, rather than the means of gratifying the irrational desire to have more than one needs. The role of money as the indispensable means is stressed when he said that where there is 'nothing . . . either because of its commonness, or perishableness, fit to supply the place of money' there no one has a reason 'to enlarge his possessions beyond the use of his family, and a *plentiful* supply to its consumption' (Sec. 48). To extend the scope of one's industry makes sense only where there is 'something both lasting and scarce, and so valuable to be hoarded up' and where there are 'hopes of commerce with other parts of the world . . .' That in the absence of a money-economy there is no reason to give way to the desire of having more than one needs, does not make money the cause of existence of this desire. Since for Locke there was always room for barter, and there were always substitutes for money, money was the accomplished instrumentality for gratifying the desire to have more than one needs and hence for extending the originally restricted proportions of inequality.

Thus, the first part of our answer to the inquiry into the changes wrought by the introduction of money remains that money enhances the inequality of property. The second part of our answer is that government is the means to secure the purpose of the sufficiency-spoilage clause. This follows from the connection between Locke's evaluation of money and his explanation why money renders the spoilage limitation practically ineffective.

[46] Strangely enough, most interpreters have either attributed to Locke the view that money was the cause of the desire to have more than one needs, or have failed to make a distinction between this proposition and its reverse. Polin, *op. cit.*, 270, 282, comes near to making the distinction but rejoins the rest of the commentators in holding that, for Locke, money puts an end to natural equality (270, 284).

B. *Ends and Means*

'The greatest part of things *really useful* to the life of man ... are generally things of short duration; such as, if they are not consumed by use, will decay and perish of themselves: Gold, silver, and diamonds, are things, that *fancy or agreement* has put the value on, *more than real use, and the necessary support of life*' (Sec. 46). Nevertheless

'a man may fairly possess more land than he himself can use the product of, by receiving in exchange for the overplus, gold and silver, which may be hoarded up without injury to anyone, these metals not spoiling or decaying in the hands of the possessor' (Sec. 50).

We are faced with a strange deduction. Nobody is injured when things which he designated in the vein of Morus as having 'but a fantastical imaginary value' (Sec. 184), are substituted for what is alone useful. In other words, in accord with the interdict of spoilage the thing most useful to the life of man – land – may be accumulated because something else, in itself useless, which is substituted for the perishable products of the land, does not spoil. This sort of argument represents a *tour de force*, reminiscent of earlier theological evasions of economically cumbersome interdicts. To be sure, money prevents the spoilage of goods by permitting their circulation. But this insight does not require the false presupposition that the intrinsic quality of metals as non-spoiling objects offsets the spoilage of consumable goods. While money spent on eatables is 'consumed' with the consumption of purchased goods, excessive buying is harmless only if the goods keep. If part of the eatables spoil, you have wasted part of your money, which, as far as your purchasing capacity is concerned, has also 'spoiled'. If you are out of cash, it is no consolation that the part of your money spent on the spoiled goods still exists and retains its purchasing power after it has passed into other hands. That your money is now your grocer's money is also of no comfort to a needy man for whom you have no money to spare and who might have used the things you have let spoil.

The argument offered by Locke is no credit to the man who was a theoretician and practitioner of public finance. However, he was not concerned here with the merely functional interpretation of money, but with the moral and social evaluation of its role. And this evaluation remains negative. Money does not lend rationality to excessive appropriation in both the moral and expedient senses,[47] and unlimited appropriation does not become the essence of rationality. According to Locke, a money-economy makes it possible for different degrees of industry to cause a gross inequality of possessions. Since he thought that to be industrious is to be rational, he may have assumed that rationality is more prevalent after the introduction of money than before. Yet for Locke this rationality is subservient to the irrational craving for more than one needs, and due to '*amor sceleratus habendi*, evil concupiscence . . .' (Sec. 111), it alters the intrinsic value of things. It is therefore at best rationality in the expedient but not in the moral sense, which has enabled the circumvention of the natural limitations on acquisitiveness commanded by the law of nature. Yet since expedient rationality is not exempt from moral censure, it is also not uncontainable. It has led to a money economy which by 'a tacit and voluntary consent. . . . men have made practicable out of the bounds of society. . . .' (Sec. 50). But political society exists for the better enforcement of the law of nature.

The chapter 'Of Property' reaches its end and apex in the clarification of what the invention of money really amounts to: the accumulation of things most useful to the life of men by means of something which by itself is useless but does not spoil. At the very point where it is impressed upon us how the spoilage prohibition is rendered illusory by the invention of money and the acquisition of land freed from any limitation we are reminded that, 'in governments the laws regulate the right of property, and the possession of land is determined by positive constitutions' (Sec. 50). Although appearing quite abruptly in its immediate context, this conclusion of the argument is not unwarranted. Almost at the beginning of the *Second Treatise*, 'the regulating and preserving of property' (Sec. 3) is defined as the major purpose of legislation. The regulation of property rights by government and law is referred to several times in the chapter 'Of Property',[48] in which we are in fact also told that 'the increase of lands and the right employing of them is *the great art of government*'.[49] The statement which concludes the discussion

[47] Macpherson, *op. cit.*, 235, makes the assertion.
[48] Secs. 35, 38, 45.
[49] Sec. 42. I have followed Goldwin, *op. cit.*, 468, in reading 'the right employing' instead of 'the right of employing'. But I must differ from Goldwin when he asserts (452) that the passage corroborates the view that government is the final step in the elimination of the natural labour and spoilage limitation. The passage concludes the

of the introduction of money recalls summarily what has been maintained all along.

It follows that while by reliance on the concept of consent the barren quality of gold and silver is transcended,[50] what this consent has made practicable 'out of the bounds of society, and *without compact*' (Sec. 50), is in turn subjected to the consent or 'compact' on which society rests. 'Where the increase of people and stock, with the use of money had made land scarce', communities regulated 'by laws within themselves, . . . the properties of the private men of their society, and so, *by compact and agreement*, settled the property which labour and industry began' (Sec. 45). Although political consent supersedes, it does not come into existence after, the non-political consent to the use of money. From its incipience a money-economy is containable by government, because, as we have seen,[51] government already existed when people lived simply and poorly in pre-monetary times. The consent to the use of common money – 'the silver money of Europe'[52] – presupposes the existence of political societies, and so does the non-political tacit consent, which established the use of money.

To maintain the claims of moral rationality over and against the claims of expedient rationality, Locke did not recommend a reversion to the pristine times, when 'it was useless as well as dishonest [for a man] to carve himself too much, or take more than he needed' (Sec. 51). Legislation can give effect to the intention of the sufficiency clause because consent is not excluded from the sphere of property relations, nor is this kind of consent regarded as intrinsically different from the consent which determines political relations.

3. CONSENT IN PROPERTY RELATIONS

When Locke distinguished the tacit consent to the introduction of money from the compact upon which law and government rest, he seemed to set consent in one sphere and in one form apart from

---

demonstration 'how much labour makes the far greatest part of the value of things' and lauds 'that prince . . . so wise and godlike as . . . to secure protection and encouragement to the *honest industry* of mankind . . .' So much for the 'elimination' of the labour limitation.

[50] Although by no means 'neatly' as Macpherson, *op. cit.*, 207, argues.
[51] See above, 97.
[52] See above, 115.

that in another sphere and in another form. But he considered the political compact, too, adequately realized by tacit consent.[53] Moreover, the spheres of property relations and political relations are not distinguished but given the same status by the declaration that the original exercise of the right of property is independent of 'any express compact of all the commoners' (Sec. 25). The validity of all natural rights is independent of consent. Yet because all are possessors of natural rights, any arrangements for the realization of these rights in interpersonal relations must be referable to consent. In other words, although all natural rights are independent of consent, all social relations between adults must be based on consent.

A. Contractual Interdependence

The nucleus of social relationships – the union in marriage – is the result of consent formalized in a contract bearing also on matters of property.[54] Property relations between families, too, are a matter of consent. Abraham and Lot, 'when their herdsmen could not agree, . . . parted by consent,' (I, 135) as was usual among people when 'there was not room enough in the same place, for their herds to feed together . . .' (Sec. 38). Within the patriarchal family – in effect a family of families – the head has no arbitrary power either. It cannot be assumed that 'Jacob had . . . the same power over every one of his family as he had over his ox or his ass, as an owner over his substance' (I, 155). Everything beyond the relationship between the appropriating subject and the appropriated object is a matter of consent between contracting parties. This applies also to the master-servant relationship, for only 'the consent of the poor man' (I, 43), subjects him to the rich proprietor.

There is nothing incongruous in Locke's referring to servants in the midst of his demonstration that property is created by individual labour.[55] The servant is a party to a contract about an exchange of

[53] See below, 219 f.
[54] Secs. 80–3; I, 47, 98.
[55] Macpherson's query (*op. cit.*, 216) whether it was absurd for Locke to suppose a master-servant relationship in the state of nature is doubly out of place. First, as Laslett points out ('Market Economy and Political Theory,' *The Historical Journal*, VI, 1 (1964), 152–3), Macpherson constantly overlooks the fact that for Locke the original framework of human existence is the patriarchal family, comprised not only of servants but often also of the sons' families. And this framework already requires the equivalent of political organization. (See below, 213) Secondly, Locke related the master-servant relationship not only in Sec. 28 to political society. The reference there to the manorial commons is matched in Sec. 85 by the distinction between the state of slavery and the state of servants with regard to civil society.

his labour for the money of another man, i.e. for the product of another's labour. According to Section 85, 'master and servant are names as old as history' and 'a free-man makes himself a servant to another, by selling him for a certain time, the service he undertakes to do, in exchange for wages he is to receive'. As a result the servant – and this still applied in Locke's time to all dependent workers[56] – is placed 'into the family of his master, and under the ordinary discipline thereof'. The master's power over the servant remains temporary 'and no greater, than what is contained in the contract between them'. Since the contractual wage-labour relationship is as old as history, it is not assumed to be a consequence of the introduction of money.[57] The character of the relationship as an exchange of labour is even more obviously assumed, when in Section 28, no contract or wages are mentioned. The contractual relationship is implied all the same, because an exchange of the products of labour is visibly involved.

Locke first says that 'the turfs my servant has cut' belong to me just as the other things which I appropriate through my labour 'where I have a right to them in common with others . . . without the assignation or consent of anybody'. If, he goes on to say, 'an explicit consent of every commoner' (Sec. 29) were

'necessary to any one's appropriating to himself any part of what is given in common, children or servants could not cut the meat which their father or master had provided for them in common, without assigning to every one his peculiar part.'

The comparison contains besides the parallel also a difference. Whether he is himself a commoner or not, the servant who grazes, turfs and mines on the common land for the master does not thereby acquire any right to the turf and grass he has cut or the ore he has dug. But this does not preclude an exchange of labour between him and the master.[58] Not being a slave, the servant has the right to receive something for his labour. It is surely on account of the labour that he has performed for the master that he does not need the latter's explicit consent to share the meat provided for the entire household. In respect of what is common to the household the servant's right parallels that of the master who needs no express

[56] Cp. Laslett, *Locke's Two Treatises*, 340.
[57] Macpherson, *op. cit.*, 214.
[58] As Polin, *op. cit.*, 266–7, maintains.

F   161

consent of the other commoners to take part of what is common. Yet, just as the turf and the grass cease to be part of the manorial commons as a result of the servant's labour, the meat which the master provides for the household can only belong to the household as a result of his labour. The patent implication is that the servant's product of labour becomes the master's property in exchange for the servant's right to some of the master's property which in the last resort is the product of the master's own exertions. If it made no difference to Locke whether the right to something was established by one's own or by purchased labour,[59] it was because he assumed that to be able to purchase labour you have to rely on the fruits of your own labour.

However dire the necessity that drives a free-man to become the servant of another, however bad the conditions of service, the servant does not become a slave. Since he has not forfeited his right to live, he can use his labour as a commodity[60] but does not become a commodity himself. That would be his fate if he were a slave. Then he would have no right to the meat provided by the master, but would have to be content with the expectations of a working animal to be fed as much and so long as it pleases the master. Even if a man sells himself in such a way as to place himself at the absolute disposal of another man, this still involves no more than a particular onerous kind of service such as 'we find among the Jews, as well as other nations . . .' (Sec. 24). Such a man sold himself 'only to drudgery, not to slavery . . . For the master could not have power to kill him, at any time, whom, at a certain time, he was obliged to let go free out of his service.' Normal service as well as drudgery involve mutual, i.e., contractual obligations, and are bounded by time. The master has the right of permanent appropriation of the servant's product of labour. He has no permanent right to the servant's labour, which would be slavery. 'As soon as compact enters, slavery ceases . . .' (Sec. 172), and like political obligation, the economic dependence of adults who are innocent of a crime deserving death is determined by compact. There is no right to contract away freedom.

---

[59] Cp. Macpherson, *op. cit.*, 215.

[60] Cp. Macpherson, *loc. cit.*, and Polin, *op. cit.*, 266. I cannot agree with Laslett, *op. cit.*, 104, that Locke's reference to 'service' instead of 'labour' makes any difference. Against this distinction speaks also the view of Laslett himself, quoted above in note 55.

B. *Consent as the Function of Freedom*

Freedom is unalienable, 'for . . . not having the power of his own life, [a man] cannot, by compact, or his own consent, enslave himself to any one . . .' (Sec. 23). Freedom would, however, practically cease to be ensured by the right of consent, if the differences in rationality were socially acquired and perpetuated by the differences in economic position.[61] If the economic position into which men are born determines their rationality, mobility in the economic sphere is excluded and consent becomes immaterial as a function of freedom.

Marx, unlike Hess, Cabet and Grün, seems to have taken no notice of Locke's critical attitude towards the enlargement of possessions and the introduction of money. According to Marx, Locke had attempted to present 'even bourgeois reason as normal reason'.[62] There are no grounds for enlarging upon this, and presenting Locke as justifying self-alienation in terms of an anticipatory compliance with Marxist causality. According to Macpherson, Locke implicitly assumes that the difference in rationality between two classes of men came about because 'men were free to alienate their freedom' so that 'the difference in rationality was a result, not a cause, of that alienation'.[63] Yet, as the quotation at the beginning of this section testifies, Locke explicitly denied the right to alienate one's freedom. Apart from contradicting the Lockeian text, Macpherson raises more questions than he answers. If different rationality is not the cause of the alienation of freedom but its result, then men were originally equally rational. If so, why do some alienate their freedom while others do not, and why do some alienate more than others? If they are equal in the first stage of the state of nature,

---

[61] Macpherson, *op. cit.*, 246, attributes this view to Locke.

[62] *Das Kapital* (Wien-Berlin, 1933), Band I, Buch 1, 903. In *Die Heilige Familie* of 1844-5 (K. Marx, *Der Historische Materialismus, Die Frühschriften*, ed. by S. Landshut and J. P. Mayer (Leipzig, 1932), 2 vols., I, 385), Marx and Engels believed that the trend of French materialism which derived ultimately from Locke culminated 'directly in socialism'. From this lineage Locke is, however, excluded. In *Die Deutsche Ideologie* of 1845-6 Marx and Engels summed up their arguments against German philosophers and socialists – including specifically Karl Grün. In this context, Hobbes and Locke figure as the originators of the subsumption of bourgeois society 'under the one abstract money and broker relationship' ('das eine abstrakte Geld – und Schacherverhältnis'. See *Sankt Max*, *op. cit.*, II, 430). Accordingly in *Das Kapital*, I, 39, 96, 106, 130, 157 and 409, Marx evaluated Locke's views about money as characteristic of the capitalist attitude. I owe the references to E. Cabet, *Voyage in Icarie* (Paris, 1942) and K. Grün, *Die Soziale Bewegung in Frankreich und Belgien* (Darmstadt, 1945), to my colleague S. Avineri.

[63] Macpherson, *op. cit.*, 246.

they must be supposed to come to terms on an equal footing with the scarcity which follows in the wake of population increase. If men cannot sustain the stress of scarcity equally well, then all were apparently not equal in the first place. As far as Locke is concerned, these are gratuitous quandaries. Having clearly and reasonably supposed differential capacities from the outset, he provided the explanation why some succeed more than others in the struggle for economic benefits. Furthermore, he did not regard class-position and inborn capacities as being transmitted unchangingly from generation to generation.

A tenant for life can accumulate property of his own, for he has 'a property in all that he gets over and above his rent . . .' (Sec. 194). A man becomes a servant by selling his labour for a given time. It is evidently assumed that when the time is over, he may be able to start out on his own or if he has not ceased to be an owner of property, he may become fully independent again after having overcome, by means of his service, the difficulties which had caused him to become the servant of another free-man. When whole regions are seen to be changing demographically and economically so much that the re-demarcation of constituencies is necessary,[64] social mobility is ostensibly part of the process. When heirs are obliged to renounce their property to free themselves from the political obligations of their fathers, the sons are supposed to join the propertyless, yet are quite certainly regarded as eligible for property of their own earning.[65]

The wage-earner of Locke's time had not much choice in consenting to the patron's conditions of contract, and Locke was not far from justifying alienation in the Marxian sense when he condoned the almost total absorption of the labourers' humanity by their toil.[66] But the point here is that as a matter of principle he ruled out a contract of perpetual subjection, as well as a negation of the right of property in those who did not inherit any.[67] Although the principle of consent is liable to cover up a person's practically irredeemable alienation of freedom, class barriers, for Locke, are not insurmountable. Consent in economic relations remains a function of freedom in view of the clearly implied assumption of

---

[64] Sec. 157.
[65] See below, 272–3, 291.
[66] See Polin, *op. cit.*, 266 and below, 173.
[67] Rashdale, in Gore, *op. cit.*, 46, imputes the negation to Locke.

socio-economic mobility. Because consent is unwaveringly upheld as the basis of the wage-labour relationship, the sphere of economic relations is kept on the same plane of principles as the political sphere. Thus the ground is provided for legal measures against preventing the labourers from seizing upon better opportunities. Cherished ideas about the nature of liberalism notwithstanding, Locke's theory sanctions the principles and forms of political action for the restraint of economic power.

4. POLITICAL AND ECONOMIC POWER

Nobody contests that Locke admitted the right of the state to regulate and protect property. But the terms of incorporation – the 'compact' – limit the defence of property as little as they prevent the state from interfering with property relations in accordance with the will of the majority.[68] Locke could have stipulated a moral interdict against the interference of government and law with property relations, if, as is often assumed, he had raised the natural right of property above all others. In this case, consent would still remain, as I have asserted earlier in this chapter, the instrument for the realization of all natural rights,[69] but the sphere of property relations could then be sealed off against the public sphere. Since consent is sanctioned by natural law, the second sets the limits to the first.

A. The Inclusion of the Economic in the Political Sphere

a. The Right of Property – A Natural Right among Others

Locke's use of the term property in an extended and restricted sense, rather than elevating property above all other natural rights, presents it as the prototype of all natural rights. As Laslett has aptly put it, it is because men's rights 'can be symbolized as property, something a man can conceive of as distinguishable from himself though part of himself, that a man's attributes, such as his freedom, his equality, his power to execute the law of nature, can become the subject of his consent . . .'[70] Thus we have on the one hand the much quoted statement: 'the great and chief end *therefore*, of men's

---

[68] Cp. Hobhouse, in Gore, *op. cit.*, 27, and Larkin, *op. cit.*, 73.
[69] See above, 159–60; see also 69.
[70] Cp. Laslett, *op. cit.*, 102.

uniting into commonwealths, and putting themselves under government, is the preservation of their property' (Sec. 124). On the other we have the fact that the same sentence is related through the word 'therefore' to the preceding one, where Locke explains 'the general name, property' to mean men's 'lives, liberties and estates'.[71] The references in Sections 138-9 to property in the restricted sense are, as Macpherson says, part of the crucial argument for the limitation of governmental power *vis à vis* property.[72] But the argument that Locke derived the right of consent to taxation from the premise that 'the preservation of property . . . [is] the end of government' (Sec. 138), does not void,[73] or render less crucial, the repeated definition of property as the prototype of all natural rights. Further, the right to consent to taxation is only a special incidence of the limitation of government by consent. For the protection of property in the restricted sense is an end and a legitimation of government insofar as it is one of the fundamental natural rights subsumed under the name property in the extended sense.

Locke's emphasis on the right of property seems to stem from his awareness that life and liberty may mainly be jeopardized through the violation of property rights – because men clash with each other on this ground most often and most violently,[74] and because the government's demands on the citizens bear most immediately and visibly on their property. That is probably why Locke made taxation contingent upon express consent in any regime.[75] But in so limiting the power of government, he subjected the enjoyment of the right of property to political decisions no less than he did the enjoyment of any other natural right. Locke does not transform the natural right of property into a conventional one,[76] nor does he give it special status through the invention of money. We cannot ascribe to Locke the view that due to a contrivance for the more effective exercise of the natural right of property, positive laws could not contain property accumulation

---

[71] Sec. 123. Similarly Sec. 87, line 5; Sec. 171, lines 5 and 17; and especially Sec. 173, lines 4–5 and 8. See also I, 92: 'Government being for the preservation of every man's right and property.'

[72] Cp. Macpherson, *op. cit.*, 198.

[73] As Vaughan, *op. cit.*, 168, 181, asserts.

[74] Cp. Lamprecht, *op. cit.*, 135.

[75] For the contradiction which follows see below, 247, note 11.

[76] Schlatter, *op. cit.*, 158–9, thinks that property in the modern world was viewed in this way by Locke.

in accord with natural law. If a human convention is apt to free property laws from compliance with natural law, this must apply to any positive law, indeed to anything authorized by political society, since it is the major human contrivance established by consent.[77] If positive laws can at all guarantee what natural law enjoins, the laws which regulate property cannot be an exception. Locke upheld the inner consistency of his natural law teaching when it comes to property. The right of property is the prototype of all natural rights. They are freedoms sanctioned by natural law and freedom is protected and bounded by positive law in all spheres of action.

b. *Law and Freedom*

Neither 'freedom . . . under government' nor 'freedom of nature' – or 'natural liberty' (Sec. 22) – are unlimited. The first is limited by 'a standing rule . . . made by the legislative power . . .' The second is the 'perfect freedom [of men] to order their actions, and dispose of their possessions, and persons as they think fit . . .' (Sec. 4). It leaves man independent upon the will of other men but does not permit him to overstep 'the bounds of the law of nature . . .' What 'holds in all the laws a man is under, whether natural or civil' is 'to know how far that law is to be his guide, and how far he may make use of his freedom, . . . how far the law allows a liberty' (Sec. 59). Since the law of nature is the law of reason and positive laws ought to accord with it, 'freedom under government' like 'perfect freedom' are rationally limited freedom. Neither is unbounded, but both are maximized freedom. Law maximizes freedom because by imposing limitations upon men it liberates them *'from restraint and violence from others'* which cannot be, where there is no law' (Sec. 57). That is why 'law, in its true notion, is not so much the limitation as the direction of a free and intelligent agent to his proper interest, and prescribes no further than is for the general good'. Locke's conception implies thus the empirical definition of liberty as the absence of constraint by others.[78] If we call this 'negative' liberty, and 'positive' liberty consists in being self-directed

---

[77] Cp. Polin, *op. cit.*, 270, note 5. Strauss' contention (*op. cit.*, 235), that the validity of natural law ceases in respect of property once society is formed, leads to the *reductio ad absurdum* I have indicated.

[78] For the elaboration of the empirical definition, see F. E. Oppenheim, 'Freedom – an Empirical Interpretation,' *Nomos IV* (Yearbook of the American Society for Political and Legal Philosophy, 1962, ed. by C. J. Friedrich), 214 f., and Oppenheim, *Dimensions of Freedom* (New York-London, 1961).

inasmuch as one is moved by reason,[79] the two liberties condition each other in Locke. This applies insofar as the difference between the two concepts consists mainly in saying the same thing in a negative or positive way, that is, on the basis of freedom as the absence of constraint imposed upon us by others.

While freedom, for Locke, is not divorced from law, the difference between them is not obscured as it was later by Hegel. Reason does not cause man to identify law and freedom but 'is able to instruct him in that law he is to govern himself by, and make him know how far he is left to the freedom of his *own* will' (Sec. 63). Similarly, a man's proper interest is not submerged in the general good although it is not divorced from it either. It is in nobody's interest to fall prey to the whim and violence of his fellow-men. A man's proper interest and that of his fellow-citizens coalesce in the true notion of law because personal freedom is not increased when individual inclinations are left unrestrained or never directed towards the general good. This is why 'the end of law is not to abolish or restrain, but to preserve and enlarge freedom'. Law fulfils this function inasmuch as 'where there is no law, there is *no* freedom' (Sec. 57). Locke did not mean that law does not constrain, but that without constraint no amount of freedom is assured. Laws serve as 'the bonds of the society, to keep every part of the body politic in its due place and function' (Sec. 219). They do not eliminate all natural freedom and leave room for self-willed compliance with natural law. This relationship between freedom and law applies as much to the realization of property rights as to that of any other natural right.

Everybody has 'a liberty to dispose, and order, as he lists, his person, actions, possessions, and his whole property, within the allowance of those laws under which he is' (Sec. 57). Although freedom under government is to live by a standing rule, 'common to every one of that society', I retain 'a liberty to follow my own will *in all things*, where the rule prescribes not' (Sec. 22). Liberty in political society is residual liberty in all kinds of activity and not specifically in property relations. Inasmuch as political society must have 'the power to preserve the property' – defined in the preceding sentence as 'life, liberty and estate' – 'all private judgement of every particular member [as regards the punishment of infractions of natural law] being excluded', the execution of laws 'decides *all*

[79] Cp. I. Berlin, *Two Concepts of Liberty* (Oxford, 1958), 16. On the distinction between negative and positive liberty, see also Cranston, *Freedom, a New Analysis*.

the differences that may happen between *any* members of that society, concerning *any* matter of right' (Sec. 87). The law instructs man 'how far he is left to the freedom of his own will' (Sec. 63). Thanks to the law he is free in matters not subject to law. For Locke, the purpose of law is not negative, although freedom exists only where men are independent of the will of other men. (Hence they are perfectly free so long as they are under no other than natural law.) Law, the hall-mark of the political order, has the positive and creative task of maximizing man's moral stature by protecting him from the arbitrariness of his fellow-men and government. Locke leaves no doubt that the prerequisite for any reconciliation of contrary private interests is the existence of a public will formalized in law. As we have shown above, Locke's conception of the state of nature, both as a hypothesis and as a real situation, provides no ground for a distinction between state and society.[80] In the same way do his views on the relationship between property and law not permit to turn him into the intellectual source of the tendency to conceive of society as an entity distinct from the political order.[81] Insofar as the aim of a liberal distinction between 'state' and 'society' is to prove the feasibility and necessity of a sphere free of direct government intervention, he saw it result from the rule of law. Exactly because 'civil interests' are expressive of men's wants in general,[82] these are for Locke politically guaranteed interests. He used 'civil society' and 'political society' synonymously because the community is the repository of the individual wills turned into the public will. This is not to break the monopoly of the political order but to ensure the public a share in the working of that order. The power to make and enforce laws independently of the will of the individuals seemed to him, and has not ceased to be, the major threat to what men may reasonably claim as their private concerns. Civil are tied to political interests because government is not merely the arbiter between private interests. It exists,

[80] See above, 88 f.

[81] Wolin, *op. cit.*, 291, 309 f., 311 f., imputes this role to Locke. I can also not follow Polin, *op. cit.*, 144, in attributing to Locke the use of the terms community, society and people in different senses. Since, in what follows, I shall make some comparisons between Locke and Hegel, I should like to point out that, in my view, Hegel's distinction between state and society is one between spheres of a different factual and moral nature which remain, as in Locke's conception, existentially inseparable. It seems that the Marxist vision of a classless and stateless society has contributed a good deal to the reification of non-political society in latter-day liberal thought.

[82] Wolin, *op. cit.*, 302.

'for the benefit of the governed, and not the sole advantage of the governors (but only for theirs with the rest, as they make a part of that political body, each of whose parts and members are taken care of, and directed in its peculiar functions for the good of the whole, by the laws of the society) . . .' (I, 93).

The body politic is not a 'whole' in the terms of organic theories,[83] but a pluralistic composite inasmuch as it includes governors and governed. The public good is the sum total of all the individual advantages and benefits recognizable by law, 'the good of every particular member of that society, as far as by common rules, it can be provided for . . .' (I, 92).

These rules guarantee property as such. To the extent that 'the preservation of property . . . [is] the end of government', this 'necessarily supposes and requires, that the people should have property...' (Sec. 138). In other words, there should be no propertyless people.[84] This remains unequivocally sanctioned by natural law and serves therefore as the binding directive for positive law. 'That the people should have property' admits of unequal acquisition as well as of the restriction of unlimited accumulation; it precludes expropriation. This is the irreducible limit set to the realization of the right of property in the restricted sense. Hence, and because property in the restricted sense is part of the right of property in the extended sense, political society is not empowered merely to guarantee small and big property alike.[85] Positive laws can also be made to cope with and to transcend what Bosanquet called 'a world, on the whole, of cash nexus and mere protection by the state'.[86]

B. The Supremacy of the Sphere of Politics

a. Moral Superiority

There is something to be said for the Hegelian view that laws and government are more than tools of the world of the cash nexus and that the moral standards which prevail in property relations are of a lower order than those which determine political decisions. In Hegelian terms, this means that the sphere of property relations – of

---

[83] Cp. Polin, *op. cit.*, 145.

[84] Larkin, *op. cit.*, 63, asserts the contrary. Monson, *loc. cit.*, 131, recognizes that all have equal rights to some property.

[85] Cp. Gough, *op. cit.*, 83; Macpherson, *op. cit.*, 300 and Polin, *op. cit.*, 274.

[86] B. Bosanquet, *The Philosophical Theory of the State* (repr. London, 1958), 256.

'civic society' – is that of 'lower reason' and is inferior to the sphere of the state. As we have seen, for Locke, too, the rationality deployed in the economic sphere is subject to the rationality evinced in the political order. The well established imagery about the liberal attitude has prevented the recognition of the fact that the practical and moral priority of the sphere of politics is implicit in Locke's conception. The misconception has been enforced by the influence of Hegel if it does not emanate from him. It was he who had stipulated the inadequacy of the principles of 'civic society' as conceived by Hobbes, Locke and the eighteenth-century Enlightenment, in apprehending the nature of the modern state. Hegel and his followers contend that the 'state' rests upon an ethical foundation – *Sittlichkeit* – different from and only 'dialectically' related to the morality manifest in the satisfaction of individual interests and aspirations.[87] With Locke, the norms of individualist morality contain a sufficient foundation for social virtues and apply equally to the economic and to the political sphere. Yet for this very reason the economic sphere reveals itself as morally inferior to the political. For both spheres are judged in the light of the postulate of natural equality. If in his valuation of politics, as compared with economics, Locke remained within the classical and Christian tradition and anticipated Rousseau and Hegel, he did so on grounds which he shared with Rousseau alone.

The moral primacy of the political over the economic sphere follows from the central axioms of Locke's theory, as we have already reviewed them. His individualist morality consecrates the principle of consent in all interpersonal relations between adults. What is consented to, in both the economic and the political sphere, may or may not be right. Although he admitted that positive laws often contravene natural law, as such consented laws have a morally unequivocal function. But he stamped the act of consent which makes it possible for the economic sphere to attain its highest stage of development as subservient to the pursuit of an irrational desire; it allows covetousness to thrive and the intrinsic value of things to change. Contrariwise, the consent on which political society rests serves to overcome the irrational desires manifest in the asocial inclinations of men. Unequal capacities cause and justify the modification in all social relations of the moral imperative of natural

[87] G. W. F. Hegel, *Grundlinien der Philosophie des Rechts* (ed. by Hoffmeister, 4th ed. Hamburg, 1955), esp. Sec. 258.

equality. But when far-going economic differentiation comes to prevail, political organization ensures a greater measure of equality in political than in property relations. Alongside equal political obligations and duties, the political effects of economic inequality are limited through the right of a considerable segment of the citizens to elect their representatives and to do so as political – but not economic – equals. In addition, the right of the majority of all citizens to give effect to their dissent through revolt, represents an unqualified concession to political equality. It follows, then, that in the light of the postulate of natural equality, the economic sphere occupies a moral status inferior to that of the political sphere. Such forms of political action are justified by Locke as render it feasible to impose on property relations that measure of equity and justice which can be attained in the sphere of political relations.

If we agree that Locke's government has the power to go beyond holding the ring, we cannot infer that he actually did not mean it to do so.[88] The inference is the less acceptable if it is agreed that abstention from direct interference is assured not by any physical limitation but by the 'trust' between governors and governed. The maintenance of the 'trust' on which non-interference depends is manifested by the abstention of the majority from resorting to the right of resistance. Locke neither assumed that such abstention would prevail without any attempt of the government at alleviating gross social distress, nor did he contradict himself on the prescriptive plane by refusing wage-earners the right of revolt.

b. *Purposes of Governmental Interference*

As an economist and political theorist Locke acknowledged the predominance of the more propertied classes and saw the clash of interests between them as the central phenomenon in the economic field. The cleavage of wealth in general, and the shortage of money in particular, result in tensions between the 'landed man, the merchant and the monied man'.[89] Normally, the contest does not extend further.

[88] As Parry, *loc. cit.*, 175, maintains.

[89] *Some Considerations of the Consequences of the Lowering of Interest and Raising the Value of Money. In a letter sent to a Member of Parliament, 1691* (sec. ed., London, 1696), 115, 116. The addressee was Sir John Somers, the chief figure in the government that carried out the famous – or by now infamous – deflation recommended by Locke. Cp. Laslett, 'The Great Recoinage,' 378, 384, 387, 391, who points out that the formation of Locke's economic views can be traced as far back as 1668. (*Ibid.*, note 21 to 379.)

172

'The labourer's share, being seldom more than a bare subsistence never allows that body of men time and opportunity to raise their thoughts above that, or struggle with the richer for theirs (as one common interest).' This holds true 'unless . . . some common and great distress uniting them into one universal ferment, makes them forget respect and emboldens them to carve for their wants with armed force: And then sometimes they break in upon the rich, and sweep all like a deluge. But this scarcely happens but in the mal-administration of neglected or mismanaged government.'

Locke probably meant among other things that a government which fails to keep the labourers down is no good. But he accepted at the same time the excessive economic distress of the labourers as a cause of revolt and did not condemn as illicit the labourers rising in arms and provoking a cataclysm. That the labourers are apt to forget respect is stated as an empirical fact, and not as something improper which the labourers ought never to allow themselves.[90] Locke did not even say[91] that a workers' revolt is illicit because by themselves the workers do not amount to a majority of the people and hence have no right to revolt except if supported by others.

Locke blamed a workers' revolt upon 'the mal-administration of neglected or mismanaged government'. This is to make government responsible for not having prevented the 'common and great distress' which causes the workers to rise in arms. Locke attacked not government interference in itself but only ill-advised interference such as the fixing of rates of interest. His primary worry is the inept meddling with private interests He censured 'the foolishness of making a law, which cannot produce the effect it is made for'.[92] Legislation on economic issues has the purpose of encouraging the flow of money 'into the current trade, for the improvement of the general stock and wealth of the nation'.[93] This requires not only legislation that removes encumbrances to all private initiative but it requires also limiting some for the benefit of others. To

---

[90] Macpherson, *op. cit.*, 224, turns Locke's statement of fact into a prescriptive statement in order to claim that he denied labourers the right of revolt. This part of Macpherson's attempt to show that Locke denied labourers membership in political society is as ill-founded as his reliance for the same purpose on the evidence in the *Reasonableness of Christianity* (see above, 55) and on the *Treatise* with regard to incorporation (see below, 290 f.).

[91] As Larkin, *op. cit.*, 37, and Polin ,*op. cit.*, 230, seem to maintain.

[92] *Some Considerations*, 164.

[93] *Ibid.*, 101.

encourage the free flow of capital, governments must discourage the concentration of capital. Credit may need regulation 'when a kind of monopoly, by consent, has put this general commodity [money] into a few hands'.[94] Non-political consent thus remains subject to political consent. Moreover, we must not forget Locke's critical attitude in the *Treatise*, towards the emergence of very large landed possessions (Harrington's influence?[95]), nor that land, like money, is regarded by him as a commodity in *Some Considerations*.[96] The government's duty to take steps against a monopolistic concentration of commodities could thus easily have been extended by him to land (in anticipation of the stand of classical economics on rent). In *Some Considerations*, as in the *Treatises*, the guiding principle to which consent in any sphere remains subjected is that 'private interests ought not . . . to be neglected, nor sacrificed for anything but the manifest advantage of the public'.[97]

The prevention of too great a concentration of capital for the sake of public interest is part of Locke's admixture of mercantilist and *laissez-faire* policies, and is not meant to identify the manifest advantage of the public with easing the situation of wage-earners. 'The labourers, living generally from hand to mouth, may well carry on their part if they have but money to buy victuals, clothes and tools.'[98] His view of unredeemable poverty is similarly uncharitable. The problem of pauperism consists in getting the poor to work, rather than in getting work for them.[99] While the assumption of scarcity was characteristic of classical economics, and determined the negative attitude towards an amelioration of subsistence wages,[100] we may nevertheless attribute to Locke the intention that government ought to prevent excessive distress and exploitation for reasons of charity and justice. We need not content ourselves with inferring the intention from his affirmation of government interference for the public good. Locke, who believed that 'the great design of God,

[94] *Ibid.*, 103.
[95] On the use of Harrington's ideas at that time – also by Shaftesbury – and on the Neo-Harringtonians in general, see J. G. A. Pocock, 'Machiavelli, Harrington, and English Political Ideologies in the Eighteenth Century,' *William and Mary Quarterly*, Vol. XXII, No. 4 (October 1965), esp. 558 f.
[96] *Some Considerations*, 37.
[97] *Ibid.*, 13.
[98] *Ibid.*, 34.
[99] Cp. Larkin, *op. cit.*, 72, who refers to *Atlantis* and the *Report of the Board of Trade to the Lords Justices* (1697).
[100] Cp. J. K. Galbraith, *The Affluent Society* (Penguin Books, 1962), Ch. 3, and Wolin, *op. cit.*, 319.

increase and multiply' (I, 41) is thwarted mainly by absolute monarchy, enunciated also principles on which a welfare policy might be grounded. 'Common *charity* teaches, that those should be most taken care of *by the law* who are least capable of taking care of themselves.'[101] A distinction between charity and justice, according to which only the principles of justice provide guidance for legislation, is thus not maintained by Locke.[102] Charity is not distinguished from but coordinated with justice. 'Justice gives *every man a title* to the product of his *honest* industry . . .' but

'God the Lord and father of all, has given no one of his children such a property, in his peculiar portion of the things of this world, but that he has given his needy brother *a right* to the surplusage of his goods; . . . so charity gives *every man a title* to so much out of another's plenty, as will keep him from extreme want . . .' (I, 42).

Ownership entails duties and responsibilities[103] and law is not prevented from implementing the rules of charity.

Furthermore, justice imposes limitations upon the political utilization of economic want. Locke was apprehensive of the compulsion which might arise out of property relations. On the level of principle, he disqualified property as a means of extorting political obedience quietly from men.[104]

'A man can no more justly make use of another's necessity, to force him to become his vassal, by withholding that relief, God requires him to afford to the wants of his brother, than he that has more strength can seize upon a weaker, master him to his obedience, and with a dagger at his throat offer him death or slavery.'[105]

The ruthless exploitation of power acquired by one's industry – 'so perverse an use of God's blessings' (I, 43) – provides no more grounds for political obligation than does the direct use of physical force and the denial of any assistance to another without which he would perish. For 'anything by this rule that may be an occasion of

---

[101] *Some Considerations*, 13.
[102] The contrary is asserted by Polin, *op. cit.*, 271–3, and Parry, *loc. cit.*, 175. Polin recognizes the importance of the point when he argues that if only justice but not charity can be implemented by law the redistribution of property is the more easily evaded.
[103] Larkin, *op. cit.*, 19, ascribes the opposite to Locke.
[104] Wolin, *op. cit.*, 301, 312, maintains the contrary.
[105] I, 42. Cp. II, Sec. 202.

working upon another's necessity, to save his life, or anything dear to him, at the rate of his freedom, may be made a foundation of sovereignty, as well as property'. Sovereignty and property are not to be founded on extortion nor does the right of private property carry with it the foundation of public authority. '. . . how will it appear, that property in land gives a man power over the life of another' (I, 41)? Even if God had granted Adam private dominion of the whole earth, Locke argued against Filmer, this would not have given him a title to sovereignty. To derive political from economic power is thus to violate the nature of political power. Neglecting the needy to the point of endangering his life, or 'anything dear to him', is no proper foundation either of property relations among free men or of sovereignty over them. Assistance can be, and to a minimal extent must be, guaranteed. For charity can be administered by law, and private interests may be sacrificed to public advantages by political authority alone.

c. *Assurances of Governmental Limitation of Distress*

'To have one rule for rich and poor, for the favourite at court, and the country man at plough' (Sec. 142) does, of course, not imply laws of economic equality. But Locke never said, as Hegel did, that growing socio-economic polarization is the necessary and unchangeable correlate of the modern state, and that in the process the rich must grow richer and the poor poorer.[106] In Locke's system the economically successful have more political rights than the unsuccessful. Such a situation does not preclude successful pressure of the underprivileged for political action in their favour; nor is the political prevalence of the propertied irreconcilable with initiative on their part for the alleviation of excessive distress. Both possibilities can be derived from Locke's views.

His moral downgrading of the rationality exercised in the excessive accumulation of property,[107] does not leave the underprivileged with a higher rationality in either the moral or expedient sense. Those who are able to gratify the desire to have more than is needed for subsistence might be considered superior, in terms of both efficient and moral rationality, to those who want more than

---

[106] Hegel, *Phil. of Right*, Secs. 243-5, and *Die Vernunft in der Geschichte* (ed. Hoffmeister, 5th ed., Hamburg, 1955), 207. Colonization was for Hegel (*Phil. of Right*, Secs. 246-8), as it apparently was for Locke, a means to relieve some poverty.

[107] See above, 158.

they need for mere subsistence but are neither rational nor industrious enough to get it. No doubt, the idea may be attributed to Locke that those who fail to make the best of their reasoning capacity are maiming their liberty and hence exposing themselves to moral censure.[108] They might also be accused of lack of consideration for others. For, according to Locke, the individual who accumulates more than others by honest industry does not cause want to others but increases the general level of subsistence.[109] To the extent that the resolving of moral issues is primarily a matter of rationality, the presence of efficient rationality facilitates the chances for conceiving correct and feasible solutions. Locke not only believed that as *homo economicus* the more talented individual benefits others, even if not moved directly by consideration for them. Apparently, he also believed that as *homo politicus*, the more talented man is capable of sitting in judgement over the *homo economicus* in himself and others. The distinguishing mark of leaders is their preference for the public over the private interest.[110]

As we have seen, Locke was aware of the tensions between the 'landed man, the merchant and the monied man', and objected to the concentration of capital in too few hands. We cannot, therefore, attribute to him as a 'hidden assumption' the Marxist oversimplification that the consent of the propertied to state regulations is unanimous, and constitutes a fool-proof means of assuring the right of unlimited accumulation.[111] When Locke strongly advised vesting the legislative in 'collective bodies of men' (Sec. 94), he accepted the grading of suffrage according to income as a matter of course, and put his trust in the public-spirited among the more prosperous. But he was alive to the danger of their voice being drowned in the contest of interests, as in the case of electoral reform.[112] He quite clearly assumed that the variety of interests and the varying degrees of public-mindedness among the propertied would turn the political process into a contest between minorities, each soliciting popular support, particularly in a revolutionary situation.[113] The conflict of interests among the propertied alone makes recourse to principles

[108] Cp. Parry, *loc. cit.*, 166.
[109] See above, 152.
[110] This is already emphasized in the early *Essays*, 206–7, 208–9, and underlies the judgement of objectionable rulers throughout the *Treatises*.
[111] Macpherson, *op. cit.*, 300.
[112] See below, 344 f.
[113] See below, 308 f.

of general interest mandatory, if anarchy is to be avoided. He required that economic policy be above the intrigues and private designs of merchants and proceed 'upon invariable reason to the general good and concern of the nation'.[114] Locke was convinced of the integrity of the intellectual, as he was suspicious of the London capitalists who floated the Bank of England, and as he was contemptuous of the squires' dabbling in economic policy.[115] But though he affirmed in principle the advancement of charity by law, he apparently did not think of legislative measures for bettering the wage-earners' lot directly. The recoinage he inspired was a forced deflation mostly paid for by the poorer people. Yet it is also characteristic of the climate of opinion prevailing among the intellectuals who served as government consultants, that Newton, with whom Locke collaborated, suggested a price-control authority.[116] In this, as in the suggestion that the monopolistic concentration of capital must be hindered by legislation, the intention obviously was to arrest the rise of prices, and thus benefit also wage-earners indirectly.

Finally there is Locke's evaluation of the political rights and influence exercised by the masses. Government must prevent the labouring masses from being driven to despair lest they forget their customary respect and revolt. In granting them this right, Locke acknowledged their ability to discern between public-minded and self-interested leaders.[117] Aware of human shortcomings in general and those of the broad masses in particular, he conceded in the *Treatise* that not every uprising which commands popular support is, for that reason alone, justified. But what makes a revolution illegitimate is not the socio-economic composition of the rebels, or the possible economic ground of their motives. Locke merely agreed that the supporters of a revolution may be misled in their judgement of the nature and intent of the government's actions.[118]

The role of elected legislators, the representatives of the propertied minorities who are always exposed to popular pressure, is directly related by Locke to matters concerning property. The

[114] This passage is taken from a paper of the year 1670 preserved by Shaftesbury. Though not written in Locke's hand, it may well be taken to express Locke's views, as Laslett, 'The Great Recoinage,' 377–8, from whom I have taken the quotation, points out. The view expressed in the paper is identical with that quoted from *Some Considerations*, above, 174, note 97.

[115] Cp. Laslett, *ibid.*, 395, note 64.

[116] For both facts see Laslett, 'The Great Recoinage,' 378, 392.

[117] See above, 54–6.

[118] See below, 310.

rulers 'must not raise taxes on the property of the people, without the consent of the people, given by themselves, or their deputies' (Sec. 142). The way is opened up for the indirect redistribution of property in the legislative struggle between the deputies and the executive and under the pressure of the popular forces. To make a last comparison between a fundamentally conservative, though modern, conception and a liberal one: In Hegel's scheme the growth of socio-economic polarization in 'civic society' accompanies the self-realization of the 'spirit' in the modern state. The process is in no way linked with the executive's becoming subject to effective control and to the formal obligation, not merely of soliciting the advice of an elected body, but of sharing with it legislative power. According to Locke, the increase of economic inequality is paralleled by the development of representative institutions which make governors effectively responsible to the governed. The Lockeian subordination of the sphere of economics, in which inequality abounds, to the sphere of politics, in which equality is more apparent than in property relations, invites the restriction of ruthless class discrimination. This restriction is possible under absolute princes only if they are 'so wise and godlike as by established laws of liberty to secure protection and encouragement to the *honest* industry of mankind against the oppression of power and narrowness of party . . .' (Sec. 42). It is no less possible to moderate excessive acquisitiveness through the competitive and mutually checking interplay between King, Lords and Commons, each representing different economic interests, and between these agencies and the people *en masse* who, by revolt, can establish a government, or a regime, that shows some consideration for their material needs.

It is evident that Locke was far from envisaging the kind of welfare policy which his principles of judgement and of action permitted. But it is likewise plain that his views on the relationship between economics and politics cannot be interpreted in the terms of pure *laissez-faire* liberalism. And yet it was Locke who freed the incipient liberal theory of property from fundamental contradictions. Having insisted that one ought not to subsume under natural equality 'all sorts of equality' (Sec. 54), he avoided the widely accepted assumption of an original propertyless order.

CHAPTER VI

THE ORIGINAL OF PROPERTY

IT has been usually taken for granted that Locke retained the traditional idea of an originally existing community of all things. No notice has been taken that it might have been contradictory to assume on the one hand that men share all things in common and on the other that individual appropriation is the necessary condition of using anything. Consequently Locke is believed to have considered labour as the final stage in the establishment of private property and also as the necessary condition for appropriating anything at all.[1] Only his rejection of the correlate of the original community of things, that is to say, of consent as the foundation of private property, has created any difficulty about Locke's argument.[2] Inconclusiveness as to his position on this point stems partly from the fact that he did not comment directly on the ideas of his predecessors about the community of all things but there also exists no adequate account of the difficulties in which the proponents of that idea had become entangled. To see that Locke wished to evade these difficulties, we must, therefore, first clarify what is involved in his predecessors' determination to base private ownership on consent. True, his theory of the foundation of property is an essential part of Locke's polemic against Filmer. But like other parts of his theory it also involves taking issue with the views of thinkers whom he did not mention by name, in this particular case, Grotius and Pufendorf. Nor did Locke care to acknowledge how much his putting a distance between himself and the major seventeenth-century proponents of the idea of an original *communio rerum* owed to Filmer's criticism of the idea.

I. THE PRIMEVAL COMMUNITY OF THINGS – GROTIUS AND PUFENDORF

A. Positive and Negative Community

Precursors of liberalism like Grotius and Pufendorf considered

---

[1] Polin, *op. cit.*, 265, and Gough, *op. cit.*, 75, respectively.
[2] Cp. Kendall, *op. cit.*, 70 f.; Macpherson, *op. cit.*, 202; and Laslett, *op. cit.*, 100.

untrammelled original liberty and the absence of private property as two sides of the same coin. In the continual discussion of the inviolability of property rights, ideologists and theorists more often than not sought to support their case by stipulations about the primeval – that is to say, the natural – order of human relations. This tendency did not always make for consistency, particularly as for a long time views about the original order, the one closest to perfection, had been made mandatory by Christian tradition. Representative seventeenth-century natural law theories reflect differences insofar as they derived private ownership from either a positive community of things or a *communio negativa*, exemplified in the common enjoyment of air and sea. It has been concluded that, because negative community signified less a community in ownership than the absence of any ownership, the idea lent itself to two purposes. First, to justify limitations of private property; second, to clearing the way for the natural right theory of property, since the idea of negative community rendered superfluous the recantation by consent of joint or overlapping original property rights.[3] But Grotius derived from originally collective ownership the same limitations of private ownership as Pufendorf did from the absence of any ownership.[4] And, since Pufendorf merely made negative community anterior to positive, private ownership continued to be derived from the latter, and an original order had in any case to be suspended by consent. Moreover, although Locke ostensibly ignored, but implicitly rejected, both points of departure, this did not create any differences between him and Grotius and Pufendorf as to the moral weight and practical scope permitted to the limitations of private property rights. Yet, when Locke broke with the long-established idea of an original community of things, liberalism became not only more consistent, but also not less other-regarding.

According to Grotius, the general right over things of a lower nature forms the basis of the original indivisible possession of all men.[5] Although eventually leading to private acquisition, the right to use what the earth freely produces gives rise in the first place to

---

[3] O. Gierke, *Natural Law and the Theory of Society*, trans. by E. Barker (Boston, Beacon Press), 103; and Schlatter, *op. cit.*, 146, 149.

[4] H. Grotius, *De Jure Belli ac Pacis*, text of 1646 (Washington, 1913), Bk. II, Ch. II, ii, 1–4; S. Pufendorf, *De Jure Naturae et Gentium*, text of 1688 (Oxford, 1934), Bk. VI, Ch. IV, 1–14; Ch. V, 2–10.

[5] *Op. cit.*, II, II, ii, 1.

property owned equally by all users. Such a communal – or, if you will, communist – order is made possible by the simplicity and mutual affection exhibited by the American Indians, the Essenes, the first Christians, and ultimately, the first men. This way of life was abandoned when men turned *ad artes varias, quarum symbolum erat arber scientiae boni et mali.*[6] We need not detain ourselves over the question whether Grotius was justified in lumping together the tribes of the Indians, the Essenes and the early Christians as not yet having tasted the fruits of the tree of knowledge. If knowledge and toil put an end to the community of property, it must have ended with the Fall. Even if, as was usual, Grotius considered Adam and Eve as symbols of the whole human race, and the chapter of communal ownership was thus not confined to a single couple, he regarded it as of fairly short duration. He agreed that the first brothers practised the most ancient arts, agriculture and grazing, along with an exchange of the commodities owned individually by each of them. It follows either that the community of all things did not last beyond the first couple, or that it was compatible with the distinction between 'mine' and 'thine'; and this, as Filmer noticed,[7] contradicts the very nature of a community of things. On these rather shaky grounds, Grotius advanced the idea of an original community of property after the Creation and again after the Deluge, so as to be able to stipulate the transition by universal agreement from common to private ownership.

Pufendorf sought more impregnable grounds. It had already been argued against Grotius that the universal right to gather something for exclusive use takes the place of proprietorship.[8] Pufendorf elaborated that commonly owned things belong to several people in the same manner as privately owned goods belong to one person. In both cases, the right to things appropriated by some people excludes the right of other people to them. Whether they are appropriated individually or in common does not matter.[9] These unexceptional truths are the corollary of the proposition that, because property is created by consent, an entirely propertyless stage has preceded both common and private ownership. This is

[6] *Ibid.*, ii, 2.
[7] Filmer, *Patriarcha*, 264–5, in Sir Robert Filmer, *Patriarcha and Other Political Works*, ed. by P. Laslett (Oxford, 1949).
[8] Boecler, as quoted by Pufendorf, *op. cit.*, IV, IV, 3.
[9] *Ibid.*, 3.

the stage of the negative community of things. It exists, says Pufendorf, 'before any deed of man and the use of anything' have any effect on other persons. Nothing belongs to anybody and everything belongs to everybody, because no object belongs to one person more than to another. As long as the use of things has no effect on other persons,[10] the right to the earth's fruits and creatures is an 'indefinite right'. God did not indicate anything concerning the manner, extent and intensity of exercising this right. He left all this to human determination.[11] As is immediately evident, the 'indefinite right' is definite in that it excludes one way of exercising men's equal right to the earth's fruits and creatures in accord with God's grant: the way by which things belong to one man and not to another. The indefinite right is definite in excluding the manner of selecting nature's products by which one individual has no right to what another has already selected; it is indefinite insofar as the ways of mutually exclusive appropriation of things are left to future determination by universal agreement.

A situation in which nothing is 'held to belong to this man rather than to another'[12] might, under one of two conditions, be regarded as preceding the universal consent to the individual appropriation of nature's products. Either 'negative community' excludes any permanent inter-family contact or it must be assumed that moral pre-dispositions of the highest order had obtained during the time when the selection of the earth's fruits and creatures did not exclude the claim of one man to what another had already selected. As Filmer said, Grotius 'takes the appetite of society and community [of goods] to be all one'.[13] Pufendorf did not confuse the two, and by logical implication at least restricted his negative community to the relation between persons and objects. Indeed, the practical examples he offered for showing that the indefinite right to things can operate effectively, actually bring home that the unadulterated negative community of goods is incompatible with any community life.[14]

---

[10] *Ibid.*, 1, 14.
[11] *Ibid.*, 4, 9.
[12] *Ibid.*, 2.
[13] *Patriarcha*, 264.
[14] This is the inference which Rousseau drew from Pufendorf's premises for his conception of the state of nature in *Quelle est l'Origine de l'Inégalité parmi les Hommes et si elle est autorisée par la Loi naturelle?*

B. Conditions for Negative Community

The first example, solitary Adam,[15] is as apposite as it is self-defeating. The use of things by Adam alone can neither affect others nor exclude the use of the same things by others, because there are no others. There remains the negative community of goods between Adam and Eve. To demonstrate the viability of the indefinite right to all things in the life of the first couple, Pufendorf further defined it as the right to apply things to reasonable and necessary uses.[16] Admittedly, reasonableness and necessity are limitations of usage which may also be considered incumbent upon a man who leads a solitary existence. But where any kind of social existence is concerned, reasonableness and necessity must also be predicated on the effect which the acts of one human being have on another. Pufendorf's own account of the first family requires this conclusion, and offends, therefore, against the term of definition of 'negative community'. The first couple is assisted by its children in the gathering of fruits. But the children are apt to misbehave by treating themselves excessively to what was intended to be their contribution to the subsistence of the whole family. Yet, Pufendorf explains, since neither dominion nor property – the two being co-existent, if not identical – characterizes the first family relationship, the children's misbehaviour is not a sin against the principle of property, but a transgression of paternal authority.[17] Hence, so long as Adam's children were minors and until they set up households of their own, 'Adam's needs were met by primitive community and neither Adam nor his sons had private dominion'.

Strictly speaking, 'primitive community' is inconsistent with Pufendorf's definition of negative community. Let us grant that the first couple's union was something out of the ordinary and that the perfect consonance of their wills prevented any question whether a thing selected belonged to the one or the other, and that in their use of things their actions did not affect each other because they acted in complete harmony. To speak of a sin against paternal authority committed by Adam's children during the harvest means, however, to acknowledge that their gathering of goods does have an adverse effect on the others with whom they live. Whether or not paternal authority can be otherwise detached from property,

---

[15] Pufendorf, op. cit., IV, IV, 3.
[16] Ibid., 6, 10.
[17] Ibid., 12.

Adam's authority over his children includes the right to determine their share of the goods gathered by the whole family. It follows that fully negative community is possible only as long as the first couple is childless; the moment the children take part in gathering there must be regulation. If the nonage of children justifies the fatherly imposition of considerations of reasonableness and necessity, it does not follow that these criteria are immaterial for adults; rather, they would be the standard by which adults must agree to abide, lest one person's gathering should impair that of others. The addition of the criteria of reasonableness and necessity to the definition of the indefinite right to all things cancels its indefiniteness and restricts negative community either to solitary existence or predicates co-existence on ideal human beings.

Pufendorf admitted that moral deterioration rendered negative community untenable. But he failed to demonstrate in the first place that a number of ordinary adults can co-exist without rules of distribution. He succeeded in proving that tenability preceded untenability only by the assumption of an ideal harmony of will between Adam and Eve and by implying that the exercise of fatherly authority over children does not constitute distinctions between 'mine' and 'thine'. Even supposing that negative community so conceived applies to ordinary families as well, it still wants demonstration that negative community is practicable between different households. Pufendorf attempts to prove this by showing the co-existence of negative community and property. But he shows us not multi-family groups which practise either the one or the other but only such groups as practise both simultaneously.

First of all, the concluding of pacts which put an end to negative community turns out to be a prerequisite for human existence and not a stage of it. The primary group is the family, and marriage is concluded by a pact.[18] Even if no more than monogamy is settled by the pact, it determines what belongs to some to the exclusion of others. Secondly, the establishment of families, with the exception of the first one, is viewed by Pufendorf in the context of relations among a plurality of families to whom things belong exclusively. Concerning property in particular, 'although the pacts of two or a few men, which bear on a thing open to all, work no prejudice to the rest, but leave them their original right unimpaired; yet if they all should enter a common pact, whether express or tacit, we

18 *Ibid.*, 11.

should not hesitate to say that a true property in things is included.'[19] Pufendorf would not have granted that a few men may institute property without prejudicing negative community, if he had not thought that property and negative community actually co-exist among people who are socially related to each other. It was, however, not reasonable to assume that the majority will be unconcerned by the attempt of a few men to create a definite right over the fruits of the earth – unless the majority are so primitive as to feel no urge to imitate the few, or so high-minded as to refrain from applying the rules of negative community to what the few declare as their exclusive property. Pufendorf's empirical demonstration of the co-existence of negative community and property rests on neither of these assumptions. It comes down to an acknowledgement of the co-existence of an indefinite right of all to things which can be used without excluding their simultaneous use by others, and a definite right of everybody to things which exclude the right of any other person to them.

There are claims of different parties to individually owned property. The state, the owner and the tenant have different rights to the same piece of land.[20] Things may also be owned in their entirety by several persons while others are denied a share in them. What represents a real instance of negative community are the things left for further use.[21] Actual use goes with negative community where it applies to air, light and the oceans; it was Pufendorf's major concern to show that these are and ought to be left in negative community, partly or wholly, temporarily or permanently.[22] None of this adds up to men living in pure negative community. Since Pufendorf acknowledged that normal family life is founded on a pact that settles matters of 'mine' and 'thine' to the exclusion of others, it is indeed not surprising to find him finally meeting the objections to the possibility of negative community by referring to peoples 'who are *little removed from* primitive community'.[23] He did not, because he clearly could not, point to groups which are not at all removed from it. 'Limited community' means that 'the bodies of things belong to no one, but the fruits after gathering are proper',

---

[19] *Op. cit.*, VIII, V, 2.
[20] *Op. cit.*, IV, IV, 2.
[21] *Ibid.*, 6.
[22] *Op. cit.*, IV, V, 2, 5–10.
[23] *Ibid.*, 13.

and this is 'the tempering of primitive community by proprietorship'. The indefinite right applies to the bodies of things which are of no direct importance to man in the stage of gathering, and the definite right to the directly consumable fruits. Grotius identified this situation with the original positive community of things. Locke also saw in this the primeval order of things, but associated it with individual appropriation and ownership.

Having attempted to show up the shortcomings of the notion of the negative community of things, which calls to mind the metaphysical play with being and non-being, we are now in a position to demonstrate how at its decisive junctures Locke's argument overcomes the assumption of either a positive or a negative community of things so as to perfect the defence of both private property and the principle of consent.

2. THE PRIMACY OF PRIVATE PROPERTY: THE RATIONAL ARGUMENT

Pufendorf anticipated Locke in conceding that the fruits of the earth are of no use if they cannot be appropriated; that is, if others can take what by our own act we have already selected.[24] He also agreed with Hobbes and other authorities that 'mine' and 'thine' does not cause war, but prevents it.[25] He sided with Aristotle against Plato and scoffed at the utopian views of More and Campanella.[26] Both Grotius and Pufendorf agreed that even the first convention, establishing the right of mutually exclusive appropriation of the fruits of the earth, was merely the ratification of previously established practice.[27] Yet to show that any property right – whether collective or individual – derives from agreement, they thought it necessary to suppose an initial propertyless stage. They also thought the derivation of property from consent to be the indispensable concomitant of basing government on consent. Forewarned by Filmer's criticism of the idea of the original community of things, Locke put property from the outset on an individual basis and at the same time went beyond Grotius' and Pufendorf's notion of government by consent.

[24] *Op. cit.*, IV, IV, 5.
[25] *Ibid.*, 6.
[26] *Ibid.*, 7 8.
[27] Pufendorf, *op. cit.*, IV, IV, 6, and Grotius, *op. cit.*, II, II, 5.

A. The Universal Common for Private Appropriation
a. God's Gifts and Men's Claims

Locke clearly joined battle on two fronts. He did not content himself with showing

'that if it be difficult to make out property, upon a supposition, that God gave the world to Adam and his posterity *in common*; it is impossible that any man, but one universal monarch, should have any property, upon a supposition, that God gave the world to Adam, and his heirs *in succession*, exclusive of all the rest of his posterity' (Sec. 25).

In other words, the first supposition underlying the theories of Grotius and Pufendorf, which poses for 'some a very great difficulty' does not cease to be wrong because the opposite supposition, i.e. Filmer's, is likewise wrong. Locke, therefore, set out to show 'how men might come to have a property in several parts of that which God gave to mankind in common, and that *without any express compact of all the commoners*'. This is the challenge which goes right to the heart of the theories of Grotius and Pufendorf. It underlies his thematic discussion of property in the *Second Treatise*, the argument against Filmer being developed in the *First Treatise*.

Locke accepted it as 'very clear, that God, as King David says, Psalm CXV. xvi. has given the earth to the children of men, given it to mankind *in common*' (Sec. 25). He used this traditional idea as an argument against Filmer, and with its help refuted the consequences previously drawn from it.[28] But he did so to justify immediate individualistic appropriation and to reject the idea that private property originated in consent and derived from collective ownership. Neither a collectivity nor ownership involving appropriation – and hence no property in the sense in which Locke used the word – is meant when he speaks of the earth as universally common to mankind. 'Mankind' denotes the sum of all individuals. Speaking first of '*men*' who 'have a right to their preservation' (Sec. 25), then going on to quote 'children of men' from the Psalms and finally referring to 'mankind', Locke did not pass surreptitiously and illogically from men as individuals to men as a collectivity.[29] 'Mankind' is used synonymously with 'men' and 'the children of men', as is made plain in his polemic against Filmer on the inter-

[28] Cp. Polin, *op. cit.*, 257, and Macpherson, *op. cit.*, 200, respectively.
[29] Laslett, *op. cit.*, 100, 303, following Kendall, *op. cit.*, 77, note 18.

pretation of the Scriptures. He explicitly defined there the species of men as all men taken individually.[30] In his demonstration of the foundation of property rights, as in any other context, Locke conceived of a community as an aggregate of individuals from whose personal rights the rights of any group emanate.

The supra-human foundation of property contains two propositions, which coalesce in establishing the right of individual acquisition. 'God . . . has given the world to *men* in common . . .' (Sec. 26). According to this proposition, 'nobody has originally a private dominion, *exclusive of the rest of mankind*'. No collective ownership by a world community but the potential ownership of everybody is stipulated over and against Filmer's claim of the proprietorship of Adam and his heirs to the exclusion of all other men. The second proposition makes it clear that 'the earth, and all that is therein' is conferred upon all men in common as the matrix of property, the substance from which each and everyone may and must appropriate for himself. God 'has also given them [men] reason to make use of it [the world] to the best advantage of life, and convenience'. God has bestowed two simultaneous gifts upon men to enable them to subsist: By God's will, nature produces goods for the use of all men; and all men are fitted with the rationality to make use of these goods. To use them is to appropriate them individually. For

'though all the fruits it [the earth] naturally produces, and the beasts it feeds, belong to mankind in common, as they are produced by the spontaneous hand of nature; . . . yet being given for the use of men, there must of necessity be a means to *appropriate them* some way or other *before they can be of any use, or at all beneficial to any particular man.*'

The means, as we know, is labour. Through labour subsistence is finally assured, because labour makes possible the private appropriation of nature's products. Survival is impossible without individual appropriation. 'The fruit, or venison, which nourishes the wild Indian, . . . must be his, and so his, i.e. a part of him, that another can no longer have any right to it, before it can do him any good for the support of his life.' The characteristic of 'negative community', the right to things already taken by others, is rejected by Locke as contrary to all logic. No state of universal propertylessness

[30] I, 23–30. See below, 204.

or the right to a share in the ownership of everything – positive community – are involved when all have an equal right to everything nature provides.[31]

Without using the term, Locke implied 'negative community' in its sole proper sense. For he considered as universally common what is indeed only negatively so, that is, either that which is not given to full appropriation – 'the Ocean, that great and still remaining common of mankind' (Sec. 30) – or that which is as yet not appropriated at all because as yet it is not used. If the wild Indian 'knows no enclosure, and is still a tenant in common' (Sec. 26), it is because his economic activity in the stage of gathering and hunting does not encompass the soil itself. He is a tenant in common in respect of the substance which he does not use directly, and, not using it directly, the question of the ownership of land does not arise. A distinction in this sense between property and commons seems also implied when Filmer says that the blessing of Noah accords him 'liberty to use the living creatures for food. Here is no alteration or diminishing of his title to a propriety of all things, but an enlargement only of his commons.'[32]

b. *Usage Requires Individual Appropriation*

The affirmation that 'nobody has originally a private dominion, *exclusive of the rest of mankind*, in any of them [the fruits], as they are thus in their natural state' (Sec. 26), means that the goods which nature spontaneously produces remain in common so long as they remain unused, and that nobody has a right to appropriate from them which is not shared by another. 'Every man had a right to the creatures, by the same title Adam had, viz. by the right every one had to take care of, and provide for their subsistence: and thus men had *a right in common*, *Adam's children in common with him.*'[33] To

---

[31] Goldwin, *op. cit.*, 443, asserts that if any man has the right to appropriate any part of what is common without the consent of the others, nobody can have property, since it is in the nature of property that it cannot be taken from a man without his consent. Goldwin thus infers propertylessness from Locke's justification of private acquisition! The right of making property which is independent of consent, because exercised over things not as yet appropriated, is turned into its opposite on the ground that, according to Locke, only consent confers the right of impinging upon property already made.

[32] *Patriarcha*, 64.

[33] I, 87. Marx followed Locke in appraising the individual right over the creatures as private property rights. He quoted Thomas Münzer to this effect in 'Zur Judenfrage,' *Der historische Materialismus*, I, 260. In his *Critique of the Gotha Programme, op. cit.*

deny Filmer's claim of the exclusiveness of Adam's title, Locke accepted that God had given the earth to men in common. Yet instead of an original community of things, which he rejected with Filmer, he stipulated that men have a common right which they must exercise if they are to subsist – the right to render private what is common.

According to Grotius, too, a man cannot take away from what another takes for his own needs, without committing an unjust act. But, as his quotation from Cicero demonstrates, Grotius believed that no more is at stake here than the right to the seat which one has taken in a public theatre.[34] Pufendorf likewise thought that the example of the theatre, like that of the Essenes and early Christians, related to commonly held property and therefore not to negative community.[35] God's conferment of the right to use the products of the earth is 'indifferent to positive community and property'.[36] Locke, unlike Tyrrell, did not avail himself of the Stoic axiom about seats in the theatre,[37] undoubtedly because it did not provide an illustration of his view that usage inevitably entails permanent individual appropriation.

Clearly aiming at Grotius' and Pufendorf's interposition of consent between the first gathering and individual ownership, Locke declared that, 'if the first gathering made them [nature's fruits] not his, nothing else could' (Sec. 28). To require 'the consent of all mankind to make them his' is out of the question. 'If such a consent as that was necessary, man had starved, notwithstanding the plenty God had given him.' He was not inconsistent when he explained the introduction of money as founded upon universal consent. Since man's subsistence does not depend on money, agreement to its introduction may be deferred. Without the exercise of the right of private appropriation through labour, subsistence is impossible. The exercise of the right cannot therefore wait for agreement, and hence cannot be contingent upon it. Whatsoever is by a man 'removed from the common state nature placed it in, it has by

555–6, Marx declared likewise that 'nature is just as much the source of use values . . . as labour', and that these are 'bourgeois phrases' according to which man has behaved from the outset 'as her owner'.

[34] *Op. cit.*, Bk. II, Ch. II, ii, 2.
[35] *Op. cit.*, Bk. IV, Ch. IV, 9.
[36] *Ibid.*, 11. See also 4.
[37] Tyrrell apparently followed Locke's line of argument without fully realizing all its implications. Cp. Laslett, *op. cit.*, 305, both on this and the vague theories of Baxter, and still vaguer hints at the labour theory in Petty and Hobbes.

this labour something annexed to it, that excludes the common right of other men' (Sec. 27). A transaction is involved, inasmuch as to call something my own, I have to give something. I do so by performing a certain action. Through the labour of gathering, not through that of boiling, eating and digesting nature's products, men 'added something to them more than nature, the common mother of all, had done; and so they became his private right' (Sec. 28). Strictly speaking, men do not add anything to the fruits by gathering them, but they add something by boiling, eating and digesting food to disintegrate it. Locke applied summarily to gathering what holds good for mixing labour with the soil. Although in the first stage, labour performs no more than the taking possession of something,[38] he appears to have taken it for granted, rather than having overlooked that in any case an act of will is involved,[39] to say nothing of man's awareness of and reaction to natural processes alongside the selective use of the means for taking possession.[40] Gathering, however, also adds something in that labour establishes the relationship between subject and object, between man and fruit, and thus secures the teleological materialization of nature's potentialities. In conformity with the labour principle, appropriation is individual in the state of gathering but production is not. To put it somewhat paradoxically, production is 'communist' only so long as men have nothing to do with it. There is no property over the means of production so long as men do not use them to produce. The wild Indian is a tenant in common with others because the land has no immediate relevance for his subsistence. The moment a thing is used, property over it begins, because nothing can be used without labour. Private acquisition is coeval with human existence. Even water must be drawn, acorns picked, apples gathered and the deer hunted.[41]

When Locke regarded individual appropriation as the necessary corollary of usage, he did not confuse the fact of acquiring property and the right of doing so.[42] Theories like those of Grotius and

[38] Cp. Polin, *op. cit.*, 262.
[39] This was Kant's objection on which Green elaborated. See M. Richter, *The Politics of Conscience : T. H. Green and His Age* (London, 1964), 277 f.
[40] H. Schmidt, 'Zur Natur der Eigentumsbildung in der Arbeit. John Locke in den Deutungen von Raymond Polin,' *Der Staat*, IV (1965), 74–5, raises these points in free elaborations on a few Lockeian themes sifted exclusively from Polin's book.
[41] Sec. 28.
[42] As Larkin, *op. cit.*, 65, asserts.

Pufendorf were an open invitation to give the labour principle its due both as a fact and a right. They deliberately ignored the factual role of labour to dispute that labour by itself provides the foundation of property. According to Grotius, the community of property depends not only on extreme simplicity; he also stipulated that no toil is involved in collecting what the earth brings forth on its own.[43] His discounting of the toil necessary for gathering is not only senseless but self-negating. Since he is actually assuming that the absence of labour is the condition for the non-existence of private property, he implies that labour – and not consent – is the foundation of private property. It would appear as if Grotius withheld from human effort its place in the collection of the fruits of the earth because he was aware that otherwise he would have had to admit individual appropriation as the basis of positive community. Pufendorf granted that most of the things that man needs require labour and that it is, therefore, improper for one who has contributed no labour to have an equal right with one who has.[44] But he declared that 'it is impossible to conceive how the mere corporal act of one person can prejudice the faculties of others'.[45] What follows is not so much that in an incidental passage Pufendorf came close to the natural right theory of labour,[46] but that Grotius and Pufendorf missed it, or rather evaded it, because they had committed themselves to base property on consent. This is why they presented the special conventions for the distinction between 'mine' and 'thine' as the ratification not of what had prevailed all along, but of the change from either collective to private ownership, or from non-ownership to ownership. In their own argumentation, the pact to this effect is not necessarily antecedent to the existence of private property. On the one hand, Grotius argued that agreement to divide must be supposed to have taken place at a time when no division of common property had yet been made. On the other, he conceded that agreement is revealed either expressly or tacitly in the very fact of division or occupation, and that it no more than confirms that whatever each had already taken possession of should remain his own.[47] Similarly, when Pufendorf included labour as a co-

[43] Op. cit., II, II, ii, 1.
[44] Op. cit., IV, IV, 6.
[45] Op. cit., IV, IV, 5. There is a similar note in Hume's criticism of the labour theory. Cp. A Treatise of Human Nature, Bk. III, part II, sec. III.
[46] Schlatter, op. cit., 149.
[47] Op. cit., II, II, 5.

determinant in the assignment of things to different persons, he actually inferred the pact for the establishment of property from the fact that labour has been employed.

It would have been consistent to reject a 'mere corporal act' as the foundation of property and maintain, as Hume later did, that property rights are a matter of expediency or of convention. But unlike Hume, Pufendorf did not detach property from the supra-conventional justice of natural law. He therefore laid himself open to the query why, according to natural law, it is just that a pact, and unjust that a corporal act, should establish the right of ownership.

B. Private and Collective Ownership

a. The Unity of Natural Law Ethics

Indeed, Locke's argument is formulated in such a way that it seems he wished to put Pufendorf right about the significance of 'the mere corporal act'. He did not rest his case solely on arguing that the requirement of a pact for the establishment of private property is unreasonable. He further explained why a corporal act results in a moral claim. But he did not simply derive a moral rule from the statement of fact that a man's body is part of himself.[48]

'Every man has a property in his own person' (Sec. 27), is no statement of fact but a judgement of value. Man has 'in himself the great foundation of property', because he is *master of himself*, and proprietor of his own person, and the actions of labour of it . . .' (Sec. 44). The right to property is anchored in the moral autonomy which attaches to the phenomenological singularity of each human being. To exist man must labour. In doing so he manifests his autonomy *vis à vis* other men. Social freedom, as Locke seems to imply, is not attainted by the necessity to work for a living. Our own wants and not our fellowmen force us to labour. And since nobody but a man himself has a right to his person, 'the labour of his body, and the work of his hands, we may say, are properly his'. His gatherings belong to him, because 'whatsoever . . . he removes out of the state that nature has provided, and left it in, he has mixed his labour with, and joined to it something that is his own . . .' (Sec. 27). Out of a realistic consideration for the only way in which men can exist, Locke maintained that labour, and not consent,

---

[48] This is maintained by Plamenatz, *op. cit.*, 245, when, in enlarging upon Hume's criticism, he finds Locke's derivation of the right of property 'quaint and obscure'.

establishes the title to invariably private appropriation. A specific response of autonomous agents to the beck and call of necessity establishes a right. The means of assuring physical subsistence accord with the moral principles which alone ensure proper human existence. The mere corporal act of labouring issues in appropriation, because this is expedient and moral. The right to one's life and estate is inseparable from the right to one's liberty.

The right to the fruits of one's exertions which flows from the right to one's personal autonomy is, like any other natural right, directly and expressly supported by natural law. 'This law of reason makes the deer, that Indian's who has killed it; it is allowed to be his goods who has bestowed his labour upon it, though before, it was the common right of every one' (Sec. 30). So far as 'this original law of nature for the beginning of property', sanctions private appropriation to the exclusion of all other forms, it is fully in line with the earlier views of the *Essays* according to which 'the strongest protection of each man's private property is the law of nature'. In the *Treatises*, labour is introduced as the instrument through which men manifest the right to private property; the authority of natural law is specially invoked to legitimate that which men must do in order to subsist.[49]

In teaching that natural law directly and immediately countenances private property, Locke took his stand against Filmer as well as against Pufendorf and Grotius. But he avoided the inconsistencies which Filmer had exposed in Grotius' theory of property. For Grotius as for Pufendorf, natural law does not directly prescribe the necessary privacy of things; on the other hand, it contains unambiguous suggestions for the abandonment of the original lack of property distinctions so as to enable men to lead cultured lives of peace and tranquillity after their numbers have multiplied.[50] Although natural equity is originally incompatible with private property, which is introduced by the will of men alone, private ownership is nevertheless made just by natural law and theft is forbidden.[51] Evidently, the relationship between property and natural law is bound to become complex if on the one side property relations are subjected to that law, but do not, on the other, owe

---

[49] Therefore I cannot see why Laslett, *op. cit.*, 223, invites us not only to compare but also to contrast *Essays*, 206-7, and *Treatises*, I, 86-7, II, 30. For the conformity between the two, see also, *Essays*, 210-1, and *Treatises*, I, 88-92, II, 38.

[50] Pufendorf, *op. cit.*, IV, IV, 14.

[51] Grotius, *op. cit.*, I, I, x, 4.

their existence to it.[52] Pufendorf and, especially, Grotius were aware of some difficulty in their argument. When Grotius made allowances for the cases in which people have a right to things possessed by others,[53] he conceded that such a view might appear strange 'since the right of private ownership seems completely to have absorbed that which has its origin in a state of community of property'. To narrow the disparity, he specified that the original intention in introducing private property had been to depart as little as possible from natural equity. Arrangements made to maintain the right of private ownership, Pufendorf suggested, may be said to belong 'reductively' to the law of nature.[54]

Filmer addressed himself to the contradiction in Grotius between private property and natural law but was wrong in invoking the authority of Thomas Aquinas whose justification of innovations in traditional natural law theories[55] Grotius and Pufendorf quite clearly followed. Filmer held that natural and Divine law do not admit of both private dominion and the community of goods. To try and make them compatible with natural law is to frame new divisions of it. This, as Filmer argued with good logic, means giving different definitions of natural law, making it changeable and self-contradictory.[56] If 'some things are by the law of nature, not *proprie* but *reductive*', if 'some things are by the law of nature, but not immutably', then man is invested with 'a double ability . . .; first to make that no law of nature, which God made to be the law of nature: and next, to make that a law of nature which God made not'.[57] Nothing else can come of saying 'that by the law of nature all things were at first common, and . . . that after propriety was brought in, it was against the law of nature to use community'.[58] When we maintain, like Grotius, that the 'community of all things should be by the law of nature, of which God is the author, and yet such community should not be able to continue', we derogate from the providence of God and make the introduction of private property

---

[52] Cp. L. Krieger, *The Politics of Discretion, Pufendorf and the Acceptance of Natural Law* (Chicago, 1965), 108, who points to the same problem in connection with the institutions of marriage and family.

[53] Grotius, *op. cit.*, II, VI, 1, 4, and Pufendorf, IV, IV, 5 and Ch. V.

[54] *Op. cit.*, II, III, 22.

[55] Cp. *Summa Theologica*, qu. 66, art. 1, and qu. 94, art. 3.

[56] *Patriarcha*, 64, 264–5, 272.

[57] *Ibid.*, 266.

[58] *Ibid.*, 274.

by human law 'a sin of high presumption'; for 'then the moral law depends on the will of men'.[59]

In the present instance, Filmer stood up for the independence of the moral law from consent so as to delete the ideas of consented human law and government from the political vocabulary. He urged that once 'we maintain the natural and private dominion of Adam to be the fountain of all government and propriety', we are rid of the 'divers dangerous and seditious conclusions' which inevitably follow from 'these two propositions of natural community and voluntary propriety'.[60] The conclusion which Filmer wished to avoid above all – and which Locke made the basis of his theory – was the right of resistance to kings, the first instalment of the political rights accorded to the people by virtue of the principle of consent. Filmer was no less correct in exposing Grotius' 'mixed negation, partly negative, partly affirmative' of the right of resistance than in considering it as connected with the idea of natural community. 'Natural community' is the fullest realization of equality, from which the principle of consent emanates. Filmer had therefore good reason to complain about those who accepted 'an error which the heathens taught, that all things at first were common, and that all men were equals', and to warn against 'the desperate inconveniences which attend upon the doctrine of natural freedom and community of all things'.[61]

Locke must have been put well on his guard by Filmer when he set out to carry the 'seditious conclusions' of Grotius further. In deriving private ownership directly from natural law, he left the moral law independent of the will of men. In accordance with Filmer's objection against Grotius' identification of 'the appetite of society and community' (of goods),[62] Locke discarded the latter as the necessary and historically demonstrable corollary of primary socialization. In defending the original right of all men to private ownership against Filmer, and in elevating this right above consent in opposition to Grotius and others, he preserved the status of natural law as independent of consent and saved the inner unity of the new conception of natural law which consecrated individual rights. At the same time he strengthened the case for consent in

[59] *Ibid.*, 65.
[60] *Patriarcha*, 71, 66.
[61] *Ibid.*, 262, 71. Filmer understandably refrained from pointing out that the 'error' had become part of the Christian tradition.
[62] *Ibid.*, 264.

human affairs as the permanent mode of applying natural law. The mode follows as a matter of right from the individuals being possessors of natural rights. Filmer's criticism of Grotius had made it clear that any prevarication about the direct derivation of the right of private property from natural law would have undermined the basis for deducing individual rights from that law. If the self-realization of personality through labour, without which existence is impossible, does not establish an incontestable right, the right of man to be 'master of himself' is open to doubt. As Locke's theory of the foundation of property likewise most emphatically and clearly illustrates, men do not arbitrarily arrogate natural rights to themselves. Those rights are not derived from facts although they tally with them; they are at once independent of consent and tenable only through consent.

b. *Liberalism Divorced from Socialism*

Although Locke enhanced the inner unity of natural law by deriving from it the primacy of private property, he thereby broke with all previous doctrines of natural law. Despite the differences between them, Hobbes, Filmer, Grotius and Pufendorf had all insisted on the derivative character of private property. As far as philosophical and ideological argumentation is concerned, this difference is important as a matter of principle. To be sure, Locke's predecessors were as ill-disposed as he was towards the ideal of a future propertyless society. Yet while otherwise hesitant liberals, like Grotius and Pufendorf, considered the community of things as definitely *dépassé* by men's agreement to private ownership, they also considered that an original propertyless condition reflected justice at its fullest. Yet the second assumption provided a better moral foundation, not so much for the limitation of property as for its re-elimination. Moreover, if private ownership is above all a matter of consent, people can as legitimately replace private by 'communist' ownership as *vice versa*. Filmer had been quick to draw this inference:

'If our first parents, or some other of our forefathers did voluntarily bring in propriety of goods, and subjection to governors, and it were in their power either to bring them in or not, or having brought them in, to alter their minds and restore them to their first condition of community and liberty, what reason can there be alleged that men that now live should not have the same power?'[63]

[63] *Patriarcha*, 273.

Locke derived the right of retracting subjection to governors and altering the form of government from the principle of original liberty. He undoubtedly eschewed the equation of original liberty with an original community of things, because he did not wish to give ground for deducing, together with the right of altering the form of government, a right to alter the form of private ownership. That this was his intention becomes readily obvious, when we consider how easy it would have been for him to reconcile the idea of an all-pervasive system of communal ownership with the primacy of private appropriation. Positive community, Grotius explained, is effected through 'the gathering of the product of the soil into a common store'.[64] A collective organization of storage can be founded on the premise that, since the products are gathered by individual effort, everybody receives from the common store in accordance with the labour he employs for gathering and the maintenance of the store-organization. On such a basis Locke might have adapted the common-store theory to his view of the primary fact and right of private appropriation. He had only to agree with Pufendorf that, like private property, positive community is a form of ownership. Then the collective organization of appropriation and distribution could have been based by him on man's natural right to the fruits of his labour. He could have argued that by consent, not only various forms of government but different forms of the organization of ownership could be established, provided they preserved the fundamental principle of property, which is the right to the product of one's labour. This right would not be affected by the collective organization of gathering and redistribution from a common store, as long as distribution was proportionate to individual effort. Positive community so considered would still have permitted Locke to reject distribution according to need.

On these grounds, it is also possible to grant collective organization beyond the stage of gathering, and, indeed, to allow for a kind of socialism which might be called liberal, inasmuch as it is based on the free consent of the individuals and their right to secure by labour an area of private concerns and individual independence. By Locke's own demonstration, the exclusive right to the fruits of one's labour in the stage of gathering is compatible with the individual non-ownership of land. With the cultivation of the soil, the land might remain under communal ownership, provided that

[64] *Op. cit.*, II, II, ii, 4. See, also, Pufendorf, *op. cit.*, IV, IV, 9.

labour continues to be the measure of rewards. The difference between Locke and Grotius would then have paralleled Marx's distinction between socialism as 'the first phase of communist society' – each according to his effort – and real communism – each according to his need.[65] Not that such a distinction would have greatly mattered to Locke and other seventeenth-century thinkers; nor should we expect him to have hit on the combination of communal and private ownership practiced today in Israel. But we are perhaps entitled to surmise that he realized the possibility of squaring his labour theory with the communal order which Grotius and like-minded theorists relegated to primitive times, and which Winstanley and his Diggers had only recently tried to put into practice. Locke's uncompromising insistence on the primacy of private property and the exclusiveness of individual appropriation seems to stem from the awareness – due to, or reinforced by, Filmer – that, if the establishment of a 'first phase of communist society' has been legitimate in the past, it cannot be stigmatized as illegitimate when suggested for the present and the future. This seems to be the reason why Locke doggedly avoided conceding the rightfulness and feasibility of any kind of all-pervasive communal ownership in any stage of history.[66] He held fast to the view that the same principle pertains to the stages of gathering and producing.

'This law of reason . . . this original law of nature for the beginning of property,' which 'allowed to be his goods who has bestowed his labour upon it' (Sec. 30), as a matter of course, applies to land as well, since 'the earth, and all that is therein, is given to men for the support and comfort of their being' (Sec. 26). 'The chief matter of property' – and increasingly so after plenty had given way to penury –

'being now not the fruits of the earth, and the beasts that subsist on it, but the earth itself; as that which takes in and carries with it all the rest: I think it is plain, that property in that too is acquired as the former . . . He by his labour does, as it were, enclose it from the common' (Sec. 32).

The exclusion of everybody else's title to what is thus enclosed

---

[65] Marx, *Critique of the Gotha Programme, op. cit.*, 565, and Lenin, *The State and Revolution*, Selected Works, Moscow, 1952, vol. II, part I, 294 f.

[66] Macpherson, *op. cit.*, 202, comments on Locke's disregard of communal ownership and labour in primitive societies, but attributes to him an adherence to the idea of the original community of things.

requires as little consent from all mankind as does gathering. The same propositions by which the individual appropriation of the earth's fruits and beasts had been justified serve for the justification of individual acquisition of the chief means of production, that is, land. God gave the world to mankind in common and made man capable of obeying his Divine command and that of man's own reason, to labour and 'subdue the earth, i.e. improve it for the benefit of life, and therein lay out something upon it that was his own, his labour'. Of the cultivation of the soil it could be said with more precision than of the gathering of fruits that man 'thereby annexed to it [the earth] something that was his property . . .' It is made perfectly clear that to be cultivated, the earth must be individually appropriated. 'God gave the world to men in common; but since he gave it them for their benefit, and the greatest conveniences of life . . , it cannot be supposed he meant it should always remain *common and uncultivated*' (Sec. 34).

No doubt, Locke passed from asserting the right of ownership over that with which a man has mixed his labour to the proposition that what a man has *first* mixed his labour with belongs to him to the exclusion of other people who might later mix their labour with it.[67] The transition from one proposition to the other evidently reflects the wish to leave no loophole for communal ownership over cultivated land. To secure the first 'mixers' and their descendants in their possessions, is not, however, to ignore the fate of those who might have to mix their labour with land upon which others have already laboured. Although Locke made no specific provisions to prevent the propertied from depriving the propertyless of the right to acquire property on their part,[68] he assumed that the more land is appropriated for cultivation, the more abundant the means of livelihood for all. Furthermore, when you mix your labour with land already belonging to somebody else, you are entitled to a reward. The sale of labour affects the argument under discussion,[69] since the right to receive wages is an alternative to the right of sharing both the land and the joint labour product. The share which, through his labour, a man has acquired in the land of another is, so to speak, bought back by the owner by paying wages to the non-owner. The wages of the labourer serve to purchase things for exclusive use and

[67] Cp. Plamenatz, *op. cit.*, 246.
[68] *Ibid.*
[69] Contrary to what Plamenatz, *op. cit.*, 246, note 1, says.

ownership. As long as no labour goes unrewarded, the exclusion of others from the ownership of the same piece of cultivated land, or over other means of production which have already been appropriated, does not involve the loss of the natural right of property by some people while others benefit from it. On Locke's principles, the people should have property. The failure to realize this right fully lies with the individual and does not detract from the validity of the natural right of the individual to acquire land and other means of production through his labour. Locke upheld this right so strictly that he regarded only individual appropriation as legitimate. Whatever view one takes of the logical and moral adequacy of such a theory of property, if its one great virtue is that it justifies property not only as a means to security or happiness, but also as a means to liberty,[70] one should not be too hard on Locke for allowing no exceptions to the right of individual appropriation.

In referring to the communal ownership of land in the form of the commons of the manorial system, he held that under it the land was used as it was in the stage of gathering, that is, not as in itself the object of private acquisition but as that which contains or by itself produces such objects. Whether things are common by nature or 'remain so by compact , . . it is the taking any part of what is common, and removing it out of the state nature leaves it in, which begins the property; without which the common is of no use' (Sec. 28). Once more the individual's right to appropriate by his own labour, and without anyone's consent, from what nature has provided for all in common, is illustrated, although by being contained within the territory of a state, commons become different from the universal common. They are 'the joint property of this country, or this parish' (Sec. 35), and therefore to be used only by their respective members. Further, 'no one can enclose or appropriate any part, without the consent of all his fellow-commoners: Because this is left common by compact, i.e. by the law of the land, which is not to be violated.' Indeed, the right of the men of the manor to send their horses to graze and their servants to turf and mine on the common land, is an extremely bad example of pristine communism prevailing in a whole society.[71] But since Locke never had such a system in mind, the example is just another illustration that 'this original law of nature for the beginning of property', the

[70] Cp. Plamenatz, *op. cit.*, 249.
[71] Cp. Laslett, *op. cit.*, 307.

right to which labour alone furnishes the title, 'still takes place' after men 'have made and multiplied positive laws to determine property . . .' (Sec. 30). Accordingly, as in the case of hunting a hare, the right to appropriate something 'out of that common state nature left it in' holds good as long as it 'is still *looked upon as common*'. The way something is looked at, that is, convention or consent as ultimately expressed in law, does not determine whether something one removes from the common is one's property. In political society, law determines whether game or land from which things can be removed by all the commoners remain common, or shall be cultivated and hence made available for individual appropriation. Communal ownership of land may exist alongside private property but does not extend over cultivated land.

3. CONFIRMATION OF THE PRIMACY OF PRIVATE PROPERTY

A. The Bible

Although the little that Locke said on the universal common is for the most part derived from biblical evidence, he nowhere adduced biblical texts as proof of original communism.[72] There is no reason to expect any such proof, except if we expect Locke to contradict himself. Indeed, the *First Treatise* which, as Laslett has shown, was written after the *Second*, buttresses the latter's rational derivations with evidence from the Bible. The rational theory of property of the *Second Treatise* is twice referred to in the *First Treatise*.[73] Further attention is drawn to the correspondence between the rational and biblical arguments in the opening statement of the Chapter 'Of Property' in the *Second Treatise*. The same conclusions, we are told, follow 'whether we consider natural reason, . . . or revelation, which gives us an account of those grants God made of the world to Adam, and to Noah, and his sons . . .' (Sec. 25).

Locke attacked Filmer's reading of the Scriptures to prove first that 'God gave no immediate power to Adam over men, over his children, over those of his own species', and secondly that 'God gave him not private dominion over the inferior creatures, but *right in common with* all mankind . . .' (I, 24). Locke argued that Adam was made monarch neither by the immediate grant of God nor

[72] Cp. Laslett, *op. cit.*, 187.
[73] I, 87, 90.

indirectly by property rights accorded him. Adam had not been given private dominion or property which first excluded the private property rights of all other men, and then served as their fountain-head. The gift of God establishes 'the dominion of the whole species of mankind, over the inferior species of creatures . . .' (I, 28). Each individual member of the higher species has the right to use the lower species. 'God blessed *them*, and said unto *them*, have dominion' (I, 29). To give dominion over the creatures to 'the species of man' is to give it to 'those who were to have the image of God, the *individuals* of that species of man that he was going to make . . .' (I, 30). Locke left no room for exegetical doubt about his interpretation of the species as the aggregate of individuals. 'The word *them* in the text must include the species of man', and cannot mean Adam alone. The scriptural text does not make sense 'if *man* in the former part of the verse [I, Genesis, 26] do not signify the same with *them* in the latter, only *man* there, as is usual, is taken for the species, and *them* the individuals of that species'. The *First Treatise* confirms by way of biblical exegesis the presupposition of the *Second Treatise* that the recipients of God's grants of dominion over the creatures are the individuals, and not the collectivity, of mankind. It also confirms that human existence is inconceivable without private property.

The children have the right to inherit from their parents, possessions 'being *personally* the parents' (I, 88). Children have 'a title, to share in the property of their parents, and a right to inherit their possessions', because, next to self-preservation, the propagation of his kind is a natural desire planted in man by God. 'Men being by a like obligation bound to preserve what they have begotten, as to preserve themselves, their issue come to have a right in the goods they are possessed of.' Natural law, universal consent and positive law coalesce on this issue, because there is no evading the fact that personal property is the condition of the continuance of mankind. The natural right of private property as supported by scriptural evidence guarantees to the utmost against the return of property 'to the common stock of mankind'. Only when no relatives can be found, and not simply when the parents die intestate, do 'the possessions of a private man revert to the community, and so in political societies come into the hands of the public magistrate' (I, 90). Outside political society they 'become again perfectly common' – that is, nobody can 'have a property in them, otherwise than in other things common by nature...' And of this Locke will 'speak in its due place'. The rational argument about property is constantly kept in mind by him and there is no deviation from it as regards the community of all things. Filmer had denied that 'a community of all things [was] instituted between Noah and his sons'. Instead, God's blessing must be understood as allowing 'the sons either *under* or *after* their father ... a private dominion'.[74] In contesting the faithfulness of Filmer's reading of the Scriptures, Locke does not defend the idea of a community of all things between Noah and his sons. He attacks the notion that the Bible confirms Noah as 'the sole heir of the world' (I, 35); and that only under or after him Noah's sons could be proprietors. According to the Bible, God's grants 'belong to Noah and his sons, *to them as much as to him*, and not to his sons with a subordination or in succession' (I, 34). Applying the sufficiency clause for the limitation of individual appropriation, Locke queried:

'What harm was done him [Noah] if God gave his sons a right to make use of a part of the earth for the support of themselves and families, when the whole was not only more than Noah himself, but infinitely more than they all could make use of, and the possessions of one could not at all prejudice, or as to any use straighten that of the other' (I, 37)?

Noah's adult sons were proprietors as independent as their father. For what 'best agrees with the plain construction of the words' (I, 32) of the Scriptures is 'a joint title in present', and not one 'in subordination, or succession'; nor do they testify to 'only an enlargement of commons' (I, 39). What was 'given in clear words' to Noah and his sons was individual property.

'If they [the words of the Scriptures] give not property, nay, property in possession, it will be hard to find words that can, since there is not a way to express a man's being possessed of anything more natural, nor more certain, than to say, it is delivered into his hands.'

What is so delivered is 'the utmost property man is capable of, which is to have a right to destroy anything by using it'.[75] As in the *Second*, so in the *First Treatise*, the right of usage is the right of private appropriation, and is coeval with human existence.

[74] *Patriarcha*, 64. My italics.
[75] I, 39. Cp. 92.

'The original community of all things amongst the sons of men' (I, 40), which Locke held up against Filmer, has nothing whatsoever to do with the community of all things as understood by Grotius or Selden, against whom Filmer inveighed. As interpreted by Locke, it excludes not private property but the proposition that God gave 'Adam monarchical absolute power over other men, or the *sole* property in all the creatures . . .' Locke's conception of the original community of all things serves in fact to link the equal title of all men to individual property with God's sole proprietorship of the world. While

'in respect of one another, men may be allowed to have propriety in their distinct portions of the creatures; yet in respect of God the maker of heaven and earth, who is sole Lord and proprietor of the whole world, man's propriety in the creatures is nothing but that liberty to use them, which God has permitted, and so man's property may be altered and enlarged, as we see it was here, after the flood, when other uses of them are allowed, which before were not' (I, 39).

In respect to God's ownership, men merely use the world as one uses a common. Otherwise the original community of all things means simply that God gave 'to man, the whole species of man', what Filmer claimed to have been given to Adam alone; it means that God gave 'them all a right, to make use of the food and rayment, and other conveniences of life . . .' (I, 41); it means that not one individual but every individual has a right to property of his own.

B. Philosophy

An Essay Concerning Human Understanding does not affect what both Locke's polemical exegesis of the Scriptures and his rational deduction of property rights reveal as regards the primacy of private property. In the context of citing examples in support of the inclusion of 'morality amongst the sciences capable of demonstration', he derived the proposition '*Where there is no property there is no injustice*' from two ideas: 'the *idea of property* being a right to anything, and the idea to which the name *injustice* is given being the invasion or violation of that right . . .'[76] In the *Treatises*, the violation of the right of property is prohibited by natural law. In the *Essays on the Law of Nature*, Locke asked: '. . . what justice is there where there is no personal property?' Although this phrase is

---

[76] *Essay*, IV, iii, 18. The italics are in Yolton's edition.

not the same as in the *Essay*, as von Leyden suggests, the contents of the statements are certainly similar.[77]

In the *Essay*, the equation of the absence of injustice with the absence of property does not refer to an actual situation; it is a logical extrapolation. It can be considered as a criterion for judging property relations similar to the hypothetical state of nature which serves as a criterion for judging political relations. Moreover, just as in the *Treatises* the complete definition of the state of nature does not exclude the existence of injustice, so in the *Essay*, the correlation between the absence of injustice and the absence of property does not exclude, but rather emanates from, the supposition that only where there is property is there room to speak of both justice and injustice. Even if we re-formulate 'where there is no property there is no injustice', and say 'where there is no property there is justice' (no injustice = justice), we can conclude that only where there is property can there be injustice, without being logically forced to say that to have property is unjust. The identification of the absence of injustice with the absence of property does not presuppose the premise that property is unjust, which Locke did not posit, but presupposes rather two things: that where there is property there is opportunity for injustice and that the violation of property is unjust. This Locke did affirm also in the *Essay*.

The Euclidean-like demonstrability of ethical propositions is first applied in regard to property, and then in the derivation of the proposition that 'no government allows absolute liberty'. In relating the spheres of political and property relationships in the *Essay* as in the *Treatise*, Locke concluded: 'Let a man have the idea of taking something from others, without their consent, what their honest industry has possessed them of, and call this *justice* if he please.' This is nothing but an example of 'the change of name, by the impropriety of speech . . .'[78] As to the proposition about the absence of property and injustice, there is a striking similarity between the *Essay* and Hobbes' *Leviathan*. Hobbes derived the conclusion 'where there is no *own*, that is no propriety, there is no injustice' from the proposition: '*justice* is *the constant will of giving to every man his own.*'[79] The dissimilarities are no less patent than the

---

[77] *Essays*, 213; see von Leyden there on 'the same phrase' in the *Essay*, and Laslett, *op. cit.*, 74, on the similarity of the statements.

[78] *Essay*, IV, iv, 9.

[79] *Leviathan*, Ch. XV. The italics are in Lindsay's edition, *Everyman's Library* (1937).

similarities. Hobbes' statement occurs in a context where property is being considered as established by contract. Further he contends that 'the names of just and unjust' are inapplicable without reference to 'some coercive power, to compel men equally to the performance of their covenant'. According to Locke, the right of property is independent of consent, and justice, though more applicable where there is a coercive power, is not inapplicable where there is none. There is more justice where men are equally compelled to do what is just, provided constraint is continuously legitimized by consent, to which Locke assigned an equally important role in both political and property relations.

Locke rendered liberalism consistent inasmuch as he detached the criteria of economic justice from the notion of an original property-less order. The dissociation from a socialist past for the sake of ensuring a non-socialist future did not entail the disowning of the hitherto accepted moral limitations of acquisitiveness. Locke's factual clarification why the natural limitations of appropriation had become ineffective went together with the moral and practical subjection of the economic to the political sphere. In both spheres, he regarded historical origins as exemplary. Economic differentiation and with it the growing dependence of the many upon the few evoked his moral reservations; yet the time in which all were dependent upon the superior talent and virtue of one man was the golden age of early government. In fact, according to Locke the exclusive political leadership of one man in the beginning goes together with both minimal government and minimal economic inter-dependence of the ruled, whereas, ultimately, economic growth and differentiation demand the limitation, yet by no means the elimination, of discretionary power.

Although Locke declared the discretionary rule of good and wise princes to be compatible with the principle of consent, this does not derogate from the fact that he made considered concessions to authoritarian leadership. He dispensed far less with fatherly authority inside and beyond the family than his long-winded and vehement polemics with Filmer would lead one to expect. Evading many of the abstractions of which he is often accused, Locke made, as we shall see, allowances for principles and forms of social and political organization in respect of which he is generally supposed to have evinced nothing but unhistorical hostility and misunderstanding.

CHAPTER VII

THE FOUNDATION OF
POLITICAL SOCIETY

LOCKE'S onslaught on Filmer's paternalism has diverted attention from his attempts to reconcile the historical precedent of patriarchal monarchy with the rational justification of the principle of consent. His assumption of the transition from the family to incorporation into political society by compact has been noticed;[1] it has even been recognized as the example of how near he could get to a historical point of view.[2] But according to the prevailing evaluation, this was by far not near enough, and an inadvertancy at that. As Vaughan says, 'only by a back door and in a blissful absent fit, [Locke] . . . admits even the most beggarly elements of history,' unaware 'that to leave even a chink open for them was to destroy his whole argument from top to bottom'.[3] Even when it is pointed out how central an issue in the *Treatises* is the structure of the family and its relevance to social and political authority, and hence to the importance of the issue of patriarchalism; even when it is admitted that concessions on these points indicate awareness of the limitations of rationalism;[4] Locke's preoccupation with relating *ius paternum* to *consensus populi* is nevertheless relegated to his first period with Shaftesbury, and is considered to be no longer equally fundamental in the final work.[5] He is therefore accused of having ignored 'the full strength, antiquity and importance of the patriarchal tradition,'[6] and it is maintained that one of the most important results of a

---

[1] Cp. Stephen, *op. cit.*, II, 140.

[2] Cp. Pollock, *op. cit.*, 244.

[3] Vaughan, *op. cit.*, 174.

[4] Cp. Laslett, *op. cit.*, 44, 67–8. The awareness of any such concessions in Locke escapes Parry, *loc. cit.*, 170 f., in his otherwise instructive attempt to reveal the insight which Locke's views on paternalism make possible into his theory of individualism.

[5] Laslett, *op. cit.*, 34. See now P. Abrams, *John Locke: Two Tracts on Government* (Cambridge, 1967), 63 f., for Locke's early intellectual conservatism. To the extent Abram's consideration of continuities (84 f.) touches upon the specifically political aspects of Locke's theory, it does so in a highly summary and often arbitrary fashion. See below, Ch. X, note 7.

[6] Laslett, *op. cit.*, 69.

critical edition of the *Treatises* is that the exhaustive refutation of patriarchalism can be seen to run throughout the *Second Treatise*.[7] Locke's early authoritarian monarchism[8] is not my concern here. I wish to establish the nature and to assess the significance of the reconciliation between patriarchalism and contractualism in his mature thinking. For this purpose, the present chapter will examine his distinction between paternal and political authority, and compare his account of the development of the family into a political society with the terms of the incorporating compact. This will provide a basis for the reconsideration of his attitude towards history, and also for the clarification, in the following chapter, of his evaluation of absolute monarchy. In this way it will become apparent to what extent concessions to historical forms of authoritarian leadership colour Locke's most fundamental tenets without blurring the divide between the politics of liberalism and of conservatism.

I. PATERNAL AND POLITICAL AUTHORITY

A. Paternal and Parental Power

'Origins', in Locke's conception, has a historical as well as an Aristotelian meaning. It denotes foundations in the sense of what is supposed to have actually existed and in the sense of generally valid principles. Thus, on the plane of principles Locke took pains to demolish Filmer's case for divinely ordained absolute monarchy, and more specifically to discredit the view that 'men are not born free, and therefore could never have the liberty to choose either governors, or forms of government' (I, 5); yet he did not reject an evolutionary connection, nor all likeness between paternal, patriarchal and political authority.

Filmer derived absolute monarchy from the natural and divinely ordained absolute authority of the father. Attacking him once more on his own ground, Locke set out to show that he had failed to prove this point from the Scriptures and by reason.[9] It was odd, he argued, to speak of paternal authority instead of speaking, in the

---

[7] *Ibid*, 45, 51.

[8] Cp. Lord Peter King, *op. cit.*, 62–3; Fox Bourne, *op. cit.*, I, 148; Lamprecht, *op. cit.*, 142–3; von Leyden, *op. cit.*, 21 f.; Cranston, *op. cit.*, 59 f., 288, and Abrams, *op. cit., passim.*

[9] I, 6–13 and *passim.*

spirit of 'reason or revelation', of parental authority.[10] Although intended to destroy the basis for an analogy between absolute rule in the family and in the state, the argument does not issue in maintaining the joint rule of parents in the family. Locke does not deny the father's supreme power,[11] notwithstanding his repeated references to the joint authority of husband and wife.

'But the husband and wife, though they have but one common concern, yet having different understandings, will unavoidably sometimes have different wills too; it therefore being necessary, that *the last determination, i.e. the rule*, should be placed somewhere, it naturally falls to the man's share, as the abler and the stronger.'[12]

Co-dominion in the family is ruled out at any event. If not the male, then the female is head of the family. Locke directed attention to 'that part of the world where one woman has more than one husband at a time' (Sec. 65), and spoke of 'one family, wherein the master *or* mistress of it had some sort of rule proper to a family' (Sec. 77). The assertion that the father has no authority 'but what a mistress of a family may have as well as he' (Sec. 86), refers therefore not to their joint rule, but to matriarchy as the alternative to patriarchy. A political element – 'the last determination, i.e., the rule' of one person – is seen to characterize family organization. The insistence on the natural superiority of the male indicates that Locke regarded matriarchy as the exception to the rule, if not as unnatural, and at any rate irreconcilable with the Christian tradition in the context of which he argued.

In his controversy with Filmer, he agreed that 'as a helper in the temptation, as well as a partner in the transgression, Eve was laid below him [Adam], and so he had accidentally a superiority over her . . .' (I, 44). This interpretation of the Fall is not meant to stress the accidental character of the male's superiority, but is part of ridiculing the Filmerian confusion of the public and the private sphere. Locke scoffed at the idea 'that God, in the same breath, should make him [Adam] universal monarch over all mankind, and a day labourer for his life'. Filmer's derivation of kingship from fatherhood is ludicrous because the curse laid on Eve, and henceforth on all women, to 'bring forth her children in sorrow and pain'

---

[10] Sec. 52. Cp. Secs. 53, 55, 58, 61, 69, 71, 72, 170, and I, 6, 11, 52, 55, 60–6.
[11] Strauss, *op. cit.*, 221 note 82, and Parry, *loc. cit.*, 172, go wrong on this point.
[12] Sec. 82. Cp. I, 47, 49, 61 and especially 48.

(I, 47), did not place a queen married to one of her subjects in political subjection to him. Yet that 'God, . . . gives not, . . . any authority to Adam over Eve' refers to proper political authority which a male may have as well as a female but neither of them merely in virtue of fatherhood or motherhood. Locke did not intend to dispute the natural preponderance of the male over the female. For what God says 'only foretells what should be the woman's lot, how by his Providence he would order it so, that she should be subject to her husband, as we see that generally the laws of mankind and customs of nations have ordered it so; and there is, I grant, a foundation in nature for it.' Hobbes was more advanced concerning the woman's natural standing. According to Locke, a woman could by convention become a queen, but as a female she is by nature and convention inferior to the male. For Hobbes, the father's authority is determined by civil law, 'whereas in the state of nature, every woman that bears children, becomes both a mother and a Lord'.[13]

For all Locke's emphasis that 'the mother too has her share with the father' in making the children 'most useful to themselves and others . . .' (Sec. 64), he nevertheless declared that 'the first part then of *paternal* power, or rather duty, which is education, belongs . . . to the father . . .' (Sec. 69). Likewise, having referred again to 'the obligation on the *parents* to bring up their children' (Sec. 72), he enumerates 'another power *ordinarily in the father*, . . . And this is the power men generally have to bestow their estates on those, who please them best.' The advance towards the equal status of women serves to tear some holes in Filmer's argument but, however genuine in intention, it is strictly limited.[14] The wife is not denied a part in educating the children and is left in full possession of 'what by contract is her peculiar right . . .' (Sec. 82). She is also at liberty to separate from her husband. But none of this affects the husband's right to the last decision in all family matters. The right is maintained and made definite precisely by its being limited 'to the things of their common interest and property . . .' With his characteristic way of reducing the weight of polemical propositions, Locke harked back from parental to paternal authority. He was ready to admit that in the family the unification of wills necessitated rulership, and most naturally that of the male.

[13] *De Cive*, ch. IX, 3.
[14] Kendall, *op. cit.*, 121, maintains contradictorily that support for women's suffrage might be drawn from Locke and that his views on women were those of his age.

B. *Father and Monarch*

a. *The Right over Life and Death*

Locke's distinction between non-political and political relationships does not exclude comparability between them. The distinction is less sharp than he makes it out to be; it is unqualified only inasmuch as the father's rule is limited in time and in the choice of penalties he can impose.

Husband and wife remain equal in so far as neither has a right over the life of the other, nor over that of their children. On this point, the family provides no analogy to political society. To follow 'Sir Robert [Filmer's] happy arguers' in finding such an analogy in the practice of exposing or selling children is to base opinion 'on the most shameful action, and most unnatural murder, human nature is capable of. The dens of lions and nurseries of wolves know no such cruelty as this.'[15] Apparently for reasons of religion and of scientific scepticism, i.e., our present ignorance of what constitutes life,[16] Locke rejected the view that procreation gave the father power over the life of his children. Moreover, 'the mother cannot be denied an equal share in begetting of the child, and so the absolute authority of the father will not arise from hence' (I, 55). Locke apparently thought that he had to remove the right to inflict the death penalty from the family relationship so as to grant the right to every adult against whoever attempted to use him like the inferior creatures. It was the defence of the right of revolt against the patriarchalists which required the novelty of deriving from individualistic premises the right of the magistrate to inflict the death penalty.[17]

The right to impose the death penalty, the decisive attribute of sovereignty, is an intrinsically public one even when exercised where there is no public authority. When a man who is a father, but not a magistrate, kills another in self-defence, he does so not by virtue of the right of fatherhood but of the right of war, which reverts to every man when he is in the woods of America or when he is assaulted by a robber. Further, 'a man in the West-Indies, who has with him sons of his own, friends, or companions, soldiers under pay, or slaves bought with money, or perhaps a band made up of all these, [may] make war and peace , . . without being a sovereign

---

[15] I, 56. As Laslett, *op. cit.*, 199, remarks, it is noteworthy that, unlike Tyrrell and Sydney, Locke failed to go behind Filmer to his source, that is, to Bodin.

[16] I, 52–5.

[17] See above, 63–4.

... ' (I, 131). Not only 'a single man for himself' but 'in voluntary societies for the time, he that has such a power *by consent*, may make war and peace , .. where they have no superior to appeal to'. Although not separable from political authority, and in no case related to fatherly authority, 'the actual making of war or peace', – which carries with it the right to kill – 'this power in many cases anyone may have without any politic[al] supremacy' (I, 132). Here is a most striking adumbration of Max Weber's view that most, if not all, functions of the sovereign authority have at one time or another been exercised by others than the sovereign.[18]

A sharp though thin line divides paternal from political supremacy. Besides the limitation of paternal authority to the nonage of children nothing sets paternal rule apart from absolute monarchy and from political rule in general but the reservation to the public authority of the monopoly of carrying coercion to its extreme by inflicting the death penalty. All other criteria adduced by Locke for distinguishing between the private character of the family relationship and the public realm turn out to be relative. The wife's liberty to leave her husband corresponds to, if it is not modelled on, the right of citizens to refuse obedience to their superiors by way of revolt or of withdrawal from the community. There remains particularly the right to make laws. But it is not so much the function of legislation, as legislation with power over life and death that is denied to the father.

b. *Legislative Authority*

Locke distinguished between 'the pronouncing of sentence of death' which 'is not a certain mark of sovereignty, but usually the office of inferior magistrates', and 'the power of making laws of life and death', which 'is indeed a mark of sovereignty . . .' (I, 129). The father *qua* father has neither the one power nor the other. It does not follow, however, that he has no functional equivalent of legislative, executive and judicial power. It is true that Locke untiringly iterated that the father's rule over his children was neither regal nor

---

[18] Cp. Max Weber, *Grundriss der Sozialökonomik*, III. Abteilung, *Wirtschaft und Gesellschaft* (Tübingen, 1925, zweite vermehrte Auflage), I. Halbband, 29. The importance of the public-private distinction as an addendum to Weber's definition of the political – in which it is not the end or what an organization does, but the means over which it has a monopoly, which is decisive – has been argued by Runciman, *Social Science and Political Theory*, 35-7. For an instructive discussion of the distinction between the public and the private sphere, see H. Arendt, *The Human Condition* (New York, Doubleday Anchor Books, 1959), Part II.

absolute because he had no right to make laws and enforce them.[19] 'For this is the proper power of the magistrate, of which the father has not so much as the shadow' (Sec. 65). But to accord the father, as Locke did, 'the last determination, i.e. the rule,' is, if anything, to equip him with the equivalent of making and executing laws at his discretion. Locke himself spoke of 'a sort of rule and jurisdiction' (Sec. 55) of parents over children – and a sort of jurisdiction presupposes a sort of law. He had no difficulty, therefore, in granting 'that a father may have a natural right to some kind of power over his children' (I, 111) and that someone 'must govern' (Sec. 59) a son during nonage. 'The father's *empire* then ceases' (Sec. 65), his 'temporary *government* . . . terminates with the minority of the child' (Sec. 67). If, then, the paternal rule is 'far from an absolute or perpetual jurisdiction' (Sec. 65), it is not absolute mainly because it is not perpetual, but not because obedience to it is otherwise restricted.

'The father's power of commanding' is confined to 'the minority of his children, and to a degree only fit for the discipline and government of that age . . .' (Sec. 74). It will not be 'a severe arbitrary government' (Sec. 170). 'God has woven into the principles of human nature such a tenderness for their offspring, that there is little fear that parents should use their power with too much rigour.'[20] Nevertheless, the power is discretionary. As demonstrated in God's 'gentle dealing with the Israelites' (Sec. 67), the severity of discipline has no other limitation than what the educator thinks is 'absolutely best for them' and is not necessarily more kind for being slack. Children are commanded obedience 'that the pains and care of their parents may not be increased, or ill rewarded'. The minor having 'not understanding of his own to direct his will, he is not to have any will of his own to follow: He that understands for him, must will for him too' (Sec. 58). Since, like political authority, educational authority without coercive power is likely to be ineffective, absolute responsibility for the children carries with it both 'the power of commanding and chastising them . . .' (Sec. 67).

The effects of paternal punishment may extend even beyond nonage. '. . . There is another power ordinarily in the father, whereby he has a tie on the obedience of his children: which . . . passes in the world for a part of paternal jurisdiction. And this is the power men generally have to bestow their estates on those, who

---

[19] Secs. 55-6, 59-60, 64, 66, 69-71, 82-91, 170, 173.
[20] Sec. 67. Cp. 63, I, 88, 89, 97.

please them best' (Sec. 72). This right is not invariably exercised by the father, – his authority may be delegated or even exercised by the mother in her own right;[21] but 'it is commonly in the father's power to bestow it with a more sparing or liberal hand, according as the behaviour of this or that child has comported with his will and humour' (Sec. 72). Like any other government, therefore, the father's government consists in determining rules of conduct and ensuring their observance with the help of efficient sanctions. In other words, it consists in the functional equivalent of making and enforcing laws. When Locke pointed out that 'these two powers, political and paternal, are so perfectly distinct and separate; are built upon so different foundations, and given to so different ends' (Sec. 71), he wished to disprove that 'all political power were only paternal, and . . . in truth . . . one and the same thing'. This is absurd, since it would follow that, 'all paternal power being in the prince, the subject could naturally have none of it'. As the prince and 'the meanest of his subjects' have the same paternal power and owe their parents the same filial duty and obedience, these relationships 'can therefore contain not any part or degree of that kind of dominion, which a prince, or magistrate has over his subject'. Locke's aim here is to expose the absurdity of confounding the foundations and ends of political power with those of paternal power. Nothing speaks against admitting at the same time the functional similarities between the father's and the magistrate's rule.

c. *Household and Commonwealth*

Locke cited Hooker, who accepted it as 'no improbable opinion . . . which the arch-philosopher [Aristotle] was of, that the chief person in every household was always, as it were, a king' (Sec. 74). There is no discrepancy between the quotation and Locke's own opinion. In the same context, Locke deals with the ease with which the father of the family becomes prince over several families and grants some resemblance of 'all these subordinate relations of wife, children, servants and slaves united under the domestic rule of a family . . . in its order, offices, and number too, with a little commonwealth . . .' (Sec. 86). He only says that 'what resemblance soever it [the family] may have . . . with a little commonwealth', it must be distinguished from a family as regards its 'constitution, power and end' (Sec. 86). As he had already pointed out, the difference is

[21] Secs. 72, 65 and I, 100-2.

apparent 'if we consider the different ends, ties, and bounds' (Sec. 77). Moreover, in these contexts, the power of the monarch and that of the master of the family – a 'very distinct and differently limited power, both as to *time* and *extent*' (Sec. 86) – are distinguished in terms not of law-making as such, but of the specific 'legislative power of life and death'. This power Locke also called 'a *political* power of life and death' (I, 48). Given the admission of the resemblance and the narrowing down of the difference between household and commonwealth, it does not come as a surprise, that he likens kings to fathers in much the same way as did the advocates of royal absolutism. He says that it is 'impossible for a governor, if he really means the good of his people, . . . not to make them see and feel it; as it is for the father of a family, not to let his children see he loves, and takes care of them' (Sec. 209).

Locke's admission of the parallel is not contradicted by his attack on Filmer's reliance on the fifth commandment. If he was repudiating a Christian and particularly a Protestant tradition,[22] he did so only insofar as the derivation from that commandment of 'an *absolute* subjection to a sovereign power . . .' (I, 64) is concerned. Locke disputed the connection in regard to 'that political dominion, which our A(uthor) would derive from it', and which created another absurd confusion of the private and public sphere. For

'if the grandfather has by right of fatherhood, sole sovereign power in him, and that obedience which is due to the supreme magistrate, be commanded in these words, *Honour thy father*, it is certain the grandfather might dispense with the grandson's honouring his father . . . But what law of the magistrate, can give a child liberty, not to *honour his father and mother*? It is an eternal law annexed purely to the relation of parents and children, and so contains nothing of the magistrate's power in it, nor is subjected to it.'

The object of disputing the applicability of the fifth commandment to political obligations is to refute Filmer's brand of patriarchal absolutism; Locke does not reject the view that beyond the fundamental distinction between the private and the public sphere there exists also a similarity. One might wish that he had formulated his distinctions less emphatically and attuned them better to his implicit and explicit admissions of the similarities.

[22] As Laslett, *op. cit.*, 205, argues in his comment on I, 64.

Indeed, Locke succeeded no better than Aristotle, whom he followed *via* Hooker, in drawing as sharp a line between the household and political society as he had promised. But the failure is an asset. The different ideological purposes which prompted Aristotle and Locke were toned down by their empirical insights. The similarity of 'ties and bonds' in any social group and particularly the similarity of the functional requirements of the unification of wills in any social setting, was not lost upon Locke. He did not merely admit by the back door many of the tenets about the political character of the family which are to be found in Filmer and in traditional philosophy as a whole. He quoted Hooker's enlargement upon Aristotle and made parallel statements as a matter of principle in his own name. He did not consider the political aspects of the family as an adjunct of the specific position of the colonial planter in the West-Indies, who by implication is likened to the biblical patriarchs.[23] In point of fact, the patriarchs, rather than the planters, are called by him political rulers. Both the patriach's and the planter's command 'over servants, born in his house, and bought with his money' (I, 130), did not make them sovereigns because it enabled them to make war and peace. Yet Esau was not only the founder of a people and a government but 'himself *prince* over them, as much as Jacob was *in his own family*' (I, 117).

There is nothing adventitious in Locke's acknowledgement of the political character of the family and in his equating the status of the patriarchs with that of princes. Alive to the historical arguments of the defenders of the patriarchial tradition, he desired to establish the validity of his propositions about the origins of political society in the sense both of principles and of historical beginnings. He had thus to demonstrate that incorporation by compact was no figment of the mind. He had to recognize the quasi-political character of the single family and relate it to the fully political character of a family of families. Far from being inimical to his ideological purposes, the admission enabled him to write, like Pudendorf and others, generically about the individuals, when he was actually speaking of the heads of households. In attributing natural rights to individuals who are already organized, Pufendorf too, had eased the passage from natural freedom to political subjection.[24] Locke could not go further

---

[23] Cp. Laslett, *op. cit.*, 255.
[24] Cp. Krieger, *op. cit.*, 113 f., also on Pufendorf's attribution to natural institutions of the terms characteristic of the civil state.

than he did in distinguishing natural from political ties, because in taking up the challenge of the paternalists, he grafted the idea of incorporation by compact on the well established opinion that political society grows out of the constitution, power, ends and ties which characterize the proper domain of paternal authority.

2. INCORPORATION BY TACIT CONSENT

A. Natural and Contractual Foundations

a. *Ius Paternum and Consensus Populi*
Although all the father's prerogatives give him

'no dominion over the property or actions of his son: yet it is obvious to conceive how easy it was in the first ages of the world, and in places still, where the thinness of people gives families leave to separate into unpossessed quarters, . . . for the father of the family to become the prince of it' (Sec. 74).

To adopt this view, Locke had to agree that the father 'had been a ruler from the beginning of the infancy of his children'. Only on this premise could he maintain that

'government . . . was likeliest it should, by the express or tacit consent of the children, when they were grown up, be in the father, where it seemed *without any change* barely to continue . . .' 'Thus it was easy, and almost natural for children . . . to make way for the father's authority and government' (Sec. 75).

The proximity between fatherly and political authority is reconfirmed in an argument set out in Sections 74–5 and elaborated upon again in Sections 105–112. It also is referred to briefly at various stages of the discourse. On each occasion it serves meeting his opponents' arguments on their own ground and adapting them to the idea of government by consent.

Having stipulated consent as its basis, he could accept the fact of the patriarchal beginning, and at the same time, detach it from legitimation *de jure divino*, 'which we never heard of among mankind, till it was revealed to us by the divinity of this last age'.[25] Locke did

---

[25] Sec. 112. Cp. Preface, lines 32–3 and I, 4 and 33. The view persisted in the liberal argument, as evidenced, e.g., by Mme. de Staël's famous slogan, that despotism is new and liberty is old. See also below, 222, Locke's defence of 'the old way' of contriving government.

THE LIBERAL POLITICS OF JOHN LOCKE

not quarrel with traditionalist views on a point of fact, but on one point of principle. The natural paternal right can become a proper political right only by the adult sons' 'permitting the father to exercise alone in his family that executive power of the law of nature, which every freeman naturally has' and 'this was not by any paternal right, but only by the consent of his children . . .' (Sec. 74). The transformation of private into public power is inevitable because to rule over grown-up children is to rule over several families. In this respect Locke followed the traditional view as re-stated by Bodin in the opening sentence of the *Six Livres de la République*: 'A *res publica* may be defined as the rightly ordered government of a number of families and of those things which are their common concern, by a sovereign power.' For Locke, however, paternal authority takes on the complexion of political authority, because, accustomed to obey their father's commands, men of their own accord 'made no distinction between minority, and full age' (Sec. 75). By way of 'express or tacit consent' the family organization naturally flows over into proper political organization. The Scriptures, like all other history, confirm the same story.

Jacob and Esau 'were both heads of their distinct families, . . . and were the roots out of which sprang two distinct peoples . . .' (I, 118). It does not matter whether there was an equivocation in Locke on the question whether Esau and Jacob were only the remote founders of peoples or already political father-monarchs. Pristine political leadership has the complexion of paternal authority even when the leader is not a father, nor a monarch in the formal sense, but a judge or general.[26] Hence no contradiction is created by the references to 'the chosen people of God [who] continued a people several hundreds of years, without any knowledge or thought of this paternal authority, or any appearance of monarchical government at all' (I, 164). That the people was appealed to for justice and 'it was the tribes and the congregation, that debated, resolved, and directed . . .',[27] does not exclude individual leadership of the tribes. Although Locke stresses the exceptional character of the establishment of the Jewish polity by direct Divine intervention, he not only stated that this 'favours not at all paternal dominion' (Sec. 101) as understood by Filmer, and argued the case in agonizing detail in the

[26] Secs. 94 and 108-10, 112, respectively. See below, 238 f.
[27] I, 165. This view of the ancient government of Israel was not uncommon in the seventeenth century. Cp. Laslett, *op. cit.*, 279.

220

First Treatise; he also dedicated the whole of Section 109 of the *Second Treatise* to showing that there is a contractual aspect to the emergence of judges and kings in Israel. He relied twice on Hooker[28] to show that the emergence of early kingship and of the authority to make laws is a matter of consent even on traditional views. In the second instance, however, Hooker's passage refers alternatively to consent and to 'express commission immediately and personally received from God'. Locke himself rules out any alternative to the origin of government in consent. On this basis alone, he conceded the traditional standpoint on the naturalness of both political society and patriarchal monarchy in its beginnings.

b. *Voluntariness and Naturalness*

The chapter 'Of Political or Civil Society' opens with the acknowledgement that 'God having made man such a creature, that, in his own judgement, it was not good for him to be alone, put him under strong obligations of necessity, convenience, and inclination to drive him into society . . .' (Sec. 77). The reaffirmation of the immanent social nature of man follows on the heels of the argument which shows family life to have predisposed the adult children to assent to the father's political rule over them.[29] As distinct from 'voluntary societies for the time' (I, 131) – 'a band made up' by 'a man in the West-Indies', the crew of a ship etc. – political society is not presented as a fully voluntary or artificial creation, although consent distinguishes it, too, from a non-political natural family-kingdom. Voluntariness and naturalness are to varying degrees part of any of the basic human associations. Conjugal society 'is made by a voluntary compact' (Sec. 78), yet is at once natural and artificial.[30] If procreation is the purpose of conjugal society, men and women could hardly avoid consenting to it. What is voluntary is the choice of partners for the pursuit of the pre-ordained end; this makes the association one of equals. But through the necessity of placing the last determination in the hands of one of the contracting parties, subordination becomes an inescapable concomitant of the voluntary union. Voluntariness in the case of both conjugal and political society means for Locke that, by their own judgement,

---

[28] Secs. 74, 134. See Hooker's *Ecclesiastical Polity*, I, i.

[29] Sec. 75. Cp. 110.

[30] Cp. Polin, *op. cit.*, 130. Cumberland had already argued against Hobbes that the social compact was not an artificial but natural agreement. Cp. Fetscher *loc. cit.*, 678-9.

men answer the call of necessity in accord with God's will. They have the choice of partners but not the freedom to dispense with the institution (except, of course, in marginal cases which confirm the rule) or with the dominion appropriate to it.

A well established tradition of appraising liberalism has blinded interpreters to Locke's awareness of the naturalness of social and political life and of men's natural predisposition to sociability. At best, the absence in his conception of any contradiction between rational artifice and natural instinct is allowed as regards the family alone,[31] or the charge that he failed to give love, natural sociability and emotional togetherness their due in respect of political society is somewhat toned down by the admission that there too he made some concessions.[32] But in dealing with the emergence of government out of the family, Locke clearly said that 'those, who liked one another so well as to join into society, cannot but be supposed to have some acquaintance and friendship together, and some trust one in another' (Sec. 107). Although compact is 'no natural tie or engagement, but a voluntary submission' (Sec. 73), it is grafted upon, and indeed unthinkable without, those natural ties which characterize the family. Rational contrivances are not made in a void, except perhaps by God, whom Locke called the 'all-wise contriver . . .' (I, 53). Locke defended 'the old way of [governments] being made by contrivance, and the consent of men making use of their reason' (I, 6), against the new way of deriving government from 'this authority of parents' called 'royal authority, . . . fatherly authority, right of fatherhood'. He did not by this argument hold himself committed to disputing the growth of political organization out of family ties. In recognition of the naturalness in the sense of the inevitability of the state as an institution, he stressed that 'without some government it would be hard for them [the grown-up sons and their families] to live together' (Sec. 74). He also presupposed naturalness in the sense of a more instinctive than reflective response. Having said that the father's rule continued 'by the express or tacit consent of the children, when they were grown up' (Sec. 74), Locke omitted the alternative between express and tacit consent and concluded that 'thus it was easy, and almost natural for children by a *tacit, and scarce avoidable* consent to make way for the father's authority and government' (Sec. 75). 'Thus the natural fathers of

---

[31] Cp. Polin, *op. cit.*, 29, 136, 143 and 105.
[32] Thus Laslett, *op. cit.*, 69, 109.

families, by an *insensible* change, became the political monarchs of them too' (Sec. 76).

Naturalness in both senses restricts Locke's view of the artificiality of the state to such an extent that the limitation of contractualism is not only set by the fact that men cannot do without political society; they have also no choice as to the form of pristine government. Accepting patriarchal monarchy as the original form of government, he purged it and, indeed, any monarchy of a paternalism which does not admit consent as its basis. Locke's concessions to patriarchalism, which are concessions not just to Filmer or Pufendorf[33] but to a tradition of political thought of the longest standing, are thus tempered by consent. Yet his idea of consent is also tempered by the concessions to patriarchalism. If incorporation by compact is historically demonstrated by the imperceptible transformation of the family into patriarchal monarchy, the compact is divested of its fictitious character but the illustration is also provided for what the consent of the people means in practice. This is one of the crucial aspects of his account of the transition from private paternal to public patriarchal rule.

c. *The Terms of the Compact*

Consent to the father's monarchical status[34] is defined by Locke in terms fully reconcilable with the terms of definition of the incorporating compact. For the establishment of political society in the form of paternal monarchy 'indeed nothing more was required to it, than the permitting the father to exercise alone in his family that executive power of the law of nature, which every free man naturally has, and by that permission resigning up to him a monarchical power . . .' (Sec. 74). The general definition of the incorporating compact reads:

'Whosoever . . . out of a state of nature unite into a community, *must be understood* to give up all the power, necessary to the ends for which they unite into society, to the majority of the community, unless they expressly agreed in any number greater than the majority. *And this is done by barely agreeing to unite into one political society, which is all the compact that is, or needs be,* between

---

[33] Cp. Laslett, *op. cit.*, 334-5, who points also to Tyrrell and William Temple.

[34] Gough, *op. cit.*, 61, sees in this a contradiction of the majority principle. But he confuses, like Kendall whom he follows here, majority-consent with majority-rule as the Lockeian condition for society to 'act or continue one body . . .' (Sec. 96).

the individuals, that enter into, or make up a commonwealth' (Sec. 99).

Locke explicitly confirms that 'all the compact that is, or needs be' is carried out by the tacit compliance of the grown-up sons with the continuance of the father's authority in the form of monarchical power. The fact that government in the beginning had been in the hands of one man 'destroys not that, which I affirm, (viz.) that the beginning of political society depends upon the consent of the individuals, to join into and make one society' (Sec. 106). Locke was justified in making this statement, for, although not immediately apparent, the form of consent is the same according to the terms of the general definition of incorporation and to those of the transition from paternal to monarchical rule.

In conformity with the shift from 'the express *or* tacit consent of the children' (Sec. 74) to 'a tacit, and scarce avoidable consent' (Sec. 75), Locke refers in his general definition to express consent only with regard to the case where the recipient of all the power is a number greater than the majority. But generally, the resigning of powers 'must be understood' to have been performed. This wording is appropriate to an inference *ex post factum* and not to the statement of an overt act, and tallies, therfore, with the acknowledgement that incorporation under patriarchal monarchy is made by tacit consent and takes the form of an imperceptible change. Apparently fashioned after the Roman legal fiction of the *lex regia* – the people's conferment of all their authority upon the emperor – the conclusion of the founding compact is set apart from legal or other specific procedures. No more is to be understood by the terms of the compact, than that we may safely assume consent to have been given in some undefined form, or that if the participants to the undertaking had been asked, they would have explained their compliance in terms of consent.

Locke's attempt to indicate social solidarity by the idea of tacit consent has appeared to one interpreter as almost ridiculous, and the contract is seen as basing legalism on a fiction.[35] An earlier interpreter was more penetrating in arguing that Locke avoided calling the compact non-existent by allowing for tacit consent.[36] Indeed, the idea of the compact has come to be recognized as an expository device, as a way of saying that society cannot exist

[35] Cp. Lamprecht, *op. cit.*, 150.
[36] Cp. Stephen, *op. cit.*, II, 142.

unless its members act as if they had negotiated a contract.[37] The contract has therefore also been compared with the notion of trust, inasmuch as both are metaphors and are not predicated on the enactment of a specific procedure and legal models.[38] Yet even if the surmise were generally accepted that political theorists had never been guilty of considering the social compact an historical event,[39] it is important not only to establish that such naiveté was avoided, but also to see how this was done and to ascertain the implications. Hence it has to be realized that Locke's general definition of the compact is deliberately phrased to legitimate incorporation by tacit and scarcely avoidable consent under the government of the father. No support is thereby provided for the two diametrically opposed conclusions that Locke had substituted for free compact the framing of government by a few wise and industrious men, who are, or become, despotic masters,[40] or that the admission of tacit compliance with incorporation enabled him to conceal an underlying anarchial tendency.[41] Rather, Locke illustrates the practical meaning of popular consent by its paradigm, the compact: express consent to incorporation is evidenced not in an act but in tacit compliance with an imperceptible process. The essential points are missed if we take the expressness of the compact literally, considering it confined either to the founding of political society or to the overthrow of the government, and hence of subordinate significance in Locke's conception.[42] Exactly because tacit and hardly avoidable consent to political incorporation under the father-monarch is an attitude rather than a formal act, it retains its importance in the political process. For Locke's equation of tacit with express consent is conditional. If the formal expression of consent on the part of the people as a whole is excluded, tacit consent can still give way to active dissent, to revolt or withdrawal. The conditional equation of tacit and express consent is consistently upheld. As I shall explain in detail in Chapter IX, Locke, who affirmed that only 'an express consent, of any man, . . . makes him a perfect member of . . . society' (Sec. 119), gave no other

---

[37] Cp. Kendall, *op. cit.*, 91.

[38] Cp. Gough, *op. cit.*, 65, 90, 136 and Laslett, *op. cit.*, 112, 115.

[39] Cp. G. E. G. Catlin, *Principles of Politics* (New York, 1930), 167.

[40] As Cox, *op. cit.*, 102-3, asserts.

[41] This is the view of Stephen, *op. cit.*, II, 142, and Th. Waldman, 'A Note on John Locke's Theory of Consent,' *Ethics* vol. LXVIII, 1 (1957), 46.

[42] Wolin, *op. cit.*, 311. According to H. Pitkin, 'Obligation and Consent – I,' *The American Political Science Review*, LIX, 4 (1965), 996, the hypothetical character of the compact renders personal consent to political obligation irrelevant.

illustration of express consent than incorporation by compact, and considered it to be reaffirmed by abstention from an overt act of dissent.

To interpret his compact as a formal and active act of consent which symbolizes the supremacy of the individual[43] would still be possible if Locke had enumerated several ways of incorporation, among which the patriarchal way was one, if the commonest.[44] If he had another way in mind, he was bound to cite it, since he had accepted the challenge to marshal concrete examples of incorporation by compact. But he did nothing of the kind.

B. Historical Incorporation – Inevitability and Choice

If history provides no examples of independent and equal men meeting together and by consent setting up government,[45] the reason is that 'Government is everywhere antecedent to records' (Sec. 101). Literature is a late product of civil society and people 'begin to look after the history of their founders, and search into their original, when they have outlived the memory of it'. Nevertheless the birth and infancy of societies can be as safely inferred as the birth and infancy of individuals. However Locke evidently felt that he had to go beyond what 'must be understood' to have occurred; he adduced historical examples of the 'manifest footsteps' of the beginning. As we have already seen, these examples do not confirm the state of nature as a pre-social and pre-political stage of historical development.[46] Even if inferences concerning the infancy of societies were meant to lead us to an historical as well as an unpolitical state of nature, this would not affect the issue under discussion: the form of original incorporation. What the examples from history confirm in this particular respect is summed up in the following words:

'I will not deny, that if we look back as far as history will direct us, towards the original of commonwealths, we shall *generally* find them under the government and administration of one man. And I am also apt to believe, that where a family was numerous enough . . . *the government commonly began in the father*' (Sec. 105).

[43] Cp. Vaughan, *op. cit.*, 139, 172, who at the same time, however, interprets the compact as the one sweeping restriction imposed on the individualist conception of the state (194).

[44] Cp. Laslett, *op. cit.*, 106.

[45] Sec. 100.

[46] Cp. Secs. 102-3, 108-9 and above, 86 f. 'Manifest footsteps' in Sec. 101 is, as Laslett, *op. cit.*, 352, points out, Filmer's own expression.

It is difficult to suppose that he had instances in mind which were neither general nor common. He gave no indication whatever of what the 'manifest footsteps' of the 'births and infancies' of commonwealths might have been, except those evidenced by patriarchal monarchy. Only the recognition that history provides no examples of the creation of political society by a formal act of incorporation, could have evoked the insistence on Locke's part that what history confirms 'destroys not that, which I affirm, (viz.) that the beginning of political society depends upon the consent of the individuals . . .' (Sec. 106). He tempered thus patriarchalism with consent as much as he tempered consent with patriarchalism. He began by equating tacit consent to patriarchal monarchy with express consent, as the only provable form of incorporation. He ended by substituting scarcely avoidable tacit for express consent. His general definition of incorporation by compact was so worded as to cover the case and he never contradicted the so tempered idea of the consent of the people *en masse*.

Locke limits free choice, but does not exclude it by the necessity of living in a political society and by the scarcely avoidable consent to incorporate under one particular form of government. The practical impossibility of choosing an alternative form and the insistence on the people's right to choose any government they like do not contravene each other. Since 'people in the beginning generally pitched upon this form' (Sec. 106), that is, patriarchal monarchy, practically the freedom to choose a form of government is the right to break away from patriarchal and thenceforth, any other government. Individuals 'when they are thus [i.e. by consent to one-man-rule] incorporated, might set up what form of government they thought fit'.[47] No two distinct compacts are envisaged – one for the establishment of society and another for the constitution of government. As Locke's phrasing and refutation of the second objection to the theory of incorporation by compact makes plain, incorporating means establishing a government, although beginning a new government does not necessarily mean founding a new political society.

It is objected, argues Locke, that men cannot incorporate freely because, 'all men being born under government, some or other, it is impossible any of them should be ever free, and at liberty to unite together, and begin a *new one*, or *ever be able to erect a lawful*

---

[47] Secs. 106. Cp. Secs. 132, 135, 136, 151, 213.

government'.[48] The first objection concerns original incorporation, and is met by the answer that the undeniable monarchical beginnings do not refute the theory of incorporation by consent. The answer to the second objection maintains the right of incorporation by consent by affirming the right of men who have already lived under a government to replace it by a new and lawful one or to withdraw and found both a new government and a new society.

Locke argues here from known facts because he wishes to refute objections against the feasibility of the right of free compact. 'There are no examples so frequent in history, both sacred and profane, as those of men withdrawing themselves, and their obedience, from the jurisdiction they were born under, ... and setting up *new* governments in other places' (Sec. 115). Notwithstanding the difference between the foundation of political society and the mere establishment of a new government, the same principle of legitimation is involved. In this respect it is irrelevant whether men are born under a government or whether 'they were born in the woods, amongst the unconfined inhabitants that ran loose in them'.[49] What legitimates the act of foundation the first time must needs legitimate its full or partial reenactment at any time. Consent justified not only the invariably monarchical beginning but the devising of other and eventually better forms of government in the course of time. Locke accepted Hooker's view that 'the inconveniences of one kind [of government] have caused sundry other to be devised' (Sec. 74), because for him it was a matter of principle what for Hooker was a possibility, namely, that 'all public regiment of what kind soever' began by 'the deliberate advice, consultation and compostion between men'.

Locke agreed that for a long time no inconveniences attached to patriarchal monarchy. The father-monarchs 'chanced to live long, and leave able, and worthy heirs, for several successions, or otherwise; so they laid the foundations of hereditary, or elective kingdoms . . .' (Sec. 76). Once Locke had removed the contradiction between consent and patriarchalism, nothing was gained by flying in the face of history and spiriting patriarchal monarchy quickly off the stage. Patriarchal government being anything but defective, the historically unavoidable consent to it was justifiable by reason and compatible with freedom of choice. Free choice was limited in a circumstantial sense rather than on principle. If in the beginnings

---

[48] Sec. 113. Cp. Secs. 100, 114.
[49] Sec. 116. The latter is clearly a hypothesis for the sake of argument.

any other choice was practically impossible, then there was also no reason for it. In the socially relevant sense, the principle of free choice is not impaired, if uncoerced by others we accept as reasonable what is commanded by circumstances. The exclusion of any other way of original incorporation than under patriarchal monarchy is indicative of the informal character of Locke's understanding of societal consent; it does not contradict the principle of free and rational choice.

Locke thus confuted the argument 'that by nature government was monarchical, and belonged to the father' (Sec. 106), without disputing that patriarchal monarchy was a natural form of government. It is natural in that nothing else would be feasible and better in given conditions. It is not natural if this means that nothing more was required to become a monarch than to be a father, or that it was unnatural eventually to displace or modify it. 'The reason, that *continued* the form of government in a single person, was not any regard, or respect to paternal authority; since . . . almost all monarchies, near their original, have been commonly, at least upon occasion, elective.'[50] Not originally, but only 'near their original', monarchies were '*upon occasion*, elective'. But whether or not primitive monarchies became elective or remained hereditary, consent is decisive and fatherhood does not strengthen the title to rulership or the right of succession. 'He comes by right of succession, to be a prince in one place, who would be a subject in another' (I, 94). If one accepts that monarchy is by God's 'positive grant and revealed declaration . . . he that will claim by that title, must have the same positive grant of God for his succession' (I, 95). Locke doubted that there is such a grant and on the strength of facts and principles denied the right to succeed the father by title of primogeniture. The son of a lawful prince might become a subject, since 'a cadet, or sister's son' may have as good a title as the first lawful prince. Although this is how William III was related to the English royal line, Locke does not uphold William's title on these grounds. His title rests on 'the consent of the people, which being the only one of all lawful governments, he has more fully and clearly than any prince in Christendom'.[51] This being the foundation of legitimacy, Locke

---

[50] Cp. Laslett, *op. cit.*, 356, on the entry in Locke's journal (25th March, 1679) in in which he quotes from Saragard's *Canada* on elective kingship, which permits the succession of the ruler's son.

[51] Preface, lines 6-8.

argues that Filmer failed to answer the question of 'Who Heir?', as the last and longest chapter of the *First Treatise* tries to show.[52] Only 'positive laws and compact, which Divine institution (if there be any) shuts out' (I, 126), can settle the question of succession. In other words, the way is always open 'for human prudence, or consent to place it [paternal regal power] anywhere else'.

Although the terms of incorporation by compact have been met by men's tacit and hardly avoidable consent to the emergence of patriarchal monarchy, the right to choose any form of government as it is implicit in these terms is not foreclosed. As they are explicated in Locke's answers to the two objections to the theory of incorporation, consent on the people's part can be presumed throughout, so long as the contrary is not proved by dissent. But this also means that, on the terms of the compact, the consent of society, though falling short of express consent, is, nevertheless, conditional and, therefore, an instrument of change. Historical precedent must not hamper development; it carries weight not as an encumbrance of rational choice, but as its embodiment.

3. REASON AND HISTORY

A. Precedent

Locke's alignment of the historical precedent of patriarchal monarchy with the principle of consent is not contravened by his insistence on the legitimacy of what by right ought to be over and against the facts of the past. 'If the example of what has been done, be the rule of what ought to be, history would have furnished our A(uthor) with instances' of people begetting 'children on purpose to fatten and eat them' (I, 57). Thus, 'at best an argument from what has been, to what should of right be, has no great force' (Sec. 103). Such a view need not stamp as fortuitous or inexplicable what one does not approve of in the past or the present, nor need it disavow that what has once been might have been justified in its time. A distinction can be made between an interpretation of human affairs in terms of causes and of reasons,[53] between the explication of facts and their valuation. There is the interpretation of the actions and convictions of men in terms of their responses to the stimuli produced by man-

---

[52] According to Laslett, *op. cit.*, 18, 219, 248, Locke's objections were often far-fetched and unfair.

[53] See M. Polanyi, *The Logic of Liberty* (Chicago, 1958), 22.

made and natural environment. This is the causal nexus of historical instances as revealed, for instance, in the explanation of the emergence of patriarchal monarchy and its duration or of infanticide and its discontinuation. There are then the criteria according to which the causal sequence is judged as justifiable or not. That there are causes for what we do is no sufficient reason that we ought to have done it. Nonetheless, what ought to be done will appear the more plausible if it can be shown to have been once done or to be otherwise compatible with factual evidence. On these lines Locke combined his reliance on reason and history.

The lessons of historical experience are not dismissed by Locke, nor are actualities held to abrogate the ethical code and history itself deemed to furnish the rules of knowledge and behaviour.[54] He answered those who invoked what had been as the justification of what was and ought to be, by saying that 'one might, without any great danger, yield them the cause' (Sec. 103). But he himself did not do so. With great determination, he made his readers see that the paternalists had better not 'search too much into the original of governments, as they have begun *de facto*, lest they should find at the foundation of most of them, something very little favourable to the design they promote'. He therefore proclaims victory over the paternalists on the two fronts of reason and history, 'reason being plain on our side, that men are naturally free, and the examples of history showing, that the governments of the world, that were begun in peace, had their beginning laid on that foundation, and were made by the consent of the people'.[55]

There is more than a polemical manoeuvre in Locke's use of history to confirm plain reason. The author of the political *Treatises* was as much aware as was the author of the philosophical *Essay* that the findings of reason must be confirmable by experience. As we have seen, reason supports the idea of a free compact; the generally accepted evidence of history affords confirmation as to the feasibility of its application. While subject to the adjudication of reason, historical facts condition the implementation of reason. In the beginnings, incorporation under paternal rule is hardly avoidable. The principle of free compact is borne out by history, but at the same time elevates men above history. It logically entails that the progeny of those who have not been a party to it may renunciate it.

---

[54] As Cox, *op. cit.*, 165, 193, rather summarily, if not contradictorily, asserts.
[55] Sec. 104. Cp. Sec. 112.

Nobody can 'by any compact whatsoever, bind his children or posterity' (Sec. 116). The arrangements which in certain conditions were in accord with reason need not be so under other conditions and cannot bind for ever. If they did, all history following the establishment of a political society would be the embodiment of reason, instead of reason being the perpetual judge of history and guide to making choices. Different estimations of a given political society are also legitimate. Yet choices are not made in the void and different estimations are not to be enacted as everybody thinks fit. The terms of the original compact are binding so long as the majority does not wish to throw off the obligations to the government under which they were born. Insofar as the dissatisfaction of single individuals occasions their desire to renounce allegiance to the political society of their forebears, they must abandon their inheritance.[56] Historical precedent has no absolute binding power but is far from being devoid of it, and institutions are not laid open to every momentary whim of the individual. This is the logical position of a thinker who pleaded for government by laws established and executed through mutually checking agencies.

There is further proof that Locke's recourse to the historical validation of the rational principles of politics cannot be brushed aside as merely incidental to a polemical purpose. Regard for historical verisimilitude prevented him from conceiving of the state of nature as a stage of development. In his conjectures he revealed a sense of historical development.[57] The absence of historical records does not hide the public conclusion of a pact of incorporation but an imperceptible transformation by tacit consent from a quasi-political family organization into a political society. In fact, the liberal who defends political change, cannot but accept the criteria of evolution. The continually valid terms of incorporation contain the principle of change. The adult children had the right not to consent to their father's rule over them. History subsequent to the beginnings shows numerous examples of the exercise of the right to dissent, which is the right to change prevailing arrangements.

History being identified with development and change, the arbitration of reason is all the more indispensable to distinguishing between good and bad, between viable and obsolete precedents, Precedent by itself is no guarantee of the propriety of men's actions,

---

[56] Secs. 73, 117, 120. See below, 274.
[57] See above, 86 f.

nor is every development a sign of improvement. Of many igno-
minies, 'there are examples . . . both ancient and modern' (I, 59).
Indeed 'if precedents are sufficient to establish a rule' (I, 58) even
Holy Writ could lead us astray. But God does not allow 'of the
authority of practice against his righteous law'. Nevertheless, we
find much in the nations' 'governments, religions, and manners'
which deserves no reverence, because often 'what folly or craft
began, custom makes it sacred'. It cannot be otherwise in the history
of man, for 'in a creature, whose thoughts are more than the sands,
and wider than the ocean, . . . fancy and passion must needs run
him into strange courses, if reason, which is his only star and
compass, be not that he steers by'. If history deviates from the course
set by reason, it also shows that men abide by reason. Men, therefore, may and do have recourse to historical precedent to defend or
retrieve an historical right. '. . . The conquered, or their children,
. . . may appeal, as Jephtha did, to heaven, and repeat their appeal,
till they have recovered the native right of their ancestors . . .'
(Sec. 176). There are rights which are natural as well as historical.

History converges with reason in matters both of property and
government, though more in earlier than in later times. But if
development was not naively identified by Locke with progress, it
did not spell hopeless deterioration either.

B. Rational Politics and Common Law Tenets

While the past remained a source of verification and inspiration,
Locke did not, like other Whig theorists, refer to the historical case
for English liberty: to the traditions of the Common Law, the
House of Commons and the 'ancient constitution'. This omission,
I think, reflects the particular turn political argumentation had taken
rather than a disregard in general of history and tradition.[58] Agreement to the historical primacy of government by royal will through
linking it with the principle of consent, might have seemed to Locke
a more appropriate way of relying on history than accepting the
major Whig myths. For this reason he might have been averse to
contradicting Filmer's exposure of some of the myths, yet unwilling
to appear in agreement with him for fear of embarrassing his fellow

[58] Laslett, *op. cit.*, 75 f., who draws the second conclusion says also (444) that Locke
required a gentleman to acquaint himself with the English constitution and the books
of the Common Law but points out that Locke never possessed or read any of these
books. Laslett thinks it unlikely therefore that the missing part of the *Treatises*, more
than half of the text, was a constitutional argument on traditional lines (77).

Whigs. Whether or not this is why he refrained from making his attitude towards the Common Law tradition explicit, there are some similarities to be noted between Locke's rational theory of politics and traditional Common Law tenets.

In the first place, Locke shared with the common lawyers the purpose of coping with change and development by reference to precedents and principles.[59] Moreover, concessions to royal prerogatives, such as he made,[60] played an essential – though, as much else in Common Law, a somewhat ambiguous – part in the Common Law tradition.[61] His attitude to law itself reveals further similarities. One might well query whether the prominence he gave to property rights does not reflect a transformation of, rather than a break with, the medieval tradition, in which the law of the land and the idea of property were so intimately connected that they assumed the place of modern constitutional and public law. The claim to 'no taxation without representation' cannot be divorced from the late medieval view of the relationship between property and sovereignty, epitomized in the aphorism of Seneca: 'ad regis enim potestas omnium pertinet: ad singulos proprietas' – to kings belongs authority over all; to private persons property.[62] Although Locke attacked the derivation of sovereignty from property,[63] he would have had no quarrel with Seneca's aphorism.

For Locke, property denotes more than men's physical possessions. It exemplifies the whole complex of their rights and liberties guaranteed in law. In this sense 'law, in its true notion, ... ill deserves the name of confinement which hedges us in only from bogs and precipices. So that, however it may be mistaken, the end

---

[59] Th. E. T. Plucknett, *A Concise History of the Common Law* (4th ed., London, 1948), 33, and *passim* for the following statements on the Common Law.

[60] See below, 242 f., 331 f. and 340 f.

[61] Bracton, *De Legibus et Consuetudinibus Angliae*, f. 5b, declared on the one hand: 'parem non habet Rex in Regno suo.' On the other hand he also said (f. 34b): 'Rex habet superiorem, scilicet Deum; item curiam suam, videlicet comites et barones, quia comites dicuntur quasi socii regis, et qui habet socium habet magistrum.' During the revival of the Common Law in the seventeenth century controversy over the doctrine of the divine rights of kings, Bracton was heavily drawn upon by such men as Sir Edward Coke. (See Plucknett, *op. cit.*, 49 f.) Locke referred not only to Hooker, who combined a rational conception of law with the traditional one of the Common Law (cp. Friedrich, *The Philosophy of Law in Historical Perspective*, 71), but quoted Barclay extensively (Secs. 232-8), as well as mentioning Bilson, Bracton and Fortescue (Sec. 239). See below, 254 f.

[62] Cp. C. H. McIlwain, *The Growth of Political Theory in the West, from the Greeks to the End of the Middle Ages* (New York, 1932), 394.

[63] See above, 175-6.

234

of law is not to abolish or restrain, but to preserve and enlarge freedom.'[64] Locke was not only anticipating Rousseau but also giving voice to the Common Law tradition, which regarded English law as the bulwark of liberty.[65] For Locke, this function of law applies to natural and positive law. The Thomistic demand that positive law be in conformity with natural law, he shared with such eminently influential ecclesiastical statesmen as Hubert Walter and Stephen Langton, who hold an honoured place in English political and legal history.[66] When he spoke of 'the fancies and intricate contrivances of men' concerning 'the positive laws of commonwealths' (Sec. 12), or of what 'the municipal laws of some countries, may absurdly direct . . .' (I, 90), he may also have meant the Common Law,[67] although he never mentioned it and spoke only of 'common laws' (Sec. 138). Yet he did not for a moment deviate from the principle he and the common lawyers professed, namely, that without law there is no freedom. If criticism of positive law was aimed at the Common Law at all, then it did not mean a wholesale rejection of its fundamental tenets. The practice of the common lawyers shows that, in their view also, laws may be mistaken. Principles of equity and justice were tied to precedents by which adjudication, and even legislation, have to abide, which for the common lawyers were hardly distinguishable from one another. Locke's 'common superior' is the 'judge on earth', who has to abide by 'the constitutions and laws of the government' (Sec. 226). These, as we have seen,[68] are rules for the conduct of government rather than laws of the government.

A distinction is made by Locke not only between natural law and positive law, but there is one implied also between positive law and 'constitutions'. The latter represent the principles embodied (by the people's consent) in institutions and procedures, rather than principles elaborated in constitutions in the modern sense. Although not predicated specifically on English history, like the common lawyers' 'ancient constitution', Locke's 'original constitution' also possesses an historical connotation. It is an arrangement that has attained an obligatory or directive character through having been

[64] Sec. 57. See also Sec. 22 and the *Essay*, IV, iii, 18.
[65] D. Ogg, *England in the Reigns of James II and William III* (Oxford, 1955), 547, has mentioned this parallel.
[66] *The Cambridge Medieval History*, VI, 218-19
[67] Cp. Laslett, *op. cit.*, 293.
[68] See above, 136.

legitimately instituted. Insofar as the 'original' of each proper political society is consent, invocation of the 'original constitution' may be that of a generally applicable principle. But 'original' also denotes something specific to different societies, such as the form of government, its organization and legislative procedures.[69] What is 'original' in both senses, 'the original and supreme act of the society' (Sec. 157) and 'the first and fundamental positive law of all commonwealths' (Sec. 134), may be appealed to against particular decisions, including, in the last instance, those of the legislative body. Locke thought this likely only in extreme cases, when the community as a whole became concerned. Nevertheless, this function of Locke's 'constitutions' paralleled that of the Common Law when cited in the attempts to control and invalidate acts of parliament. Of course, Locke's 'constitutions' generalize, if they do not abstract, ideas which the common lawyer substantiated by constantly overlapping references to the findings of courts, to charters, laws, statutes and custom. The more fundamental and general the juridical and political validity attached to precedents, the more doubtful, in some cases at least, was the historical reality of what was fastened upon. After all, it was not the original *Magna Carta* but rather the myth attendant upon its vicissitudes, which in time became a frame of reference in Common Law. It provided therefore not much more of a true historical precedent than Locke's 'original' of government.

The few points which I have made merely indicate the lines along which the differences and affinities between Locke's approach and that of the exponents of the 'ancient constitution' might be further investigated. Enough has been said to permit the conclusion that Locke's attitude towards history and tradition in the *Treatises* cannot be identified with outright animosity or lack of understanding, and that the *Treatises* do not fail to reflect 'the plain historical method' of the *Essay*.[70] Admittedly, the appeal to history serves to vindicate political ideas and practices. Since Machiavelli's time, such appeals had become increasingly part of political philosophy and polemics. Both traditionalists and rationalists have ever since referred to history when they wished to clinch a political argument. This has not prevented agreement on facts, or what were considered to be such. Locke's and Filmer's factual statements

---

[69] Cp. Secs. 1, 134, 141, 153, 154, 198.
[70] As Simon, *loc. cit.*, 398 and Laslett, *op. cit.*, 83, maintain.

concerning paternalism are a case in point. It is mainly a matter of bias if one says that rationalists in particular have misinterpreted and misconstrued historical facts. It can hardly be shown that Filmer had more consideration for historical facts and a more fitting view of the historical process than Locke. Although it is almost axiomatically accepted in the distinction between a liberal and a conservative approach, detailed investigation does not bear out the assumption that the proper understanding of the nature of history and tradition is invariably bound up with the conservative's proclaimed reverence for the past.[71] Being prejudiced against change usually prevents a man from acknowledging what the past was really like. Conjuring up the authority of the past rarely entails an indiscriminate acceptance of past commitments. It rather consists in the selective resort to precedents, to say nothing of the arbitrary interpretation of what is fastened upon. The recognition that history involves change is necessary, if one wishes to attenuate the arbitrariness of patterns of thought which each present tends to impose upon the past.[72] Consciousness of bringing rational criteria – and forthwith those extraneous to the past itself – to bear upon historical and political tradition implies the distinction between criteria of uniqueness, continuity and timeless validity, all of which are essential components of historical knowledge and judgement. The distinction and co-ordination of these criteria is an essential part of Locke's subjection of history to reason, and is much less evident in Filmer's attempt to do the reverse.

Since what has existed in the past has not, according to Locke, continuous validity, he was free to acknowledge the adequacy of a form of government in one stage of development and dispute it in another. He could consider the continuation of patriarchal monarchy as legitimate and still reserve judgement on royal absolutism.

---

[71] See M. Seliger, *The Conception of History of the French Historians of the Restoration (1815–1830) in their Treatment of French History* (unpublished doctoral thesis [in Hebrew], the Hebrew University of Jerusalem, 1956).

[72] Cp. N. Rotenstreich, *Between Past and Present, An Essay in History* (New Haven, 1958).

CHAPTER VIII

ONE-MAN RULE IN HISTORICAL PERSPECTIVE

I. PREREQUISITES FOR CONTINUITY

A. *Predispositions and Environment*

The same conditions as make for the emergence of patriarchal monarchy make for its duration, that is, for the government of one man: the continuation of the psychological predispositions of children in adults, the socio-economic situation and the quality of the ruler. It was natural for 'children even when they were men' (Sec. 105) to obey their father. 'The custom of obeying him, in their childhood, made it easier to submit to him, rather than to any other.' The custom does not have to find its focus in the father. Where 'a family by degrees grew up into a commonwealth, and the fatherly authority being continued on to the elder son, every one in his turn growing up under it, tacitly submitted to it...' (Sec. 110). Obedience to the father and the affection characteristic of family-ties breed a propensity towards father-like authority, to one-man rule as such.

'The father's government of the childhood . . . having accustomed them to the rule of one man, and taught them that where it was exercised with care and skill, with affection and love to those under it, it was sufficient to procure and preserve to men all the political happiness they sought for, in society. It was no wonder, that they should pitch upon, and naturally run into that form of government, which from their infancy they had been all accustomed to; and which, by experience they had found both easy and safe.'[1]

The obedience accorded to the father, and most willingly and naturally to the good father, continues to be accorded to his successor, who is no longer the father of the adult males of the commonwealth. Obedience is also rendered from the outset to a chief who is no more than a father-substitute. What psychologists call a transference is implied by Locke to account for the fact that 'perhaps at first . . . some one good and excellent man, having got

[1] Sec. 107. Cp. Sec. 112.

a pre-eminence amongst the rest, had this deference paid to his goodness and virtue, as to a kind of *natural authority*, that the chief rule . . . by a tacit consent devolved into his hands' (Sec. 94). In this way 'they used their natural freedom, to set up him, whom they judged the ablest, and most likely, to rule well over them' (Sec. 105). Locke, like Machiavelli before and Montesquieu, Rousseau and Hegel after him, did not take exception to heroes as leaders and founders of infant states. But he insisted that their legitimation consisted in consent, assuming for this purpose the existence of tacit consent, evidenced by abstention from exercising the right of active dissent. The family-bred habit of obeying the father increased the likelihood of deference being voluntarily paid, especially to a person of distinction.

'Whoever, nations, or races of men, labour to fetch their original from, may be concluded to be thought by them, men of renown, famous to posterity for the greatness of their virtues and actions; but beyond these they look not, nor consider who they were heirs to . . .' (I, 141).

To reject 'fatherly authority to be the original of government' is for Locke to deny its Filmerist foundation, namely 'that it descended from Adam to his heirs' (I, 158). Inherited authority, detached from personal merit, cannot be claimed for Moses and Joshua, nor for mythical or historical heroes like Ogyges, Hercules, Brahma, Tamberlain and Pharamond.[2] Locke asked concerning the judges of Israel, 'cannot God raise up such men, unless fatherhood have a title to government' (I, 158)? Filmer himself 'seems to confess, that these judges, who were all the governors, they then had, were only men of valour, whom they *made* their generals to defend them in time of peril'. The modern theory of charismatic leadership is adumbrated and explained by the natural inclination of adults to the father-substitute, by the yearning to seek shelter from the growing perils and complications of life outside the family under the wings of a father-like authority. The advocacy of the right of revolt – abstention from which legitimates the father's monarchical power – lends itself also to explication in Freudian terms. The anthropological myths of the origin of human society often imply the slaying of the primal father as the complement of the predisposition to obey him.

[2] I, 141, 157.

The readiness to accept fatherly authority is particularly fostered by the specific conditions of early societal development.

'Thus, whether a family by degrees grew up into a commonwealth, ... or whether several families, or the descendants of several families, whom chance, neighbourhood, or business brought together, uniting into society, the need of a general ... and the great confidence the innocence and sincerity of that poor but virtuous age ... gave men one of another, made the first beginners of commonwealths generally put the rule into one man's hand ...' (Sec. 110), craving for that 'paternal affection [which] secured their property, and interest under his care ...' (Sec. 105).

The continuance of family-like affection beyond the family, the need of protection and common economic concerns 'of a simple poor way of living' (Sec. 107) pointed to authoritarian yet minimal one-man rule. '... monarchy being simple, and most obvious to men' who as yet had not experienced 'the ambition or insolence of empire ..., they put themselves into such a frame of government, as was ... also best suited to their present state and condition; which stood more in need of defence against foreign invasions and injuries, than of multiplicity of laws'.[3] Whether or not the examples from the Bible, from Greek and other mythology will bear out the assumption of interior harmony and backwoods simplicity, Locke assumed that, under these conditions, discretionary one-man rule was natural. In fact, it was as imperative that such was the form of government as it was that the rulers acquitted themselves successfully of their task. For 'unless they had done so, young societies could not have subsisted: without such nursing fathers tender and careful of the public weal, all governments would have sunk under the weakness and infirmities of their infancy; and the prince and the people had soon perished together' (Sec. 110).

A poor and honourable way of living and the propensity of adults to behave as political infants make for the management of the commonwealth by able nursing fathers. This was 'the golden age before vain ambition, and *amor sceleratus habendi*, evil concupiscence, had corrupted men's minds into a mistake of true power and honour ...' (Sec. 111). Men had to revise their attitude – or, as we may say, were compelled to become political adults – when 'ambition and luxury, in future ages would retain and increase the

[3] Sec. 107. Cp. Sec. 75.

power, without doing the business, for which it was given, . . . and
. . . taught princes to have distinct and separate interests from their
people . . .' The change of behaviour of the rulers, though related
to socio-economic differentiation, becomes the principal cause of the
growth of a different attitude towards one-man rule. The influence
of economic change notwithstanding, the confidence of the ruled
waned as the result of political experience *per se*. Locke remained
faithful to the view that economics depended more on politics than
vice versa.

B. The Ruler's Quality

Absolute power developed out of men's positive experience with
fatherly monarchy, 'the easiness and equality of it not offending
anyone, everyone acquiesced, till time seemed to have confirmed it,
and settled a right of succession by prescription' (Sec. 110). Discretionary one-man rule became defective, however, 'when time,
giving authority, and (as some men would persuade us) sacredness
to customs, which the negligent, and unforeseeing innocence of the
first ages began . . .' (Sec. 94). Yet what happened in the course of
times does not reflect adversely on one-man rule in the beginning,
nor could lack of foresight be blamed in

'men, whom neither experience had instructed in forms of government, nor the ambition or insolence of empire had taught to beware
of the encroachments of prerogative, or the inconveniences of
absolute power, which monarchy, in succession, was apt to lay
claim to, and bring upon them . . .' (Sec. 107).

In point of fact, the quality of the ruler rather than the nature and
extent of his power remained decisive throughout the greatest part
of history. The tender but authoritarian solicitude of rulers for the
public good is the prerequisite for transcending the equality and
ease of an uncomplicated but poor way of life. 'The increase of
lands and the right employing of them is the great art of government' (Sec. 42). The advancement of economic growth is indeed a
princely art.

'That prince who shall be so wise and godlike as by established laws
of liberty to secure protection and encouragement to the honest
industry of mankind against the oppression of power and narrowness
of party will quickly be too hard for his neighbours.'

The laws of liberty are evidently of the prince's own making, or at least decisively dependent upon his will and protection. Godlike princely rule during the phase of economic expansion, just as 'the easiness and equality' of one-man rule in the beginning, does not offend any of the subjects; it protects against 'the oppression of power and narrowness of party'. Efficient and beneficent one-man rule does not cease to be appropriate when it is no longer mainly concerned with external defence. Rather, defence is made easier as the result of the godlike prince's protection of honest industry. In other words, the persistence of men's natural predisposition to abide by father-like authority depends less on socio-economic conditions, or on danger from neighbour-states, than on the quality of the rulers. Locke cited the history of England without any reference to a specific stage of economic development, or to external issues, when he argued 'that prerogative was always largest in the hands of our wisest and best princes' (Sec. 165). Indeed, *whenever* they acted without or contrary to the letter of the law', the people 'acquiesced in what they did, and, without the least complaint, let them enlarge their prerogative as they pleased . . .'[4]

Although in this context Locke reminds us that 'princes are but men, made as others' (Sec. 165), he did so to justify the people's acquiescence in rule by prerogative even 'if any human frailty or mistake . . . appeared in some small declinations' from the public good. The important thing was that 'it was visible, the main of their [the princes'] conduct tended to nothing but the care of the public'. In virtue of their being godlike such princes 'indeed had some title to *arbitrary* power, by that argument, that would prove absolute monarchy the best government . . .' (Sec. 166). It was not contradictory for Locke to add: 'upon this is founded that saying, that the reigns of good princes have been always most dangerous to the liberties of their people.' The statement is usually misunderstood because the habit of disregarding Locke's allowances for one-man rule has made it natural to ignore the next sentence and its connection with the first. Locke continued: 'For when their successors, managing the government with different thoughts, would draw the actions of those good rulers into precedent, . . . it has often occa-

---

[4] Sec. 165. For Locke's use of the verb 'to acquiesce' as regards the beginnings and later stages, see also Sec. 110 – 'every one acquiesced' in the transmission of fatherly authority; Sec. 164 – the people's 'acquiescing in it when so done,' i.e., in the exercise of prerogative.

sioned contest, and sometimes public disorders . . .' The inference is clearly not that it would have been better to have foregone the good and edifying precedents so as to be spared the insidious sequel. In the first place, not the precedent of exercising prerogative, but its exercise with 'different thoughts' is condemned, 'as if what had been done only for the good of the people, was a right in them [the successors] to do, for the harm of the people, if they so pleased'. Secondly, Locke immediately reaffirmed that it was 'very possible, and *reasonable*, that the people should not go about to set *any* bounds to the prerogative of those kings or rulers, who themselves transgressed not the bounds of the public good'. He had already declared it a general rule that, where a rational creature

'finds a good and wise ruler, he may not perhaps think it either necessary, or useful to set precise bounds to his power in all things . . . For . . . a good prince, who is mindful of the trust put into his hands, and careful of the good of his people, *cannot have too much prerogative*, that is, power to do good' (Sec. 164).

Consequently, exception is taken to the tendency of

'a weak and ill prince . . . to make or promote an interest distinct from that of the public, [which] gives the people an occasion, to claim their right, and limit that power, which, whilst it was exercised for their good, they were content should be *tacitly* allowed.'

The prerogative to be accorded to a good and wise ruler is not prejudiced by the experience of wicked and foolish rulers, although it serves them as a pretence for doing harm.

Kingship by divine right is rejected by Locke; but not unbounded prerogative of godlike princes. The founders' greatness and virtue give 'a lustre to those, who in future ages could pretend to derive themselves from them' (I, 141). This becomes dangerous under unworthy successors. The continuance of prerogative rule, as established by the founders, was legitimate by tacit consent, so long as the performance of princes had been sufficiently godlike and whenever it subsequently proved to be so. The question to be faced, therefore, is: how are we to reconcile the foregoing with Locke's famous diatribes against absolute monarchy, which accompanied the advocacy of a mixed constitution?

2. ABSOLUTE MONARCHY AND ARBITRARY RULE

A. Arbitrary Power and the Form of Government

The legislative and executive power derived from the renunciation by everyone of his right to pronounce and execute judgement on offences against natural law. 'And herein we have the original of the legislative and executive power of civil society . . .'[5] Having added no more than that only the exercise of these functions by government permits us to speak of political society, Locke went on: 'Hence it is evident, that absolute monarchy, . . . is indeed inconsistent with civil society, and so can be no form of civil government at all' (Sec. 90). Rather than following from what Locke said before, the conclusion follows from what he said afterwards: 'For he being supposed to have all, both legislative and executive power in himself alone, there is no judge to be found' (Sec. 91).

If we accept this categorical assertion as Locke's considered opinion, we may say that he allowed legislative and executive power to be exercised by the same body of persons or the same person, yet at the same time disqualified absolute monarchy;[6] but we must add that Locke was inconsistent. If we argue that he embraced both views because he considered all forms of government to be equally founded on consent,[7] the question remains how could he disqualify one particular form? Nor does the solution lie in regarding the theory of governmental forms as inconsistent with his theory of majority consent,[8] unless we take majority consent to mean majority rule, which it does not. The solution lies in that for Locke, as later for Rousseau, each form of government is legitimate if it can be related to the public good and the consent of the people.[9]

If each form of government can be established by majority consent, there can be no reason against uniting the legislative and executive power in one person. The prohibition against it would override the principle of consent, instead of being a further application of it. As quoted above, Locke's disqualification of absolute monarchy renders pointless his strenuous efforts to reconcile the beginning of political society under one-man rule with the principle

[5] Sec. 88. Cp. Secs. 87, 89, 124-6, 128-30.
[6] Laslett, *op. cit.*, 119.   [7] Goldwin, *op. cit.*, 457.
[8] Kendall, *op. cit.*, 127.
[9] Sec. 132. *Contract Social*, III, XVII. There is a decisive difference between Locke and Rousseau. According to Locke, legislative supremacy can rest with one, a few or the people. Rousseau's distinction between the forms of government has no bearing at all on the placing of legislative authority, it always remains with the people.

of consent, and the prevalence of that rule both in English and in general history. If we were not faced with an instance of emphatic but careless wording Locke must be deemed so inadvertent as to justify the distribution of governmental powers by reference to the ultimate supremacy of the people, only to contradict this supremacy and demolish his endeavours to show history as confirming the verdict of reason that political society rests on consent. If so, outdoing Jules Verne's Phineas Fogg, Locke not only stoked the boilers of his ship with the expendable woodwork, but used the very timbers that held the ship together.

The previously quoted statement on the inadmissibility of absolute monarchy is an overstatement and is reformulated later on. To show that the initial and not the subsequent statement is inaccurately formulated, we must first keep in mind that Locke attached the right to choose any form of government to the terms of the compact, but supposed the right to be applicable only after political society had been established under patriarchal monarchy, and existed under it for a considerable time. The sharing of governmental power is, therefore, conceived to have followed the concentration of power as an historical sequel. Degenerate rulers caused men 'to think of methods of restraining any exorbitances of those, to whom they *had given* the authority over them, and of balancing the power of government, by placing several parts of it in different hands' (Sec. 107). Locke juxtaposed shared and absolute power in historical perspective on the basis of the legitimate conferment of one-man government by consent.

A second and decisive consideration suggests itself for the view that Locke did not intend to identify absolute government as such with non-civil government. On the one hand he distinguished absolute power from arbitrary power. On the other, this is not the only instance where he did not abide by his own terminological distinctions. Despite the pejorative meaning which he usually attached to 'arbitrary', he spoke, in one and the same section, first of the 'arbitrary power in some things left in the prince's hand '(Sec. 210) – meaning his legitimate prerogatives – and then of 'several experiments made of arbitrary power' – meaning actions which are reprehensible and give just cause for revolt. Conversely, despite the pejorative meaning which he also attached to 'absolute', in the thematic discussion of the nature and extent of legislative power, he stated that 'even absolute power, where it is necessary, is not arbitrary by being absolute, but is still limited by that reason, and confined to those ends, which required it in some cases to be absolute' (Sec. 139). This is said on military discipline, and therefore predicated on the most stringent of emergencies. Yet the development of political society is also a matter of emergency, since without authoritarian nursing fathers society would never have progressed beyond its beginnings. Besides, he justifies military discipline on the same terms as political authority. The power of life and death which the officer exercises over his subordinates is the hallmark which sets monarchical and all political authority apart from paternal authority. That the officer has no immediate authority over the possessions of his subordinates applies to any bearer of official authority. There can be little doubt that the distinction between 'arbitrary' and 'absolute' power is intended to justify absolute power in politics. The distinction is spelled out only after Locke had reformulated the proposition that, on account of legislative and executive authority being united in one person, 'absolute monarchy, . . . is indeed inconsistent with civil society, and so can be no form of civil government at all' (Sec. 90). A few sections after the statement that the majority 'may put the power of making laws' also 'into the hands of one man' (Sec. 132), he joined 'arbitrary' to 'absolute', and said: '*Absolute arbitrary power*, or government without settled standing laws, can neither of them consist with the ends of society and government . . .' (Sec. 137).

Arbitrary rule is first and foremost rule without 'declared and received laws', for 'by stated rules of right and property to secure their peace and quiet' is what men ask of society and government. Secondly, the exercise of absolute arbitrary power is not allied with monarchy alone. In accordance with the right of the people to institute monarchy, aristocracy or democracy – or 'make compounded and mixed forms' (Sec. 132) – it is stressed that 'the legislative, *whether placed in one or more*, . . . is not, nor can possibly be absolutely arbitrary over the lives and fortunes of the people' (Sec. 135). What 'it cannot be supposed that they should intend' is not to choose a monarch as their legislator, but 'to give to any *one, or more*, an *absolute arbitrary* power over their persons and estates . . .',[10]

[10] Sec. 137. In this section, Locke spoke three times of 'absolute arbitrary power', and also mentioned 'arbitrary power' but never 'absolute power'. Likewise in Secs. 135, 138, 171, 172. Only in the summary of Sec. 174 is 'absolute dominion' again referred to as not being 'one kind of civil society'. But it is 'absolute dominion, *however placed*,' i.e., not confined to one-man rule.

so as to allow 'one or a few men . . . to force them to obey at pleasure the exorbitant and unlimited decrees of their sudden thoughts . . .' Although Locke knew that even 'good and equitable laws' (Sec. 138) are not always a sufficient safeguard against arbitrariness, rule by law is the *desideratum*. Hence,

> '*whatever form the commonwealth is under*, the ruling power ought to govern by declared and received laws, . . . that both the people may know their duty, and be safe and secure within the limits of the law, and the rulers too kept within their due bounds, and not to be tempted, by the power they have in their hands . . .' (Sec. 137).

Absolute arbitrary rule is possible under any form of government. It is evident wherever no respect is paid to the subjects' 'right to the goods, which by the law of the community are theirs . . .' (Sec. 138). For 'government into whatsoever hands it is put , . . the prince or senate . . . can never have a power to take to themselves the whole or any part of the subjects' property, without their own consent'.[11] Disregard of property rights, and arbitrary absolute rule in general, quite apart from not being confined to absolute monarchy, are not even most frequent under it alone. They are greatest where 'the legislative is in one lasting assembly always in being, *or* in one man, as in absolute monarchies' (Sec. 138).

B. The Legitimacy of Absolute Monarchy

It may be said that Locke entertained a horror of personal authority,[12] if this means that he abhorred the exercise of authority by personal whim. Absolute monarchy fosters but does not create this tendency. Anticipating Lord Acton's famous dictum, Locke said that to advance a claim to an unlimited power is to 'flatter the natural vanity and ambition of men, too apt of itself to grow and increase with the possession of any power' (I, 10). Hence 'he that thinks absolute power purifies men's bloods, and corrects the baseness of human nature, need read but the history of this, or any other age to be convinced of the contrary . . . For what the protection of

[11] Sec. 139. If either the majority or their representatives must consent to taxes (Sec. 140), it is difficult to see how taxes can be imposed under a prince who is the sole law-maker, or else, as Plamenatz, *op. cit.*, 230, points out, why, if a prince can rightfully be the sole law-maker, he needs to secure express consent to taxation. If Locke was aware of the inconsistency in his argument – which he shared with Bodin – and wished to convey something, then it probably was that in the long run a mixed form of government was unavoidable.

[12] Cp. Kendall, *op. cit.*, 85.

absolute monarchy is, what kind of fathers of their countries it makes princes to be', can be learned from any chapter of history and especially from countries 'where this sort of government is grown to perfection . . .' (Sec. 92). Like Lord Acton, he did not say that rulers invariably succumb to the temptations of absolute power. He disputed only the purifying effect of absolute monarchy upon the ruler's personality. Much depends on the personal quality and intentions of the ruler:

'He that would have been insolent and injurious in the woods of America, would not probably be much better in a throne; where perhaps learning and religion shall be found out to justify all, that he shall do to his subjects, and the sword presently silence all those that dare question it.'

Institutional patterns and ideological trappings provide an opening and inducement for the personal predispositions of the rulers towards arbitrariness. The absolute power of the monarch invites abuse, because it gives rise to the *non sequitur* that 'because he has power to do more hurt and wrong, it is right when he does it' (Sec. 93). In view of the ends and reasons of government, Locke denied the contention that, although for the subjects 'there must be measures, laws, and judges, for their mutual peace and security', the ruler, because he is held to preserve law and order, 'ought to be absolute' (Sec. 93). Absolute power is dangerous because it is conducive to wrongdoing; but only by wrongdoing does absolute government like all other government become arbitrary rule and hence disqualified.

Even in his vehement outburst against absolute monarchies, Locke conceded that they were actually a form of government like all others but doubted whether the subjects were afforded 'an appeal to the law, and judges . . . from a true love of mankind and society, and such a charity as we owe all one to another'.[13] He judges absolute monarchies according to the criteria of reasons and ends by which the absolute power of the officer is set apart from arbitrary power, and good and wise rulers are distinguished from unworthy successors. If he believed that no just appeal to the law was available on principle under absolute monarchy, Locke ought to have claimed not that 'there is reason to doubt', but that there is no reason for any doubt that, under such a government, 'a true love of mankind'

[13] Sec. 93. See also above, 104-5.

cannot guide the maintenance of law and order. He would have maintained that an absolute ruler never does anything but 'what every man who loves his own power, profit, or greatness, may, and naturally must do, keep those animals from hurting and destroying one another who labour and drudge only for his pleasure and advantage'.[14] Locke wished to justify revolt 'against the violence and oppression of this absolute ruler', but not to reject absolute monarchy unconditionally. It is for this reason that he dismissed the assumption

'that all of them but one, should be under the restraint of laws, but that he should still retain all the liberty of the state of nature, increased with power, and made licentious by impunity. This is to think that men are so foolish that they take care to avoid what mischiefs may be done them by pole-cats, or foxes, but are content, nay think it safety, to be devoured by lions.'

If this famous denunciation of absolutism were meant to apply unqualifiedly to absolutism, and not to arbitrary or degenerate absolutism, then Locke might be expected to have gone on to say that, whenever one man is the sole legislator and chief executive of political society he is in the state of nature. Instead, he said that only when 'they have no appeal on earth against any harm they *may* receive from him, they are apt to think themselves in the state of nature . . .' (Sec. 94). What is more, in the next sentence, he reaffirmed the legitimacy of 'some one good and excellent man', having at first 'the chief rule, . . . by a tacit consent devolved into his hands, *without any other caution, but the assurance they [the people] had of his uprightness and wisdom*'.[15] And as in the context of justifying prerogative rule,[16] he insisted that 'successors of another stamp' had no claim to such authority. As related to each other by Locke himself, the various strands of argument relevant to one-man rule coalesce in the view that only when it does them harm does absolute monarchy, like all other forms of government, forfeit the people's

[14] Sec. 93. Cp. 163 and I, 156.
[15] Sec. 94. Locke referred here to 'the following part of this discourse'. Laslett, *op. cit.*, 347, takes this to mean Secs. 162 onwards. However, the reference would seem to apply first and foremost to Secs. 105-12, where what happened 'at first' is shown 'more at large', and for the second time at that. For it is the contents of Secs. 74-5 which are enlarged upon in Secs. 105-12. Locke's carelessness in his cross-references should put us on our guard lest, like Cox, we read too much into the inexactness of his references to other writers' works.
[16] See above, 242-3.

trust and evoke the transformation of their tacit consent into active dissent. As early as Section 17, indeed, Locke said that 'he who attempts to get another man into his absolute power, does thereby put himself into a state of war with him'. But he immediately qualified the statement by speaking of the one 'who would get me into his power *without my consent*'. That absolute power can be legitimated by consent is kept in mind from the outset and never intentionally gainsaid. In his classification of the legitimate forms of the commonwealth,[17] appears therefore also that form in which the monarch unites legislative and executive authority in his hands. What was in accord with the terms of the compact in the beginning is expressly recognized as legitimate at later, if not at all, times.

Thus, though most likely to jeopardize the people's safety, absolute monarchy is not precluded from providing it. The personal authority which Locke feared was authority made subservient to the personal motives of rulers. This is what renders power arbitrary and not who, or how many, wield it. Besides ruling by settled and promulgated laws the reasons and ends count which may require power to be absolute and at the same time determine whether political has degenerated into despotic power, no matter what the regime.

'For wherever the power that is put in *any* hands for the government of the people, and the preservation of their properties, is applied to other ends, and made use of to impoverish, harass, or subdue them to the *arbitrary and irregular* commands of those that have it: There it presently becomes tyranny, whether *those that thus use it are one or many*.'[18]

3. ROYAL ABSOLUTISM AND FILMERISM

Locke's recognition of the legitimacy of an absolute monarch, who ruled for the public good through settled and promulgated laws, is most suggestively confirmed by the way in which he played off King James' definition of tyranny and the views of less exalted champions of royal absolutism against Filmer. In fact, his preoccupation with discrediting Filmer's version of absolute monarchy seems to explain the overtones of Locke's censure of that form of government and its contradictory disqualification in one instance.

[17] Cp. Secs. 132, 133.
[18] Sec. 201. The 'many' are the thirty tyrants of Athens and the *decemviri* of Rome. No democracy, and consequently no 'tyranny of the majority', is meant. One of its important aspects was, however, envisaged by Locke. See below, 311.

A. *Lawful Kingship, Tyranny and Usurpation*

Filmer stands accused of confounding usurped and legitimate kingship by his incoherence. All means to obtain kingship can be justified, says Locke, by stretching the principle of fatherhood as Filmer does. On these grounds, what makes 'any one properly a king, needs no more but governing by supreme power', or else 'no kingdom by this natural right, can be bigger than a family'.[19] To isolate Filmer, Locke capitalized on the traditional absolutists' endeavour to distinguish tyranny from kingship. In his definition of tyranny, he relied on the views of James I, the royal advocate of monarchical prerogative, whom Filmer quoted extensively.[20]

Locke quoted from two speeches delivered by the king in 1603 and 1609 respectively, and approved 'that learned king who well understood the notions of things', for showing 'the difference between a king and a tyrant to consist *only* in this, that one makes the laws the bounds of his power, and the good of the public, the end of his government; the other makes all give way to his own will and appetite' (Sec. 200). He also quoted James' reference to the king's 'making of good laws and constitutions' and to the ruler being 'bound to observe that paction made *to* his people by *his* laws . . . according to that paction which God made with Noah, after the deluge'.

It was not merely to obtain a better stick to beat Filmer with that Locke quarrelled neither with the king's idea of the 'paction', nor with the view that to be lawful, a king need only observe his own laws and occupy his sovereign will with the pursuit of the public good. Locke himself defined tyranny as 'the exercise of power beyond right' (Sec. 199). Right means here as much natural as positive law. After all, a tyrant might rule through settled standing laws of his own making no less than a lawful king. Only by reference to natural law or constitutional custom can he be said to exercise power beyond right. Also, for the sake of the public good, the chief executive may use his prerogative and transgress laws without becoming a tyrant. Not in this respect alone are the 'good prince' and the 'tyrant' comparable;[21] they are no less indistinguishable

[19] I, 78, 142. Cp. I, 72, 79–80, 121, 134, 149. As Laslett, *op. cit.*, 219, points out, it was not very charitable of Locke to reproach Filmer perpetually with his justification of usurpation, knowing that it was written under Cromwell and that he himself had published at that time nothing except an eulogy of Cromwell.

[20] Cp. Laslett, *op. cit.*, 417.

[21] Cp. Goldwin, *op. cit.*, 460.

where legislation is concerned. Mindful of this, Locke supplemented the statement that 'wherever law ends, tyranny begins', with the rider: '*if the law be transgressed to another's harm*' (Sec. 202). The definition of tyranny is narrowed down to the transgression of law to another's detriment, because actions for the public good cannot always be actions according to positive laws. But according to Locke, action for the public good cannot even be in invariable accord with the laws or customs that regulate the designation of persons who are to bear rule. He elaborated on the terms in which, in full accord with King James, he had distinguished between proper political power and despotic power, to distinguish between usurpation and tyranny. As a result, he left King James behind, envisaging the transformation of a usurper, a conqueror or a tyrant into a lawful ruler.

'As conquest may be called a foreign usurpation, so usurpation is a kind of domestic conquest, with this difference, that a usurper can never have right on his side' (Sec. 197). Usurpation, nevertheless, is 'a change only of persons, but not of the forms and rules of the government'. The forms and rules, that is, the constitution, are affected by usurpation, insofar only as the usurper 'is got into the possession of what another has right to'. Hence, he is not a tyrant unless he 'extend his power beyond, what of right belonged to the lawful princes, or governors'. A usurper becomes a tyrant on the same terms as a lawful ruler, as is logical, since 'the exercise of power beyond right, . . . *nobody* can have a right to' (Sec. 199). What sets a usurper apart from a lawful ruler emanates then from the one fact that 'in all lawful governments the designation of the persons, who are to bear rule, is as natural and necessary a part, as the form of the government itself, and is that which had its establishment originally from the people' (Sec. 198). On these terms the usurper can achieve legitimacy. What has been established by the people may be altered or revoked by the people. Although

'he is not the person the laws have appointed, and consequently not the person the people have consented to . . .' he 'or any deriving from him' remain usurpers 'till the people are both at liberty to consent, and have actually consented to allow, and confirm in him, the power he has till then usurped' (Sec. 198).

The right of the people to shake off 'the usurpation, or tyranny, which the sword has brought in upon them' stands 'till their rulers *put them* under such a frame of government, as they willingly . . . consent to' (Sec. 192). The new rulers have to establish 'a full state of liberty' and provide for 'such standing laws, to which they [the people] . . . *or* their representatives' assent. It is worth noting that as far as the people are concerned, their legitimation of conquest, usurpation – and, correspondingly, of the nullification of the claims of those who by established law are the rulers – consists in tacit acquiescence. For Locke did not grant suffrage to the majority of the people. Hence, just as 'that which has its establishment originally from the people' derives from their tacit consent, so do their further legitimations. Inasmuch as popular consent is evidenced by the absence of active dissent, no more is implied by the willing consent of the people to a usurper or conqueror than that the majority refrain from revolt against him either in conformity with, or against, the will of their representatives who are directly responsible to a minority of the people.

Exactly because Locke upheld the right of revolt, he had to leave the door open for the legitimation of usurpation. The right to resist rulers cannot be fully effective unless the forcible seizure of power is permitted. Otherwise only an elected, but never a hereditary, ruler could be rightfully expelled from the throne. Since the right of war holds good in respect of any rulei who may be considered to have put himself in a state of war with his people, any ruler or form of government which avoids or overcomes this state of affairs is, or can become, legitimate. Just as absolute monarchy as such is not illegitimate, but may become so, usurpation, although it is illegitimate because illegal, may in the event become legitimate. 'The injury and the crime is equal, whether committed by the wearer of a crown, or some petty villain. The title of the offender, and the number of his followers make no difference in the offence, unless it be to aggravate it' (Sec. 176). The equality of the crime destroys the authority due to titles. That is why the title to authority must necessarily go with whoever avenges the crime and amends the offences. When 'the governor, however entitled', who 'makes not the law, but his will, the rule', and uses his power 'not for the good of those, who are under it . . .' (Sec. 199), becomes a tyrant and may be dealt with like any villain, one who is legally a villain must also be allowed to bceome the wearer of the crown.

No lack of perspicacity caused Locke to rely for the advancement of these views on King James' distinction between a lawful prince and a tyrant and yet to censure Filmer's no more than inadvertent legitimation of usurpation.

B. The Use of Traditionalist Views and the Abuse of Filmer

By their distinction between a lawful prince and a tyrant, the traditional absolutist doctrines provide an opportunity for raising the question of the right to resist the ruler who defies natural law. As exceptions to the interdict of resistance were admitted, consent could be claimed as the missing link for rendering these theories consistent. This was their advantage, from Locke's point of view, over the theories of Hobbes and Filmer. For as both knew, to make any concession to the right of resistance was a surrender to the principle of government by consent.

Hobbes owned, like Locke,[22] that the government is dissolved when the prince subjects his country to foreigners, or abandons execution of the laws. Yet this served him to circumvent the acknowledgement of a right to overturn the government. He could not but acknowledge the fact of revolt – sovereignty is 'not only subject to violent death, by foreign war; . . . it has in it, from the very institution, many seeds of a natural mortality, by intestine discord'.[23] But the death of sovereignty is not the rightful self-assertion of the citizens against the ruler. Hobbes presented it as the self-cancellation of the government. At times, his attitude too was that, if facts did not fit the theory, so much the worse for the facts. To Barclay and other traditional absolutists it could be imputed that in allowing for resistance in exceptional cases, they advanced towards the criterion of moral forfeiture. Although 'Barclay himself, that great assertor of the power and sacredness of Kings' (Sec. 232) 'denies it to be lawful to resist a King in any case . . ., he . . . assigns two cases, whereby a King may un-King himself' (Sec. 235), namely, if he intended, like Nero, to destroy his kingdom or to subject it to a foreign power. These cases are those regarded by Hobbes and Locke respectively as instances of self-abolition and of moral forfeiture. Hence Locke's assertion that they 'differ little from those above mentioned, to be destructive to governments' (Sec. 239), that is, from those adduced by Locke himself. He, indeed, could with equal justice find that he had, in practice, claimed no more than Barclay had and that Barclay had

[22] Secs. 213, 219.
[23] Leviathan, Ch. 21.

'omitted the principle from which his doctrine flows; and that is, the breach of trust, in not preserving the form of government agreed on, and in not intending the end of government itself, which is the public good and preservation of property'. Critics of divine kingship had by now come to insist on the concessions to resistance in absolutist thought.[24] Locke did so to drive a wedge between Filmer and the old-fashioned champions of absolutism. Seizing upon what lent itself to justification of resistance in traditional theories, Locke criticized them merely for limiting it unrealistically[25] and for failing to give full credit to the principle of consent from which the right of resistance followed. Although their 'omission' of the principle put them on the same side of the fence with Filmer, although by reference to the principle of consent Locke corrected their royal absolutism as he did Filmer's patriarchalism, he dubbed not Barclay, Bracton, Bilson, Fortescue and Hooker, but innovators like Filmer, as 'Egyptian under-taskmasters' and 'servile flatterers, who . . . would have all men born to, what their mean souls fitted them for, slavery' (Sec. 239). He asserted that Filmer himself confessed that 'the great vindicators of the Right of Kings' (I, 67) – in this instance Hayward, Blackwood and Barclay – had not succeeded in denying 'the natural liberty and equality of mankind'.[26] In admitting both the principle and the conclusion only in part, argues Locke, the old school of absolutists stopped halfways; it is much worse to dispute the principle, base one's case upon the conflicting principles of divine appointment, fatherhood and property, and cap all this by inadvertently implying the most revolutionary conclusions. This comes of the 'very quick-sighted' attempt of Filmer 'to spy out fatherhood, where nobody else could see any the least glimpses of it' (I, 144). If, as must follow, 'all the world must be only one empire by the right of the next heir', all existing governments become unsettled and nothing but confusion, anarchy and violence become justified.[27] Indeed, 'this new nothing , . . this fatherhood which is to design the person, and establish the throne of monarchs, whom the people are to obey, may, . . . come into any hands, . . . give to democracy royal authority, and make a usurper . . . lawful' (I, 72).

[24] Cp. Laslett, *op. cit.*, 443.
[25] Sec. 235.
[26] *Ibid.* Cp. also I, 4.
[27] I, 142. Cp. I, 72, 104-6, 126, 142-3, 148, 191.

By implication Filmer's is put on a par with Hobbes' theory which legitimized all who succeed in maintaining themselves in power. Filmer is isolated as a dangerous innovator by the man who, more than anyone else down to his time, overcame the hesitations re-engendered by the Reformation concerning the right of displacing rulers; who himself owned that usurpation can become lawful and who argued that, as a matter of principle, government may come into anyone's hands. He made Filmer's theory appear to be more destructive than anything advanced by himself, although his advocacy of the right to resist any regime furnishes the basis for the acceptability of every regime.

Locke himself did not find every regime equally acceptable. His alternation of vehemence and calm language in his treatment of absolutism reveals itself as a device for turning the tables on both traditional and Filmerist absolutists. He sought to confer respectability upon his views by presenting the principle of obedience conditioned by consent as merely an enlargement of the exceptions of Barclay and others to absolute obedience. As a matter of fact, he gave coherence to what he found incoherent especially in Filmer, and supplemented the respectable absolutists' theories in such a way as to make it possible to account in a straightforward manner for the undeniable occurrence of the twin-phenomena of revolt and the legitimation of usurpers. Although his theory of the acceptable regime reflects his concessions to royal absolutism and patriarchal monarchy, it takes its cue from his refutation of the claim of royal absolutism to be the only justifiable form of government. Locke's metapolitics and the lessons which he drew from historical experience culminate in – or buttress – this conclusion.

The examination in the following part of the practical politics he recommended carries, therefore, to its conclusion the elucidation of the central tenets of Locke's political theory and in this sense sums up the argument of the book as a whole. A synopsis of the grounds we have traversed so far recommends itself at this point.

SYNOPSIS

In the first part we have seen that Locke's theory of political action and obligation rests on the belief in the necessary predominance of objective rational criteria. These, he thought, were embodied in the law of nature. He was aware of the difficulties involved in making dictates of reason prevail. Inasmuch as the injunctions of natural law, like any standards that cover a multiplicity of cases, are necessarily of a rather general nature, they are plain to all rational creatures and eventually also to the majority. The specification of such standards and their application to particular cases must, equally necessarily, be more complicated and controversial. Neither an enthusiastic nor a modest belief in the function of rationality in politics has got around this fact. In this respect, there is also no difference between the traditional doctrine of natural law and Locke's version of it, or between his *Treatises* and his *Essay*. There, too, he took it for granted that men on occasion know with certainty. And although very little knowledge is certain, the probable knowledge, i.e. 'the grounds and degrees of belief, opinion and assent' which men can achieve, is sufficient for their needs.[28] Although philosophy is restricted to determining the limits of knowledge, political knowledge is not limited to 'tentative probabilities'.[29] A natural law of self-preservation and human dignity obligates and is realizable, though never fully, and it provides the foundation of specific individual and collective rights and duties.

Related to each other, Locke's statements on the knowability and applicability of natural law reflect a division of labour between the more and the less enlightened members of society. He distinguished clearly between a moral imperative of equality and the actual fact of inequality, the second necessarily and justly modifying the first. The student of natural law perforce faces the difficulty of communicating his superior knowledge to the ignorant or to those whose bias and interests distort their judgement. Those who know better consequently face the difficulty of inducing the many to respond to the commands of rational ethics. The many are capable of response, not primarily as a result of reasoning, but by virtue of commonsense or deep-seated convictions. Tradition and scriptural teaching are of help inasmuch as they tend to confirm the voice of reason. The important feature which sets Locke's version of natural law apart, not only from the traditional version but also from that of Hobbes, is his stipulation of the realization of natural law by consent. To be implemented most effectively and fairly, it sanctions besides the institutional diversification of political authority the permanent

---

[28] *Essay*, I, i, 2, 4.
[29] As Wolin, *op. cit.*, 229, argues.

uninstitutionalized right of ordinary men – not extended to colonial peoples – to appeal directly to the eternal rule of reason at critical junctures and to act upon it.

The defence of the extension to the common people of the right to veto by revolt their betters' particularizations of the eternal rule explains the complexity of Locke's teaching about the state of nature for it is a theory about human nature as revealed in patterns of behaviour relevant to politics. Its place in the history of political philosophy is determined by its two related presuppositions. On the one hand, in admitting the warlike aspects of the state of nature, he took up the well established point of reference in traditional theory – the Fall – for the necessity of coercion as well as of force and violence in human relations. Hobbes had only secularized the Christian derivation of government from the Fall, although Aquinas had already retrieved domination from the sphere of human sinfulness by pointing to the existence of subjection among men *ante peccatum* and of dominion among the angels.[30] On the other hand, Locke's emphasis on the peaceful aspects of the state of nature does not attest the disparagement of the state and a belief in the reinstatement of the state of innocence; it testifies to the conviction that the extension of consent in political relations, and above all of the right of dissent, is feasible and desirable. Both Hobbes' and Locke's conception of the state of nature appears to have been shaped in the light of their evaluation of the phenomenon of revolution. The state of nature was for Hobbes the state of war of all against all, because revolution spelled only senseless anarchy. Absolutely sovereign government was the only one fit for individualists. Locke evaluated government without consent as anarchy, and revolution as its ultimate remedy. This reversal demanded the conversion of Hobbes' negative into positive individualism, an individualism according to which social responsibility and a public will arise from the will of the individual. Methodological individualism spills over into ideological individualism, or rather the first implies the second.

The postulate of the validity of natural law is linked to the hypothesis of the state of nature, because the latter illustrates social propensities and rights of men. Natural law and with it rational politics are applicable, given the intrinsically social and political nature of the human condition. A governmentless state of nature is

[30] *Summa Theologica*, I, qu. 96, art. 1-4.

an hypothesis and a real state of nature can only occur inside political society or between members of political societies who, whether princes or ordinary men, meet in no-man's-land. Within a political society, it is a state of war between morally disqualified rulers and their society. The dissolution of government from within does not entail the dissolution of society. Society can persist as a revolutionary democracy. The state of nature, the state of war and political society are related to each other in principle because they are considered as co-existent in practice. The state of nature and the state of war denote specific situations, reflecting the two basic propensities to peacefulness and contentiousness, the poles of consensus and conflict between which political life fluctuates.

In principle, Locke judges interstate relations by the same criteria as internal relations. As a result, prescriptively overloaded principles are imposed by him upon war between states. High-mindedness is exercised with a vengeance. The distinction between just and unjust war outlaws any form of conquest – and justifies slavery. The exception made for colonial conquest implies that the application of natural law need not have identical results for all nations.

Also as regards the nations to which natural law equally applies, Locke's argumentation is consistently permeated by the awareness of the fateful link and tension between what men are able to do and what men have a right to do, between power and authority, might and right. Force is required to make right prevail, because the unequal possession of what constitutes might invites its use in excess of right. To prevent the utmost evil, which is tyranny-cum-anarchy, political authority must be guided and judged by objective values, immutably embodied in, yet never perfectly derivable from, natural law.

The metapolitical foundations which Locke's doctrine of natural law provides serves therefore to justify a conception of politics as a continuously competitive process of maintaining or re-establishing, by reference to rational criteria, a tolerable balance between powers which represent individual rights and capacities. This power-right configuration includes property relations.

Locke's contribution towards the emergence of the spirit of capitalism is determined by the fact that individual labour remains the foundation of property and consent the basis of property relations. Notwithstanding the circumvention by men's consent to use money of the specifically other-regarding sufficiency limitation, the right of property is no more than the prototype of all other natural rights. The validity of each natural right is equally independent of consent, although through consent men guarantee the enjoyment of all natural rights. All interpersonal relations between adults are contractual and in principle consent remains a function of freedom because law guarantees a reasonable amount of freedom in all spheres of action. Since the right of consent is derived from the ideal postulate of natural equality, and its realization in fully-developed property relations falls short of the equality attained in properly-developed political organization, the economic sphere is not only practically dependent upon, but also morally inferior to, the political sphere. Neither principles nor organization are lacking for politics to interfere with economics in the spirit of equity and justice. If this relationship between politics and economics cannot be summarily identified with nineteenth-century *laissez-faire* liberalism, especially Spencer's brand, it is no less true that Locke seems to have laid the ground for conclusions which far exceed those that he was ready to underwrite.

Modern liberalism began by evincing the traditional reverence for the ideal of absolute equality manifested in the original community of all things. It relegated, however, such an order to the irresuscitable past. Locke drew a clear line between socialism and liberalism both in retrospective and perspective. He lent consistency to incipient liberalism in that the natural limitations of appropriation are no longer associated by him with an originally propertyless order but with the primacy of private property. The demonstration why the natural limitations of acquisitiveness eventually became ineffective do no more than clarify what had been admitted all along in a roundabout manner. Historical origins remain exemplary. In the past, men led poor and simple, but virtuous, lives, equality being reflected in small but not equal possessions. To the extent that Locke rationalized the notion of the Fall, it attached not to the distinction between 'mine' and 'thine', but to the factors which caused and enabled possessions to become very large.

Locke's rejection of the idea that individual property owes its justification to consent, strengthens rather than weakens the case for liberty and for consent as the only instrumentality for realizing natural rights in society. Since man has a right to his person and therefore to the product of his labour, his consent is required as much for making him the servant of another as for subjecting him to rulers. If in property relations far-reaching dependence is reconcilable with consent, the political dependence of all upon the wisdom and virtue of one man can also be a matter of consent. Locke accepted one-man rule in the beginning without any of the moral reservations made against the increase of possessions. The reason was not so much that, in the 'golden age' of early government, patriarchal monarchy coincided with the smallness of individual properties. Rather, he could not carry his distinction between the authority of the father and that of the monarch to the point of effacing the fundamental resemblance between the two. The ends and ties by which the family and political society are distinguished from each other remain comparable, for incorporation by compact turns out to be a process which transforms family into political ties. Contractualism and the naturalness of political organization are reconciled.

The 'express' consent of the compact is identified by Locke with tacit consent to a process of change and growth, almost imperceptible to those involved. This tacit consent, in the nature of the case, rests on no evidence other than the absence of dissent. The natural inclination to live in society and seek shelter under father-like authority make for the natural and scarcely avoidable acquiescence in one-man rule in the beginning. This is the only form of incorporation verified by history. It does not disprove but confirms that all government rests on consent. The right to choose any form of government is not prejudiced by the objective necessity to choose a particular form which is best suited to the circumstances.

History, which exemplifies the validity of the findings of reason, also illustrates the deviations from the rule of reason. Even what once was in accord with reason need not always be so. History provides precedents for obligations and patterns of government which should not be lightly shaken off. But precedents by themselves do not provide standards of action. History, which bears out reason, is also judged by it. Locke invaded the territory of history as a rationalist and for polemical purposes. But his feeling the need for the empirical verification of his propositions prevented him from flights into unhistorical fancy. Thus the 'state of nature' reveals itself as a psycho-sociological model on the one hand, and as the socio-political key-concept for the analysis of the extremities of the political condition on the other. Incorporation by compact is not conceived as an act but as embedded in a process. Both reason and the empirically possible are invoked for stipulating the primacy of private acquisition. Although he did not rest his case on the Common Law tradition, there are important similarities between its fundamental tenets and those of his rational theory of politics. Locke demonstrated that a liberal had no reason to be an unyielding enemy of history and tradition in general.

The tactical purpose in Locke's use of tradition is particularly evident in his reliance on the authority of King James I and Barclay. The aim was to isolate Filmer, the most influential advocate of royal absolutism in Locke's time, and to show the advocacy of the right of resistance merely as the logically required step beyond what respectable absolutist theories had conceded. But there remain the concessions which Locke was prepared to make to patriarchal monarchy and royal prerogative when viewed in historical perspective. He replaced monarchy by divine right by monarchy based on consent, yet considered the natural inclination of men to adopt one-man rule as dependent not so much upon primitive economic conditions as upon the goodness and wisdom of princes. Godlike princes are entitled to as much prerogative as they see fit to claim. Monarchy is absolute without being arbitrary and a prince is no tyrant if he rules through standing and promulgated laws of his own making and devotes himself to the public good. On these terms tyranny is possible whether the rulers are one or more. Resistance is, therefore, justified under any form of government. Equally, non-resistance generally testifies to the legitimacy of any form of government, and, as far as the majority of the people is concerned, to the legitimation of usurpation and conquest. On this basis, the right of the people to a regime which is to their liking is made part of the terms of the original incorporation, and presumed to become effectual only long after the beginnings of society and government.

Locke's positive evaluation of the historical role of monarchy in strengthening nascent and developing societies neither diminishes, nor is obliterated by, the awareness of the dangers inherent in excessive prerogative. The experience with wicked and foolish rulers teaches that the best provision against the degeneration of proper political power into despotic power is to vest legislation in collective bodies and to place executive and legislative powers in different hands.

To show to what extent the practical politics which Locke recommended represent a consistent application of the metapolitical principles and the forms of political action which he had justified as regards the beginnings of political society and its subsequent history, we shall first ascertain whether the people's right to consent to anything, or to empower anyone to act on their behalf, remains a matter either of tacit consent or of its converse, revolutionary dissent. After having determined what individual consent and popular participation amount to in the regime which he recommended, we shall appraise Locke's constitutionalism by investigating his conception of the institutionalized sharing of power, and of the direct representation in the constitutional framework of the tacit will of the many by the will of the chief executive.

PART THREE

THE ACCEPTABLE REGIME

CHAPTER IX

INDIVIDUAL CONSENT

IT is conceivable and not without historical foundation that absolutist rule will guarantee individual rights and interests. Yet if, as in Hobbes' theory, this is explicitly upheld as the prime purpose and justification of authoritarian government, it is assumed to derive ultimately from consent. In contrast to a genuinely liberal theory, consent is not claimed by Hobbes as the mode of political action through which the individuals defend their rights. As a paradoxical consequence of the rooted misconceptions about liberal theory, the acceptance of this claim, and not its rejection, has become associated with a negative or passive attitude towards political obligation. It is, however, neither logical nor borne out by facts that, because consent renders obedience, and, at the limit, membership in political society, conditional political obligation is robbed of a secure foundation. What better basis than consent is there for the self-willed commitment of individuals to the political order and which other form of commitment can be more effective after a society has become permeated with individualist consciousness?

It is a central theme of Locke's theory that the individuals furnish the government with the moral right and the physical means to act for them and in the process also to constrain them. The individuals realize their rights and interests by legitimatizing and supporting the agency which is to protect them from each other but also by defending themselves against it. If Locke's liberalism is characterized by the compatability of natural and contractual foundations, contractualism by itself is incompatible with a predominantly passive attitude of citizens towards government. Its major purpose is to forestall and eventually resist the government's trespassings; and this requires the individuals' intermittent political activity and the constant alertness of special bodies of citizens. Even if fear of governmental encroachments were the only motive of contractualism, a negative view of those who normally carry out the government might be involved, but neither lack of personal commitment to the political order, nor indifference to the functioning of government can be presupposed. The restriction of suffrage closes to the many an avenue for demonstrating identification. Individual consent is nevertheless regarded as the strongest and most dignified foundation of political obligation when the non-exercise of the right of contracting out of established obligations – the right Locke granted to each member of a new generation – is equated with express acceptance of membership.

For two reasons I shall demonstrate in detail what otherwise might seem a minute point, i.e. that Locke gave no other indication of 'express' consent to membership than abstention from specific acts of dissent. First, he conceived on the same basis the political participation of the masses. Secondly, his stand in both instances bears testimony to the fact that, concerning the consent of all members of society, he made no distinction between the past and the present. All this means that the practical significance he attached to the people's consent and participation is much more restricted than his semantics would lead one to expect. The nature of the dichotomy between words and facts has not changed, although awareness of it has become more explicit and refined in the age of democracy and empirical political science.

1. ACCEPTANCE AND REJECTION OF MEMBERSHIP

A. Reaffirmation

a. The Indirect Evidence for Acceptance

'Nobody doubts,' wrote Locke, that only 'an express consent, of any man, entering into any society, makes him a perfect member of that society, a subject of that government' (Sec. 119). He postulated that individuals renewed their consent to obey the government in each generation, but also maintained that a man who inherited his father's property thereby consented to obey the government as his father had done. We might justly wonder what to make of the argument about express consent, for there seems to be an abrupt transition from a strong to a much weaker form of individual consent.[1] But the point is that Locke did not come up with a procedure for directly expressing reaffirmation of membership in the first place.

He referred to 'a common distinction of an express and a tacit

---

[1] Gough, *op. cit.*, 65, and Plamenatz, *op. cit.*, 218, respectively.

consent, which will concern our present case' (Sec. 119), and re-marked that 'the difficulty is, what ought to be looked upon as a tacit consent . . .' What sounds like a promise to explain the dif-ference between express and tacit consent, issues in shifting all the weight on tacit consent. The central argument is that the compact of one generation does not automatically oblige the next generation. The continuously contractual character of political society requires that each generation has the choice of accepting membership and with it the obligation to obey the government. But the obligation of obedience applies to members and non-members alike. At first sight it seems as if only the resident's consent to obey the govern-ment could be given tacitly, whereas express consent would be required of a full member of the society. One questions, however, what express consent could add to the obligation to obey the government if 'every man, that has any possession, or enjoyment, of any part of the dominions of any government, does thereby give his tacit consent, and is as far forth obliged to obedience to the laws of that government, during such enjoyment, as anyone under it' (Sec. 119). Tacit consent is implied, moreover, not only in the holding of property but also in 'lodging only for a week; . . . barely travelling freely on the highway; and in effect, it reaches as far as the very being of anyone within the territories of that government'. Every person that finds himself in a country is held tacitly to have agreed to comply with its laws. No difficulty in the argument is created by Locke's making this claim and yet concentrating on the consensual significance of property rights.[2] He never placed resi-dents who hold property on the same footing as the original covenanters and their progeny, except insofar as citizens and residents (whether they own any property or not) are alike obliged to abide by the law. As the foregoing quotations confirm, he did not maintain either that citizenship was the condition for the tenure of land,[3] nor that the tenure of land was the condition for being obliged to obey the government. It is his claiming that the posses-sion of land entailed the obligation of obedience on the part of citizens and residents alike which created a difficulty as far as the distinction between the tacit consent of the resident and the express consent of the citizen is concerned. For the specific rights and obligations of a citizen, not merely the obligation to obey the

[2] As Wolin, *op. cit.*, 311, argues.
[3] Vaughan, *op. cit.*, 191, asserts the opposite.

government, are also linked by Locke with the possession of land.

Through incorporation into a political society, a person 'annexed also, and submits to the community those possessions, which he has, or shall acquire . . .' (Sec. 120), and the father 'may indeed annex such conditions to the land, he enjoyed as a subject of any commonwealth, as may oblige his son to be of that community, if he will enjoy those possessions which were his father's'.[4] The political rights and obligations of the heir are tied to his inheritance, because in joining a political society, or remaining within it, his progenitors had to submit their possessions to its jurisdiction.[5] Yet the submission of possessions to the jurisdiction of a government is a matter of tacit consent, whether one is a citizen or a mere resident. The government's jurisdiction extends 'only over the land, and reaches the possessor of it, (before he has actually incorporated himself in the society) only as he dwells upon, and enjoys that' (Sec. 121). Ownership of land by itself can thus be no indication whether the owner has bound himself to a society by express consent. Consequently Locke required that in relation to his landed or other inheritance the son of a 'perfect member' must enter 'actual agreement', by 'express declaration' (Sec. 121) or 'positive engagement, and express promise and compact' (Sec. 122). Yet it seems as if Locke had coupled the manifestation of express commitment to accept the father's political status with the inheritance of his possessions, so as to be able to admit that 'the consent of free-men, born under government, which only makes them members of it, being given separately in their turns, as each comes to be of age, and not in a multitude together; *people take no notice of it . . .*' (Sec. 117). Express declarations or positive engagements on the part of the sons of members who assent to being members go unnoticed because they are made individually and all the time. But what, according to Locke, is actually done daily cannot but pass unnoticed, because he meant no more than that heirs of propertied members refrain from renouncing their inheritance. Nothing else is

---

[4] Sec. 116. Cp. Sec. 73. Not only the eldest son is meant. Although according to the law of England 'heir . . . signifies the eldest son, who is . . . to have all his father's land' (I, 37), Locke denied the rightfulness of primogeniture (I, 74, 91, 93, 101-3, 140).

[5] There is no confusion of paternal and political power here, as Gauthier, *loc. cit.* 38-40, thinks. Not paternal but political jurisdiction is under discussion. The father is obligated to set conditions relating to political obligation on inheritance and has no choice whatsoever in the matter.

mentioned in the *Treatise* as evidence of the express acceptance of membership.

Evidently, if to accept one's inheritance is tantamount to an express declaration, it is difficult to see why, in doing so, only the son of a full member and not also the son of a resident should be considered to have made an express declaration – the son of a member for the acceptance of membership and the son of a non-member for the acceptance of the obligations of a mere resident.

If, however, the acceptance or refusal of one's inheritance as such does not permit a distinction between members and non-members, we may nevertheless safely assume that, in addition to a specific act by which foreigners become naturalized, Locke also had in mind different legal procedures by which the heirs of members and non-members succeeded to their inheritance. He probably thought that an express declaration was included in the procedure. But the purpose of such a declaration normally relates to establishing the identity of the heir as the son of a citizen and as the lawful claimant to his father's property, rather than to his agreement to continue as a member of the political society. Of course, the second can be inferred from the first; but for this very reason it cannot be identified with an express declaration. We are therefore left with the fact that 'positive engagement, and express promise and compact' may be reasonably inferred as 'being given separately in their turns' by the sons of members because they have accepted their inheritance. In other words, the evidence for an 'express declaration' is a substitute for the declaration. No act is demanded which directly serves to re-affirm individual membership.

A specific act would seem to be called for not only by Locke's emphasis on an 'express promise and compact' but also because his concentration on property as the medium of manifesting consent to membership is not based on the assumption that property and political rights and obligations are inseparable.

b. *The Separability of Property and Political Rights and Obligations*
The stipulation that by accepting his inheritance a person also accepts the government's conditions for holding property does not contravene[6] the principle that the natural right of property is prior to government, and to consent. All natural rights, and not only the right of property, are prior to government in the sense of being the

[6] As Plamenatz, *op. cit.*, 225-6, argues.

ends for which government exists and not its apanage. Since it is given no choice but to protect natural rights, the fact that the government must have the right to set down conditions to fulfil this function does not prejudice the 'priority' of any natural right. This is particularly true if the government rules by consent. If the authority of government and political consent do not absorb the right of property, the reverse is also not the case.

Although a man's consent to obey the government is evidenced first and foremost in relation to property, it is consent, not property, from which the duty of obedience arises. The age at which a man becomes mature for political consent and the age at which he may acquire property coincide. 'What gave him a free disposing of his property according to his own will' is a 'state of maturity', that is, 'such a state of reason, such an age of discretion made him free', in which 'he is presumed to know . . . how far he may make use of his freedom, . . . how far the law allows a liberty' (Sec. 59). The right to dispose freely of inherited property depends upon the son's ability to know and exercise his civic rights and duties. This implies a distinction between the possession of property rights and civic rights, as a significant gap in Locke's argument reveals. On attaining the age of discretion, the adult son must manifest his assent to membership in relation to his inheritance. Locke does not consider that quite often the son comes of age while his father is still alive. If the father has not settled some property on his son when he comes of age, he cannot do what he must to refuse membership, i.e. 'by donation, sale, or otherwise, quit the said possession' (Sec. 121). He can only renounce the right of his inheritance and emigrate. His renunciation is then manifested, not in relation to any property in his possession, but at best only in relation to his expectation of property. Likewise, the son who wishes to accept membership can do no more than assent, expressly or tacitly, to the provisions of his father's will. As a rule, no specific procedure is required for this purpose, nor does Locke indicate one. Therefore, since the decision about membership must be made when the son comes of age, though at that time he is not necessarily a proprietor, consent to membership is taken to be manifested otherwise than through the medium of property. For this very reason either a specific undertaking for the acceptance of citizenship ought to have been pointed out by Locke or no public affirmation at all be demanded, certainly not an 'express promise and compact'. That adult sons may have property of their own making does not make any difference. The product of his labour becomes his property only when the son becomes a freeman like his father.[7] He can demonstrate his acceptance or rejection of citizenship even less in regard to self-acquired property than in respect of his future inheritance.

Although Locke failed to mention the possibility that the decision about membership may be demanded at the moment when the son has no property, he furnished the premises for inferring this possibility and hence for the separability of accepting the political rights and obligations and the possession of property. As we shall see in the second part of this chapter, the intention of admitting propertyless persons to citizenship must be attributed to Locke. The inference that property cannot invariably serve as the medium for manifesting the acceptance or rejection of political obligations is further substantiated, since Locke claimed that, in specific circumstances, the holding of property is no proof of the acceptance of political obligations towards a government which protects property.

The enjoyment of property does not prove the acceptance of political obligation under the rule of a conqueror. Unless the vanquished consent to his rule, a conqueror who respects their property is not entitled to their obedience; but they remain entitled to their possessions.[8] The argument in favour of the immunity of private property from conquest conforms fully with the moral and practical primacy Locke accorded to the political over the economic sphere.[9] The holding of property can be no evidence for submission to the conqueror's government, because consent, not property, gives rise to obedience, and only legislation related to consent is binding. If there is no freedom of consent, property ceases to be the medium of manifesting consent.

Lastly, the right of property and civic rights and duties are in fact also separable in the case which exemplifies the intimate connection between them. Just as, in the extreme case of conquest, the right to preserve property does not invalidate the right of withholding consent, so in a proper political society the right to withhold consent does not invalidate the right of property. The rights of property and of consent are not confused, or the principle retracted

---

[7] Secs. 59, 65, 69. Child-labour is thus justified (Sec. 64).
[8] See above, 111–2.
[9] See above, 170 f.

that the father's consent cannot bind his children, if the son of a member must choose between accepting the political commitments of his father and renouncing them together with his inheritance.[10] The choice between accepting or renouncing paternal consent is real even if sons who want to contract out have to give up their inheritance or self-acquired property without receiving anything in return. Individual dissent would then demand an extraordinarily heavy sacrifice and, in fact, annul the natural right of property and of inheritance. Political obligation and property would be inseparable, but freedom of choice would still exist. The cost of freedom from political obligation is not prohibitive, however. The dissenter has the right 'by donation, sale, or otherwise' (Sec. 121) to dispose of his inheritance or self-acquired property. He has to quit his estate just as anybody has to give up what he sells. (And there is little reason why he should quit otherwise than by selling.) He may suffer material loss, up to the amount of the difference between the value of inherited or self-acquired property and the price he can obtain for it. Such a risk is unavoidable in any commercial transaction.

In principle, the repudiation of the political commitments of previous generations does not run counter to the natural right of property, and, in practice, repudiation is not tied to conditions that nobody can be expected to fulfil. Political obligation and property are inseparable, inasmuch as the acceptance of inheritance – except under conquest – carries with it the acceptance of political obligation. Political obligation and property are separable insofar as the acceptance of political obligation by the still propertyless is concerned, and insofar as the rejection of political obligation does not entail the loss of property rights under a conqueror, or the loss of the counter-value of the inheritance or of self-acquired property in a proper political society.

c. *The Dispensability of an Express Declaration*

We have seen that Locke stipulated express consent for demonstrating acceptance of membership but did not indicate a specific and direct act for this purpose. That he ought to have done so seems to be all the more imperative as he treated property as the most conspicuous medium, but not the always available nor invariably

---

[10] Plamenatz, *op. cit.*, 227, who discounts the alternative, makes the two last-mentioned objections.

necessary or even valid medium through which acceptance of political rights and obligations can be manifested. Nevertheless, there is no inconsistency in Locke's applying the adjective 'express' to indirectly evidenced acceptance. He simply and logically considered reaffirmation of membership effected on the same terms as original incorporation. In both instances he spoke of express consent, while accepting tacit as the equivalent of express consent, by virtue of the fact that express dissent was not manifested. Concerning both incorporation by compact and its individual reaffirmation, the negating evidence is more tangible and requires more resoluteness than the affirmative.

Over and against the affirmative evidence of tacit compliance with the insensible transformation of paternal into political rule, the negating evidence consists in breaking away from the habitual. The positive action of accepting membership is an unspecified part of the acceptance of one's inheritance – the act which is performed daily and passes unnoticed, but is not necessarily performable at the time when the son comes of age. Rejection of membership involves, however, doing something out of the ordinary: the renunciation of one's actual or expected inheritance, and, in any case, emigration. True, when a man fulfils his civic duties and exercises his civic rights, his acceptance of citizenship is demonstrated in action. But simply to go on doing what one has done as a minor or what one's predecessors have done, is not nearly as close to an express manifestation of assent as leaving one's country and/or disposing of one's property approximates an express manifestation of dissent. Yet Locke consistently labelled the behaviour in the first two cases as express consent.

The issue is not clarified if one says that, for Locke, tacit consent also binds; that both members and non-members consent either tacitly or expressly; and that he was more concerned with the content than with the form of consent.[11] The point is that, where the consent of all members is concerned, Locke invariably accepted the possibility of express dissent as the means for turning tacit into the equivalent of express consent. Yet however much the idea of

[11] The first explanation is advanced by Gough, *op. cit.*, 65 f. and Polin, *op. cit.*, 148, and all three explanations are proffered by M. Waldmann, 'A Note on John Locke's Theory of Consent,' *Ethics* LXVIII, 1 (1957), 57-8. I disagree with the imputation to Locke of a disregard of the forms of consent as the indicators of the contents of consent. See below, 299 f., in connection with Plamenatz's diametrically opposed opinion that Locke neglected the contents of consent as against its forms.

consent was thus watered down, it permitted that which *The Fundamental Constitutions of Carolina* prohibit. Their interdict of the right of revolt, and not only regard for the specific requirements of a new and sparsely populated dependency,[12] bears on the issue in hand in such a way that the details which the *Constitutions* provide in this respect cannot, as in the case of suffrage,[13] serve as an illustration of Locke's intentions in the *Treatise*.[14]

The *Constitutions* lay down that acceptance of their contents be made in writing before the registrar of the precinct. No person of 'what condition or degree soever', above the age of seventeen, who has not so subscribed, can enjoy 'estate, or possession or the protection of the law'.[15] As distinct from the *Treatise*, aliens are denied the right of landownership and even the protection of the law. But they become naturalized by subscribing like any freeman who wishes to stay in the colony.[16] The fundamental difference between the two documents consists in the fact that, although the formality of subscribing is demanded of all persons above seventeen, this does not attest the principle of universal consent to incorporation as reaffirmation of membership by a new generation does in the *Treatise*. The 'compact' of the *Constitutions* was concluded by the eight lord-proprietors alone and denied even to their heirs the right of making any changes. 'We the lords and proprietors ... have agreed to this following *form of government to be perpetually established* amongst us, unto which we do oblige ourselves, our heirs and successors, in the most binding way that can be devised.'[17] By subscribing to the *Constitutions*, the obligation is entered to preserve faith and allegiance to King Charles II, his heirs and successors, as well as to maintain the once established form of government of the colony.[18] In contradistinction to the *Constitutions*, the *Treatises* stipulated that the original covenanters comprised all the members of the society, and that the right to change the form of government is implicit in the terms of incorporation. In other words, the com-

---

[12] Fox Bourne, *op. cit.*, I, 238, 240, thought that this consideration actuated both Locke and those who commissioned him to draft the *Constitutions*, notwithstanding the possible divergencies of views between Locke and the lord-proprietors on specific issues.

[13] See below, 288.

[14] Laslett, *op. cit.*, 365, makes this assumption.

[15] Article 117.

[16] Art. 118

[17] Preamble, *Works*, X, 175. Italics supplied.

[18] Art. 117.

mitment to belong to the society and the commitment to a form of government are separable. In the *Constitutions* the two commitments are inseparable, so as to guarantee the perpetuation of a social and political feudal hierarchy.

This difference explains why a formal affirmation of membership was necessary in the one case and inexpedient in the other. Since, on the one hand, any change of the colony's regime was prohibited, and on the other, voluntary affiliation was the only way to assure the colony's development, it was logical to require a specific formal undertaking from everybody which tied the assent to belong to the society to the obligation of honouring its order as now immutably established. Even if Locke had a formal reaffirmation of membership in mind when he wrote the *Treatises*, it could not have been the provision of the *Constitutions*. The *Treatises* which deal with a long-existing political society acknowledge, above all, that alienation from one's society and its order generally stems from the unsatisfactory conduct of government and justify revolution as an alternative to compliance besides individual withdrawal. Maintaining the right of citizens to change the political order by revolt, Locke was well advised to abstain from demanding a specific formal undertaking for the reaffirmation by each generation of its forbears' obligations. He probably found it no less embarrassing to demand a formal undertaking, which included a promise to keep up the existing form of government, than to demand one which excluded that promise.

To forgo a formal declaration was a matter as much of expediency as of consistency. In virtue of his conditional equation of express and tacit consent, Locke kept the way in which each generation affirmed membership consonant with the way in which original incorporation was effected. But there remains one doubt as to the conditional character of the equation. It becomes unconditional to the extent that the alternative to affirmation of membership is ruled out. In one instance, Locke appears to do so by denying the right of emigration to those who may be supposed to have expressly consented to belong to the political society of their fathers. If no effective right of emigration were granted to full members of political society, the commitment to belong to it would lose much of its self-willed character, notwithstanding the right of revolt. To speak of each generation's renewal of its commitments in this case would be to hide an essentially illiberal, or, in Kendall's terms, collectivist, conception of political obligation behind an individualist smoke screen.

B. Emigration

a. The Restriction

The contradiction in Locke's argument is not removed if one suggests first that, according to Locke, consent subsequent to original incorporation was tacit, and then accepts that he denied the right of renouncing membership to those who had once expressly agreed to it.[19] Once consent to membership is tacit, it is beside the point to stipulate that express consent annuls the right of emigration. If we maintain that, according to Locke, membership can be affirmed by either tacit or express consent,[20] the question surely is: What makes the act of accepting one's inheritance (performed, moreover, by sons of members and of non-members) on one occasion identifiable as express consent, which annuls the right of emigration, and on another as tacit consent, which does not annul it? Locke provides no direct answer but quite clearly equates the consent of non-members with tacit consent alone. Kendall, who alone is fully aware of the contradiction in Locke's argument, seems therefore to be on the safest ground in concluding that Locke conceded the right of emigration only to residents and hence did not make the individual's obligation to his society dependent on an effective right of emigration.[21]

The only passage which explicitly restricts the right of emigration reads:

'He, that has once, by actual agreement, . . . given his consent to be of any commonweal, is perpetually and indispensably obliged to be and remain unalterably a subject to it, . . . unless by any calamity, the government, he was under, comes to be dissolved; or else by some public act cuts him off from being any longer a member of it.[22]

Although withdrawal by the citizen's own initiative is excluded, it does not follow that the commitments to society are perpetual so

---

[19] Vaughan, op. cit., 139.

[20] Polin, op. cit., 148, 190-1.

[21] Kendall, op. cit., 89, and note 71.

[22] Sec. 121. In Sec. 73, the words 'whilst they are in that freedom' might indicate what Sec. 121 makes explicit.

long as the established government persists. Government can be dissolved, yet society continues to exist. The commitment to belong to society and the commitment to abide by its government are separable, inasmuch as the revolutionary dissolution of a government does not free individuals from allegiance to their society.[23] Revolution is the collective way of repudiating obedience to a government; it is not a way of withdrawing from one's society. In speaking of a 'calamity' in connection with the right of emigration, Locke could hardly have thought of the dissolution of both government and society by conquest or in some other manner. The right of seceding from society is irrelevant where nobody has any social obligation, where nothing is left to which he can be held obliged. If, then, Locke was dealing with the individual withdrawal from a properly functioning political society, there appears to be only one justification for the emigration of an individual member, namely, that the government 'by some public act cuts him off'. In other words, only expulsion seems to render emigration of members permissible.

If Locke had allowed emigration only to residents or to sons of members prior to their acceptance of membership, he practically would have left no alternative to compliance except revolt. While withdrawal and revolt are equally means of realizing the right of dissent, the one may take the weight of the other. The concern for stability might induce a proponent of the right of dissent to permit emigration not only to diminish the chances of revolt, but even to rule out revolt. Conversely, only a proponent of the right of dissent who does not wish to diminish revolutionary pressure would recommend frequent revolt and make it difficult to contract out of political society or deny this right altogether.[24] The most sensible course for an advocate of the right of revolt would be to affirm withdrawal as an alternative outlet for the revolutionary repudiation of obedience, so as to avoid frequent revolt. This was Locke's position, and a denial of the right to emigrate is as irreconcilable with it as it is with the details and main line of his argumentation. I suggest, therefore, that it must have been his intention that both members and non-members had the right to emigrate, i.e., that the solitary

---

[23] See above, 128.

[24] Although Kendall does not relate both issues, he ascribes to Locke the affirmation of frequent revolt – wrongly, as shown below, 311 f. – and the intention of withholding an effective right of emigration.

statement restricting emigration is another of his ill-considered overstatements. It is as much out of tune with its immediate context and the basic principles involved, as is the statement which suddenly attributes inequality of possessions to the introduction of money.[25] To demonstrate this is to confirm and to rely upon what I have tried to show so far, namely, that in Locke's view express consent to membership was solely evidenced by abstention from its rejection.

b. *The Evidence to the Contrary*

In the very context in which the passage under discussion occurs, the right of withdrawl is linked with the most fundamental proposition of the *Treatises*, that political society rests on consent. In fact, the most decisive argument against accepting the qualification of the right of withdrawal as Locke's considered opinion is that this right is presented by him as the correlate of the right to erect a lawful government. The collective and individual way of exercising natural freedom in and towards political society flow from the same principle and the contradiction of the one ought to have entailed that of the other. Yet Locke defended the core of his theory and invoked history to demonstrate that the liberty to establish a new government at home is the same as establishing one elsewhere, or as incorporating into another commonwealth.[26]

'. . . There are no examples so frequent in history, both sacred and profane, as those of men withdrawing themselves, and their obedience, from the jurisdiction they were born under, and the family or community they were bred up in, and setting up new governments in other places' (Sec. 115). 'This has been the practice of the world from its first beginning to this day: Nor is it now any more hindrance to the freedom of mankind, that they are born under constituted and ancient polities' (Sec. 116).

The right to 'go and make distinct commonwealths and other governments', is upheld without any qualifications to the effect that only men who have never expressly accepted citizenship are permitted to avail themselves of the right. In fact, no rider of this kind could have been appended. Otherwise, the patent absurdity would have followed that, apart from aliens, only the sons of members who, on reaching maturity, decided to repudiate membership had

[25] See above, 153 f.
[26] Sec. 100 onwards and Sec. 113 onwards.

been instrumental in the multiplication 'of petty commonwealths in the beginning of ages', and in 'setting up new governments in other places' from times immemorial. The absurdity is avoided if all persons who have no property, or only negligible property, are excluded from membership. Since anybody who stays in a country is bound to obey the government, it would still have been necessary to stipulate for the propertyless, too, the right of 'withdrawing themselves, and their obedience, from the jurisdiction they were born under'. But Locke did not exclude the propertyless from membership.[27] The refusal to actual members of the right of individual secession would thus have left unexplained what Locke presented as the most striking result, and confirmation of this right, the multiplication of distinct commonwealths. This holds true, even if we allow that Locke had also the predominance, among emigrants, of the junior members of families in mind.

Still, the solitary contradiction of the right to emigrate might perhaps be mitigated by reference to Locke's statement that only after becoming a freeman could the heir become a proprietor, especially since, despite disregarding the possible time-lag between the two events, he acknowledged instances in which property and political rights did not coincide. He might therefore have assumed that the son of a member could not be expected to demonstrate fully his attitude towards membership until he entered on his inheritance or acquired some property by his own efforts. Till then, his abstention from emigration could be regarded as provisional assent to membership, to be invested with its definite – and in this sense 'express' – meaning the moment he entered into his inheritance. If, at that moment, he decided to leave, he need not have repudiated an 'express' assent, i.e., an assent definite in contents and indirect in form. If we may assume that Locke distinguished in this way between the provisional and definite contents of consent, we might perhaps go a step further and suggest that he thought it admissible to impute to any member who disposed at any time of his property so as to emigrate that on coming of age he had accepted membership only provisionally. Consent which is 'express' in respect of its content, but always indirect or tacit in its form, could then be supposed to have been given if property was not disposed of, and as never having been given if it was. The plausibility of this interpretation is increased by the fact that, while property serves as the most adequate medium through which to demonstrate acceptance of membership by the son of a member, the *Treatise* gives no indication of a specific formal act for the purpose. I can see no other interpretation which reconciles the prohibition of the emigration of actual members with the emphatic affirmation of the right of withdrawal, the right borne out by 'the practice of the world from its first beginning to this day', and, by virtue of the principle of government by consent, indissolubly linked with the right of revolt. We may accept the proposed modification of the prohibition or rule out its literal meaning as an inadvertence. In either case we retain that if Locke equated express and tacit consent for original incorporation on account of the presumable absence of active dissent, it was only consistent to hold the same as applicable when original incorporation was reaffirmed by successive generations.

It is not exegetical pedantry which has evoked the foregoing attempt to account for the gaps and for a patent contradiction in Locke's argument. Its difficulties reflect problems which are still with us. The question whether or not to belong to one's particular political society has more and more lost its academic character. The advances in technology and communication have not led us to dispense with the assumption that in a long-established society, affirmation need not be formally expressed but can be presumed to be expressed, because it can be presumed to be implicit in certain actions and in abstentions from others. We do, like Locke, infer an affirmative attitude towards a free society from the fulfilment of civic duties and the exercise of civic rights, although none of such acts, including voting, is directly performed to answer the question whether people agree to belong to their political society or accept its regime. Affirmation is also deduced still from abstention from such acts as the decision to revolt or from decisions which the citizens refrain from making in matters whose private character is guaranteed by public authority. Among these, the issue of emigration is not everywhere faced without ambivalence. In a free country, like Britain, the emigration of scholars and scientists is nowadays a matter of grave public concern. Although publicly recognized as a private matter, in Communist countries, emigration is made either virtually impossible or, where permitted for a certain category of people, is not publicly acknowledged.

INDIVIDUAL CONSENT

Negation is now, as it was in Locke's conception, more directly evidenced than affirmation. But none of this, least of all his conditional equation of express with tacit consent, impairs the assumption that the principle of consent is conterminous with the self-willed commitment to political obligation. Rather, it all reveals the consonance of Locke's insights with the deflation in modern political theory of the concrete meaning of the people's consent and sovereignty. For those who believe in democracy, this consonance should be of some interest, since in Locke's conception the people's supremacy is compatible with the rejection of general suffrage.

2. SUFFRAGE AND CITIZENSHIP

A. Suffrage for the Propertied

Few interpreters have made it clear that Locke had not much faith in the majority.[28] Some are aware that he was no radical or democrat because he maintained the right of revolt.[29] Most have, in one way or another, accepted at their face value and therefore in a democratic sense Locke's statements on consent, majority-decision and the supremacy of the people. Some of these commentators have simply ignored the criterion of general suffrage[30] (or, in deference to historical development, at least of universal manhood suffrage), which is a necessary, though not a sufficient, condition of democracy. Other interpreters have attributed to Locke the intention of advocating general suffrage,[31] or have asserted that he merely failed

---

[28] Strauss, *op. cit.*, 233, and Laslett, *op. cit.*, 96, have done so.
[29] Cp. Ch. Bastide, *op. cit.*, 238, 240; Gough, *op. cit.*, 39, 41, 59, 68, 113, 131-3; Cranston, *John Locke*, 211; Macpherson, *op. cit.*, 198, and *passim*, and Plamenatz, *op. cit.*, 234. E. Barker, *The Social Contract* (Oxford, 1946), xxxiv, rather vaguely remarked that Locke 'did not press the idea of democracy.'
[30] E. Smyniades, *Les Doctrines de Hobbes, Locke et Kant sur le droit de l'insurrection.* (Paris, 1921), 71-2, 83; Vaughan, *op. cit.*, 166, 201; Monson, *loc. cit.*, 129, 131, 133 and Cox, *op. cit.*, 117, 133-4.
[31] H. Laski, *Political Thought in England from Locke to Bentham* (New York, 1919), 38-9 and Polin, *op. cit.*, 151, 235-6. Polin's searching interpretation of Locke in Kantian – and at times even Hegelian – terms, is not only by itself hardly conducive to democratic conclusions, which Kant avoided and Hegel rejected strongly. Polin is also aware that according to Locke, the multitude comes into its own only in revolution (141, 156). This has also been clear to Laski and Vaughan, who moreover abide by their view of Locke's commitment to democracy despite their recognition of the connection between Locke's theory and the non-democratic system of government in Locke's England. (Laski, *op. cit.*, 18, 42-3 and Vaughan, *op. cit.*, 143, 186.)

283

to make his acceptance of general suffrage plain enough.[32] He is also said to have ignored the need to work out techniques for forming and revealing the will of the majority, because majority-rule and universal suffrage seemed to him sufficiently accounted for by the equal right of individuals to form part of a revolutionary majority.[33] In interpretations which take liberties with the notion of general suffrage the sporadic exercise of a residuary revolutionary power is in fact equated with the regular exercise of residuary power according to constitutional provisions, the revolutionary with the constitutional participation of the majority in politics.[34] Yet Locke gave little cause for such misinterpretations even though he said again and again that the consent of the people was the only justifiable foundation of political society.

a. The Thesis

'That equal right that every man has, to his natural freedom' (Sec. 54) is converted by consent into the rule of law and that of its

---

[32] Lamprecht, *op. cit.*, 140, note. Lamprecht accused Locke of inexactness in his use of juridical and political terms (151), but himself worked with a rather loose conception of democracy and was, moreover, not consistent as regards Locke's attitude towards democracy. Cp. *op. cit.*, 3, 139, 140. Aaron, *op. cit.*, 271, 258, 304, maintains in one instance that Locke would not grant general suffrage and in another that it is not clear whether he meant to withold it.

[33] Kendall, *op. cit.*, 121, note 5. In keeping with his insistence on institutional arrangements (19, 98) and on the proper definition of majority rule (18), Kendall, therefore, concludes that Locke was a majority-rule democrat in all but one respect (53, 67, 99, 108, 113, 119, 124). Although Kendall concedes that the right of revolt was 'a tardy attempt' (127) to compensate for the lack of 'political machinery by means of which the popular (or majority) will may express itself' (124), he accepts revolutionary participation as the means for securing 'an equal voice in the making of laws' (121), i.e., as the substitute, if not the equivalent, of universal manhood suffrage.

[34] Cp. Friedrich, *Constitutional Government*, 130, on the distinction in terms of the 'constituent' and 'constitutional' power. Vaughan, *op. cit.*, 150, was much less clear. Lamprecht, *op. cit.*, 146, says that the social contract establishes 'narrow legal limits' for the right of revolution. Laski, *op. cit.*, 41, said that, through the right of revolt, Locke inserted the social contract 'into the interstices of public statutes'. Barker in his comment on Gierke also somewhat confuses the issues, whereas Gierke himself (*op. cit.*, 149, 349) and Gough, *op. cit.*, 114, recognize Locke's distinction between legal and extra-legal power; so do Wolin and Goldwin although at the cost of defining the right of revolt as a non-political right. (See above, 128, note 45). Pollock, *op. cit.*, 247-8, too, correctly explains Locke's right of revolt as the reserved power of the people, but regards it not so much as an extra-legal but as an anarchical one. While one should say with Laslett, *op. cit.*, 114, 119, that the residuary power of the people to change their governors and form of government was 'Locke's idea of what we now think of as popular sovereignty', this needs qualification because according to Locke the people's supremacy is not exercised under the constitution.

makers and officers. Laws render all men politically free because they protect each from the arbitrary will of the other. 'For who could be free, when every other man's humour might domineer over him' (Sec. 57)? Equality before the law does not mean equal political rights for all. Although Locke stressed especially the necessity of the people's consent to taxation, he took care in speaking in this and other connections of the consent of the people *or* of its representatives,[35] that is, he equated one with the other. Locke's answer to the question 'Who elects the representatives?' must determine whether or not he related the consent of the representatives to the consent of the people in a way consonant with democracy. Government by consent is democratic if, besides other things, the right to govern depends on a formal expression of will on the part of a majority of the governed.[36] Election-studies have led empirical theory to the conclusion that national elections express no more than the first preferences for candidates and are somewhat unreliable as indicators of majority preferences for policies. Empirical theory does not deny that the plea of traditional democratic theory for elections held on the basis of political equality constitutes a crucial control of leaders.[37]

Locke was far from ignoring the question who actually authorizes the holders of political power. In the first paragraph of the *Second Treatise* he stated it as his object to suggest an appropriate 'way of designing and knowing the persons that have it'. For, 'the great question which in all ages has disturbed mankind', and caused the greatest afflictions, 'has been, not whether there be power in the world, nor whence it came, but who should have it'. Hence, 'a reformer of politics . . . should lay this sure, and be very clear in it.'[38] Locke made it clear that the masses were to have no share in the election of their representatives. 'Every one who enjoys his share of the protection, should pay out of his estate his proportion for the maintenance of it' (Sec. 140). The 'proportion' determines whether one has the vote or not. The right 'to be *distinctly* rep-

---

[35] Secs. 88, 89, 131, 140, 142, 192, 212.
[36] Cp. Friedrich, *op. cit.*, Ch. XIV; J. P. Plamenatz, *Consent, Freedom and Political Obligation* (Oxford, 1938), 4 f., and his contribution in *Democracy in a World of Tension*, (Unesco, Paris, 1951), 304. See also, H. Kelsen, 'Foundations of Democracy,' *Ethics*, LXVI, 1, part 2 (1955), 2-3, and A. Ranney and W. Kendall, *Democracy and the American Party System* (New York, 1956), 21 f., and *passim*.
[37] Cp. Dahl, *A Preface to Democratic Theory*, 3, 125, 131.
[38] I, 106. Cp. I, 126.

resented , . . no part of the people however incorporated can pretend to, but *in proportion* to the assistance, which it affords to the public' (Sec. 158). Assistance is afforded to the public through the payment of taxes. The right to vote depends on whether one has taxable property or not, and is, moreover, graded proportionately to taxable property. We cannot therefore say that, according to Locke, everyone who works is a proprietor, and hence not only a citizen but also an elector.[39] The right 'to be *distinctly* represented' (i.e. not indirectly or virtually) depends on the proportion of the monetary assistance rendered to the public.

The plain assertion of unequal suffrage occurs in the context in which Locke deals with the problems created by rotten boroughs such as Old Sarum. In the spirit of the electoral reform proposed by Shaftesbury, the reform supported in the *Treatise* involves redrawing the map of electoral districts in conformity with 'the reasons it [representation] was at first established upon' (Sec. 157). The reapportionment of seats is to be effected in accordance with demographical and economic change: 'people, riches, trade, power, change their stations; . . .' 'To have a fair and equal representative' (Sec. 158) means representation proportionate to the wealth and number of inhabitants of the constituencies. An argument in favour of democratic representation would have referred to population alone. And when he referred only to numbers he added the non-egalitarian restriction, for he spoke of 'the true proportion, . . . of representation, [which] regulates, not by old custom, but true reason, the number of members, in all places, *that have a right to be distinctly represented*'. To 'choose . . . representatives upon just and undeniably equal measures' is to prevent a situation where a place inhabited by a solitary shepherd sends 'as many representatives . . . as a whole county *numerous in people, and powerful in riches* . . .' (Sec. 157). It does not mean to go by numbers alone and give shepherds or their like the right 'to be distinctly represented'. Thus, what justifies the exercise of the right of revolt – i.e., the political right shared equally by all – when either the executive or the legislature abuses its power, is the fact that 'the people cannot be judge, so as to have *by the constitution* of that society any superior power, *to determine and give effective sentence*' (Sec. 168). Locke did not mean that the electorate had no power whatsoever to pronounce effective sentence under the constitution. He meant that, because

[39] Polin, *op. cit.*, 272-3.

the majority of the people was disfranchised, they could judge only whether or not to appeal to heaven.

That the defence of unequal suffrage should be accompanied by so much talk of majority consent and popular authorization of government will not surprise anyone familiar with the 'stock-in-trade' Whig language of the period.[40] Its practical meaning was well understood by contemporaries. When the Whig Exclusionists pamphleteers talked as if Parliament and the people were the same thing, their opponents did not fail to retort that the Commons represented only one-sixth of the people.[41] The *Treatise* endorses as a matter of course the principle underlying this state of affairs. Its explicit defence of virtual representation rejects implicitly that measure of manhood suffrage demanded by the Levellers. This is the consistent application to politics of Locke's view that the many lagged behind the few in the comprehension of natural law, that 'the industrious and rational' (Sec. 34) come first; in short, Locke proceeded according to his distinction between natural and 'all sorts of equality'.[42]

b. *The Application*

For an elaborate illustration of the principle of undemocratic representation we may turn to the *Fundamental Constitutions of Carolina*. For in this point, as distinct from individual reaffirmation of membership,[43] the details given in the *Constitutions* conform to the principles enunciated in the *Treatise*.

As in the *Treatises*, political status is here linked to social class. It is also emphasized that socio-economic stratification does not merely reflect political organization but is guaranteed by it. In a manner strikingly reminiscent of Harrington, 'the balance of government' is associated with the distribution of land. The political constitution guarantees that one-fifth of the land belongs to the lord-proprietors, another fifth to the lesser nobility and the remaining three-fifths to the free-holders.[44] The preponderance of the political institutions which are in the hands of the lord-proprietors and other members of the nobility is also assured

---

[40] For the term, see Gough, *op. cit.*, 71.
[41] Cp. O. W. Furley, 'The Whig Exclusionists: Pamphlet Literature in the Exclusion Campaign, 1679-81,' *The Cambridge Historical Journal*, XIII (1957).
[42] Sec. 54. See above, 51 f. and 144 f.
[43] See above, 276.
[44] Article IV.

through the composition of parliament. Each county comprises four precincts, eight baronies, all of which have their own representatives.[45] Each of the four precincts is represented by a freeholder, but not all freeholders have the right to elect and be elected. To qualify as a candidate, one must possess not less than 500 acres of freehold within the precinct, 'nor shall any have the ,vote in choosing the said member that has less than 50 acres of freehold within the said precinct'.[46]

No doubt, these far-going concessions to feudal privilege conform to the wishes of the lord-proprietors. Whether or not Locke agreed to the details as being required by the particular conditions of colonization, we can certainly hold him already at that time committed to the restriction of the franchise. When in his later years he drew the more radical conclusions from the idea of consent, he abided, as the *Treatise* shows, by the principle of unequal representation, which underlies the provisions made for the suffrage of freeholders in the *Constitutions*. Nor is it difficult to see why the details are found in the *Constitutions* and not in the *Treatise*. A legal document like the *Constitutions* had to be specific concerning not only wherein it differed from, but likewise where it imitated, the usages obtaining in the mother country. Conversely, as an instrument in the ideological struggle over the desirable order in England, the *Treatises* had no need to dwell on details where the principles defended were in line with prevailing practice. We can therefore assume neither that Locke lacked definite views about popular suffrage at any time nor that his views about it underwent a considerable change. For the public that he addressed and the cause which he served, universal manhood suffrage was anything but a pressing issue. Consequently, the plea for a democratic reform of suffrage made during the English Revolution[47] evoked from Locke no more than a short and distinct reaffirmation of the principle according to which the individual right to vote depended on property qualifications.

Despite the fundamental differences between them, the *Constitutions* anticipate the *Treatises* insofar as the aim stated in the preamble is 'to avoid erecting a numerous democracy'.[48] This appears to be a

---

[45] Article LXXI.
[46] Article LXXII.
[47] On the Levellers' restrictions of the franchise, see Macpherson, *op. cit.*, 107 f.
[48] *Works*, Vol. X, 175. Maurice Cranston has drawn my attention to the expression.

strange way of putting things in an obviously undemocratic document. Why use the term 'democracy' at all? The reason can best be clarified in connection with a slightly different use of the word 'commonwealth' in the two *Treatises*. In the *First Treatise* Locke intended the meaning which had become prevalent especially during the English Revolution. Juxtaposed to monarchical government, 'commonwealth'[49] denoted all forms of government in which the sovereign consisted of more than one person. Although a republic in the first place, and not necessarily a democracy, a 'commonwealth' allowed a multiplicity of persons to share sovereign power. For this reason, a commonwealth which avoided being a 'numerous democracy' might nevertheless be regarded as more democratic than a monarchy.

In the *Second Treatise*, any identification of 'commonwealth' with a specific form of government is emphatically ruled out, and particularly the exclusive identification with a democracy. 'By commonwealth, I must be understood all along to mean, not a democracy, or any form of government, but any independent community which the Latins signified by the word *civitas*' (Sec. 133). As compared with the *First Treatise*, 'commonwealth' seems to cover all forms of government and not only those in which sovereign power is shared. Nevertheless, the stance in both *Treatises* is the same. While 'commonwealth' is more consistently used in the Second *Treatise* than in the First, it denotes in both an independent community ruled according to the principles of government by consent. Since the principle is rejected by Filmer, his conception of monarchy is stamped by Locke as inconsistent with all proper forms of commonwealth. If all legitimate forms of government derive from the consent of the people, a democratic element may be said to inhere in all of them. Probably for this reason Locke saw fit to stress that not all commonwealths were democratic and explicitly identified democracy with direct democracy.

The same considerations seem to underlie the reference to a 'numerous democracy' in the *Constitutions*. It apparently connotes a regime based on the equal, and hence most numerous, participation of citizens in politics, if not in the direct wielding of sovereign power. 'To avoid erecting a numerous democracy' does not demand the exclusion of everything characteristic of democracy, least of all elections. In providing for a non-democratic representation of the

---

[49] I, 132, 133, 146, 147.

people according to property qualification, the *Constitutions* anticipate and illustrate the principle enunciated later in the *Second Treatise*.

B. *Citizenship for the Propertyless*

It remains to clarify to what extent citizenship and suffrage are associated in Locke's conception. Generally, they are inseparable in any regime inasmuch as only citizens have the vote, whereas the right to vote is not invariably a condition of citizenship. Only in a democracy are all adult members of society usually both citizens and voters. If, on the other hand, in a non-democratic regime – such as prevailed in Europe and elsewhere until this century – citizenship were confined to those entitled to vote, full membership of political society would be denied to non-voters. Locke did not assume what neither logic nor historical experience confirms, namely, that, because the vote is not accorded to all citizens, only those who have the right to vote must be regarded as citizens.

Although in his treatment of the reaffirmation of membership by 'express' consent, Locke demanded that either citizenship be accepted or the inheritance disposed of, he allowed for cases in which property rights and political obligation do not coincide. But even if we acknowledge no more than that he broadened the doctrine of express into one of tacit consent because he could not demonstrate express consent on the part of all members, we cannot conclude[50] that he assigned the status of non-members to those whose property was insignificant, or who had none at all. We can draw this conclusion the less, if we stipulate that the right of controlling the government is the mark of citizenship and acknowledge the right of revolt to serve the purpose of control. In this case we accept the right of concerted dissent as the substitute of the right of express consent. And if we concede that citizens are, for Locke, all who possess the right to revolt, then not estate owners alone are citizens. For there is no foundation for saying that he confined the right of revolt to owners of land, or otherwise to a minority.[51] What is more, the wording itself of the clause which restricts suffrage bears out that the restriction does not affect citizenship. To repeat: 'a right to be distinctly represented, . . . no part of the people *however*

[50] As Macpherson, *op. cit.*, 249-50, does.
[51] See above, 173.

incorporated can pretend to, but in proportion to the assistance, which it affords to the public' (Sec. 158). Property distinctions do not divide the people into those who are incorporated and those who are not, but they divide the incorporated into several categories; and to be incorporated means to be a citizen. The restriction of suffrage creates a distinction between citizens and not between members and non-members of political society.

Locke furnishes us with a still more direct admission of the inclusion of the propertyless. As Macpherson agrees, Section 120 qualifies the exclusion of the propertyless from incorporation. It refers to the man who, by incorporation, annexes to the commonwealth 'those possessions, which he has, *or shall acquire*'. Those who have no more than expectations of property are admitted as parties to the compact, i.e. as citizens. Locke does not here merely qualify the exclusion of the actually propertyless from citizenship, but quite clearly concedes them citizenship. This corroborates my interpretation of that part of Section 158 which I have re-quoted.

Both pieces of evidence, but particularly the passage in Section 120, support also my previous inference of the possible non-coincidence of proprietorship and citizenship in the case of a son of a member who comes of age when his father is still alive.[52] It is confirmed that, although the refusal of citizenship obliges the heir to dispose of his inheritance, proprietorship is not the condition of citizenship. The separability of property and political rights and obligation reveals itself now as working both ways, that is, as applicable to rejection and acceptance. The rejection of political obligation does not demand the renunciation of property rights under a conqueror or entail the renunciation of the equivalent of one's estate in a proper political society. The exercise of civic rights and duties by a son of a member and incorporation into another political society depend not upon the actual possession of property but at most upon the expectation of acquiring property in the future.

If the expectation of property qualifies for citizenship, it could only be withheld from part of the propertyless, if a distinction were possible between the propertyless labourers who have and those who do not have expectations of property. Even if Macpherson had faced this implication on which his interpretation rests, he could not have suggested the criterion which Locke might have had in mind for distinguishing between working men who have no property but

[52] See above, 272 f.

expectations of it, and those who have neither the one nor the other. Apart from dividing *ex post factum* those who are fit and willing to work from those who are not, only one sensible *a priori* distinction can be safely inferred, viz., between the sons of property-owners, who may be propertyless until they inherit, and the sons of impecunious fathers. But this distinction is of no help nor is any other which does not enable us to discern beforehand which persons among the propertyless who are admitted as parties to the incorporating compact will or will not live up to the expectation of acquiring property by their own efforts. Prediction of this kind was obviously beyond Locke's purpose. He conceded the faculty of acquiring property to every normal being inasmuch as everybody, if he is to live, is under the necessity to secure external goods through work. Everyone who works can thus be regarded proprietor enough to qualify for citizenship and count among those who share political rights 'in *proportion* to the assistance' they afford to the public. Political rights are graded not so much according to whether men have property or not as according to the proportions of it.

Locke's state is, to be sure, a 'class-state'.[53] There has never been any doubt about it. But his – or any other liberal's – conception is not predicated on the impossible distinction between those propertyless who possess expectations of property and those who lack them. Socio-economic mobility is presupposed by Locke,[54] and economic proficiency determines in truly liberal fashion the extent of political rights.

Political freedom depends on the existence of effective and morally unobjectionable alternatives.[55] In the self-willed identification of the individual with the fate of his political society, it does not only matter whether acceptance of political obligation and participation are formal or not, but above all, whether there are legitimate alternatives to obedience, such as withdrawal by emigration or concerted dissent to change the governors or the form of government. Usually the more the individual participates in the political life of his society, the greater his sense of commitment to it. In a

[53] Cp. Macpherson, *op. cit.*, 251.
[54] See above, 164.
[55] Cp. Berlin, *Two Concepts of Liberty*, 15, note 1.

free democratic mass society, differential capacities are the main cause why the positive avenues for demonstrating and developing one's sense of commitment are not equally open to all. Locke's liberal contractualism is inconsistent with an exclusively passive attitude on the part of the mass of citizens; but it does go together with the closing to the majority of constitutional avenues for demonstrating active concern with the political order. Yet having adopted the right of revolt as the sole realization of the people's collective right of consent, he saw himself free to speak of the right of the people to choose, appoint, or authorize representatives so as to declare their decisions as normally reflecting the will of the people. The idea that the liberty of the individual must be safeguarded by the limitation of governmental power and that, to be limited, political power must be shared, is the common and basic denominator of liberal ways of thought. They are, as not only Locke shows, adjustable to elitist, authoritarian and extra-constitutional notions, because stipulating multilateral consent as the basis for sharing power does not necessarily amount to stipulating democratic or invariably constitutionally expressed consent.[56] Conversely, the criteria of a democratic theory are to be found not in the rejection of the rights and responsibilities of an élite, but in the procedure through which an élite attains its special rights.[57] A fundamental tension results if universal or majority consent is postulated as the fount of legitimation while general suffrage is restricted. In Locke's case, this tension is resolved – or partly resolved – by his permitting an occasional outburst: revolution.

[56] See my 'Napoleonic Authoritarianism in French Liberal Thought.'
[57] Cp. Lasswell and Kaplan, *Power and Society*, 202.

CHAPTER X

POPULAR CONSENT - A THEORY OF REVOLUTIONARY ACTION

LOCKE'S attempt to align the principle of popular consent with that of political inequality by admitting the right of popular resistance raises a question. Locke held the majority of the people to be unfit to participate in the election, and hence in the judgement, of their representatives. If this was his opinion of the people's power of judgement in more or less normal circumstances, how could he at the same time admit the people's umpirage when they were ill-treated and made miserable to the point of despair: that is to say, when the last thing one could expect of them was a judicious judgement? Locke answered the question by extending his distrust of the majority to its revolutionary umpirage. His views on revolution add up to a circumspect theory of the nature of revolutionary action, which is consistent with his attitude towards democracy.

I shall try to prove his awareness of the logical and practical implications of his defence of revolution by dealing with questions pertinent to any theory of revolution in particular, and of the political participation of the masses in general. First, to what extent was Locke's argument intended to grant to the majority the competence of judging the policies of their representatives and rulers, and if it were not so intended, can his doctrine of resistance be considered as a doctrine of consent? Secondly, did Locke assume that the power of the majority is used only, and prevails invariably, in support of just causes? What, in fact, is the nature of the majority decision implied in the appeal to heaven? Thirdly, does Locke's justification of the right to revolt amount to advocating frequent revolt? Lastly, there is the question of what is modern in his conception of revolution.

I. THE NATURE OF THE PEOPLE'S JUDGEMENT

A. Disapproval of Wrongs Inflicted by Rulers

In accordance with his views on the knowability of natural law by the common man, Locke carefully limited what exactly the people judge in deciding on revolt. The answer to 'the old question': 'Who shall be judge?' is that the people have, and can never abandon, the right 'to judge whether they have just cause to make their appeal to heaven'.[1] The decision on the rightness or wrongness of their appeal represents the people's judgement on whether the prince or the legislature, or both, are acting contrary to their trust, whether the wrongs done to the people by their rulers are worth bearing or not. By their conscience or feeling,[2] the people decide whether there exists a serious threat to their lives, liberties and fortunes. Neither knowledge of, nor a direct judgement upon, the right and reasonable way to secure life, liberty and fortune are demanded but knowledge and judgement as to when and whether security and dignity are unduly endangered by the rulers. One need not know specifically what is ultimately right to be able to judge by generally accepted standards of right and wrong what is unbearable, and to declare it to be wrong.

Men, Locke thought, are more likely to judge correctly present rather than future enjoyment and suffering. Yet while for the most part, 'the greatest present uneasiness is the spur to action', the ability to pass an objective judgement depends on the mind's 'power to suspend the execution and satisfaction of any of its desires'.[3] Since the people greatly lacked this ability, it was as moral to justify their revolutionary judgement which was occasioned by the greatest and most pressing public 'uneasiness', as it was logical to limit the exercise of this adjudication to negating what the established leaders were doing. Locke asked: 'Are the people to be blamed, if they have the sense of rational creatures, and can think of things no otherwise than as *they find and feel them*' (Sec. 230)? It is not the people who have put 'things in such a posture'. The 'manifest evidence' of what is practised by their rulers, in patent contradiction to the explanations which they give, makes the people fear their rulers' further intentions. If only fully-fledged tyranny, not the steps by which it develops, furnishes evidence of wrongdoing which can be discerned and opposed, 'this is . . . no more than to bid them first be slaves, and then to take care of their liberty'.[4] The Hobbesian *summum malum*

---

[1] Sec. 168. The question 'who shall be judge?' is posed or implied also in Secs. 13 19-21, 89, 93, 123, 131, 136, 181, 240, 241.

[2] Secs. 21, 209 and 94. See above, 55-6, 65.

[3] *Essay*, I, Bk. II, Ch. xxi, 64-5, 40 and 47 (Cp. 52, 56), respectively.

[4] Sec. 220. See also Secs. 221-3 and 16.

is the compass of Locke's power-hedonism,[5] as far as the design of others on one's life and property is discerned and judged politically by the people. In respect of this threat, 'this question, (who shall be judge?) cannot mean, that there is no judge at all'.[6] It means that the constitutional arrangements are either ineffective or abused and that the people must be called upon to take the law of virtuous self-preservation into their own hands, or rather reject its insidious implementation by others, and support those who will guarantee its more appropriate discharge. The majority broaches the question of the appeal to heaven only after the minority has expressed its grievances in the first place. For 'if a controversy arise between a prince and *some* of the people', then 'the proper umpire . . . should be the body of the people' (Sec. 242). Although the people are guided by a minority, the ultimate decision on revolt is reserved to the majority, since for the people 'to act as one body . . . is only by the will and determination of the majority'.[7]

The determination does not carry further than passing sentence on the rulers' wrongdoing, although the majority is granted not only the right to reject an existing regime but to choose any form of government which they think fit.[8] However, the determination of a new form of government cannot be attributed to the direct endorsement of the majority. Locke admitted direct democracy only for the conduct of revolution. Although he allowed for any mixture of the traditional forms of government, his rejection of general suffrage did not admit of incorporating principles of perfect demo-

---

[5] Cp. Strauss, *op. cit.*, 250. Strauss' view that, for Locke, rights originate from sufferings and defects is particularly borne out by the negative character and function of the people's judgement, as it has been interpreted here. But, as I have explained in Chapter II, it does not follow that all natural rights have only a negative point of reference.

[6] Sec. 241. Cp. 168, 93.

[7] Sec. 96. Plamenatz, *op. cit.*, 233, 259, asserts, like Macpherson, (see above, 173) that Locke granted the right of revolt only to the minority. He speaks of a right of 'rebellion' – which, according to Locke, nobody possesses (see below, 316) – and ignores what his line of argument ought to have led him to consider, i.e. the evident connection between the repeatedly posed and always identically answered 'old question . . . "who shall be judge" ' (see note 1) and the majority principle. In fact, because Locke justified only majority resistance, it might be said that he made no provision for a duty of resistance. Cp. Pitkin, *op. cit.*, *The American Political Science Review*, LX, 1 (1966), 41. However, the duty is implicit in the moral foundation of the right. Abrams fails to make it clear why in one instance (*op. cit.*, 91) he says that *Two Treatises* allow action against the magistrate and in another (105) that they are 'more ambiguous' in this respect than the early writings which deny the right.

[8] Secs. 132, 149, 168, 176, 220, 243.

cracy in another form of government. True, the revolutionary displacement of a government or regime is not usually effected by electoral procedure. But then active participation in the revolution and acquiescence in it do not necessarily attest more than the people's will to resist the government, not the majority's legitimation of the permanent new governors or new form of government. Usually repudiating a government also implies identification with positive revolutionary aims. But ascertainment of such an identification is ruled out if the people may express their preferences only by exercising the extreme and summary right to overthrow the governors or the form of government. The voting by representatives or new elections must be considered as the final means of endorsing the new regime. If suffrage is severely restricted, the electoral decision reflects the will of the minority of citizens, or of their representatives. For all intents and purposes Locke thus assumes that, as soon as the people desist from active resistance, they can be supposed to have consented to what the politically articulate minority has found to be acceptable. Since no means of pressing any point is open to the people save revolt, once engaged in revolt the people can express no judgement of the achievements of the revolution except by abstaining or not abstaining from a further revolution.

Just as the existence of political society testifies to the agreement of all the incorporated to evade the 'inconveniences' of the hypothetical state of nature, the majority's verifiable response to revolutionary objectives is restricted to the repudiation of an obnoxious regime. As distinct from the right of express dissent manifested in the attempt at overthrowing the government, the right of the people to choose a government to their liking remains a matter of tacit consent. Peaceful incorporation into society remains the paradigm of majority consent.

B. The Adequacy of Locke's Theory of Consent

a. Dissent and Consent

Since only through revolutionary dissent the people as a whole may realize the principle of majority consent, it appears that, just as Filmer had negated the idea of consent in order to deny the right of revolt, Locke adopted the principle of popular consent solely for the purpose of justifying revolt. Even so, his theory may be confronted with two questions: First, whether society can assign to government the power to do that which society approves; and secondly, whether the government has the power to do to society that which society disapproves of.[9] Locke's theory stands the test of both questions, provided we accept as an answer that society's approval of government action is revealed in tacit compliance, and its disapproval in lending support to – or tacitly complying with – those who call for revolution. This is to accept the absence of the act of dissent as evidence for the existence of majority consent. Stripped of its nominalistic inflation, Locke's conception of majority consent thus turns out to be rather a hypothesis about an attitude than a statement about an act,[10] but it remains a theory of consent.

Abstention from the overt act of revolutionary dissent is, of course, not invariably an indication of the existence of an attitude, or mental state, of tacit consent; it might equally reflect mute resignation and withdrawal. The attitude of dissent might exist even if it is not expressed in concerted action. Yet so long as the conclusive criterion of the people's attitude towards their rulers consists in whether or not the ruled appeal to heaven, any regime must be regarded as sustained by consent until it is challenged by revolution. Even if tacit consent on these premises means 'mere acceptance of what you are powerless to reject', unless the implication is that it is beyond your power to reject anything at any time, it does not follow that Locke misrepresented a doctrine of resistance as a doctrine of consent.[11]

Although there is a difference between dissent and consent, they are connected inasmuch as their effect is identical in a decisive respect. The right of dissent like the right of consent renders obedience conditional and abstention from dissent may, and in a number of circumstances definitely does, indicate consent. Montesquieu saw no difference between the right to approve and the right to disapprove, and even derived the first from the second.[12] If we do not rule out tacit consent altogether as a sensible assumption but

[9] Kendall, *op. cit.*, 97. For the comparison between Locke and Filmer, see above, 196–7, 255 f.

[10] For the terminology used, see below, note 16.

[11] Plamenatz, *op. cit.*, 231, 239, suggests the derivation rejected here.

[12] *De L'Esprit des Lois.* Ed. par G. Turc, Classiques Garnier, Paris, n.d., 2 vols, I, Bk. XI, Ch. VI, 168. Formal disapproval is what Montesquieu called 'la faculté d'empêcher', i.e., 'le droit de rendre nulle une résolution prise par quelque autre; . . . Et quoique celui qui a la faculté d'empêcher puisse avoir le droit d'approuver, pour lors cette approbation n'est autre chose qu'une déclaration qu'il ne fait point d'usage de sa faculté d'empêcher, *et dérive de cette faculté*.' (Italics supplied.)

consider it, with Plamenatz, as consent in its weakest connotation, then Locke cannot be refused the claim of having made consent the grounds for obedience. This is the less deniable since obedience depending on consent in its weakest form meant for him abstention from dissent in its strongest. True, formal disapproval permits the rejection of proposals, whereas revolutionary dissent bears chiefly on accomplished facts. Formal disapproval fulfils the function of consent more accurately than revolutionary disapproval. It does so also more effectively because it distinctly eliminates everything disapproved and indirectly indicates, very precisely, what is approved. But, although formal dissent demarcates the area of consent more clearly and effectively than informal, both formal and informal dissent demarcate an area of consent indirectly. Neither on logical nor practical grounds can Locke's doctrine of resistance be divorced from a doctrine of consent. We can only object that the principle of popular consent is imperfectly applied if it is not democratically institutionalized. This and nothing more, follows from the criticism of Locke which asserts that his fundamental error was to look for the difference between strong and weak consent in the manner of giving consent instead of in its contents.[13]

It is feasible to distinguish two ways of consenting not merely by the manner of their expression. We could call consent direct or strong, insofar as it grants authority to persons, or establishes or alters a system of government, and term it indirect when it does not bear on matters like these.[14] Yet, on Plamenatz' own showing, the manner of expressing consent continues to matter. Although for his definition of indirect consent he requires the unwarranted stipulation that inaction should not be understood as preference for an alternative, the correlation between the contents and the form of consent is sustained when he says that indirect and weak consent are given only tacitly. Tacit consent is a form of consent, even if it is consent which is indirect in virtue of its content; it is related to the forms of giving consent precisely because it cannot be formally expressed but can be inferred only from certain forms of behaviour. Yet rather than distinguish between forms and formless consent, Plamenatz seems to distinguish between a strong and a weak form when he says that consent which is strong in its content can be given expressly or tacitly. And this is to accept what is criticized

---

[13] Plamenatz, *op. cit.*, 235.
[14] Plamenatz, *op. cit.*, 238-9.

in Locke, i.e. his equation of tacit with express consent in matters which are, in Plamenatz's terms, objects of strong consent. Locke, moreover, avoided confusion as he did not hold that in all matters consent to the same things can be expressed in different ways. The minority of the people who have the vote, and the representatives whom they elect, exercise consent which is strong in its contents, inasmuch as they grant authority to persons; they do so by consent which is direct in its form. Their right of formal approval and disapproval does not include the authority to establish or alter a system of government. To do that, they must join the people and embark with them on revolution.[15] In this case, consent which is strong in its contents is indirect in its form – for it is abstention from dissent. But insofar as the formal consent of part of the people, and of the representatives chosen by that part, stands for the tacit consent of all, consent to the same things is assumed to be expressed differently.

Indubitably, the existence of tacit consent can be presumed with greater certainty when formal consent, even if it is the preserve of a minority of the people, has its place beside the informal, because extra-constitutional, dissent of all. In leaving the majority of the people with nothing but the choice between tacit consent and expressing dissent either through emigration or revolution, Locke offered an insufficiently developed, rather than an insufficiently grounded, case for government by consent. In fact, if appraised as it actually operates, the democratic idea of consent betrays a considerable affinity with Locke's non-democratic idea of consent.

b. Acts and Attitudes

Earlier in this chapter, I defined Locke's notion of majority consent as a hypothesis concerning an attitude rather than an act. I applied terms which have lately been suggested as suitable for defining the democratic consent of the governed in a realistic and reasonable way.[16] According to this approach, when we speak of consent, we assume the people's belief in the moral right of the

---

[15] Sec. 218.

[16] The terms are those of W. Cassinelli, 'The Consent of the Governed,' *The Western Political Quarterly*, XII, 2 (1959), 406–7. I have found Cassinelli's insights most helpful for making Locke's position clear, although Cassinelli's own references to Locke do not point that way. On the meaning of democratic consent, see also D. Spitz, *Democracy and the Challenge of Power* (New York, 1958); Dahl, *A Preface to Democratic Theory*; Sartori, *Democratic Theory*, and Runciman, *Social Science and Political Theory*.

rulers to govern, on the supposition that, if the people had an opportunity to give voluntary assent, they would give it. It would not seem to matter greatly that, in making the same assumptions, Locke gave the people no opportunity for express assent. On the modern view, the same objections apply to overt consent – the electoral test – as to tacit, especially as far as the ascertainability of consent to an existing constitution is concerned.[17] One may object that in the majority of cases consent to the existing constitution underlies participation in the electoral test. It provides, in any case, a reasonably explicit confirmation of the rulers' moral right to govern. Nevertheless, the express act of consent by the same persons in respect of one issue – 'Who is to govern?' – permits no more than the presumption of the tacit and indirect consent of most of these persons in respect of another issue, viz., the affirmation of the existing constitution. Likewise, elections are supposed also to decide issues of policy. They do this directly much less than they designate those who are to rule and shape national policy. The same objections apply to express and tacit consent, because not all that is to be decided by the overt act of consent can be taken to be expressly decided by it. Besides express and direct answers, the overt act is presumed to indicate indirect and tacit answers not only to questions that are asked, but also to those that are not asked at all.

The empirical analysis of democratic consent is not as far removed from Locke as it pretends to be. Locke did not state explicitly that express consent was open to the same objections as tacit consent. But his awareness of their affinity underlies his conditional equation of the two forms of consent as far as concerted popular consent and the individual assent to membership is concerned. His restriction of suffrage affects the dimensions, moral and practical, rather than the fundamental nature, of the implementation of government by consent. Modern analysis of the conclusiveness of the electoral test reduces the significance of the consent of the governed. Consequently, the distance between operative democratic theory and Locke, who advocated non-democratic suffrage, is also diminished. If in the one instance the moral right of the rulers to govern does not cease to be effectively related to the consent of the governed, this must to a considerable extent be true also of the other. This applies the more since the right of revolt guarantees, not only for Locke, the relatedness in each regime between the right to govern

[17] Cp. Cassinelli, *loc. cit.*, 391, 400.

and the consent of the governed. Modern critics of the notion of consent do not confine consent as an attitude to a specific form of government; they, too, relate the attitude to the frequency and intensity of revolt.[18] The affinities between modern empirical theory and Lockeian assumptions are astonishing only at first sight. After all, if modern empirical theory found out that the democratic process is not as democratic as ideology would have it, Locke did not conceive of the political process in terms of democratic ideology in the first place. Moreover, although Locke equated a doctrine of resistance with a doctrine of consent, he remained critical in appraising the power of the majority and the quality of its judgement when it came to revolutionary action itself.

2. THE MAJORITY'S POWER AND ITS USE

T. H. Green, who seems to be responsible for quite a number of misconceptions about Locke, claimed that he had been unaware of 'all sorts of questions' attendant upon the implementation of the majority's right to revolt.[19] Locke overlooked, as it were, that it is impossible to say whether a revolution is the act of the people; a sectary or a revolutionary can claim to have the people on his side, without this being actually the case. Neither failure nor success is proof that the majority has supported a revolution: a minority may be strong enough to cause its failure or its success.[20] Other interpreters have elaborated in this vein on Locke's lack of precision with regard to the circumstances in which, and the organs through which, revolution takes place.[21] Green quite correctly held that the same applies to revolution as to incorporation. One might, therefore, ask what can there be wrong about his objections if, as we have shown so far, Locke was not interested in the direct ascertainability of the will of the majority? What is wrong with the objections of

[18] Cp. *ibid.*, 408.
[19] T. H. Green, *Lectures on the Principles of Political Obligation*, Sec. 60.
[20] *Ibid.*, Sec. 61.
[21] J. W. Gough, *The Social Contract* (2nd ed., Oxford, 1957), 144; W. Simon, 'John Locke: Philosophy and Political Theory,' *The American Political Science Review*, XLV, 1951, 295; Laslett, *op. cit.*, 108, 119. Kendall, *op. cit.*, 129–30, does not really meet the objections of Green and his followers but rather adds to their assertions that of Locke's confidence in the commonsense of the people. For the same assertion see also Bastide, *op. cit.*, 238–9; Smyrniades, *op. cit.*, 106, 109–10; Vaughan, *op. cit.*, 151, and Polin, *op. cit.*, 161–2, 234.

Green and like-minded critics is that they accuse Locke of an oversight whereas in point of fact they overlook that his rejection of political equality has its faithful counterpart in the appraisal of the nature of the majority's revolutionary umpirage. Locke was consistent in regard to the relation between the few and the many in terms of right and might.

A. The Majority Principle and the Greater Force

On the face of it, Locke's justification of the majority principle appears to indicate that the majority must inevitably prevail. 'It being necessary to that which is one body to move one way; it is necessary the body *should* move that way whither the greater force carries it, which is the consent of the majority: or else it is impossible it should act or continue one body' (Sec. 96). Ostensibly the absolute majority of members is appraised by Locke in terms of mechanics as the greater force. But a law of mechanics, rather than stating that the body *should* move in the direction in which the greater force carries it, would have laid down that the social body invariably moves the way in which an inert body does. This difference in formulation need not be taken to attest an intention to indicate the dissimilarity between the laws of movement which govern, respectively, a social and an inert body. The similarity is not disturbed by the fact that the acceptance of the majority principle is necessarily implicit in original incorporation[22] and, according to Locke's historical demonstration, practically effected by tacit consent. The identification of the majority with the greater force is not precluded if original incorporation is by universal tacit consent, and if, once society exists, majority consent, which replaces and has the validity of universal consent, remains tacit. In concerted dissent, the majority may be held to represent the greater force. Consequently it can be regarded as prevailing when tacit consent exists, since tacit consent is presumable only in the absence of active dissent.

It makes sense to consider the majority of the whole social body as the greater force, provided we have in mind the absolute majority of all members, their equality in terms of force and their equally active and intense participation in the political process.[23] On these grounds Locke's position would have been unexceptionable but

[22] Secs. 95-7, 99.
[23] Cp. Kendall, *op. cit.*, 117, and Goldwin, *op. cit.*, 456.

unworthy of serious consideration.[24] But he was not commited to any of these assumptions. Demonstrating the application of the majority principle by reference to the practice of assemblies – 'assemblies empowered to act by positive laws' (Sec. 96) as well as 'the public assembly' (Sec. 98) – he presupposes that the majority which carries a decision usually is not the majority of all the members present. As part of his argument about the impossibility of requiring universal consent, he points to 'the infirmities of health, and avocations of business, which in a number, though much less than that of a commonwealth, will necessarily keep many away from the public assembly' (Sec. 98). He must have been aware that this same argument, which requires the foregoing of universal consent, also demands the acceptance as binding of decisions of a majority smaller in numbers than both absentees and opponents taken together. And this is to deviate from the simple mechanistic equation of the majority with the greater force. Accordingly, his justification of the majority principle is from the outset adapted to the requirements of human expediency by the intermediacy of the law of morals.

In the section in which Locke identified the majority with the greater force, he declared: 'The act of the majority passes for the act of the whole, and of course determines, as having *by the law of nature and reason*, the power of the whole.'[25] In the same section, the practice of assemblies is referred to, which implies that those who have actually 'the power of the whole' are not usually the absolute majority of members. Evidently, the moral law is resorted to as a means to justify what by a mere law of mechanics would simply not make sense. It is, then, no accident that the law of movement of a social body speaks of the direction in which 'the body *should* move', i.e. it is formulated not with an inert body in mind.

Expediency bids us rest content not only with less than unanimity but also with less than the consent of the absolute majority of all members. As a result, the majority principle must be anchored in moral grounds. Although universal consent would best conform

[24] Cp. Kendall, *op. cit.*, 119.

[25] Sec. 96. Most interpreters agree on the moral basis of Locke's argument. The exceptions are Cox, *op. cit.*, 117-18, who maintains that Locke's majority principle has a purely mechanical meaning in terms of strength, power and will, and Goldwin, *op. cit.*, 455-6, who discerns some limitations in the applicability of 'the law of greater force'.

with it, the law of nature does not ordain the inexpedient, and least of all the impossible. If morality were never compatible with expediency, it would not serve any human purpose.[26] It follows as a rule of right rather than of force that among those who actively concern themselves with an issue, the decision of the greater number prevails over that of the smaller and obligates all members, both where the express consent of assemblies and voters and where the tacit consent and active dissent of the masses are concerned. The majority of the people is, in terms of mechanics, the greater mass; in terms of human action, the greater mass – either the relative or the absolute majority – is not necessarily the greater force. In conformity with the use of 'should' in the quasi-mechanical formulation of the majority principle, Locke propagated that the moral right of the majority of the people to be decently governed *should* determine in which direction the social bodies move. He did not think the physical strength of the majority always sufficient to ensure this.

Revolution is a state of war which 'levels the parties, cancels all former relation of reverence, respect, and superiority: And then the odds that remains is, that he, who opposes the unjust aggressor, has this superiority over him, that he has a right, *when he prevails*, to punish the offender' (Sec. 235). Nothing is said here – or elsewhere – to the effect that the odds are that the righteous will prevail. Only for the sake of argument did Locke suppose that 'victory favours the right side' (Sec. 177), for he wished to stress that 'the practice of the strong and powerful, *how universal so ever it may be*, is seldom the rule of right' (Sec. 180). There can be no other foundation of government than the consent of the people, but for the most part 'this consent is little taken notice of'.[27] No contradiction follows from what Locke had said earlier: 'Where the majority cannot conclude the rest, there they cannot act as one body, and consequently will be immediately dissolved again' (Sec. 98). Locke meant to stress here that social life cannot be based on the consent of every

---

[26] While it may be said on a number of rules which Locke ascribed to the law of nature, that he merely asserted but did not prove them, this does not apply to the majority principle. Kendall, *op. cit.*, 117, Gough, *op. cit.*, 21 f., 61 f., and Laslett, *op. cit.*, 351, who make this charge, do not consider the implicit connections, which I have tried to make explicit, between the different parts of Locke's argument which culminate in the majority principle. See also above, 69 and 75 f.

[27] Sec. 175. On the strength of the relationship established between conquest and arbitrary rule (see above, 109 f.), I feel justified to rely on Sec. 175 also for internal relations.

individual and not that the will of the majority must invariably prevail if society is to exist. As we have seen, society is not 'immediately dissolved' under the absolute, or even arbitrary, rule of one or a few.[28] His whole advocacy of the right of revolt is predicated on the rulers' frequent disregard of the right of consent, on the opinion that the right of the majority has all too often given way to the might of the few.

For Locke, the right of the many is far from being commensurable with their might. Yet the commensurability of right with might is not only contingent, because the might of the majority falls often short of their right. The success of a majority cannot be assumed – any more than can that of a tyrant or a minority – to be a sign of the victory of right over might. Locke believed as little in the invariable rightness of the majority's will as in their ability always to impose that will.

B. The Improvidence of the Majority

a. Support of Arbitrary Rulers and Conquerors

On the premise that, individually, 'the greater part [of men are] no strict observers of equity and justice' (Sec. 123), one cannot expect the majority unerringly to espouse the cause of justice and prudence. Man's powers of wrongdoing increase through organization. It is much worse to be 'exposed to the arbitrary power of one man, who has the command of a hundred-thousand' than to 'the arbitrary power of a hundred-thousand single men' (Sec. 137). The distinction between the weight of power of an unorganized and an organized multitude is here part of an argument obviously levelled against Hobbes. The salient point is, however, that the organization of the multitude comes about because 'they shall have armed one or a few men with the joint power of a multitude, to force them to obey at pleasure ...' Locke acknowledges that a multitude is capable of lending its force willingly to an arbitrary ruler. Otherwise, there would be no reason to go on and point out how illogical it is for men 'to put themselves into a worse condition than the state of nature' and that 'all the power the government has, . . . ought not to be arbitrary and at pleasure'. What is denied is not the fact that a multitude has 'disarmed themselves, and armed him', but the moral validity and the prudence of such a course of action.

[28] See above, 104 f., 246 f.

Locke knows that 'the practice of the strong and powerful' often receives the support, however ill-advised, of those who are the victims of that practice and ought to be its judges.

In fact, the corrupting influence of absolute power[29] feeds also on the mass-appeal of political extremism, the corollary of the eruption of irrationality in politics. 'The busy mind of man [can] carry him to a brutality below the level of beasts, when he quits his reason, which places him almost equal to angels' (I, 58). Those who are capable of knowing better are carried away by their imagination, which 'is always restless and suggests variety of thoughts, and the will, reason being laid aside, is ready for every extravagant project; and in this state, *he that goes farthest out of the way, is thought fittest to lead, and is sure of most followers*'. Locke impressed upon his readers how little harm a single man can do by himself, even if he is safely placed at the pinnacle of power. A prince may as well be constitutionally sacred, 'the harm he can do in his own person, not being likely to happen often, nor to extend itself far; nor being able by his single strength to subvert the laws, nor oppress the body of the people' (Sec. 205).

In external no less than internal politics popular acquiescence in, and support of, arbitrary power can be obtained. In external emergencies as well as for the execution of laws the government is entitled 'to employ all the force of all the members when there shall be need'. In war, moreover, 'a blind obedience is necessary to that end for which the commander has his power, viz. the preservation of the rest'.[30] Yet to condone and support an unjust war is morally as reprehensible as to support arbitrary government in one's own political society. Locke judged internal and external arbitrariness by the same moral criteria, among other things also because he envisaged the possibility of popular participation in an unjust war[31] in the same way as popular support for despotism at home.

b. The Will of the Majority : Its Indifference and Forbearance

To speak of the possible participation in aggression of the majority, or even of all the men of the community, is to imply the possible involvement of the entire community in issues concerning

---

[29] See above, 247-8.
[30] Secs. 88 and 139. Cp. Secs. 130, 145.
[31] See above, 113.

its prestige and power. This is characteristic of the rationale of nationalism.[32] But in speaking of the involvement of the whole people in both revolution and war, Locke, of course, followed the conventions of ordinary speech. I venture to suggest that he did so with a clear understanding of what was glossed over – or taken for granted – in that manner of speech.

In his time, it was as impossible as it is in ours to determine the proportion of the population which actually participates in a revolution. It is still difficult to ascertain at the outbreak, or during a war or revolution, whether the majority desires or abets it. This difficulty is a boon to the leaders inasmuch as it enables them to claim majority consent to their actions on the strength of no more than the absence of weighty evidence to the contrary. There is no point in joining Locke's critics and blaming him for overlooking the difficulty of assigning to a definite proportion of the population the decision concerning the exercise of a non-legal right like that of revolt, or of determining whether a revolution is the work of a minority or of the majority. Instead, we should infer that because he was aware of these difficulties he allowed himself to make such a show of the majority principle. In every context in which he refers to the consent of all members and to the will of the majority, their ascertainability turns out to rest on no other than presumptive evidence. It will not do to attribute this to muddled thinking. Only because he would not admit any other evidence did he deem it expedient and, above all, safe, to invoke the will of the majority at all. This is what underlies his acceptance of the majority's revolutionary umpirage and his rejection of equal suffrage and removes any contradiction between the two. The umpirage is accepted because it is impossible to ascertain with any accuracy the will of the majority in revolution. Suffrage is limited because through it the will of the majority can be accurately ascertained, at least as regards some issues, including the confirmation of a revolutionary

---

[32] Cp. Cox, *op. cit.*, 125-6. The same applies, according to Vaughan, *op. cit.*, 156, to the assumption of the continuance of political union as implied in Locke's distinction between the dissolution of government and of society. There is also Locke's insistence on the right of the conquered to liberate themselves (Secs. 192, 196); his awareness of the connection between nation and language (I, 4, 144-6) and the implicit equation of statehood and nationhood. In fact, Locke's example shows that most of the tenets of modern nationalism can be found in political theory well before the age of nationalism. See my 'Locke, Liberalism and Nationalism,' in *John Locke : Problems and Perspectives*, ed. by T. W. Yolton, Cambridge U.P. (forthcoming).

change. Locke's intention to legitimize the management of political society by reference to the will of the majority, his mistrust of the majority's judgement, and his realistic appraisal of its power, are part of a consistent line of thought. To acclaim the supremacy of the will of the majority on these grounds does not indicate a depreciation of popular support. It means among other things awareness of the difficulties which a right-minded minority is liable to encounter in its attempt to secure such support. According to Locke, the inadvertence and indifference of the majority were mainly to the advantage of high-handed rulers. He emphasized the facile compliance of the people with rule by prerogative, their customary toleration of any government and their insensitiveness to the niceties of constitutional government.[33] Their inclination to tolerate to the utmost any government stems from their disinclination to espouse the cause of the one or the few who are wronged. The people will not stir 'till the mischief be grown general, and the ill designs of the rulers become visible, or their attempts sensible to the greater part' (Sec. 230). Locke did not think, however, that because it took a long time for the people to stir, they were more callous towards the sufferings of a minority than towards their own. Only after acknowledging that the people 'are more disposed to suffer, than right themselves by resistance', did he continue: 'the examples of particular injustice, or oppression of here and there an unfortunate man, moves them not'.[34]

Rulers who are far from being irreproachable are relatively secure and an opposing minority bent on revolt is unlikely to receive popular support unless illegal acts on a considerable scale affect the majority or – and this is very much the same thing – 'if the mischief and oppression has light only on some few, but in such cases, as the precedent, and consequences seem to threaten all, and they are persuaded in their consciences, that their laws, and with them their estates, liberties, and lives are in danger' (Sec. 209). To be thus persuaded is a matter of the majority's being guided by the example of the more sensitive and sensible men who are the first and, indeed, the only ones to voice their dissatisfaction. But there is no assurance that right-minded will fare better than wrong-minded initiators of revolt in gaining the people's support. True, this line

[33] Secs. 161, 223. See below, 311 f., 320 and 356 f.

[34] *Ibid.* Kendall, *op. cit.*, 103, relies only on the last part of the quotation to conclude that Locke was totally unconcerned with the fate of minorities.

of argument forms part of the attempt to allay apprehensions about the affirmation of the right of revolt. Yet while he argues that the acknowledgement of this right is no incentive to frequent revolt, the reasons he gives for the difficulty of putting the masses into a revolutionary frame of mind are not such as to inspire confidence in their sense of justice. He holds out no assurance that, if the masses eventually stir, they will countenance those whose intention to amend wrongs is unquestionable.

We have dwelt at some length on Locke's admissions of the possible concurrence of the majority in oppression and unjust war. We have done this, not because he did not explicitly admit that a wrong-minded minority might carry through an unjust revolt with the connivance of the people, but to show that his direct admission cannot be waived aside as an uncharacteristic inconsistency.

We are told that the people are not apt to follow 'a raving madman, or heady malcontent' (Sec. 208), 'busy head, or turbulent spirit' (Sec. 230) whenever it shall please such people to overturn the government. But to say that the people react thus in most cases is not to maintain that they do so in all. Indeed, we are also told 'that the pride, ambition, and turbulency of private men have sometimes caused great disorders in commonwealths, and factions have been fatal to states and kingdoms' (Sec. 230). 'Ill-affected and factious men may spread amongst the people' that the prince or legislature is acting contrary to their trust 'when the prince only makes use of his due prerogative' (Sec. 240). Locke did not refute that such an occurrence is unlikely, but simply reaffirmed the right of revolt: 'To this I reply, the people shall be judge.' Although they can be inveigled into supporting unjustified rebellion, just as oppressive and conquering rulers, the people as a whole must not be denied the right that private men possess in their particular cases, i.e. to discard their trustee or deputy. As Locke said, in stressing the preventive function of the right to revolt: 'Why should it be otherwise . . . where the welfare of millions is concerned, and also where the evil, if not prevented, is greater, and the redress very difficult, dear, and dangerous?'

The right of the majority to decide on the appeal to heaven is morally irrefutable, although the decision which is actually made is neither necessarily a just one, nor if it is, bound to obtain. Locke's insight that the majority may not only be the victim of wrongdoing, but may be impervious to it and condone it, contains the essential meaning of what later came to be mistermed 'the tyranny of the majority'. No doubt it makes a difference whether mass influence is exerted with or without suffrage. The more universal suffrage is approximated the greater the influence of the masses on legislation. Madison and Mill rightly viewed the problem of the 'tyranny of the majority' from the angle of 'class legislation' – Bentham's 'sinister interests'.[35] Yet Mill, who has probably done more than anybody else to make 'the tyranny of the majority' a household word in politics, understood that 'the will of the people . . . practically means the will of the most numerous *or* the most active part of the people; the majority *or* those who succeed in making themselves accepted as the majority'. That aspect of the impact of mass influence which permeated Locke's views resounds also in those of Mill, who, moreover, spoke also of 'the slavery of the majority to the least estimable portion of their numbers'.[36]

There remains one more point to consider. If Locke did not regard actual revolt as a fool-proof corrective for misgovernment, did he nevertheless advocate, or intend to lay the basis for justifying, a frequent resort to revolutionary resistance?[37]

3. THE FREQUENCY OF REVOLT

For all governments, 'the most dangerous state which they can possibly put themselves in' is that in which, by their own fault, they are 'generally suspected of their people'. In that event, 'they are the less to be pitied, because it is so easy to be avoided'.[38] Locke blamed resistance on the rulers, for according to his view of the

[35] Cp. *The Federalist*, No. X, ed. by Max Beloff (Oxford, 1948), and Dahl, *op. cit.*, 12, note 21, and Ch. I in general, on the contradiction in Madison's argument. For Mill, see *Representative Government*, Ch. VI, in *Utilitarianism, Liberty and Representative Government*, Everyman's Library.

[36] *On Liberty*, ibid., 88-9; *Representative Government*, ibid., 357. Cp. 90-1, 165-6. Italics for 'or' supplied.

[37] Vaughan, *op. cit.*, 147, 150, 168-9, makes contradictory statements. Similarly, Barker in Gierke, *Natural Law and the Theory of Society*, 299, 348, on the one hand, and in *Social Contract*, xxxiii-iv, on the other. To lend some plausibility to his equation of revolutionary action and suffrage in regard to legislation (see above, 284, note 33), Kendall assumes 'short periods' (*op. cit.*, 109) between revolutions without producing a shred of textual evidence. Smyrniades, *op. cit.*, 234, Bastide, *op. cit.*, 238, and Gough, *op. cit.*, 133, have pointed out that Locke did not regard revolt as a frequent occurrence, but have failed to notice the problems of interpretation which arise. Similarly, Lamprecht, *op. cit.*, 145 f., and 149 f., and Polin, *op. cit.*, 234.

[38] Sec. 209. Cp. 168, 230.

people's character their trust is easily maintained. The rulers need observe no more than a minimum of the conditions of tolerable government set forth in the *Second Treatise*. On the one hand, Locke attempted to make the right of revolt more palatable by insisting on the easy avoidance of the event. He did also not take lightly the dangers attendant upon it. On the other hand, if he was convinced of the rulers' propensity to succumb too easily to the temptations of power, his saddling them with the responsibility for revolutionary situations need not reflect his belief that it is possible to avoid revolt for any length of time. There are statements, or – to be exact – there are parts of statements, from which it would appear that, in his eager and repeated defence of the right of revolt, Locke entangled himself in contradictions also as to the rarity of revolution. Must we, after all, range him among those who, impatient of the existing state of affairs, adopted a theory of the inevitable revolutionary breakthrough, which the apathy of the masses can only temporarily delay?

A. '*Many Revolutions*'

Revolution is imminent 'if all the world shall observe pretences of one kind, and actions of another', so that no man can be mistaken as to what lies ahead of him, and no one can be prevented 'from casting about how to save himself' (Sec. 210). The examples of actions which give the lie to pretences refer to what had constantly occurred in recent English history.[39] As the advocates of the Exclusion Bill, who failed in their campaign against royal pretences, had occasion to witness, it is doubtful whether 'all the world', when it is told what to see, will see it that way and act accordingly. Perhaps with a trace of bitterness, Locke pointed out that, even when everybody sees an opportunity to amend original or adventitious defects 'introduced by time, or corruption; it is not an easy thing to get them changed . . .' (Sec. 223). He added,

'this slowness and aversion in the people to quit their old constitutions, has, in the *many revolutions* which have been seen in this kingdom, in this and former ages, still kept us to, or, after some interval of fruitless attempts, still brought us back again to our old legislative of King, Lords and Commons: And whatever provoca-

---

[39] Secs. 209, 210 and 212-22.

tions have made the crown be taken from some of our princes' heads, they never carried the people so far, as to place it in another line.'

We are faced with a curious proposition. We can understand that, although revolutions have always led back to the old legislature, they are nevertheless most dangerous to rulers. But, if the people are so averse to having their constitution and dynasty changed, how could they possibly have been induced to support a revolution in the first place – and many revolutions at that? Is this an instance of esoteric writing, the contradiction being intended to convey that, so far, revolutions have not been worth their while because they have never gone far enough? Faint reverberations of a spurious republicanism may have found their way into the original version of the *Treatises* and survived their revision.[40] It would nevertheless be far-fetched to impugn Locke with an attitude of hypocrisy towards the Glorious Revolution. His intimate connection with the new regime and its origins need not preclude reservations but makes it unlikely that he thought it only slightly better than that of the Stuarts. Rather we may take our bearing from the fact that Locke never intimated that a successful revolution put an end to the further applicability of the right of revolt. The moral and practical impossibility of denying this right 'is an inconvenience . . . that attends all governments whatsoever, when the governors have brought it to this pass, to be generally suspected of their people' (Sec. 209). The threat continues to exist and so ensures, also, the proper working of what has been no more than a renewal of the 'old constitution'. The spectre of revolt must never fade if it is to serve as an effective incentive for governors to refrain from 'provocations' so as not to lose their crown, as happened to some princes in the 'many revolutions'.

As for the retention of the crown in the same line – Mary, the

---

[40] Locke possessed a number of Exclusionist pamphlets when he wrote the *Treatises* (Laslett, *op. cit.*, 52) and in them civil war was not ruled out. Cp. Furley, *loc. cit.*, 29, 34 f. The final version of the *Treatises* allows an inference as to Locke's attitude not only towards the Exclusion controversy but also towards the Glorious Revolution, for two reasons. First, as Laslett, *op. cit.*, 65, explains, some twenty-five paragraphs seem to have been written between February and August 1689, and the general revision of the text went on, as Laslett says, 'until the very last possible printer's moment'. Secondly, there is a basic likeness between the fundamental ideological issues which were at stake during the Exclusion controversy – in connection with which, as Laslett has shown, most of the *Treatises* were composed – and the Glorious Revolution.

daughter of the deposed James II, was co-sovereign – Locke may have wished to claim that the line was uninterrupted so as to stress, as was common, the 'legality' of the event. On the other hand, in the Preface to the *Treatises*, he speaks of William alone. But William's mother was a sister of Charles II and James II and 'a cadet, or sister's son, must have the preference [over the first-born] in succession, if he has the same title the first lawful prince had . . .' (I, 95). Although the title in question was 'the immediate appointment of God', Locke certainly held the same to apply when the title derives from consent. At any rate, on the strength of the possible preference of 'a cadet, or sister's son', he could minimize the fact that the crown was put in another line and at the same time maintain, since a ruler was forced to abdicate, that a far-reaching revolution had been effected.[41]

While no crypto-radical intent needs to be read into these statements, we are still left with the basic contradiction: In the first of the sole two instances in which Locke used the word 'revolution' – in the plural – he spoke of 'the many revolutions' that had occurred. This does not tally with the avowed purpose of the argument started in Section 203 and taken up in Sections 223 and 225, in which the term 'revolutions' occurs. The purpose is to refute the notion

'that the people being ignorant, and always discontented, to lay the foundation of government in the unsteady opinion, and uncertain humour of the people, is to expose it to certain ruin; and no government will be able long to subsist, if the people may set up a new legislative, whenever they take offence at the old one' (Sec. 223).

Locke rejected this conclusion by suggesting a more comforting, but hardly more flattering, version of mass psychology. The ignorance and discontent of the masses do not endanger governments, because people cleave to 'their old forms' and 'are hardly to be prevailed with to amend the acknowledged faults, in the frame they have been accustomed to'.[42]

The subsequent section has the same objective: to refute the

[41] Thus one need perhaps not assume, as Laslett, *op. cit.*, 432, does, that the statement in Sec. 223 on the continuance of the crown in the same line applies to the Restoration of 1660. Moreover, like Lamprecht, *op. cit.*, 140, Laslett himself (209) has drawn attention to the possible allusion of I, 95, to William. On this passage, see also above, 229–30.

[42] Sec. 223. Cp. 230. These sections do not, therefore, as Polin, *op. cit.*, 164, suggests, controvert the unflattering opinions about the people's character. See also Secs. 203–4, 228 and 230, for the refutation of the view that to grant the right of revolt is to court disorder and anarchy.

hypothesis that the right of revolt 'lays a ferment for frequent rebellion'. But Locke goes on: Whatever the legal status of governors, when the people are made miserable by 'the ill-usage of arbitrary power' [note: not simply by the use of arbitrary power], they 'will be ready upon any occasion to ease themselves of a burden that sits heavy upon them. They will wish and seek for the opportunity, which, in the change, weakness, and accidents of human affairs, seldom delays long to offer itself' (Sec. 224). On the face of it, we have here an affirmation of the inevitable frequency of revolt. A careful reading of the sentences shows that they contradict neither the stated intention of Sections 223 and 224, nor Locke's opinion of the apathy of the people. What invariably happens when the people are ill-treated and their protest goes unheard is that they become ready to revolt and seek an opportunity to do so and that this opportunity will seldom fail to offer itself. What is unknown to one who has 'lived but a little while in the world' and 'must have read very little . . .' (Sec. 224) is, however, not an example of the fact that the people have actually seized the opportunity to revolt. For it is immediately stressed that 'such revolutions happen not upon every little mismanagement in public affairs' (Sec. 225). Even 'great mistakes in the ruling part, many wrong and inconvenient laws, and all the slips of human frailty will be borne by the people, without mutiny or murmur'. Only 'a long train of abuses, prevarications, and artifices, all tending the same way' is apt to rouse the people.[43] When Locke used 'revolutions' for the second and last time, he reaffirmed, therefore, that popular resistance was far less frequent than the misdemeanour of rulers might justify. And since the section in which he used the word for the first time has the same purpose, it is probable that, in that section, 'many revolutions' does not mean numerous instances of rightful resistance.

B. Rebellion and Rightful Resistance

To resolve the difficulty in this way is not to make a case for Locke's consistency by taking liberties with the text. He explicitly distinguished between rightful resistance and rebellion, but occasionally used the latter term also to mean rightful revolt.

Mobilizing his opponents' arguments for his own purpose, as he

---

[43] Sec. 225. Cp. Secs. 210, 230, and Laslett, *op. cit.*, 433, for the similarity of the last statement with the one in the American Declaration of Independence.

was wont to do, he demonstrated that, on Barclay's own showing, 'all resisting of princes is not rebellion' (Sec. 232), because, according to Barclay again, the people may in some cases resist their king. Rightful resistance is thus distinguishable from rebellion, 'rebellion being an opposition, not to persons, but authority, which is founded only in the constitutions and laws of the government'; the likeliest and best situated to engage in such opposition are those 'who are in power' (Sec. 226). The term 'rebellion', which had been applied to the Civil War – the Great Rebellion – and the Commonwealth, is used to denote the arbitrariness of rulers.⁴⁴ This turning of the tables was neither unprecedented nor complete.⁴⁵ In medieval thought, it had not been uncommon to regard the *princeps iniquus et tyrannicus* as a rebel.⁴⁶ True and proper rebels are those '*whoever they be*, who *by force* break through, and *by force justify their violation of them*' [the laws]. In other words, rebels are those who have been customarily called by that name and those who have only rarely been accused of rebellion. For Locke all are rebels who violate laws on no other grounds than the power which they possess to do so, and not, as in just revolt or in the exercise of just prerogative, on the authority of natural law and by reference to the public good. Although rebellion does not come solely from above – for the people's support may be forthcoming to countenance resistance to a just government – particularly rulers 'do *rebellare*, that is, bring back again the state of war, and are properly rebels' who violate laws merely by virtue of 'the pretence they have to authority,

---

⁴⁴ Murray's *New English Dictionary*, Oxford, 1914, Vol. VIII, does not quote Locke but cites St. Pierre's distinction of 1796, according to which 'rebellion is the subversion of the laws, and revolution is that of tyrants'. Smyrniades, *op. cit.*, 103, note, was aware of the pejorative meaning of the term 'rebellion' in Locke's usage. Vaughan, *op. cit.*, 144, 148, mentioned the definition of 'rebellion' and left it at that. Polin, *op. cit.*, 230, 233, explains correctly that Locke did not maintain a right of 'rebellion'. The implications which the use of the term has for Locke's attitude towards the frequency of revolt have so far not been considered.

⁴⁵ Goldwin, *op. cit.*, 461, who maintains this, raises the question why Locke did not warn the people against the use of force – which in effect Locke did (Secs. 137, 176, 231) – and whether, therefore, Locke had not 'simply played a trick on his readers by a clever reversal of terminology'. It seems that according to Goldwin the trick consists in that the preference of the word 'rebellion' over the rarely used word 'revolution' illustrates that there is no right to overturn the government, 'there is only a right to resist upon the *return of war*'. As it happens, Locke explicitly opposed such a distinction (Sec. 235–9) and in the section which defines rebels he says: '. . . this doctrine of a power in the people of providing for their safety anew by a new legislative . . . is the best fence against rebellion . . .' (Sec. 226).

⁴⁶ Cp. Thomas Aquinas, *Summa Theologica*, III, 2, qu. xliii, art. ii.

the temptation of force they have in their hands . . .' (Sec. 226). Locke did not make it clear that, on his own terms, 'rebellion' from above is possible without a violation of the laws of government. Those who possess legislative authority need never break constitutional and positive laws. In the absence of judicial review, which Locke did not stipulate, they can make or unmake any law to suit their policies. Rebellion is a violation of authority because it is the use of force without moral authority. It is therefore a violation, not so much of particular laws and of particular constitutional provisions – although this may be the case, too – as of what natural law requires positive laws to stand for in any regime.[47] Since rebellion is opposition not to persons but to authority, it follows that revolution is an opposition not to authority but to persons. It is 'legal' in consideration of what proper laws and constitutional provisions ought to be and to ensure.[48] Revolution is the use of force with authority, less on the strength and in defence of positive or constitutional laws, than on the strength and for the sake of just principles. Revolution is after all, the legitimate re-enactment of the terms of the incorporating compact upon which political society and its legal arrangements rest. It is caused and justified by rebellion. Rebellion causes the harm which endangers states and kingdoms; and 'impartial history' shows 'whether the mischief has oftener begun in the people's wantonness . . . or in the rulers' insolence' (Sec. 230).

Since, however, Locke used 'rebellion' also for rightful resistance,[49] we may assume inconsistency also in his use of the word 'revolutions'. In speaking in Section 223 of the 'many revolutions' in the same sentence in which he refers to the people's aversion to revolt, he must be understood to mean above all many 'rebellions'. The interrelatedness of revolution and rebellion is stressed in the sentence that precedes the definition of rebellion and restates the

---

[47] See above, 136.

[48] The term 'legal' was used not only by Blackstone and Burke in their vindication of the Revolution settlement, but earlier, in the publication known as: *State Tracts from the Year of 1689. Now published in a Body to Show the Necessity and Clear the Legality of the Late Revolution* . . . (London, by Richard Boldwine, 1692). E. Rosenstock, *Die Europäischen Revolutionen* (Jena, 1931), 8, has quoted these tracts to illustrate their motive of stressing the morality of the event and of setting it apart from sedition.

[49] Immediately after Locke had defined *rebellantes* in the last sentence of Sec. 227, he began Sec. 228 by using 'rebellion' for 'revolt'. Likewise, in Sec. 224, he spoke of a 'ferment for frequent rebellion,' meaning the frequent exercise of the right of resistance, because he went on to say in Sec. 225 that 'such revolutions happen not . . .' See also Sec. 93, 196, 218, 232.

purpose of these sections in the words: 'this . . . power in the people of providing for their safety anew . . . is *the best fence against rebellion*, and the probablest means to hinder it' (Sec. 226). It does not seem that 'the probablest means' is always effective. When Locke speaks of 'many revolutions', the emphasis is on the 'provocations' from above on the one hand and on the 'fruitless attempts' at dynastic and constitutional changes on the other. Provocations from above, and not revolutions, must be frequent occurrences. Indeed, 'the disorders ambition has filled the world with, . . . the noise of war, which makes so great a part of the history of mankind . . .' have caused many to mistake 'the force of arms, for the consent of the people' (Sec. 175). This is said of 'conquest', which, however, epitomizes arbitrary power irrespective of whether it is exercised at home or abroad.[50] We may therefore interpret Locke's intention to the effect that rebellion, or for that matter conquest, may be mistaken for revolution, although *rebellantes* have prevailed, while revolution, the enactment of popular consent, has not occurred at all. In fact, the interrelatedness between rebellion and revolt is the same as between conquest and revolt. Both are situations which justify revolution or change but are seldom followed by it. While

'conquest is as far from setting up any government, as demolishing a house is from building a new one in the place . . . it often makes way for a new frame of a commonwealth, by destroying the former; but, without the consent of the people, can never erect a new one' (Sec. 175).

Reasons and opportunity to reframe the government offer themselves frequently, but are not as often realized. The noise of conquest – or rebellion – drowns the voice of consent, and victory does not usually favour the right side.[51] Locke thus enlarges upon what Plato had said and Saint Augustine repeated: 'Great robbers punish little ones, to keep them in their obedience, but the great ones are rewarded with laurels and triumphs, because they are too big for the weak hands of justice in this world, and have the power in their own possession, which should punish offenders' (Sec. 176).

Revolution is not as frequent as rebellion, also because revolution

---

[50] See above, note 27.
[51] See above, 305.

is not the only answer to rebellion. As we have seen in the preceding chapter, individual withdrawal in the form of emigration, which Locke justified on the same grounds as revolution, is an alternative way of establishing a new and lawful government. Besides revolution, there is also one more direct way of dealing with the iniquities of government, when the normal governmental procedures are of no avail. As I shall show in detail in the following chapters, the chief executive, too, may concern himself with 'establishing the government upon its true foundations' (Sec. 158). Both revolution and executive prerogative have this function in similar, if not the same, exigencies.[52] The chief executive's prerogative is such that it can cope with the conditions which might otherwise create revolutionary situations. Considering that revolutionary situations may be solved through discretionary power, it is not surprising that 'many revolutions' should have led back to the 'old legislative'. Princes may be presumed to have a vested interest in maintaining the old frame of government, which provides them with considerable prerogatives. No contradiction arises from identifying the 'many revolutions' both with revolutionary situations caused by 'rebellion' from above, and with the successful prevention from above of resistance from below. Prerogative may not only be mistaken for rebellion, but, in the hands of foolish and wicked princes, it serves rebellious purposes. The agency which has the power to cope with revolutionary situations in disregard of the letter of the law has for this reason also the best opportunity to abuse its power and to create or aggravate internal crises. Yet the granting of emergency powers to a constitutional authority is also compatible with a concern with stability. It is this concern which is reflected in Locke's approval of the majority's indifference either to the wrongs suffered by the few or to the inducements to revolt offered by malcontents. It is an empirical observation that 'a few oppressed men' will be as little able 'to overturn a well-settled state' as a 'raving madman, or heady malcontent . . .; the people being as little apt to follow the one, as the other' (Sec. 208). Thus even where a prince is not legally sacrosanct, 'this doctrine of the lawfulness of resisting all unlawful exercises of his power, will not upon every slight occasion endanger him, or embroil the government' (Sec. 207). Locke did not retract the prescriptive statement that the infringement of the right of 'one or a few oppressed men' (Sec. 208) is as good a cause

[52] Secs. 224, 157, respectively, as regards revolt and prerogative.

for revolt as the infringement of the rights of the many. In coupling the plight of the few with the indifference of the many, he did not so much wish to reemphasize that right is not necessarily co-extensive with power[53] as to endorse the plea of *raison d'état*, that it was 'safer for the body, that some few private men should be sometimes in danger to suffer, than that the head of the republic should be easily, and upon slight occasions exposed' (Sec. 205). For 'a busy head, or turbulent spirit, to desire the alteration of the government' as often as it shall please them, 'will be only to their own *just* ruin and perdition' (Sec. 230). The commonwealth ought not to be easily exposed to subversion, for

'this I am sure, whoever, either ruler or subject, by force goes about . . . and lays the foundation for overturning the constitution and frame of any just government, is guilty of the greatest crime, I think, a man is capable of, being to answer for all those mischiefs of blood, rapine, and desolation, which the breaking to pieces of governments bring on a country'.

Thanks to the obtuseness of the majority towards misgovernment, governments are comparatively stable and commonwealths remain relatively secure from the horrors of civil war. The apathy of the masses is a factor of stability and attains the stature of a civic virtue. For the compliance of the majority with an existing order does not result only from indifference to the sufferings of the few, but from the readiness of the majority to put up with a predicament which is at least as considerable as that of the few who are wronged.[54] The *Second Treatise* does not support the repeated and extremist recourse to the right of revolt. Inaccurate language rather than confused thought accounts for Locke's reference to 'many revolutions'. Indeed, if closely examined in its various aspects, Locke's views on revolution are neither as naive nor as superficial as Green and like-minded critics would have them be. Rather, he proffered more answers and exhibited a more sophisticated and responsible theory of revolution than the queries of his critics would seem to warrant.

4. TOWARDS A MODERN CONCEPTION OF REVOLUTION

As the irony of fate will have it, Locke gets not so much as a mention in the attempts to trace the emergence of the modern conception of

[53] Polin, *op. cit.*, 150, thus explains Sec. 208.
[54] See above, 309.

revolution,[55] or, if his name is mentioned,[56] his views are evaluated in such a way as to justify those who do not find him worth mentioning. This disregard is hardly excusable. Although his theory of revolution has so far not received detailed attention, the importance he attached to the right of revolt has long been noted. In concluding this chapter, I desire to demonstrate briefly that what has been regarded as specifically characteristic of the seventeenth-century concept of revolution is absent in the *Second Treatise*; whereas what is said to be still absent in that concept is at least adumbrated in the *Treatise*.

It is maintained that seventeenth-century agents and interpreters did not consciously acknowledge revolution as a change from what has been to what has never existed. They raised revolution above human responsibility and moral doubt by having recourse to 'the astronomical-astrological concept of a revulsion in nature' (*Naturumwälzung*).[57] However, Locke's political theory, like his philosophy, is free of the notion of determinism, which, in the wake of the French Revolution, began to occupy a central place in political and historical thought. He had also no all-pervading circular movement of *revolvere* in mind, when he spoke of upheavals leading back to the old constitution but particular instances of English history. His references to it do not contradict the fundamental postulate that men are free to choose any form of government, whether or not it once existed. He derived power from its 'original' (Secs. 1, 4), to demonstrate generally valid principles. The appeal to principles of an unchangeable original right and to a natural rational and God-willed order is part of most concepts of revolution,[58] due allowance being made for the secularization of the God-willed order. For Locke, such an appeal does not preclude – as is said to be the case in a non-modern concept of revolution[59] – the idea of a break with whatever has been actually in existence. 'An argument', he wrote, 'from what has been, to what should of right be, has no great force' (Sec. 103). Together

---

[55] E. Rosenstock, *op. cit.*, and K. Griewank, *Der Neuzeitliche Revolutionsbegriff* (Weimar, 1955). The untimely death of Professor Griewank has prevented him from carrying out his intention of dealing at greater length with the English scene. One wonders whether, even in a preliminary outline, the omission of Locke is pardonable.
[56] Arendt, *On Revolution*, Ch. 1.
[57] Rosenstock, *op. cit.*, 8. Griewank, *op. cit.*, 171, 173, who, however, made some qualifications as to the prevalence of this concept (177). Arendt follows Griewank.
[58] Rosenstock, *op. cit.*, 13.
[59] Griewank, *op. cit.*, 2, 4, 7.

with the idea of a conscious break with the past – based upon the subjection of history to reason, yet not upon the dismissal of history by reason – other aspects of the revolutionary process, which are held to have emerged only at the end of the eighteenth-century, were recognized by him.[60]

The *Treatises* contain, if anything, a programme and hence an ideology for proper government. They also ally the revolutionary process with the conscious conceiving of revolutionary ends. This is implicit in Locke's defence of the right of the people to institute, through revolt and a leading minority, a form of government to their liking.

He was well aware that disorders and troubles – 'all those mischiefs of blood, rapine, and desolation' – and the use of force by movements from below are the necessary corollary of a *Staatsumwälzung*, of the overthrow of a regime. This awareness caused his extremely guarded attitude, not towards the right of revolt, but towards the desirability of its frequent and extremist implementation. The reaction of non-democratic liberals in France to the Revolution and the Empire was not unprecedented.[61] To realize, as Locke does, the difficulty of raising the masses, and of moving them the right way when aroused, is to underline at least one major complexity of revolutionary processes. Opponents of revolution, its reserved adherents and its most ardent advocates may, after all, hold similar views on this point. No doubt the French Revolution had bred deeper insights; but even before, Locke had understood some of the fundamental problems of modern revolutions and propounded them as valid beyond that insular experience which he had primarily in mind.[62]

The idea of the social contract, to be sure, lends itself to the sanctification of any existing constitution and to the condemnation of arbitrary and violent change.[63] Locke was in favour of adjustments to social changes made by established authorities. But he did not rule out the use of revolutionary violence for bringing changes about.

---

[60] For the aspects discussed, see Griewank, *op. cit.*, 7, 154, 233.

[61] See my paper mentioned in Ch. IX, note 56. Even as regards France, Griewank, *op. cit.*, 267, errs in taking 1830 as the starting point for such an attitude.

[62] One can certainly not assert the contrary, as Griewank, *op. cit.*, 181–2, does, except if one entirely ignores Locke.

[63] Cp. Stephen, *op. cit.*, II, 133–4. See also Bastide, *op. cit.*, 253, and Vaughan, *op. cit.*, 202, who distinguished in this respect between the fate of Locke's theory in England and in France.

He knew revolutionary tensions to be attendant upon the prevention of political changes as upon the infliction of unreasonable ones. Elected co-legislators are also prone 'to grasp themselves, or put into the hands of any other an absolute power . . .' (Sec. 222). Princes and competing minorities are responsible not only for adapting the political order to changing conditions or preventing change, but also for creating tensions through ill-advised changes. In either case the right of the majority to intervene by force and their power and will to do so are provided an opening for their exercise. Although institutionally unchannelled, this will and power, rather than being dormant, are a constituent factor in the political process. Because it can be translated into overt revolutionary dissent, the attitude of popular consent acts as an ever-present brake on rulers and as an indirect indicator of popular aspirations which it is dangerous to thwart. This is not controverted by the assumption that Locke accepted the majority's right of revolt not because he overlooked, but because he realized, the difficulty of ascertaining the weight and tendency of popular aspirations. Although these are more influential and more easily discernible in a constitutional democracy, general suffrage still leaves constitutional democracy open to objection in respect of the conclusiveness of express electoral consent and of the importance, if not the existence, of a will of the majority. Indeed, to recognize the actual preponderance in the political process of the role of minorities and minority interests is deemed today indispensable to make both political science and democracy safe from the excesses of ideology.[64] What accounts for the modernity of Locke's theory of popular participation in politics and of revolutionary action in particular is surely the fact that chiliastic expectations had invaded politics well before the French Revolution. It seems safe to assume that the all-encompassing aspects of the Puritan Revolution were not entirely lost upon Locke and his contemporaries, nor that repugnance had caused no more than a restriction of the field of vision. In fact, without assuming the contrary one would find it rather difficult to account for Locke's circumspect insights into mass behaviour.

[64] Cp. J. A. Schumpeter, *Capitalism, Socialism and Democracy* (3rd ed., New York, 1950). Dahl, *A Preface to Democratic Theory*, and E. Shils, 'Primordial, Sacred and Civil Ties,' *The British Journal of Sociology*, VIII, No. 2. For a perceptive analysis of these theories, see P. H. Partridge, 'Politics, Philosophy, Ideology,' *Political Studies* (October, 1961), esp. 225 f.

CHAPTER 11

EXECUTIVE AND LEGISLATURE

LOCKE'S theory of revolutionary action reveals that he was concerned no less to restrict popular interference than to create safeguards against monarchical absolutism. Both considerations determine his constitutional theory, which, while not democratic, is also not unfavourable to effective executive leadership. His insistence that the right of revolt is the indispensable safeguard against arbitrary rule; that absolute monarchy is particularly prone to fall prey to the temptations of power; and, above all, his plea for government by law have obscured the fact that his most widely acclaimed contribution to liberal constitutionalism – the theory of the supremacy of the legislature – admits weighty executive prerogatives. Yet while his theory of the distribution of governmental power, too, has evoked mutually exclusive interpretations, most writers use as their yardstick the identification of liberal constitutionalism with rigid legalism.

One interpreter perceives that the Lockeian legislature, though supreme, is dependent on the executive.[1] According to another view, the executive, although a strong one, is in all domestic matters in practice subjected to law and ultimately to a well-defined legislative assembly.[2] Yet Locke is also found disappointing in respect of those strict and explicit institutional limitations which are likely to prevent the abuse of power.[3] A number of interpreters of Locke, and other writers on government, claim him at least as a forerunner of the idea of a rigid separation of powers which Montesquieu is supposed to have perfected. Those who have been disturbed by Locke's admission of the executive's share in legislation have concluded that he had no clear view of the nature and residence of sovereignty,[4] that he was vague concerning the relation between the branches of government,[5] and that his attempt to determine the division of power by rigid categories ends in confusion.[6] But he is also held not to have empha-

---

[1] Smyrniadis, op. cit., 96.
[2] Strauss, op. cit., 233.
[3] Polin, op. cit., 223.
[4] Barker, Social Contract, xxxii.
[5] Lamprecht, op. cit., 142.
[6] Laski, op. cit., 52.

sized the separation of the legislature and the executive, but to have considered separation as a matter of convenience rather than a vitally important dogma.[7]

Some of these interpretations are more correct than others. None connects Locke's views in the matter as adequately as his own statements permit, nor do most dispense with inadequate ideas about the 'separation' of powers. Although he was not as systematic in expounding his views on the implementation of the supremacy of the legislature as one might have wished,[8] his consistency becomes apparent once we realize that in treating of the relationship between the branches of government, he adhered to the traditional idea of balancing powers by distributing the power of government among its different branches.[9] We must recognize, however, that the aim of balancing the power of government is not best served, but is rather made impracticable, by the complete subordination of the executive to the legislature, or by the strict separation of the two.

I. SOVEREIGNTY

The fact that interpreters have not appreciated the nature of Locke's concern with balancing governmental power may be the reason why they have accused him of failing to grapple with the idea of sovereignty, if not of rejecting it altogether, or of being guilty of this as well as of the flagrant theoretical and practical misuse of the principle of sovereignty.[10] But these doubtful accusations are as much in harmony with the frequently maintained liberal aversion to the power of the state as are the patently false contentions that Locke never even used the term sovereignty in the way his contemporaries did, or avoided it because of the use Hobbes had made of the word.[11]

Locke discussed the expression 'mark of sovereignty' (I, 129, 133) in Bodin's sense. In connection with two of these 'marks' – the authority to legislate and the power over life and death – he dis-

---

[7] Vaughan, *op. cit.*, 142, Barker, *op. cit.*, xxvi–viii; Laslett, *op. cit.*, 118, and Plamenatz, *op. cit.*, 218.

[8] Cp. Polin, *op. cit.*, 207.

[9] Cp. Laslett. *op. cit.*, 118.

[10] Lamprecht, *op. cit.*, 148–9, and Vaughan, *op. cit.*, 134, 193, respectively.

[11] Green, *op. cit.*, Sec. 59, and Gough, *op. cit.*, 41, 114–15. Similarly Laski, *op. cit.*, 36. The mistake has been pointed out by Laslett, *op. cit.*, 253; Cox, *op. cit.*, 108–9, and R. Singh, 'John Locke and the Idea of Sovereignty,' *The Indian Journal of Political Science*, XX, 4 (1959), 320 and note 3.

tinguished between paternal and proper political power and fore-shadowed modern insights as to what renders the exercise of a given function an attribute of sovereignty.[12] He also stated the traditional criterion of sovereignty. He regarded 'the form of government depending upon the placing [of] the supreme power, which is the legislative . . .' (Sec. 132); 'there can be but one supreme power, which is the legislative, to which all the rest are and must be subordinate . . .' (Sec. 149). Further, a clear distinction, like that made later by Dicey and Bryce, between legal and political sovereignty governs his approach.[13] Although the legislature is 'only a fiduciary power' and 'there remains still in the people a supreme power to remove or alter the legislative . . .' (Sec. 149), the supremacy of the people was conceived by him in such a manner as not to interfere with the legal and constitutional supremacy of the legislature. What 'the community perpetually retains' is no more than 'a supreme power of saving themselves from the attempts and designs of anybody'. Only in this respect may the community be said 'to be always the supreme power, *but not as considered under any form of government*'. The people's supremacy is extra-legal since it 'can never take place till the government be dissolved'. The distinction between legal and political supremacy thus made in principle, was never contravened by Locke. It served him well in arguing the case of both exclusive and shared, besides extra-legal and legal, supremacy.

In his usage, 'supreme power' means exactly the same as 'sovereign power'. He did not shun the term 'sovereignty'. Apart from 'mark of sovereignty',[14] he spoke of 'an undoubted right to dominion and sovereignty', of 'absolute sovereignty and power of life and death', of 'paternal sovereignty' and 'moderate sovereignty'.[15] He differed from Bodin, Hobbes and Filmer in recommending 'moderate sovereignty' – '*gouvernement modéré*' as Montesquieu was to call it – that is to say, the allocation of various sovereign functions to different agencies and the sharing by different agencies in the wielding of the same sovereign power.

This recommendation is expounded extensively in the *Second*

---

[12] I, 132. See above, 213 f.

[13] Cp. A. V. Dicey, *Introduction to the Study of the Law of the Constitution* (9th ed., London, 1948), 72–4, and J. Bryce, *Studies in History and Jurisprudence* (Oxford, 1901), 505 f. Cp. Gough, *op. cit.*, 115, and especially Singh, *loc. cit.*, 321 and note 8, for a critique of the distinction and the defence of Locke against the confusion of issues.

[14] I, 129, 131, 133

[15] Secs. 4, 83, 115, 108.

Treatise, where the terms 'sovereign' and 'sovereignty' appear rarely and 'supreme' and 'supreme power' for the most part replace them, as they well might. The *First Treatise* teems with the words 'sovereign' and 'sovereignty',[16] and they appear in the context of the rejection of Filmer's idea of sovereignty. The purpose of the discourse is the same in both *Treatises*. They do not attack the notion of sovereignty but the notion that sovereignty ought to belong to one man and cannot be shared. They stamp as self-contradictory and irreconcilable with reality Filmer's idea of absolutely unlimited and indivisible sovereignty. Filmer's derivation of absolute sovereignty from paternal authority leads, in Locke's view, to the absurdity of 'two absolute unlimited powers existing together' (I, 69), that of Adam over his posterity and that of the parents over their children. 'Adam, by a natural right of father, had an absolute, unlimited power over all his posterity, and at the same time his children had by the same right absolute unlimited power over theirs.' Thus all the children of Adam 'are slaves and absolute princes at the same time'. The absurdity, of course, extends beyond the relationship between Adam and his direct offspring. If fatherhood 'does give royal authority, then every one that has paternal power has royal authority, and then by our A's [author's] patriarchal government, there will be as many kings as there are fathers' (I, 70). If we limit kingship to the true heir of Adam we avoid one absurdity at the price of committing another. Supposing we were able to determine who was the true heir of Adam, 'then all the kings and princes of the world ought to come and resign up their crowns and sceptres to him' (I, 104). Hence, if 'there may be lawful kings . . . then kings' titles and power depend not on it,' i.e., on 'this right in nature, of Adam's heir, to be king . . . or else all the kings in the world but one are not lawful kings'.[17]

The *reductio ad absurdum* of Filmer's attempt to prove the unbounded sovereignty of the ruling princes serves to demonstrate that, if not only absurdity but also anarchy is to be avoided, consent must replace both fatherhood and divine appointment as the legitimation of those whom citizens are to obey. Consent also makes it possible to justify what Bodin, Hobbes and Filmer had found inconsistent with sovereignty: the distribution of sovereign powers between the people, the legislature and the chief executive.

[16] Cp. Cox, *loc. cit.*
[17] I, 105. Cp. I, 142, 149.

A. The Balance of Power and the Balance between the Branches of Government

Locke untiringly proclaimed the supremacy of the legislature over the executive as the principle which ought to determine the relationship between the two branches of government.[18] But to show history to be in accord with reason, he related all traditional forms of government, including absolute monarchy, to the consent of the governed by virtue of the morally and practically irrefutable right of revolutionary dissent. In conjunction with its ideological purpose, this conception of mass consent incorporates the empirical observation of the ever-present interplay between the physical power and the moral authority of the rulers over the ruled, and the reaction of the ruled towards their rulers' exercise of power and authority. This interplay is not in its entirety defined by legal rules and contained within constitutional forms. By and large this is the rationale of the political process in any regime. Locke was justified in relating all regimes to consent, inasmuch as each regime represents a power-system, and rests on a balance of power which includes the ruled.[19] Indeed, for Locke, there is nothing special about political power; it is not different from the power possessed by all men, except insofar as it is collective. In this sense, he discusses a power-system throughout his book,[20] or rather the various levels of such a system and their interaction.

To the extent that Locke supposed patriarchal monarchy to have coexisted at one time or another with the democratic institution of a general assembly, the relations between monarch and people made up what may be called the constitutional power-field. These relations turned extra-constitutional the moment the formal political participation of the people was dispensed with. Only in an internal emergency and in both an extra-legal and extra-constitutional form of action, does that occur which is legal and constitutional in a perfect democracy, namely that 'the people shall be judge' because 'he who deputes him , . . must, by having deputed him have still a power to discard him' (Sec. 240). Historical experience teaches the necessity

---

[18] E.g., Secs. 13, 22, 88, 89, 131, 134, 135, 138, 149, 150, 153, 157, 212.
[19] See above, 137.
[20] Cp. Laslett, *op. cit.*, 107, 116.

of supplementing this extra-constitutional power-field, in which the prince and the people face each other, by a multilaterally organized constitutional power-field. This is achieved by the institutionalization of express consent on two levels. First, the suffrage provides part of the citizenry with the possibility of formally expressing approval or disapproval of their representatives and thus also of their government; second, two governmental agencies may approve or disapprove of each other mainly in the field of legislation. Government by consent eventually required this twofold institutionalization of consent.

Locke did not merely prefer, but insisted on, an elective assembly.[21] Of course, consent is institutionalized when governmental power is shared, and therefore balanced between constitutional agencies, whether one of them is elected or all are hereditary. But if neither the executive nor any of the bodies engaged in legislation is elective, the constitutional power-field remains closed to the ruled. Express consent is institutionalized only for those of the governed who share in legislation and belong more to the rulers than to the ruled of the country. Yet Locke spoke as a matter of course of those who 'have a right to be *distinctly* represented' (Sec. 158). He meant people who are not only virtually represented, but take part in the election of their representatives. The institution of an elective assembly is part and parcel of the remedy against 'the inconveniences of absolute power, which monarchy, in succession, was apt to lay claim to . . .' and which had caused men to think about 'balancing the power of government, by placing several parts of it in different hands' (Sec. 107) . . . 'the people finding their properties not secure under the government, as then it was, . . . could *never* be safe nor at rest, nor think themselves in civil society, till the legislature was placed in collective bodies of men, call them senate, parliament, or what you please' (Sec. 94). This is not to leave the question of an elective assembly open. Locke insisted that the property of subjects is least endangered 'in governments where the legislative consists, wholly or in part, in assemblies which are variable' (Sec. 138), that is to say, elective. In the regime Locke preferred, the constitutional which supplements the extra-constitutional power-field reaches beyond the relationships between governmental bodies.

As to the division of governmental power, we must bear in mind

---

[21] Plamenatz, *op. cit.*, 237, makes this distinction and attributes a mere preference to Locke.

that it is designed to enable the balancing of power. For this reason the subordination of one agency to the other cannot be absolute. Locke showed no preference for the regimes which did not permit more than a mere delegation of powers, as was the case with the three principal forms of government. In a 'perfect democracy', the majority, having 'the whole power of the community, naturally in them, may employ all that power in making laws for the community . . . and executing those laws by officers of their own appointing' (Sec. 132). No special mention is made of the chief magistrate, in connection with the execution of laws. Locke classed him apparently among the officers that execute the law. In a more or less perfect democracy discretionary power passes into the chief executive's hands as the generalissimo in time of war 'which admits not of plurality of governors' (Sec. 108). Since normally all executive officers are directly responsible to the legislating majority, no executive officer can counterbalance the legislature, except in such ways as the officials of any regime are capable of influencing or obstructing it. This has never been understood by Locke, or by anybody else, as a constitutional balancing of powers. In an aristocracy – or oligarchy, as Locke called it – the executive is constitutionally no less at the mercy of those who depute him than in a democracy, although in an aristocracy those on whom he is dependent are not the people. Whereas in a direct democracy and in an oligarchy, the total subordination of the executive to the legislature precludes a balance between them, in a monarchy, where the chief executive alone exercises legislative authority, there is neither a subordination nor a balance of powers.

From the very little that Locke wrote on democracy and aristocracy, it emerges that he distinguished them from a one-man executive-cum-legislature, insofar as the legal sovereignty in those systems was vested in a number of people. In this case the power of government may be said to be balanced in the following sense: the sovereign will is expressed either by the majority of all citizens, (as in a democracy) or by the majority of 'a few select men, and their heirs or successors' (Sec. 132), (as in a hereditary or elective oligarchy). In either instance, this sovereign will is a composite of individual wills to be formed and re-formed when decisions are called for. Such an interplay of individual wills may enable a balancing of the power of government within constitutional limits. In a democracy, it operates between the plurality of men who form one branch of government, the legislature; in an aristocracy, there is an additional balance between the legislature and those who elect it. But all this is as far removed from the constitutional balance of governmental powers as is the relationship between executive officers and the legislature in a direct democracy. Yet, for Locke, the vesting of legislation in collective bodies of men is a means to the end of balancing the power of government. He meant not merely the placing of governmental power in different hands, but a distribution of 'several parts of it' by which two branches of government can hold each other in check. '. . . where the legislative is in one lasting assembly always in being, or in one man' (Sec. 138), the neglect of the citizens' interest is likely to be greatest. In saying this, he stamped a legislating monarch, a perfect democracy and a hereditary oligarchy equally inopportune. He must, therefore, be credited with the awareness that the greater the extent of subordination, the smaller the scope for an effective balancing of power. For no balance is possible where all the weight is on one side. Constitutionally, no weight is shifted by a mere delegation of powers. To confuse the delegation of powers or the social dispersion of power with a balance of governmental power is to undermine the very notion of constitutionalism. Locke evidently preferred what he called 'compounded and mixed forms of government' (Sec. 132), because they permit an effective constitutional balance of powers at the cost of the complete subordination of one to the other.

B. *The Executive's Share in Legislation*

The mixed form of government with which Locke dealt at length reserves the democratic dispersal of political power for extra-legal action; on the constitutional level, it provides for a dispersal of it which is characteristic of an elective oligarchy; it places the executive into the hands of a monarch and grants him supra-legal prerogatives as well as a share in legal sovereignty. The last provision, in particular, has aroused the objection that, in his endeavour to come to terms with the prevailing shifts and compromises of English constitutional practice, Locke offended against his own principles. The charge is unfounded but typical inasmuch as it derives from the fact that a strict 'separation' of powers is the most vaunted liberal *credo*, though it had been postulated neither by Locke nor by Montesquieu.

When Locke agreed to the chief executive's share in legislation, he introduced the balance of powers into the legislative process. This is not to violate the principle that, where one man has 'both legislative and executive power in himself alone, there is no judge to be found' (Sec. 91). The chief executive who participates in legislation does not legislate alone. He does not possess all legislative power in himself and consequently is not in the exclusive possession of both legislative and executive authority. This was the way in which Locke understood the principle of the distribution of powers. As far as the principle is concerned, it does not matter whether the executive participates in legislation or not. It matters only that he does not legislate alone. Thus 'in *well-ordered* commonwealths, ... the legislative power is put into the hands of divers persons who duly assembled, have *by themselves, or jointly with others,* a power to make laws' (Sec. 143). Out of the two forms of a mixed constitution which distinguish 'well-ordered commonwealths', Locke was concerned, and obviously identified himself, with that in which the legislative is 'placed *in the concurrence of three distinct persons*' (Sec. 213). He used 'persons' for the members who make up an assembly as well as for each governmental body or agency. The 'persons' in the latter sense who concur in legislation are: 'A single hereditary person having the constant, supreme, executive power ... An assembly of hereditary nobility ... An assembly of representatives chosen *pro tempore* ...'

We are left in no doubt that where the chief executive 'vested in a single person ... has also a share in the legislative; there that single person in a very tolerable sense may also be called supreme ...' (Sec. 151). He wields more than supreme executive power, from which 'all inferior magistrates derive all their several subordinate powers, or at least the greatest part of them'. He has 'also no legislative superior to him, there being no law to be made without his consent, which cannot be expected should ever subject him to the other part of the legislative ...' The executive in such a regime is no more subordinate and accountable to his co-legislators 'than he himself shall think fit, which one may certainly conclude will be but very little' (Sec. 152). Locke stressed that only 'the executive power placed anywhere but in a person, that has also a share in the legislative, is visibly subordinate and accountable to it, and may be at pleasure changed and displaced'. Thus 'it is not the supreme executive power that is exempt from subordination, but the supreme executive power vested in one, who having a share in the legislative, has no distinct superior legislative . . . farther than he himself shall join and consent.'

If Locke had thought that the division between executive and legislature ought to be such as to subordinate the executive power most effectively to the legislature, he ought to have rejected their association in the legislative process, as those of the Whigs intended who wished the Revolution settlement to provide for an elective monarch. We shall never know for certain whether Locke's innermost thoughts were of this kind, and how conditional was his compliance with the facts as they were finally established by the Revolution settlement. Yet it is very doubtful that he regarded the settlement as a *pis aller*. We might say that he indicated how the mixed constitution, confirmed by the Revolution settlement, could be amended to protect the polity against the abuse of the chief executive's power as co-legislator. But in his treatment of executive prerogatives, the differences between the two mixed forms of government recede more and more into the background. This they well might, if the major consideration was to ensure against the legislature's utter dependence on the executive.

In the first place, although in a constitution where the supreme executive has a share in legislation the legislature cannot change and displace the chief executive, he is not immune from deposition. Whatever the position of the executive as regards legislation, serious encroachments of the executive upon the proper functioning of the legislature justify revolt.[22] Locke did not suppose that a legislature in which the executive had no share could actually depose him without the revolutionary interference of the people. Secondly, the difference between the two mixed forms of government is narrowed further, since the monarch, without whose consent no law can be made, cannot make law alone. '. . . there that single person in a very tolerable sense may also be called supreme, not that he has in himself all the supreme power, which is that of lawmaking' (Sec. 151). In the legislative process, the consent of the other 'persons' is as decisive as his own. Since the combination of all legislative and executive powers in one person is prevented, whether or not the executive is strictly subordinated to and separated from the legislature, Locke was entitled to call both forms of mixed constitution 'well ordered commonwealths, where the good of the whole is so considered, as it ought . . .' (Sec. 143).

[22] Secs. 155, 205.

Thirdly, in the only two instances where Locke spoke of the powers being 'separated', he neither meant the 'separation' of powers in the sense it has become popular, nor considered the mixed forms of government different in respect of the 'separation' he discussed. He referred to the occasions when the members of the legislative assembly, whether they legislate alone or together with the executive, after having legislated for a time, are 'being separated again' (Sec. 143). Consequently 'the legislative and executive power come often to be separated' (Sec. 144), meaning that the two agencies separate on the adjournment or the dissolution of parliament. This separation is wholesome 'because those laws which are constantly to be executed, and whose force is always to continue, may be made in a little time' (Sec. 143).

'It is not necessary, no nor so much as convenient, that the legislative should be always in being. But absolutely necessary that the executive power should, because there is not always need of new laws to be made, but always need of execution of the laws that are made.'[23]

During the temporary separation of the powers – and only in this context Locke uses the verb 'to separate' – the executive has the field of government to himself. Whether it is a partner in legislation or not, Locke sees no need to subject the executive to the constant supervision of the legislature.

Since legislation can be intermittent, it is not the most important practical function of government, although it is the highest rated function.[24] The possessor of a superior right does not necessarily occupy the foremost place in the actual conduct of government. As Thiers said: 'le roi règne, il ne gouverne pas.' For Locke this applies *mutatis mutandis* to the people's supremacy and to that of the legislature, to the political and the legal sovereign. The legislature 'is the soul that gives form, life, and unity to the commonwealth' (Sec. 212). But the executive, too, has a share in this soul, and by virtue of the execution of laws and the conduct of foreign affairs, is much more in evidence than the legislature. What is more, those who are exclusively engaged in legislation and the holder of the executive office are both likely 'to grasp at power' (Sec. 143). Although the apprehension is justified first and foremost when 'the

[23] Sec. 153. Cp. 143, 144, 156.
[24] Cp. Goldwin, *op. cit.*, 459.

same persons who have the power of making laws, . . . have also . . . the power to execute them', the same apprehension compelled Locke to recommend the dispersal of the members of the assemblies from time to time. They will only realize the effects of their legislative power when, 'being separated again, they are themselves subject to the laws, they have made; which is a new and near tie upon them, to take care, that they make them for the public good'. Since the reasons for 'separation' and its expected educational results are the same whether or not the prince shares in legislation, this kind of 'separation' does not affect the actual predominance of the executive function, or determine its exact relation to the legislature. In point of fact, the balance of powers is at least as efficiently ensured when different governmental agencies have authority in one and the same field as when they have not. In the second case we are faced, if not with a merely theoretical stipulation, at least with a formality which obscures how things are really done. Locke's views thus lend themselves equally well to justifying a presidential executive, like the American, or a parliamentary one, like the British,[24a] in the form which it assumed after the perfection of the Cabinet system. Although different in form and effect, the influence of both kinds of executive on legislation is constitutionally provided for;[25] it is legal and not merely political.

There is no more convincing illustration of how the constitutional principles on which both forms rest can be linked with Lockeian principles, and thus reaffirm our interpretation, than Montesquieu's theory itself and Madison's evaluation of it.

C. Locke-Montesquieu-Madison

The sharing of legislative authority which Locke observed and supported makes possible the utmost balance, viz., inaction. Without agreement between the chief executive and his co-legislators, no law can be passed. If legislation is not to come to a standstill, co-operation through mutual concessions is imperative. This is the unmistakable implication of what Locke found acceptable in English constitutional practice as reformulated in the Revolution settlement. This was spelled out in Montesquieu's elaboration on the English constitution.

[24a] See now also M. J. C. Vile, *Constitutionalism and the Separation of Powers* (Oxford, 1967), 60. The book reached me too late for making further references to Vile's views or taking issue with them.

[25] Cp. K. C. Wheare, *Modern Constitutions* (rev. ed., London, 1960), 35 f.

Just like Locke, Montesquieu laid down that: 'lorsque dans la même personne ou dans le même corps de magistrature, la puissance législative est réunie à la puissance exécutrice, il n'y a pas de liberté.'[26] Like his predecessor, he meant that one person or branch of government should not possess a monopoly of all the legislative and executive power. He, too, was therefore logically right in considering as legitimate the executive's share in legislation 'par sa faculté d'empêcher'.[27] He formulated the essence of Locke's treatment of the issue in a striking manner:

'Voici donc la constitution fondamentale du gouvernement dont nous parlons. Le corps législatif y étant composé de deux parties, l'une enchaînera l'autre par sa faculté mutuelle d'empêcher. Toutes les deux seront liées par la puissance exécutrice, qui le sera elle-même par la législative. Ces trois puissances devraient former un repos ou une inaction. Mais comme, par le mouvement necéssaire des choses, elles sont contraintes d'aller, elles seront forcées d'aller de concert.'[28]

Locke and Montesquieu differed in their emphasis on some details. These differences do not necessarily attest a greater fidelity to facts on the part of one or the other. Prescription accompanies description in the expositions of both. Montesquieu, for example, insisted that the sacredness of the person of the chief executive and his right to

[26] *De l'Esprit des Lois*, (ed. par G. Turc, Classiques Garnier, Paris), 2 vols., Vol. I Bk. XI, Ch. VI, 164.

[27] *Ibid.*, 171–2. Charles Eisenmann, 'L'esprit des Lois et la Séparation des Pouvoirs,' *Mélanges de Carré de Malberg* (Paris, 1933), 190 f., and *La Pensée constitutionelle de Montesquieu*, Recueil Sirey, 133 f., has dealt with the myth of Montesquieu's theory of the rigorous separation of powers. See also L. Althusser, *Montesquieu, la politique et l'histoire* (Paris, 1959), Ch. V, for an enlargement on Eisenmann's findings. If Locke is not acclaimed as the precursor of Montesquieu's supposed rigorous separation of powers, a difference between Locke and Montesquieu is asserted both on the supposition that Montesquieu's separation was complete, and on the supposition that it was not entirely so. Thus Pollock, *op. cit.*, 247; Vaughan, *op. cit.*, 142; Laslett, *op. cit.*, 118–19; Polin, *op. cit.*, 181, 207, 219, and Plamenatz, *op. cit.*, 210, 282–4. Gough, who deals with the question more extensively than other commentators on Locke, rightly rejects the idea that Locke and Montesquieu actually originated the separation of powers (*op. cit.*, 100). Still, Gough maintains the parallel between both thinkers on the basis of the supposed contradiction between the prohibition of uniting legislative and executive authority in one hand, and Locke's and Montesquieu's accurate description of the English constitution as regards the executive's participation in the legislature (95, 102–3).

[28] *Ibid.*, 172. It seems that 'ces trois puissances' are here Locke's 'three distinct persons' who form the legislature, rather than legislature, executive and judiciary. The legislature is composed of two parts, being 'confiée, et au corps des nobles, et au corps qui sera choisi pour représenter le peuple . . .' (168).

veto the resolutions of the legislature were the major means of preventing the legislature from becoming despotic.[29] He also pointed out that 'la faculté d'empêcher' does not require the chief executive's participation in the debates of the legislature or the right to propose laws.[30] Locke did not insist on the sacredness of the prince's person but admitted that 'there cannot be a wiser constitution' (Sec. 205). Contrary to Montesquieu, he conceded the legitimacy of refusing the executive a share in legislation and pointed out the advantages of such an arrangement. But he did not particularly recommend it. On the question of the executive's initiative in legislation and his participation in debate, Locke was silent. He apparently felt no need to elaborate on the established usage of the crown's exerting influence through its parliamentary agents within the bounds set to the executive's constitutional share in legislation.

Locke and Montesquieu are often said to have differed most widely on the issue of the judicial power. But here, too, they were closer than appears at first sight. Both considered the judicial power as part of the executive power.[31] Also, while the separation of the judicial from the other two branches may have been most important to Montesquieu, it is as a separation only in name.[32] Montesquieu admitted that among the 'trois puissances . . . celle de juger est en quelque façon nulle. Il en reste que deux'.[33] Locke did not speak of a judicial power but he, too, had in mind a body of appointed but independent judges. 'And so whoever has the legislative or supreme power . . ., is bound to govern by established standing laws, promulgated and known to the people, and not by extemporary decrees; *by indifferent and upright judges*, who are to decide controversies by those laws' (Sec. 131).

None of the divergencies mentioned affects the agreement between Locke and Montesquieu on the principle of the distribution of legislative authority. Perhaps nothing can illustrate this better than the fact that Montesquieu, who has been associated more than any other thinker with the 'separation' of powers, never uses the noun 'séparation' and hardly ever 'séparer', in his famous chapter 'De la Constitution d'Angleterre', or indeed in the whole of Book XI of *L'Es-prit des Lois*. He generally used the words 'distribution' or

---

[29] *Ibid.*, 170.   [30] *Ibid.*, 171-2.   [31] Cp. Gough, *op. cit.*, 97-8.
[32] Cp. Plamenatz, *op. cit.*, 297, 281, 283-4.   [33] *Espr. des Lois, ibid.*, 168.

'distribué',[34] occasionally 'arrêter' and 'empêcher', once 'borner', 'balancer' and 'contrebalancer', all of which best expressed what he described and prescribed. As it happens, it was Locke who spoke of the powers 'being separated', but this, as we have seen, made no difference.

Already Madison had to grapple with the myth of 'separation'. He took up 'the more respectable adversaries to the constitution', who described the document as violating 'the political maxim, that the legislative, executive and judiciary department ought to be separate and distinct'.[35] He retorted that Montesquieu

'did not mean that these departments ought to have no *partial agency* in, or no *control* over, the acts of each other. His meaning, as his own words import, and still more conclusively as illustrated by the example in his eye [viz., the British Constitution], can amount to no more than this, that where the *whole* power of one department is exercised by the same hands which possess the *whole* power of another department, the fundamental principles of a free constitution are subverted.'[36]

Like Locke and Montesquieu, Madison interpreted the British constitution to the effect that the concurrence of divers branches of government in legislation adequately embodied the principle of the non-concentration of all executive and legislative power in one person or branch of government. Since Madison further argued that, on the subject of the distribution of powers, the proposed constitution did not differ from the British, he can be taken to testify indirectly to the fact that the distribution of powers, as elaborated by Locke, furnished common ground for the justification of a presidential and eventually also of a parliamentary executive; it furnished no ground whatsoever for dubbing as self-contradictory Locke's acceptance of the executive's share in legislation.

But the myth about Montesquieu's separation of powers has proved stronger than the truth. This seems, partly at least, to account for the failure to see that with Locke it was a matter of principle to have what Madison called a 'free constitution' permit substantial executive prerogatives. Even when noticed, Locke's concession of vital prerogatives to the chief executive has remained largely unex-

[34] *Ibid.*, 174, 175, 178, 181, 187, 191, 193, 195.
[35] *The Federalist* (ed. by Max Beloff, Oxford, 1948), Number XLVII, 245.
[36] *Ibid.*, 247.

plained,[37] or it has been summarily asserted that he was coming to terms with prevailing practice either in conformity with his principles[38] or in deviation from them.[39] No serious attempt has been made to uncover the intimate connection between the fundamental assumptions of his theory and his concessions to 'this power to act according to discretion, for the public good, without the prescription of the law, and sometimes even against it, . . . which is called prerogative' (Sec. 160).

3. THE EXECUTIVE'S PREROGATIVES VIS-À-VIS THE LEGISLATURE

Locke often begins the treatment of a topic some sections before he dedicates a separate chapter to it. The second half of Chapter XIII, which precedes the Chapter 'Of Prerogative', already deals with the prerogatives of the convocation, adjournment and dissolution of the legislature and with the prerogative of reforming the franchise. In linking these issues, Locke elaborates in advance on executive prerogative in the generally applicable terms on which the treatment in Chapter XIV of prerogative in a mixed constitution proceeds. In the same chapter, reference is made to what history teaches and reason confirms on prerogative in the patriarchal beginnings and in the reign of good and wise, or godlike, princes. Locke establishes here directly the connection between all the layers of his argument relevant to the issue under discussion. Prerogative emerges as the operational link between the spheres of legal and extra-legal action, the sphere of express consent and that in which either tacit consent or revolutionary dissent alone are practicable. The chief executive has a standing in both spheres. The representatives, although virtually representing also the majority who is debarred from voting, are confined to legal and the people to extra-legal action. The institutionally unmediated representation of the will of all by the chief executive does not make him independent of either the people or the legislative process, but permits him to regulate this process and on occasion to disregard it.

[37] Aaron, *op. cit.*, 281; Strauss, *op. cit.*, 233, Cox, *op. cit.*, 127–8, and Goldwin, *op. cit.*, 458.

[38] Smyrniadis, *op. cit.*, 96; Laski, *op. cit.*, 41, and Gough and Kendall as referred to below, 346, notes 50, 51.

[39] J. F. Stephen, *Horae Sabbaticae* (2nd ed., 1892) IX, 154–5; Lamprecht, *op. cit.*, 141–2, and Vaughan, *op. cit.*, 146, 187, note.

A. *Adjournment and Dissolution*

First, there is the question of convening and adjourning Parliament. Where the legislators have the right to change the executive, they assemble as 'either their original constitution, or their own adjournment appoints, or when they please; if neither of these has appointed any time, or there be no other way prescribed to convoke them' (Sec. 153). The concluding clause leaves open the possibility that the executive convene and adjourn the legislature otherwise than by merely implementing constitutional provisions or the express will of the legislature. Only because the discretionary decision of the executive turns out to be the most likely procedure where the executive shares in legislation, does it seem that the same is entirely unlikely where the executive has no such share. However, no difference in this respect seems to be intended between the two forms of government because Locke made none when it came to fixing dates for the election of representatives and consequently for the dissolution of Parliament. 'If the legislative, or any part of it' consists of elected representatives who 'return into the ordinary state of subjects, and have no share in the legislature but upon a new choice', the right of electing them must be exercised 'either at certain appointed seasons, or else when they are summoned to it: and in this latter case, the power of convoking the legislative, is ordinarily placed in the executive . . .' (Sec. 154). Locke adduces here no other criterion than the existence of an elected body of representatives. He makes no distinction between the two forms of government he is speaking of in that the legislature itself can have no say in the dissolution of parliament and its convocation after an election. It seems therefore improbable that he made a distinction between the two forms in regard to adjournment and subsequent convocation.

The choice is between 'certain appointed seasons' according to the 'original constitution', in which case 'the executive power does nothing but ministerially issue directions for their [the legislators'] electing and assembling, according to due forms: Or else it is left to his [the chief executive's] prudence to call them by new elections, when the occasions or exigencies of the public require . . .' The exclusion of the legislature from the determination of its renewal and the reliance either on the executive's observance of constitutional provisions or on his discretion are feasible because there is always the ultimate safeguard against the abuse of power: the people's interference. The executive, who, 'being possessed of the force of the commonwealth, shall make use of that force to hinder the meeting and acting of the legislative, when the original constitution, or the public exigencies require it', involves himself in 'a state of war with the people, who have a right to reinstate their legislative . . .' (Sec. 155). Irrespective of the differences between one kind of mixed constitution and another, the assurance that the legislature will not be prevented from fulfilling its legitimate function depends in the last resort on the extra-legal relationship between prince and people. As in a patriarchal or any otherwise unmixed monarchy, the executive continues to be the people's trustee, though by now he is not the only one.

'The power of assembling and dismissing the legislative, placed in the executive, gives not the executive a superiority over it, but is *a fiduciary trust*, placed in him, for the safety of the people, in a case where the uncertainty, and variableness of human affairs could not bear a steady fixed rule' (Sec. 156).

Attendant upon the higher rating of the legislative function, the legislature is the superior trustee of the people. This does not disqualify the executive from serving for his own part as a direct guardian of the people's trust in all cases where fixed rules are inexpedient.

Evidently, if the dissolution and return of Parliament are one of the cases in which the uncertainty and variableness of human affairs do not permit reliance on fixed rules, the alternative of relying on the 'original constitution' is ruled out. As Locke actually admitted, one cannot really expect that

'the first framers of the government should, by any foresight, be so much masters of future events, as to be able to prefix so just periods of return and duration . . . in all times to come, that might exactly answer all the exigencies of the commonwealth' (Sec. 156).

To all intents and purposes now speaking of summoning and proroguing in addition to dissolution and election,[40] he agreed that 'the best remedy . . . was to trust this to the prudence of one, who

---

[40] Cp. Laslett, *op. cit.*, 389.

was always to be present, and whose business it was to watch over the public good' (Sec. 156). It does not seem to have occurred to him that the executive might be allowed to use prerogative in exceptional cases only within the periods fixed by the constitution. Rather illogically, he repeated that the condition for resorting to the remedy of executive discretion remains that 'the original constitution' does not provide for 'the regulation of times'. This is clearly not considered as practical if one asks, with Locke:

'What then could be done, ... to prevent the community, from being exposed sometime or other to eminent hazard, on one side, or the other, by fixed intervals and periods, set to the meeting and acting of the legislative, but to entrust it to the prudence of some, who being present, and acquainted with the state of public affairs, might make use of this prerogative for the public good? And where else could this be so well placed as in his hands, who was entrusted with the execution of the laws, for the same end?'

Locke had no doubt as to the past, nor did he say that the chances of predetermining the periods for the sitting of parliament had improved in the course of time. But he apparently did not wish to commit himself as to the future. This, rather than uncertainty as to the present, induced him to remark that it was not his business to enquire whether it was better to have settled periods for assembling and dismissing the legislature, to leave this to the discretion of the prince, or to have a mixture of the two. Indeed, he had made it his business to show that the executive might have the prerogative, but was not thereby superior to the legislature. To do so it was especially apposite if one insisted, like Locke, that nothing else or nothing better could have been done. It was inconsistent to affect an indecisive attitude, except if this meant that, although so far no solution other than the executive's prerogative had proved itself adequate, the question might in time be faced anew. After all, Locke had no quarrel with the fact that 'the power of calling parliaments in England, as to precise time, place, and duration, *is* certainly a prerogative of the king ...' (Sec. 167). He justified the arrangement in the present, as he had justified it in the past, by the unforeseeability of events and occasions. Hence, the prerogative of choosing 'the fittest place ... and ... best season ... was left with the executive power, as might be most subservient to the public good, and best suit the ends of parliaments'.[41] This prerogative, like any other, has only one condition attached to it, to wit, that 'this trust . . . shall be made use of for the good of the nation'. The nation itself is the ultimate judge of its good. The exclusion of the legislature from determining the times of its dissolution and election and the deliverance of this authority into the hands of the executive thus leads to the reiteration of the right of revolt.[42] Likewise, the unqualified admission of the king's prerogative to call Parliament is capped by one of the major revolutionary sections.[43] Princely prerogatives become fully acceptable because it is rightful to check their abuse by popular resistance. The prince's prerogatives of calling Parliament and issuing writs for new elections are connected, on this basis, with the most striking concession to the chief executive: the reform of the franchise.

B. The Reform of the Franchise

a. The Pragmatic Justification

Locke linked the right to convoke the legislature and the reform of the franchise in stating that 'if, therefore, the executive, who has the power of convoking the legislative . . . regulates . . . by . . . true reason, the number of members, in all places' (Sec. 158), he is merely exercising prerogative for the public good. Locke subscribed to the practice of issuing royal writs for the formation of new constituencies. The practice had already been attacked under Charles II. The Commons had declared void the writs which Shaftesbury as Lord Chancellor had issued in anticipation of the reassembling of the parliament prorogued in April 1671. Yet it was Locke, apparently, to whom fell the task of hunting up the precedents for the prerogative of issuing writs.[44]

When it suited them, Whigs had no compunction about relying on royal prerogative. They had urged Charles II to use it to exclude his brother from the succession. In March 1679 – in the first parliament which they controlled – they and Shaftesbury had also

---

[41] Sec. 167. The conclusion reached already in Sec. 156 by a typically Lockeian reduction of alternatives is therefore henceforth maintained, as Secs. 167 and 213 show. Sec. 213 ought not to be opposed to Sec. 156, as is done by Laslett, *op. cit.*, 426, who takes it to indicate a change of ground.

[42] Secs. 154 and 155.

[43] Secs. 167 and 168.

[44] Cp. Fox Bourne, *op. cit.*, I, 279–80.

introduced a bill for the reform of the franchise and the electoral districts.[45] This way of approaching the problem does not correspond, however, with the position adopted in the *Treatise*. The introduction of a bill amounts to associating the legislature with whatever is decided on, which is what the *Treatise* rejected in principle. The Whigs' attitude towards executive prerogatives was neither unequivocal nor uniform. Yet considering especially the prerogatives actually accorded to William III, Stephen was unhistorical in scoffing at Locke for propagating that the king and not parliament possessed the right of disenfranchising Old Sarum. Stephen was right that this was a matter of principle with Locke. But we should qualify his verdict that this was 'the oddest illustration of the fanciful character of the results to which Locke's abstract principles led him in relation to civil government'.[46] I said qualify and not reject, for while there is nothing fanciful about the pragmatic derivation of Locke's conclusions, their justification is incongruous on the level of fundamental principles.

On the pragmatic level, the argumentation is simple and straightforward. The major reason for turning from the legislature to the executive in the matter of the disenfranchisement of rotten boroughs and the creation of new constituencies is of the same nature as that which prompted Locke to insist upon the periodical dispersal of the legislators: to prevent them from abusing their power. The deficiencies in the proportions of representation are due to 'private interest often keeping up customs and privileges, when the reasons of them are ceased . . .' (Sec. 157). Since he sought redress through the executive, Locke obviously feared the vested interest of members and local magnates to stand in the way of reform. If so, why should it be strange that he accepted the dependence of the Board of Trade on the Crown, yet ignored this dependence in his theory as an issue pertaining to the 'separation' of powers?[47] Fearing the distorting influence of private interests on the shaping of economic policy[48] as on electoral reform, it was as logical to turn to the executive in the one case as it was in the other. It was likewise natural that he should comment only on electoral reform in his treatment of the distribu-

[45] Cp. D. Ogg, *England under the Reign of Charles II*, (Oxford, 1955) 2 vols., II, 480 f.

[46] J. F. Stephen, *Horae Sabbaticae* IX, 154–5.

[47] Laslett, *op. cit.*, 199, and 'The Great Recoinage,' *loc. cit.*, 395, raises the question.

[48] See above, 177–8.

tion of powers, since he dealt exclusively with executive preroga- tives related to the functioning of legislation. The problem to be faced was that private interests sustained 'the following of custom, when reason has left it' (Sec. 157). That is why economic and demographic changes result in such 'gross absurdities' as 'when we see the bare name of a town, of which there remains not so much as the ruins . . . sends as many representatives . . . as a whole county numerous in people, and powerful in riches'. This strangers stand amazed at, and everyone must confess needs a remedy. 'Though most think it hard to find one . . .', the difficulty Locke envisaged refers not to what should be done, but to how it could be justified.

b. *The Incongruous Argument*

The problem presented by Locke was of his own making. It did not arise because he solved it by recommending prerogative on the grounds of *salus populi suprema lex*.[49] He created a difficulty because, in considering that electoral reform involved an alteration of the legislature, he contradicted the terms on which recourse to pre- rogative may be had.

The remedy is 'hard to find' – or as he ought to have said once he had suggested it – the remedy is hard to justify,

'because the constitution of the legislative being the original and supreme act of the society, antecedent to all positive laws in it, and depending wholly on the people, no inferior power can alter it. And therefore the people, when the legislative is once constituted, having in such a government as we have been speaking of, no power to act as long as the government stands; this inconvenience is thought incapable of a remedy' (Sec. 157).

The difficulty Locke presented rested on the self-contradictory character of the proposition. Only the people's will, he says, legiti- mates the alteration of the legislature, and that will cannot be invoked as long as the government is standing. The contradiction results because he defined electoral reform as an alteration of the legislature, and yet, to justify action by the executive, he regarded the government as standing. For on his own terms, if the govern- ment is standing, no alteration of the legislature is involved, and so the legislature is not prevented from attending to electoral reform. If such a reform involves the alteration of the legislature, the govern-

---

[49] As Laslett, *op. cit.*, 391, argues.

ment cannot be regarded as standing and only the people are entitled to act.

It is therefore quite wrong to say that, once Locke had adopted the people's right of altering the legislature, he had no alternative but to endorse the prevailing practice of issuing royal writs for the creation of new constituencies.[50] On the contrary, the affirmation of this right, and its invocation on the issue of electoral reform, ought to have led him to demand, if not a referendum (which was and still is alien to English constitutional practice), then at least the holding of elections on this particular issue. The option for prerogative certainly does not follow from any democratic principle.[51] Locke's theory was not democratic, nor is discretionary interference with the electoral map generally accepted as arising from democratic principles. Locke wished to avoid the incongruity of recommending revolutionary action for electoral reform no less than he wished to disqualify the legislature from attending to this matter. He failed to make out a case against both forms of action in the light of the principles he himself was adducing for this purpose. Moreover, his reference to what is involved in the constitution of the legislature rendered it far-fetched for him to identify electoral reform with an alteration of the legislature.

In the government 'we have been speaking of', as in all proper governments, the legislature is constituted by 'the original and supreme act of the society, antecedent to all positive laws in it' (Sec. 157). Likewise, 'the first and fundamental positive law of *all commonwealths*, is the establishing of the legislative power', which is 'sacred and unalterable in the hands where the community have once placed it'.[52] In other words, the people decide where legislative power resides, they determine the form of government. The establishment of the legislature and, with it, the form of government are considered in one statement as an act antecedent to positive law and in another as a first positive law – as distinct from 'the first and fundamental natural law, which is to govern even the legislative itself' (Sec. 134). The same point is stressed, in spite of the terminological difference. The first and fundamental positive law which establishes the legislative power is 'positive' in that it is a particularization of natural law. The first fundamental 'law', like 'the

[50] Gough, *op. cit.*, III, note 3.
[51] As Kendall, *op. cit.*, 130, note 11, seems to argue.
[52] Sec. 134. Cp. Secs. 141, 142, 149, 150, 168.

original and supreme act', of the people are the condition, and not the subject, of legislation, or indeed of any governmental action. Accordingly, it is likewise 'a law antecedent and paramount to all positive laws' (Sec. 168) that the people should have the right to alter through revolt the form of government and decide with whom legislative authority should thenceforth rest.

Clearly, the original determination of the form of government is generally not influenced by an electoral reform, and certainly not in 'such a government as we have been speaking of' by the kind of reform Locke had in mind. If he nevertheless identified electoral reform with an alteration of the legislature, he ought to have referred the decision to the people. The assignment of the task to the executive entails the paradox that, although no power inferior to the people can alter the legislature, the power which must do so is inferior both to the people and to the legislature. This conclusion, as we have seen, does not follow from the premise that the people cannot act as long as the government stands, for the assumption that the government stands cannot be reconciled with the need to alter the legislature. It is also of no help to infer that, in accordance with his distinction between the moral and the practical 'dissolution' of government,[53] Locke might have meant that the legislature was only morally disqualified. He did not even hint at a distinction between a disqualification of the legislature which dissolves, and one which does not dissolve the government, or between the different effects which the disqualification of either the legislature or the executive exercises upon the dissolution of government. Lastly, to add to the contradictions, he changed his ground in another context, when he stated that only the chief executive's participation in legislation prevented the alteration of the legislature by law, that is by the legislature itself. 'The other parts of the legislative . . . can never in opposition to him, or without his concurrence, *alter the legislative by a law*, his consent being necessary to give any of their decrees that sanction' (Sec. 218).

When all is said and done, there is little doubt that Locke did identify electoral reform as an alteration of the legislature which dissolves the government. Had this not been so, it would surely have been pointless on his part to define, as he did, the difficulty of justifying his solution. There is another instance in which he seems to prevaricate, but which clinches his adherence to the

[53] See above, 107 f.

definition of the case without retrieving it from the fundamental contradiction. He appears to show regard for the fact that, when executive prerogative is exercised, one cannot very well speak of the government as not standing, least of all where the exercise of just prerogative is concerned. He said that in redressing disproportionate representation, the executive 'cannot be judged, to have set up a new legislative' (Sec. 158). But he added that it must be judged 'to have restored the old and true one'. The restoration is appraised as an alteration of the legislature subsequent to a dissolution of government. In conformity with his reliance for the purpose in hand on the first fundamental act or positive law of all commonwealths – to establish a legislative agency – Locke hailed the chief executive who undertakes just electoral reform as 'an undoubted friend, to, and *establisher of the government*'.

The contradiction is unusual even by Lockeian standards. But his intention in the present case is unmistakable. The chief executive is the 'establisher of the government' inasmuch as he is the head of the established government. That is why Locke contradicted his proposition that the alteration of the legislature entailed the dissolution of government. Two reasons for doing so are immediately obvious: First, to eliminate an issue that was bound to recur with relative frequency from the agenda of the people's revolutionary umpirage and that of the legislature. Secondly, recent abuses of prerogative in respect of elections made it desirable to classify electoral reform as an alteration of the legislature so as to associate with it the people's revolutionary umpirage as a counterweight to the executive's prerogative. Yet if these were the only reasons for the contradictions, there was no reason to get involved in them in the first place. His pragmatic argument of raising the issue above vested interests was sufficient to explain his option for action by the executive on behalf of the true interests of the community on the grounds of *salus populi suprema lex*, the supposition being that the chief executive was checked in this, as in all other instances of prerogative, by the people's judgement.

An additional reason suggests itself to explain why he raised the issue of the alteration of the legislature, which was extravagant by his own standards and entangled his argument so hopelessly. A further contradiction is involved in connection with which the nature and extent of Locke's concessions to prerogative will fully emerge. The wish of having prerogative wrought into the fundamental propositions of his theory was certainly enforced by the fact that he generally justified prerogative in sudden, unforeseen emergencies but was aware that the problem of electoral reform arose in the course of a protracted process. It is not suddenly, that 'people, riches, trade, power, change their stations; flourishing mighty cities come to ruin, . . . whilst other unfrequented places grow into populous countries . . .' (Sec. 157). Whether or not Locke consciously tried to overcome this contradiction by anchoring prerogative in his fundamental tenets, he had to do so also because not only in connection with electoral reform does the justification of prerogative by emergency conditions become improbable. For this reason, too, the particular case is of general significance. The question whether prerogative in matters specifically preserved for it is properly executed, as well as the question which situation calls for discretionary action, both find their answer in the mutually checking and supporting confrontation between the prince and the people. The indications for the answer are simple, indeed too simple for a fully developed constitutional framework: If the people acquiesce with the chief executive's action, the answer is positive; if not, it is negative.

CHAPTER XII

AUTHORITARIAN REPRESENTATION AND CONSTITUTIONALISM

1. CONFRONTATIONS

A. Executive, Legislators and Revolt

In Locke's system, the executive's right occasionally to act alone in domestic affairs is legitimate because

'it is fit that the laws themselves should in some cases give way to the executive power, or rather to this fundamental law of nature and government, viz. that as much as may be, all the members of the society are to be preserved' (Sec. 159).

Acting according to the law of nature, the chief executive is guided by *'salus populi suprema lex*, [which] is certainly so just and fundamental a rule, that he, who sincerely follows it, cannot dangerously err' (Sec. 158). Such discretionary action is appraised as implementing the people's will. 'For it being the interest, as well as intention of the people, to have a fair and equal representative [fair and equal in proportion to the assistance, which the people affords the public]; whoever brings it nearest to that, is an undoubted friend, to, and establisher of the government, and cannot miss the consent and approbation of the community.'[1] The people's disapproval determines that the prince's discretionary action is not compatible with the pursuit of the public good and that the laws ought not to have been dispensed with.

'For in cases where the prince has a trust reposed in him, and is dispensed from the common ordinary rules of the law; there, if any men find themselves aggrieved, and think the prince acts contrary to, or beyond that trust, who so proper to judge as the body of the people, (who, at first, lodged that trust in him) how far they meant it should extend' (Sec. 242)?

---

[1] 'Whoever' can only mean the executive since both the people and the legislature are debarred from attending to the task.

Locke's conception of prerogative is apt to open the door to the most authoritarian hypotheses, although it is intended to serve *raison d'état* and is strictly subordinated to the public good. It is precisely because the real limitation proceeds from the people,[2] that is, because prerogative can be checked only by popular resistance, that the authoritarian possibilities assume considerable proportions. For prerogative is not only checked by revolt but serves also as its substitute.

In the same context in which he called the chief executive effecting electoral reform an 'establisher of the government', Locke went on to say:

'Prerogative being nothing, but a power in the hands of the prince to provide for the public good, . . . *whatsoever* shall be done manifestly for the good of the people, and the *establishing the government upon its true foundations, is, and always will be just prerogative*' (Sec. 158).

Not in one particular measure, but 'whatsoever' is done to establish the government on its true foundations is just prerogative. This is to substitute prerogative for revolt, since establishing the government upon its true foundations by the people itself is to 'remove or *alter* the legislative, when they find the legislative act contrary to the trust reposed in them . . . *whenever* that end [the preservation of the community = the pursuit of the public good] is manifestly neglected, or opposed . . .' (Sec. 149).

When Locke stated the case for revolt in connection with electoral reform so as to have the case settled by prerogative, he proceeded on the general rule that the chief executive's discretionary power had a revolutionary function, which when properly fulfilled, made revolution superfluous.

Although the execution of prerogative often involves extra-legal action, the authority of the prince who occasionally acts according to his sovereign will for the good of all, has a constitutional foundation. It consists not in his share in the trusteeship of the legislature, but in having 'a trust reposed in him' (Sec. 242) which exempts him from the ordinary rule of law. The continuance of either legislative or executive trusteeship depends on the ability of each trustee to avoid the conversion of the people's tacit consent into active dissent.

[2] Cp. Polin, *op. cit.*, 213, note 2; 222.

The chief executive has a definite advantage over his co-legislators. He can *ex officio* override the laws and the will of his co-legislators in the name of the public good and the will of the people. They can obstruct the executive in the process of law-making just as much as he can obstruct them. But *qua* legislators, as holders of governmental authority, they cannot otherwise thwart him. They cannot pass over him as he can pass over them. Apart from the prince,

'no other part of the legislative, or people is capable by themselves to attempt any alteration of the legislative, without open and visible rebellion, . . . the prince . . . having the power of dissolving the other parts of the legislative, and thereby rendering them private persons . . .' (Sec. 218).

Unlike the chief executive, his co-legislators cannot in their official capacity act alone in the people's name. Even if he does not render them private persons, they can associate themselves with popular resistance only as private persons. On this point, Locke furnishes us with an example of consistency which is the more striking since it is also somewhat misplaced. It puts in a false light the event which was foremost in his mind when he published his *Treatises*.

The *Preface* expresses the hope that the book would be

'sufficient to establish the throne of our great restorer, our present King William; to make good his title, in the consent of the people, which being the only one of all lawful governments, he has more fully and clearly than any prince in Christendom: And to justify to the world, the people of England, whose love of their just and natural rights, with their resolution to preserve them, saved the nation when it was on the very brink of slavery and ruin.'

Once more Locke speaks of 'the king, and body of the nation' and of 'prince and people'. He never so much as hints at the two Houses of Parliament whose role in the Glorious Revolution was as conspicuous as it was decisive.[3] In strict conformity with the constitutional theory of the *Treatise*, the alteration of the legislature is a

---

[3] *The Treatises* do therefore not represent 'an argument on behalf of the quite real parliamentary grant of the Crown to William,' as is maintained by H. H. Rowen, 'A Second Thought on Locke's *First Treatise*,' *Journal of the History of Ideas* XVII (1956), 132. Since the *Preface* seems to reflect the view expressed in Sec. 218, as I have quoted it, the section need not be regarded, with Laslett, *op. cit.*, 424, as too hypothetical for a Whig commentary on the Revolution to have been written after the event.

matter between the prince and the people. Locke might well have argued that the legislature had been 'altered', and the government 'dissolved', first by King James' trespasses and then by his elimination as one of the legislating 'persons'. Thus, if he wished to remain true to his constitutional theory, he could have referred to the members of the two Houses only as the individual spokesmen of the revolutionary majority, thereby denying their claim to any constitutional authority. The easiest way out was to omit any reference to Parliament. This enabled him to escape the quandary of either declaring the role of Parliament unconstitutional or of contradicting that only where the chief executive did not share in legislation could he be changed by the legislature. The omission proves Locke's strict adherence to two principles: That the co-legislators by themselves cannot represent the people; that the restoration of the legislature, whether it means electoral reform or replacement of the most important among the 'persons' who share in legislation, is outside the competence of the legislature. So, also, is the judgement of the exercise of prerogative.

B. Just and Unjust Prerogative

It is not self-contradictory to address both the ruling prince and whoever replaces him as 'the establisher of the government'. Only the excesses of royal prerogative give just cause for revolt; properly utilized for the public good, discretionary action realizes the will of the people. Discretionary interference even with one and the same established practice may well on one occasion be just and on another unjust, once for the public good and acceptable to the people, and another time not. It will help us to fathom how far Locke really went in his attempts to present prerogative power as effectively limited in the regime acceptable to him, if we first compare his examples of the excess of prerogative which alter the legislature and dissolve a government with the issues he had previously reserved for the discretion of the prince.

Of the five instances which constitute an alteration of the legislature of the English type and dissolve the government from within, the first three and the fifth relate to the abuse of the executive's prerogative. The fourth contingency, 'the delivery . . . of the people into the subjection of a foreign power' (Sec. 217), may be the responsibility either of the prince or of the legislature, or of both.

First, the legislature is altered through the abuse of prerogative when the prince 'sets up his own arbitrary will in place of the laws, which are . . . declared by the legislative', that is to say, 'when other laws are set up, and other rules pretended, and enforced, than what the legislative, constituted by the society, have enacted . . .' (Sec. 214). At the other end of the scale, the most obvious and extreme case of the dissolution of government is indicated by the fifth instance, viz. 'when he who has the supreme executive power, neglects and abandons that charge, so that the laws already made can no longer be put in execution' (Sec. 219). On neither count does Locke question the previously maintained executive prerogative of compensating for legal *lacunae* and the deficiencies of the legislative process. Locke disqualifies the unconstitutional enactment of laws or the neglect of their execution on one side and sees on the other the need for a temporary suspension of laws or for actions which cannot, or should not, for whatever reason be authorized by law or undertaken by the legislature. Constitutionalism is in no sense impaired by such distinctions, the less so, since they set apart from each other not only legal and illegal, but also legal and extra-legal action. The fact that electoral reform is carried out by the executive and cannot be repudiated by the legislature does not make the prince the sole law-giver or indicate a tendency on his part to neglect and abandon his charge as the executor of the laws.

The second instance of the alteration of the legislature which dissolves government from within concerns the prince's prerogative of convoking and dissolving the hereditary and elective assemblies 'within certain periods of time' (Sec. 213). The legislature must be regarded as altered if it is prevented from assembling 'in its due time' (Sec. 215), or from acting with 'freedom of debating, and leisure of perfecting, what is for the good of . . . society'. For, as Locke remarked in anticipation of modern evaluations of the legislative process, 'it is not names, that constitute governments, but the use and exercise of those powers that were intended to accompany them' (Sec. 215). Again, there is here no departure from the views expressed on the same issue in Chapter XIII of the *Treatise*. Locke does not here specify the duration of 'due seasons' or of the aforementioned 'certain periods'. All the expressions he uses are rather vague. Yet he does not say that these periods should invariably be equal, though he undoubtedly means that they should be certain, i.e. in the sense of being clearly known and observed, having once been fixed for each single occasion or for more. He does not touch upon the question of whether the legislature should determine either these periods or the rules of free debate. He carefully avoids saying anything which could be interpreted as a remonstration against the prince's prerogatives in these matters. In other words, Locke voiced the reproaches of the Whigs against the Stuarts but did not simply adopt Whig policy. Although the provisions of the Bill of Rights are hardly more specific than his words here, it had been Whig policy for some time to demand more definite safeguards against the easy dispensation with Parliament. The *Treatise* does not reflect that in 1689 such demands had found their way into the provisions of a draft bill.[4] Nor does it foreshadow the Triennal Act of 1694 which settled that Parliament must be summoned at least once every three years with its period of office limited to three years.

The third instance of the alteration of the legislature illustrates still more than the others how little Locke was deflected from his views on prerogative by its abuse on the part of the Stuarts. In Sections 157 and 158, he had taken great pains to justify the entrusting of electoral reform to the executive. He now made the prince's change in the method of election loom large among the instances which justified revolt. The explanation is that in Sections 157 and 158 Locke classified electoral reform as an alteration of the legislature so that he could denounce in Section 216, and still more violently in Section 222, the attempts of Charles II and James II to secure the return of docile members as a valid ground for resistance. In so doing, he did not contravene his previous positive stand on the prerogative of electoral reform. The legislature is altered and government dissolved 'when by the arbitrary power of the prince, the electors, or ways of election are altered, without the consent, and contrary to the common interest of the people'.[5] Discretionary interference with the 'ways of election' is not condemned unconditionally. The first condition is the assent not of the prince's co-legislators but of the people. No less than before, the issue is considered to be beyond the competence of the legislature. The second condition is the observance of the common interest. As

---

[4] Cp. Ogg, *England under James II and William III*, 490–1.

[5] Sec. 216. Laslett, *op. cit.*, 427, points out that Locke's words and meaning here are not as close to the *Bill of Rights* of 1689 as is often assumed.

before, prerogative is evaluated according to the extent to which a measure serves the public good or common interest. No contradiction is thus involved when Locke declares the prince's interference with the ways of election now just and now unjust. As in all other cases of prerogative, it is for the people to judge whether 'the arbitrary power of the prince' is properly employed. Indeed, only if men 'were so void of reason, and brutish' that they permitted princes to pursue purposes manifestly other than 'their mutual good', and were 'to be looked on as a herd of inferior creatures', only then would prerogative 'be, what some men would have it, an arbitrary power to do things hurtful to the people' (Sec. 163).

C. Limitation by Consent and Trust

If the people are the only judge whether a discretionary action is injurious to them, and if 'there is a latitude left to the executive power, to do *many things* of choice, which the laws do not prescribe' (Sec. 160), a very considerable latitude is indeed involved. We need not infer this from the fact that, for Locke, popular consent is confined either to tacit consent or to overt dissent. He himself said:

'For the people are very seldom, *or never* scrupulous, or nice in the point: they are far from examining prerogative, whilst it is in any tolerable degree employed for the use it was meant; that is, for the good of the people, and not *manifestly* against it' (Sec. 161).

On this basis, 'the tendency of the exercise of such prerogative to the good or hurt of the people, will easily decide that question', viz., 'if there comes to be a question between the executive power and the people, about a thing claimed as a prerogative'.

Evidently, if the people are seldom, or never, 'scrupulous, or nice in the point', the point, though easily settled, will in fact rarely be raised. Locke had no quarrel with this fact. It favoured his preference for established authority and stability.[6] In the context of his violent denunciation of quite recent and blatant abuses of royal prerogative in respect of the functioning and composition of parliamentary representation, he does not recommend curtailing such prerogatives. He does no more than underline the fact that the great latitude left to the prince to do many things by choice for the

[6] See above, 320.

public good makes him liable far more than any other governmental agency to dissolve the government from within. 'In such a constitution as this, the dissolution of the government in these cases is to be imputed to the prince, . . . because . . . he alone is in a condition to make great advances toward such changes, under pretence of lawful authority . . .' (Sec. 218).

If the arbitrary power of the prince to act for the good of the people enables him more than others to act to its detriment with every prospect of success, this is due to the constitutional advantage he has over both legislature and people. As we have already noted, he has a trust reposed in him which exempts him from the ordinary rule of law. Whether or not he is the bearer of a 'double trust' (Sec. 222) – the executor of laws as well as a participant in legislation – *qua* executive, he possesses 'the trust of prerogative' (Sec. 210). Indeed Locke deals with 'another way whereby governments are dissolved, and that is, when the legislative, or the prince, either of them act contrary to their trust' (Sec. 221). Yet the instances constituting the dissolution of government from within by breach of trust are the same as by alteration of the legislature.[7] Locke merely added the legislature's invasion of property rights, in the two senses of possessions and liberties. Also his language is much more vehement as regards the pre-engagement of electors and representatives by 'solicitations, threats, promises, or otherwise' (Sec. 222). In focusing on the 'trust', he introduces no legally enforceable limitation of prerogative. His conception of trust is fashioned only remotely – if at all – after a juridical model.[8] Here it definitely implies no more than the extent to which the prince can be trusted. Trust in the sense of confidence is forfeited by setting up

[7] Thus in Secs. 212, 221. Cp. 156, 203, 210, 223, 227, 270. A comment on a technical point is in order here. In Secs. 212–20, Locke deals with instances of the dissolution of government from within under the heading of the alteration of the legislature. From Sec. 221 onwards, he deals with the dissolution of government under the heading of breach of trust. Each heading is counted. The 'secondly' in Sec. 221 relates therefore not to the 'First' of Sec. 214, line 1, as Laslett suggests (*op. cit.*, 430), but to the 'First' of Sec. 212. The instances enumerated under the first heading – the alteration of the legislature – the 'First' of Sec. 212, comprise: The 'First' of Sec. 214, the 'Secondly', 'Thirdly' and 'Fourthly' of Secs. 215–17. The 'secondly' of Sec. 221 designates the second heading, namely actions contrary to the trust. These are also subdivided, yet the 'First,' i.e., the first example of when 'the legislative acts against the trust' (Sec. 221), is not followed by a 'secondly' but by: 'He acts *also* contrary to his trust, when' . . . (Sec. 222, line 31. Italics supplied.)

[8] See Laslett's succinct appraisal (*op. cit.*, 113) and Gough, *op. cit.*, Ch. VII, for a detailed and competent treatment of the matter.

'the declared abettors of his own will, for the true representatives of the people . . .' (Sec. 222). This

'is certainly as great a breach of trust, and as perfect a declaration of a design to subvert the government, as is possible ... What power they ought to have in the society, who thus employ it contrary to the trust [which] went along with it in its first institution, is easy to determine; and one cannot but see, that he, who has once attempted any such thing as this, *cannot any longer be trusted*.'[9]

Prerogative limited by 'trust' is the same as prerogative limited by consent.

When Locke justified the prince's prerogatives and removed their exercise from parliamentary control and legal impeachment, he was as far from unconsciously infringing his conception of trust[10] as he was when he recognized discretionary action as the most likely cause of revolt. The people's confidence in the goodness and wisdom of the father, or of any other excellent individual, is the original 'trust'. Like a provision attributed to the Common law, Locke's 'trust' is assumed to have accompanied incorporation on the grounds of no more than the absence of evidence that it had, formerly, not prevailed.[11] On the same terms, trust or confidence in the ability and intentions of rulers accounts for the continuation of rule largely, if not exclusively, by prerogative. Likewise, in a mixed constitution, whether acts exceed the limits set by one of the most fundamental constitutional principles – namely that the king ought not to substitute his will for the laws – is determined by the trust which the people repose in the intentions of the chief executive.

Therefore, by virtue of the 'trust', which underlies the institution of society and any regime not revolted against, it is easy enough to determine what power ought to be wielded by those who 'cannot any longer be trusted' (Sec. 222) – for they ought to wield none at all. Indeed, only in a restricted sense could Locke mean that the people will find it easy to decide if and when the chief executive transgressed his prerogatives. The decision is easy insofar as there

---

[9] In Laslett's text a 'which' or a 'that' is missing in Sec. 222, line 59.

[10] Although Vaughan, *op. cit.*, 146, note 1, rightly recognizes that 'Locke did not object to the "dispensing power" as such, but only to its abuse,' he argues that Locke was unaware of 'how deep a gash he was making in the "sacred and unalterable" character of his trust.'

[11] Thus on the Common Law, F. D. Wormuth, *The Royal Prerogative*, 1603–1649 (Ithaca-New York, 1939), 29.

is no doubt with whom it rests and on what grounds it is to be made; it rests with the people, and the criterion is whether or not they feel themselves gravely harmed. But the matter will not easily come up for a decision. Locke's evaluation of the people and their attitude towards prerogative forbade it to hold the people capable and eager to decide as often as might be warranted whether the same measures are illicit alterations of the legislature and breaches of trust, or just prerogative; whether the suspension of law and action against its letter are in the common interest or against it.

But the question poses itself: was not his association of prerogative with emergency conditions and his insistence on the supremacy of law conducive to allowing limitations of prerogative other than by revolt, or at least to supplying clues for the people's judgement of prerogative in addition to far-reaching encroachments on their lives, liberties and fortunes? In other words, was Locke really so superficial or so determined about authoritarian prerogative that he admitted no alternatives for limiting prerogative other than the prince's self-restraint or a collision between him and the people which threatens the very existence of the regime?

2. SPECIFIC CONDITIONS AND LIMITATIONS

A. Emergency Conditions

Locke supplies not only the very general criteria, by which the results of discretionary action are judged. He also specifies the situations and purposes calling for it, by giving the reasons why discretionary action is unavoidable where legislation is vested in collective bodies of men. First, 'the law-making power is not always in being, and is usually too numerous, and so too slow, for the dispatch requisite to execution' (Sec. 160). Second, 'it is impossible to foresee, and so by laws to provide for, all accidents and necessities, that may concern the public'. Third, laws must not be executed 'with an inflexible rigour, on all occasions, and upon all persons'. To act 'without the prescription of the law' is therefore required by the first and second reason. To act 'sometimes even against it' [the law] is required by the second and third reason. The second reason predicates prerogative directly on an emergency situation, the first and third do so indirectly. All three reasons seem to provide the public with tolerably specific clues for judging when discretionary action is apposite. However, the specifications as to when prerogative may be used are not as hard and as fast rules as Locke makes them out to be; nor is the criterion for judging of the purpose and the results of what is done by prerogative, i.e. that the action should be 'conformable to the foundation and end of all laws, the public good' (Sec. 165). Neither the situational specifications nor the criterion of the public good help Locke to establish a clear divide between what belongs to prerogative or legislation. His qualification of the distinctions, and indeed their convergence, can be best illustrated in his treatment of electoral reform.

In the first place, his reliance on an additional criterion – the purpose of restoration – does not make it easier to determine whether an action is for the public good or against it. Electoral reform is not intended to restore a once existent order but to adapt principles to changing conditions in the light, not of 'old custom, but true reason' (Sec. 158), in this case to prevent setting up 'one part, or party, with a distinction from, and an unequal subjection of the rest'. The aim and the criterion of judgement remain nothing less than political justice, the realization of which, by Locke's own account, the king's co-legislators are sure to dispute in this particular instance. Moreover, an informed judgement on such an issue is not expected from a people whose greater part is held unfit to participate in the choice of its representatives.

The same example also illustrates that Locke did not abide by the relatively clearest indication of when to exercise prerogative – a condition of emergency. The people, whose judgement is bound to simplify issues, can be supposed to understand the nature of emergency conditions that require discretionary authority of the 'federative' power in foreign relations, and especially in war. They may also identify as an emergency at least some of the 'many things there are, which the law can by no means provide for, . . . [or] wherein a strict and rigid observation of the laws may do harm; (as not to pull down an innocent man's house to stop the fire, when the next to it is burning) . . .' (Sec. 159). We can classify as a category by itself the discretion to pardon and reward an offender against the law, when the action so deserves and is without prejudice to the innocent. The notion of an emergency, however, becomes senseless if applied to the necessity of redistributing seats. Locke himself presented this as the predictable result of a protracted demographic change and clearly said that 'the power of erecting new corporations, and therewith new representatives, carries with it a supposition, that in time the measures of representation might vary . . .' (Sec. 158). If he nevertheless associated electoral reform with 'such cases, which depending upon unforeseen and uncertain occurrences, certain and unalterable laws could not safely direct', then his view of emergency conditions was too equivocal to supply a criterion for the people's or anybody's judgement.

We might all the same concede that, although the causes and the actual fact of disproportionate representation were neither new nor unforeseeable, the drawing of the practicable conclusion from the 'supposition' of changing measures and the demanding of the correction of the disproportion was relatively new and was not yet provided for by law. An emergency could be said to exist in all cases where legal and legislative precedents afforded no guidance. At this point the flexibility of the situational distinction shows itself together, and indeed combined with, that of the distinction between the purposes of either legislation or prerogative. For Locke, the nature of the legislative process had definitely ceased to be veiled by the idea of adjudication based on precedents. New laws have to be made and prerogative has not just the function to come instead of laws, but to the extent the absence of legislation constitutes an emergency, prerogative serves also to make legislation possible. The prerogative of the executive to summon Parliament is the best way of convening legislators 'when the occasions or exigencies of the public require the amendment of old, or making of new laws, or the redress or prevention of *any inconveniences*, that lie on, or threaten the people' (Sec. 154). The legislature can respond to any requirement; and the scope of legislation in internal affairs is virtu-ally unlimited. Prerogative serves to set the legislative process in motion and in addition is a temporary expedient to ensure against the legislators' inability 'to foresee, and provide, by laws, for all, that may be useful to the community . . .' (Sec. 159). The chief executive 'has by the common law of nature, a right to make use of it [his power], for the good of the society, in many cases, where the municipal law has given no direction, *till the legislative can con-veniently be assembled to provide for it*' (Sec. 159).

In principle, new requirements can be met by legislation, and discretionary action is in many cases merely the means to enable the legislature to deal with public exigencies. Since at least some of the exigencies might well be called emergencies, either discretionary or legislative action may cope with emergencies, though the first should be followed by the second. While this was Locke's intention, he did not define the objectives of policy nor the demands of the situation in such a way as to draw a clear limit up to which the discretionary power ought to make good the shortcomings inherent in the legislative process. It appears that this was no fault of omission, but that he was willing to leave to the prince great latitude to decide not only when an issue should come up for legislation, but to a considerable extent also which issue should be reserved for prerogative. To put it differently: As a corollary of the prerogatives inherent in the nature of the regime – the right to veto legislation and summon, prorogue and dissolve Parliament – Locke's prince seems to have the right to declare a situation to be an emergency. However, even if this right were considered a necessary concomitant of the possession of discretionary power, instead of being at variance with constitutionalism,[12] it does not follow that whoever possesses this right is the true sovereign.[13]

B. Direct Legal Limitation

In Locke's mixed constitutions, a natural limit is set to the duration of rule by prerogative. Unless the regime is to be regarded as subverted, the legislature cannot be dispensed with for too long, because the prince needs the consent of his co-legislators to impose taxes. But a more fully developed constitutional theory suggests further and more direct restrictions. The duration of emergency powers can be directly restricted by law or determined by an agency other than the one wielding emergency powers. Experience has also taught that the legislative process can be maintained in many emergencies. Many, if not all, the contingencies in which discretionary action is permitted, and especially the instances in which it is ruled out, can be defined by legislation. Of this possibility Locke was aware. As the result of the abuse of prerogative 'the people were fain by express laws to get prerogative determined, in those points, wherein they found disadvantage from it' (Sec. 162). The people have a right to do this, for

[12] Cp. Friedrich, *Constitutional Government and Democracy*, 581. See 580 *passim* for the discussion of modern constitutional limitations.

[13] C. Schmitt, *Politische Theologie, Vier Kapitel zur Lehre von der Souveränität*. (2 ed. München – Leipzig, 1934), 11, has propagated the view: 'Souverän ist, wer über den Ausnahmezustand entscheidet.'

'they have a very wrong notion of government, who say, that the people have encroached upon the prerogative, when they have got any part of it to be defined by positive laws . . . And those only are encroachments which prejudice or hinder the public good' (Sec. 163).

Yet on the terms here enunciated, a limitation of prerogative by positive laws is highly unlikely, if not impossible, in the regime which Locke discusses.

Except in a direct democracy, the people do not make laws. In the regime under discussion, the people can only indirectly procure legislation that limits prerogative – by first changing the regime. Locke had to call the people on the scene since he justified the limitation of prerogative by law in terms of an alteration of the form of government. 'For the end of government being the good of the community, whatsoever *alterations* are made in it, tending to that end, cannot be an encroachment upon anybody' (Sec. 163). In other words, the regime which Locke has in mind is not conducive to the limitation of prerogative by law. Where the prince's assent to legislation is necessary, his co-legislators 'can never in opposition to him, or without his concurrence, alter the legislative by a law' (Sec. 218). Such a prince who 'is no more subordinate than he himself shall think fit . . .' (Sec. 152), is not expected to assent to laws which limit his prerogative. Locke is therefore not speaking inadvertently of the alteration of the government, nor of the question about the proper use of prerogative being an issue between prince and people.

Although to provide directly and permanently by law against the abuse of prerogative demands the change of regime, this is not the inevitable aim and result of the people's interference. A show of force may be sufficient to rescind particular prerogative encroachments and teach the prince to refrain from repeating them. The abuse of prerogative by unworthy successors of good and wise princes, 'has often occasioned contest, and sometimes public disorders, before the people could recover their original right, and get that to be declared not to be prerogative, which truly was never so' (Sec. 166). Such a declaration is not necessarily tantamount to a constitutional change. That 'which truly was never so' was not anchored in any legal arrangements either, but was an informal arrangement according to which the 'power which they [the people] indefinitely left in his [the prince's], or his ancestors', hands, to be exercised for their good, was not a thing, which they intended him, when he used it otherwise' (Sec. 163). Moreover, a legal limitation did not recommend itself to Locke, since it fitted not all rulers alike. He did not think that good rulers ought henceforth be hamstrung on account of the precedent established by bad ones.[14] He even favoured the custom of the sacredness of the king's person despite 'the inconvenience of some particular mischiefs, that may happen sometimes, when a heady prince comes to the throne . . .' (Sec. 205).

Assuming then, as we must, that Locke was genuinely committed to the regime which emerged from the Glorious Revolution – and assuming also, as we may, that he had not unconditionally shelved the tenets of Whig extremism of the time of the Exclusion Bill controversy, the following conclusion offers itself: In speaking of legal barriers against prerogative, he merely made it clear, once again, that the way was open to institute a regime in which the executive had no share in legislation, and in which prerogative could be fully subjected to legal provisions and procedures. His emphasis of the sanctity of law, which invites a final query as to the inner consistency of his constitutionalism, will afford further proof that Locke did not find the vicissitudes of history so discouraging and the new order so lacking in safeguards as to dictate the direct legal restriction of princely prerogative.

C. Indirect Legal Limitation

Liberal constitutionalism, in particular, is usually identified with the tenet 'Rule by laws and not by men'. Locke expressed this in a less misleading way by saying: 'Against the laws there can be no authority' (Sec. 206). Yet this being so, how are we to account for authority to act without, and even against, the prescription of the laws?

One answer is, of course, that the prince's prerogative is by definition the exception to the rule and confirms it inasmuch as, by using prerogative, wise princes 'did nothing herein to the prejudice of their laws, since they acted conformable to the foundation and end of all laws, the public good' (Sec. 165). The other answer is, as the context shows, that the prince's unjustifiable transgression of the laws does not annul their validity but justifies resistance. Resistance can be confined to the king's officers and initially at least need not

14 See above, 243.

aim at injuring the prince's position and authority. It is characteristic of Locke's attitude to the 'ancient constitution'[15] that, unlike other Whigs, he did not refer to it when he adopted the compromise between the traditional absolutist principle that 'the king can do no wrong' and the principle of ministerial or otherwise delegated responsibility. On the basis of this compromise Locke conceived prerogative as limited by popular action which relies on the laws and expresses itself in civil disobedience, not in revolution.

Where the executive has no share in legislation, the legislature has the power to oust the executive from office by virtue of its authority 'to punish for any maladministration against the laws' as well as for the misconduct of foreign affairs, for the executive and federative power are 'both ministerial and subordinate to the legislative' (Sec. 153). Whether 'other ministerial and subordinate powers' under this regime are directly impeachable by the legislature, Locke does not make clear. We merely learn that they 'are all of them accountable to some other power', whatever 'the different customs and constitutions of distinct commonwealths' (Sec. 152). At any rate where the executive shares in legislation, it is from him that 'all inferior magistrates derive all their several subordinate powers, or at least the greatest part of them' (Sec. 151). Although all executive officers are accountable only to the prince in this regime, too, – where the chief executive is up to a point sacred by law – 'allegiance . . . [is] nothing but an obedience according to law'. Any of the king's officers 'may be questioned, opposed, and resisted, who use unjust force, though they pretend a commission from him, which the law authorizes not' (Sec. 206). The commission itself is void to the extent that it goes beyond

'the limitations of the law, which if anyone transgress, the king's commission excuses him not . . . But, notwithstanding such resistance, the king's *person and authority* are still both secured, and so no danger to governor or government.'

The sanctity of the king's person and authority is not immediately endangered when he authorizes action against the law. 'Whatever he commands, or does, his person is still free from all question or violence, not liable to force, or any judicial censure or condemnation' (Sec. 205). The different constitutional standing of the king and his officers serves Locke to uphold against both parties the inviolability of the laws and yet to accord a conditional lease of life to the principle of the king's immunity. Opposition is not unconditionally confined to resistance to 'the illegal acts of any inferior officer, or other commissioned by him'. The prince is secure 'unless he will by actually putting himself into a state of war with his people, dissolve the government . . .' So long as the people do not believe that the prince has forfeited the right to rule over them, their resistance to his orders is civil disobedience, which is thus clearly distinguished from revolution.

Both forms of resistance operate on the same level as prerogative, that is, outside the confines of law and legislation. Like revolt, civil disobedience is a political, as distinct from a legal, limitation of prerogative. However, it derives its justification more immediately from the laws than revolution. Laws can be suspended by prerogative but not changed or made. Laws once enacted are not even always rendered ineffective by prerogative. Their violation by the king's commands justifies resistance in the form of civil disobedience, and eventually revolt. If no resistance is forthcoming, this may mean that there exists popular consent to the infraction of laws. In this case, the laws which have been transgressed are entirely ineffective; but they stand until changed by legislative procedure. And as long as it stands, the law may at any moment cease to be ineffective. The people need only change their mind about the executive's suspension of laws and be justified to resist their violation. In this way any positive law indirectly fulfils the function of those laws which may be directly devised to restrict prerogative.

Specific legal provisions no doubt make for clarity and above all enable the solution of conflicts over the use of prerogative within the constitutional and legal framework. But a chief executive bent on breaking laws will not be deflected from his course merely in virtue of laws limiting his prerogative. Whether or not Locke was moved by considerations of this kind, in his conception legal and extra-legal action intersect, but their terms of reference remain distinct. The principle that there is no authority against the laws is not offset by the prerogative to act without or even against the law, because Locke placed the principle of the sanctity of law within a system of legal and political checks and balances. Where they conflict, the constitutional authority of the prince and of enacted positive laws checkmate each other. The prince's authority is not automatically affected when he issues commands contrary to law, and the validity of laws is not anulled by their violation, whether the violation is for the public good or not. Enacted laws provide the grounds for extra-legal resistance to the king's illegal commands, and prerogative those for temporarily overruling laws and legislators. Resistance to the infraction of laws does not guarantee their execution. But the threat of civil disobedience, and eventually of revolt, is an inducement to the king and his co-legislators to co-operate and rule by law. The forces which operate in the extra-legal sphere are thus as much influenced by the constitutional balance of powers as they influence it. Although the government is normally entitled to exact obedience through positive laws alone, positive laws and even constitutional arrangements are sacrosanct, and at the same time changeable since, after all, they are apt to be imperfect realizations of natural law. On the combined grounds of a metapolitically founded legalism and the requirements of practical politics, the chief executive is at the centre of it all, playing a decisive role in the legislative process and possessing the constitutional authority to act permanently in external affairs; and, when he finds it necessary, also in internal affairs, as the sole and authoritarian representative of the will and interest of the people.

Since liberalism is commonly supposed to oppose concessions to the authoritarian representation of the will of all by the will of one, it were well, in conclusion, to assess the limits which Locke's authoritarianism and constitutionalism impose on each other. This is to sum up where his liberal politics supersede the politics of conservatism in his time.

3. THE GODLIKE 'REPRESENTER'

Although the substitution of monarchy by consent for divine king-ship neither leaves Locke's prince as godlike as Filmer's nor makes him identical with Hobbes' 'representer', he is not entirely unlike either.

We recall that Locke styled as 'godlike' those princes who 'by established laws of liberty' secured 'protection and encouragement to the honest industry of mankind', and whose prerogative it was not reasonable to limit because they 'transgressed not the bounds of the public good' when they ruled 'without law to that end'.[16] They had

[16] Secs. 42, 166, 165.

'*some* title to arbitrary power, by that argument, that would prove absolute monarchy the best government, as that which God himself governs the universe by: because such kings partake of his wisdom and goodness' (Sec. 166). Absolute government is not the best government, because not all princes are wise and good. Even so, godlikeness attaches to the office of all princes. Some of the effects of the purely personal charisma, to use Max Weber's terms, become institutionalized.

Any monarch is in a position to make promises, grants and oaths. Unlike other men, but like God, the prince Locke was speaking of is not subject to ordinary jurisdiction. But irrespective of whether 'princes are exempt from the laws of their country; . . . they owe subjection to the laws of God and nature' (Sec. 195). Whether personally godlike or not, all holders of the princely office are reminded that the obligations of the eternal law 'are so great, and so strong, in the case of promises, that omnipotence itself can be tied by them', which shows how much more so this applies 'to princes of the world who all together, with all their people joined to them, are in comparison of the great God, but as a drop of the bucket, or a dust on the balance, inconsiderable nothing'. The moral obligation of which the royal 'drops of the bucket' are particularly reminded, is not only that which obligates God but also that which binds everybody, even outside the bounds of their own political society. 'Truth and keeping of faith belongs to men, as men, and not as members of society' (Sec. 14). As holders of their office who have godlike responsibility for a whole society, princes are constantly in the situation of ordinary members of different political societies who meet in a no-man's land. Their different situations put both categories of men beyond the reach of the laws of their society, but not beyond those which are the foundation of positive law. And natural law puts the ruler – unlike God or men in no-man's land – within the reach of the revolutionary umpirage of his society.

Hobbes' sovereign prince remains in the state of nature; society is bound by his laws but his subjects retain no right against him. Locke's prince normally hovers, so to speak, on the brink between the state of nature and political society. If he rules according to law and the majority of his subjects acquiesces in his transgressions of the law, he is as much above his subjects as he is part of their political society. But they can expel him when, by his own fault, he places himself in a state of war with his people. If their unique position lays princes more open than it does others to becoming truly and properly rebels, 'who by force break through, and by force justify their violation of them' (Sec. 226) – that is of the laws – it is because from the beginning theirs had been the task of advancing society towards greater security, well-being and justice. Benevolent one-man-rule had saved nascent societies from ruin. Discretionary leadership had launched society on the road of economic expansion when godlike princes could themselves make 'laws of liberty'. They continue to be charged with securing more just and more equal proportions of representation.

In the context of Locke's liberal politics, too, no single individual has more power over other men than the prince; no other governmental agency can employ the force of all the members of the community. As distinct from the politics of conservatism, the chief executive's unique position is allied with the principle of consent, the balance of powers, the supremacy of law and the legislature. In a mixed constitution, with which liberal politics becomes identified, the prince retains only the right to exercise his discretion for specific purposes. Yet a breakthrough from above with acquiescence from below becomes feasible whenever the prince judges the public good to require it, notwithstanding the supremacy of law and of the legislature. In specific issues and in emergency situations, their definition being ultimately a matter for the discretionary decision of the prince, the will of the entire society is embodied in him alone. Then he is godlike by virtue of his office, yet becoming subhuman when he abuses its privilege – or, more exactly, when the people regard the abuses as of sufficient moment to rise against him. To elaborate on what Aristotle said of men in general, Locke's prince is on the threshold of being a god, although he is just as likely to become a beast. By his subjects' adjudication he is either the one or the other. In this way, Locke's liberalism tempers the traditionalist view of monarchy decisively by consent – with some borrowing from Hobbes' idea of the representation of the multitude.

According to Hobbes, 'a multitude of men, are made one person, when they are by one man, or one person, represented; . . . For it is the unity of the representer, not the unity of the represented, that makes the person one . . . And unity, cannot be otherwise understood in multitude.'[17] Locke, for his part, designated the chief executive 'as the image, phantom, or representative of the common-

[17] *Leviathan*, Ch. 16.

wealth . . .' (Sec. 151). It might appear that he used Hobbesian language for entirely antithetical purposes,[18] because he went on to say that the chief executive could be considered as the representative of the commonwealth when 'acted by the will of the society, declared in its laws; and thus he has no will, no power, but that of the law'. But what he says does not cut him off from his predecessor's idea of representation. Hobbes might well have agreed that the 'representer' had no will other than that of the laws, provided it was agreed that his will alone was law. Locke's chief executive cannot legislate by himself but without his will no law can be made. Although legislation demands the concurrence of a plurality of agencies, the idea that the unity of the representer is the condition for the unity of the represented is retained. Locke puts his legislature in the place of Hobbes' sovereign[19] when he says that 'in their legislative, . . . the members of a commonwealth are united, and combined together into one coherent living body. This is the soul that gives form, life, and unity to the commonwealth' (Sec. 212). For Locke, as for Hobbes, the existence of the law allows to speak of a society and laws are determined by an act of will on the part not of the society but of the legislating authority. In its 'decisions the people acquiesced and united, as to that of their own will' (Sec. 227). The executive is the representative of society as the executor of laws made by him and his co-legislators – that is, when they – and not society – act as one 'person' and have one will. The represented are made one person by an act of will other than their own, also in the strictly Hobbesian sense, i.e., when the chief executive exercises discretionary power for the public good. In these instances, the representative function of Locke's prince is unmediated and he fulfils the terms of Hobbes' definition, according to which 'a multitude of men are made one person, when they are by one man, or one person, [i.e., one governmental agency] represented'.

Locke did thus not use Hobbesian language for entirely antithetical purposes. Yet at precisely the area in language and content that they come nearest does their fundamental difference stand out. The authoritarian representation of all by one person is not the essence, but merely a part, of Locke's political system. It is carefully and consistently distinguished from legislation. The relation of both

---

[18] Laslett, *op. cit.*, 386.

[19] Cp. Laslett, *op. cit.*, 425, who points also to passages which are similar to *Leviathan* in Grotius and Pufendorf.

the legislative process and of authoritarian representation to institutionalized and non-institutionalized consent constitutes the vital difference between Locke's constitutionalism and kingship *iure divino* or the *Leviathan*. As distinct from that of Hobbes and Filmer, Locke's constitutionalism does not merely circumscribe the structure of government, especially from the point of view of the legal arrangements. It has the specific purpose of safeguarding individual concerns against the arbitrariness of government.

Locke's constitutionalism is liberal inasmuch as it belongs to the category best described as *garantism*. [20] Traditional authoritarianism supplements his constitutionalism not just for reasons of efficiency and *raison d'état*. It is also the antidote to the subjection of the public good to the group-interests of the king's co-legislators. Locke admits non-legal action, which is arbitrary in the formal sense, because man-made laws may be arbitrary in their contents. He made concessions to both authoritarianism and revolutionism because he abided by the distinction between moral and legal norms not only to enable the judgement of the latter *in foro interno*, but also to carry out such judgements in the political process. By reference to the moral code of natural law the two governmental agencies engaged in legislation, and the chief executive collaborate and check each other; and are on their part sustained or counteracted by the electorate and the entire people. For Locke the majority of the people are the ultimate fount and umpire of the use of political authority, but must not pass judgement except by resistance. This heightens the importance of the legally unspecified interplay between the government and the people. Both from the point of view of liberal ideology and empirical insights this view of the political process persisted in its outlines.

The authoritarian vein and what continued to sustain it – the distrust of the masses – were not swiftly overcome. A case in point is the favourable attitude of liberals towards Bonaparte's *Eighteenth of Brumaire*, and much else in the Napoleonic dictatorship. The French Revolution and its heritage are distinguishable in these respects from its two Anglo-Saxon predecessors and sources of

[20] G. Sartori, 'Constitutionalism: A Preliminary Discussion,' *The American Political Science Review*, LVI, 4 (1963), 855, uses the term 'garantism' to distinguish a specific and indeed the proper kind of constitutionalism from others. See also Friedrich, *op. cit.*, 26 f., 121 f. and K. Loewenstein, *Political Power and the Governmental Process* (Chicago, 1957), 12, 14, 29, 51-2, for a definition of constitutionalism as the opposite of autocracy, and his threefold classification of constitutions (147 ff.).

inspiration, the Glorious Revolution and the American Revolution. But the difference lies in the attitude towards military dictatorship as the means of breaking through the shackles of old custom and group partiality, rather than in the evaluation of executive prerogatives and of popular influence. As John Stuart Mill attests, liberalism bears the imprint of these attitudes well into the nineteenth-century. Locke was aware that laws and law-making procedures, which are the core of the political process, may become more sacrosanct than he himself thought necessary in his time. He is the harbinger of a liberal constitutionalism which is stricter and more unqualified than the constitutionalism with which he was satisfied. He thought it feasible that a regime may be instituted in which the most formidable of all holders of power, the chief executive, has no share in legislation and is made fully accountable to the legislature, while his prerogatives are clearly circumscribed by positive laws. But he also reduced the differences between such a regime and the one he found acceptable.

The longevity of the ideological patterns forged by Locke has its counterpart in the continued validity of a good many of his insights. The advent of modern democratic and liberal constitutionalism; the proliferation of intermediate and mediating forms of action and communication in and between the spheres of government and all other social relations and the awareness of all this in modern political science has caused it to take its cue from what underlies Locke's understanding of the political process. Namely, that politics cannot be confined to legal and constitutional categories. But the metaphysical dimension of this transcendence remains also a legitimate concern of political science.

BIBLIOGRAPHY

Aaron, R. I. – *John Locke* (2nd ed., Oxford, 1955).
Aarsleff, H. – 'Leibniz on Locke on Language,' *American Philosophical Quarterly* 1, 3 (1964).
Akzin, B. – 'Analysis of State and Law Structure,' in *Law, State and International Legal Order : Essays in Honor of Hans Kelsen* (University of Tennessee Press, 1964).
Althusser, L. – *Montesquieu, la politique et l'histoire* (Paris, 1959).
Aquinas, T. – *S. Thomas Aquinatis Opuscula Omnia* (Paris, 1927), 5 vols.
Arendt, H. – *The Human Condition* (New York, Doubleday Anchor Books, 1959).
Arendt, H. – *On Revolution* (London, 1963).
Aronson, J. – 'Shaftesbury on Locke,' *The American Political Science Review*, LIII, 4 (1959).
Barker, E. – *The Social Contract* (Oxford, 1946).
Bastide, C. – *John Locke, ses théories politiques et leur influence en Angleterre* (Paris, 1907).
Bay, C. – 'Politics and Pseudopolitics: A Critical Evaluation of Some Behavioral Literature,' *The American Political Science Review*, LIX, 1 (1965).
Beloff, M. (ed.) – *The Federalist* (Oxford, 1948).
Berlin, I. – *Two Concepts of Liberty* (Oxford, 1958).
Berlin, I. – 'Does Political Theory Still Exist?' in P. Laslett and W. G. Runciman, *Philosophy, Politics and Society* (sec. ser., Oxford, 1962).
Berlin, I. – 'Hobbes, Locke and Professor Macpherson,' *The Political Quarterly*, XXXV, 4 (1964).
Bode, I. – 'Ursprung und Begriff der parlamentarischen Opposition,' *Sozialwissenschaftliche Studien*, Heft 3 (Stuttgart, 1962).
Bodin, J. – *The Six Books of the Commonwealth* (Latine copies done into English by Richard Knolles).
Bosanquet, B. – *The Philosophical Theory of the State* (repr., London, 1958).
Bourne, H. R. F. – *The Life of John Locke*, 2 vols. (London, 1867).
Bracton, H. (de) – *De Legibus et Consuetudinibus Angliae* (Wiesbaden Kraus reprint, 1964).
Brogan, A. P. – 'John Locke and Utilitarianism,' *Ethics*, LXIX, 2 (1959).
Brown, K. C. (ed.) – *Hobbes Studies* (Oxford, 1965).
Bryce, J. – *Studies in History and Jurisprudence* (Oxford, 1901).
Buchanan, J. M. and Tullock, G. – *The Calculus of Consent : Logical Foundations of Constitutional Democracy* (Ann Arbor, 1962).
Cassinelli, W. – 'The Consent of the Governed,' *The Western Political Quarterly*, XII, 2 (1959).

Catlin, G. E. C. - *Principles of Politics* (New York, 1930).
Cherno, M. - 'Locke on Property, A Re-Appraisal,' *Ethics*, LXVIII, 1 (1957).
Clark, G. - *War and Society in the Seventeenth Century* (Cambridge, 1958).
Cousin, V. - *Philosophie de Locke* (Paris, 1829; 4th ed., 1861).
Cowling, M. - *Mill and Liberalism* (Cambridge, 1963).
Cox, R. H. - *Locke on War and Peace* (Oxford, 1960).
Cranston, M. - *Freedom, A New Analysis* (London, 1953).
Cranston, M. - *John Locke, A Biography* (London, 1957).
Cropsey, J. - 'On the Relation of Political Science and Economics,' *The American Political Science Review*, LIV, 1 (1960).
Dahl, R. A. - *A Preface to Democratic Theory* (Chicago, 1956).
Democracy in a World of Tension (Unesco, Paris, 1951).
Dicey, A. V. - *Introduction to the Study of the Law of the Constitution* (9th ed., London, 1948).
Easton, D. - *The Political System* (repr., New York, 1959).
Easton, D. - *A Framework for Political Analysis* (Englewood Cliffs, N. J., 1965).
Eisenmann, C. - *La Penseé Constitutionelle de Montesquieu* (Recueil Sirey).
Eisenmann, C. - 'L'Esprit des Lois et la Séparation des Pouvoirs,' *Mélanges de Carré de Malberg* (Paris, 1933).
Fetscher, I. - 'Der gesellschaftliche "Naturzustand" und das Menschenbild bei Hobbes, Pufendorf, Cumberland und Rousseau,' *Schmollers Jahrbuch für Gesetzgebung, Verwaltung und Volkswirtschaft*, LXXX (1960).
Filmer, R. - *Patriarcha and Other Political Works*, ed. by P. Laslett (Oxford, 1949).
Friedrich, C. J. - *The New Belief in the Common Man* (Boston, 1942).
Friedrich, C. J. - *Constitutional Government and Democracy* (rev. ed., New York, 1950).
Friedrich, C. J. - *The Philosophy of Law in Historical Perspective* (Chicago, 1958).
Friedrich, C. J. - 'Authority, Reason and Discretion,' in *Authority* (ed. by Friedrich, *Nomos* I. Cambridge, Mass., 1958).
Friedrich, C. J. - *Man and His Government* (New York, 1963).
Furley, O. W. - 'The Whig Exclusionists: Pamphlet Literature in the Exclusion Campaign, 1679-81,' *The Cambridge Historical Journal*, XIII, 1 (1957).
Galbraith, J. K. - *The Affluent Society* (Penguin Books, 1962).
Gauthier, D. P. - 'The Role of Inheritance in Locke's Political Theory,' *The Canadian Journal of Economics and Political Science*, XXXII, 1 (1966).

Geertz, C. – 'Ideology as a Cultural System,' in D. E. Apter (ed.), *Ideology and Discontent* (Glencoe, 1964).

Gierke, O. –*Natural Law and the Theory of Society* (ed. by E. Barker, Boston, Beacon Press).

Goldwin, R. A. – 'John Locke,' in L. Strauss and J. Cropsey (eds.), *History of Political Philosophy* (Chicago, 1963).

Gough, J. W. – *John Locke's Political Philosophy* (Oxford, repr., 1956).

Gough, J. W. – *The Social Contract* (2nd ed., Oxford, 1957).

Green, T. H. – *Lectures on the Principles of Political Obligation* (new impr., London, 1959).

Griewank, K. – *Der Neuzeitliche Revolutionsbegriff* (Weimar, 1955).

Grotius, H. – *De Jure Belli ac Pacis* text of 1646 (Washington, 1913).

Hegel, G. W. F. – *Die Vernunft in der Geschichte* (ed. Hoffmeister, 5th ed., Hamburg, 1955).

Hegel, G. W. F. – *Grundlinien der Philosophie des Rechts* (ed. by Hoffmeister, 4th ed., Hamburg, 1955).

Hinsley, F. H. – *Power and the Pursuit of Peace* (Cambridge, 1963).

Hobbes, T. – *De Cive or The Citizen* (ed. by S. P. Lamprecht, New York, 1949).

Hobbes, T. – *Leviathan* (Lindsay's edition, Everyman's Library, 1937).

Hobhouse, L. T. – 'The Historical Evolution of Property in Fact and Ideas,' in C. Gore, *Property, Its Duties and Rights* (New ed., London, 1915).

Hooker, R. – *Of the Laws of Ecclesiastical Polity* (Everyman's Library, London, 1954).

Jouvenel, B. (de) – *Du Pouvoir* (rev. ed., Genéve, 1947).

Jouvenel, B. (de) – *The Pure Theory of Politics* (Cambridge, 1963).

Kelsen, H. – 'Foundations of Democracy,' *Ethics*, LXVI, I, 2 (1955).

Kendall, W. – 'John Locke and the Doctrine of Majority-Rule,' *Illinois Studies in the Social Sciences*, XXVI, 2 (1941).

King, (Lord) Peter. – *The Life of John Locke with Extracts from his Correspondence, Journals and Common Place Books* (London, 1829).

Krieger, L. – *The Politics of Discretion: Pufendorf and the Acceptance of Natural Law* (Chicago, 1965).

Lamprecht, S. P. – *The Moral and Political Philosophy of John Locke* (New York, 1918).

Larkin, P. – *Property in the Eighteenth Century, with Special Reference to England and Locke* (Dublin, 1930).

Laski, H. – *Political Thought in England from Locke to Bentham* (New York, 1919).

Laslett, P. – 'John Locke, the Great Recoinage and the Origins of the Board of Trade: 1695–8,' *The William and Mary Quarterly*, 3rd ser., XVI, 3 (1957).

BIBLIOGRAPHY

Laslett, P. – 'Market Economy and Political Theory,' *The Historical Journal*, VI, 1 (1964).

Lasswell, H. D. and Kaplan, A. – *Power and Society* (Third Printing, New Haven, 1957).

Lenin, N. – *The State and Revolution* (Selected Works, Moscow, 1952).

Leyden, W. (von) – 'John Locke and Natural Law,' *Philosophy*, XXI (1956).

Lindsay, A. D. – *The Modern Democratic State*, vol. 1 (London 5th impr., 1951; 1st ed. 1943).

Lipset, S. M. – *Political Man* (New York, 1960).

Locke, J. – *The Works of John Locke*, 10 vols. (London, 1823).

Locke, J. – *Essays on the Law of Nature* (edited with an Introduction by W. von Leyden (Oxford, 1954).

Locke, J. – *Two Tracts on Government* (edited with an Introduction by P. Abrams, Cambridge, 1967).

Locke, J. – *An Essay Concerning Human Understanding*, 2 vols. (edited with an Introduction by J. W. Yolton, Everyman's Library, London-New York, 1961).

Locke, J. – *Two Treatises of Government* (edited with an Introduction by P. Laslett, Cambridge, 1961).

Locke, J. – *Some Considerations of the Consequence of the Lowering of Interest and Raising the Value of Money. In a letter sent to a Member of Parliament, 1691* (sec. ed., London, 1696).

Loewenstein, K. – *Political Power and the Governmental Process* (Chicago, 1957).

Luethy, H. – 'Once Again: Calvinism and Capitalism,' *Encounter*, XXII, 1 (1964).

McIlwain, C. H. – *The Growth of Political Theory in the West, from the Greeks to the End of the Middle Ages* (New York, 1932).

Macpherson, C. B. – *The Political Theory of Possessive Individualism* (Oxford, 1962).

McShea, R. J. – 'Leo Strauss on Machiavelli,' *The Western Political Quarterly*, XVI, 4 (1963).

Marx, K. – *Der Historische Materialismus, Die Frühschriften* (ed. by S. Landshut and J. P. Mayer, 2 vols. Leipzig, 1932).

Marx, K. – *Critique of the Gotha Programme* in *Selected Works* (edited by V. Adoratsky, 2 vols. London, Martin Lawrence Ltd., no date).

Marx, K. – *Das Kapital* (Wien-Berlin, 1933).

Michels, R. – *Political Parties* (Dover Books, 1959).

Mill, J. S. – *Utilitarianism, Liberty and Representative Government* (Everyman's Library, London, 1910).

Monson, C. H. – 'Locke and his Interpreters,' *Political Studies*, VI, 2 (1958).

Montesquieu, C. L. de Secondat de – *De L'Esprit des Lois* (Ed. par G. Turc, Classiques Garnier, Paris, no date).

More, T. – *Utopia* (Everyman's Library, London, 1951).

Moulds, H. – 'John Locke's Four Freedoms in a New Light,' *Ethics*, LXXI, 2 (1961).

Neumann, F. – *The Democratic and the Authoritarian State* (Glencoe, 1957).

Niebuhr, R. – *The Children of Light and the Children of Darkness* (London, 1945).

Ogg, D. – *England in the Reigns of James II and William III* (Oxford, 1955).

Ogg, D. – *England under the Reign of Charles II*, 2 vols. (Oxford, 1955).

Oppenheim, F. E. – *Dimensions of Freedom* (New York – London, 1961).

Oppenheim, F. E. – 'Freedom – an Empirical Interpretation,' in *Nomos* IV (1962).

Parry, G. – 'Individuality, Politics and the Critique of Paternalism in John Locke,' *Political Studies*, XII, 2 (1964).

Parsons, T. – 'The Political Aspect of Social Structure and Process,' in D. Easton, *Varieties of Political Theory* (Englewood Cliffs, N.J., 1966).

Partridge, P. H. – 'Politics, Philosophy, Ideology,' *Political Studies*, IX, 3 (1961).

Pitkin, H. – 'Obligation and Consent,' *The American Political Science Review*, LIX, 4 (1965) and LX, 1 (1966).

Plamenatz, J. P. – *Consent, Freedom and Political Obligation* (Oxford, 1938).

Plamenatz, J. P. – *Man and Society*, 2 vols. (London, 1963).

Plucknett, T. E. T. – *A Concise History of the Common Law* (4th ed., London, 1948).

Pocock, J. G. A. – *The Ancient Constitution and the Federal Law* (Cambridge, 1957).

Pocock, J. G. A. – 'Machiavelli, Harrington and English Political Ideologies in the Eighteenth Century,' *The William and Mary Quarterly*, XXII, 4 (1965).

Polanyi, M. – *The Logic of Liberty* (Chicago, 1958).

Polin, R. – *La Politique Morale de John Locke* (Paris, 1960).

Pollock, F. – 'Locke's Theory of State,' *Proceedings of the British Academy* (1903–4).

Popper, K. – *The Open Society and its Enemies* (Princeton, 1950).

Pufendorf, S. – *De Jure Naturae et Gentium* (text of 1688, Oxford, 1934).

Ranney, A. and Kendall, W. – *Democracy and the American Party System* (New York, 1956).

Rashdall, H. – 'The Philosophical Theory of Property,' in C. Gore, *Property, Its Duties and Rights* (New ed., London, 1915).

Richter, M. – *The Politics of Conscience : T.H. Green and His Age* (London, 1964).

Rogow, A. A. – 'The Revolt Against Social Equality,' *Dissent* IV (1957).

BIBLIOGRAPHY

Rosenstock, E. – *Die Europäischen Revolutionen* (Jena, 1931).
Rotenstreich, N. – 'Rule by Majority or by Principles,' *Social Research*, XXII, 4 (1954).
Rotenstreich, N. – *Between Past and Present, An Essay in History* (New Haven, 1958).
Rothman, S. – 'The Revival of Classical Political Philosophy,' *The American Political Science Review*, LVI, 2 (1962).
Rousseau, J. J. – *Du Contrat Social. Quelle est l'Origine de l'Inégalite parmi les Hommes et si elle est autorisée par la Loi naturelle?* (Classiques Garnier, Paris, 1954).
Rowen, H. H. – 'A Second Thought on Locke's *First Treatise*', *Journal of the History of Ideas*, XVII, (1956).
Ruggiero, G. de – *The History of European Liberalism* (transl. by R. S. Collingwood, Beacon Press, 1959. First publ. Oxford, 1927).
Runciman, W. G. – *Social Science and Political Theory* (Cambridge, 1963).
Sartori, G. – *Democratic Theory* (Detroit, 1962).
Sartori, G. – 'Constitutionalism: A Preliminary Discussion,' *The American Political Science Review*, LVI, 4 (1962).
Schlatter, R. – *Private Property : The History of an Idea* (London, 1951).
Schmidt, H. – 'Zur Natur der Eigentumsbildung in der Arbeit. John Locke in den Deutungen von Raymond Polin,' (*Der Staat*, IV, 1965).
Schmitt, C. – *Politische Theologie, Vier Kapitel zur Lehre von der Souveränität* (2 ed., München-Leipzig, 1934).
Schulz, I. – *Prinzipien des Römischen Rechts* (Berlin, 1954).
Schumpeter, J. A. – *Capitalism, Socialism and Democracy* (1942. Harper Torchbooks, 1962).
Seliger, M. – *The Conception of History of the French Historians of the Restoration (1815–1830) in their Treatment of French History* (unpubl. doctoral thesis [in Hebrew], the Hebrew University of Jerusalem, 1956).
Seliger, M. – 'The Idea of Conquest and Race-Thinking during the Restoration,' *The Review of Politics*, XXII, 4 (1960), 545–67.
Seliger, M. – 'Napoleonic Authoritarianism in French Liberal Thought,' in A. Fuks and I. Halperin (eds.), *Scripta Hierosolymitana*, vol. VII (Jerusalem, 1961).
Seliger, M. – 'Locke's Theory of Revolutionary Action,' *The Western Political Quarterly*, XVI, 3 (1963).
Seliger, M. – 'Locke's Natural Law and the Foundation of Politics,' *Journal of the History of Ideas*, XXIV, 3 (1963).
Seliger, M. – 'Locke, Liberalism and Nationalism,' in *John Locke: Problems and Perspectives* (ed. by J. W. Yolton. Cambridge, forthcoming).
Shils, E. – 'Primordial, Sacred and Civil Ties,' *The British Journal of Sociology*, VIII, 2 (1957).
Simon, W. – 'John Locke: Philosophy and Political Theory,' – *The American Political Science Review*, XLV, 2 (1956).

Singh, R. – 'John Locke and the Idea of Sovereignty,' *The Indian Journal of Political Science*, XX, 4 (1959).

Singh, R. – 'John Locke and the Theory of Natural Law,' *Political Studies*, IX, 2 (1961).

Smyrniades, E. – *Les Doctrines de Hobbes, Locke et Kant sur le droit de l'insurrection* (Paris, 1921).

Spitz, D. – *Democracy and the Challenge of Power* (New York, 1958).

Stephen, J. F. –*Horae Sabbaticae* (2nd ed., 1892).

Stephen, L. – *English Thought in the Eighteenth Century*, 2 vols. (3rd ed. London, 1902).

Strauss, L. – *Natural Right and History* (Chicago, 2nd impr., 1957).

Strauss, L. – 'Locke's Doctrine of Natural Law,' *The American Political, Science Review*, LII, 2 (1958).

Talmon, J. L. – *The Origins of Totalitarian Democracy* (London, 1952).

Talmon, J. L. – *Political Messianism* (London, 1960).

Tawney, R. H. – *Religion and the Rise of Capitalism* (New York, 1926).

Taylor, O. H. – 'Economics and Liberalism,' *Harvard Economic Studies*, XCVI (1955).

Vaughan, C. E. – *Studies in the History of Political Philosophy Before and After Rousseau*, 2 vols. (new ed., Manchester, 1939). Vol. I.

Vile, M. J. C. – *Constitutionalism and the Separation of Powers* (Oxford, 1967).

Waldman, M. – 'A Note on John Locke's Theory of Consent,' *Ethics*, LXVIII, 1 (1957).

Watkins, F. – *The Political Tradition of the West, A Study in the Development of Modern Liberalism* (Cambridge, Mass., 1948).

Weber, M. – 'Die Protestantische Ethik und der Geist des Kapitalismus,' *Archiv für Sozialwissenschaft und Sozialpolitik*, XX–XXI (1904–5).

Weber, M. – *Grundriss der Sozialökonomik, III. Abteilung, Wirtschaft und Gesellschaft* (Tübingen, 1925, zweite vermehrte Auflage).

Wheare, K. C. – *Modern Constitutions* (rev. ed., London, 1960).

Wolin, S. S. – *Politics and Vision* (London, 1960).

Wormuth, F. D. – *The Royal Prerogative, 1603–1649* (Ithaca-New York, 1939).

Yolton, J. W. – *John Locke and the Way of Ideas* (Oxford, 1956).

Yolton, J. W. – 'Locke and the Law of Nature,' *The Philosophical Review*, LXVII (1958).

Aaron, R. I., 45, 61, 63, 119, 142, 284, 339
Aarsleff, H., 49, 59
Abrams, P., 31, 209 f., 296
absolutism, 24 f., 40, 110, 217, 237, 249, 251, 254–6, 262, 365
Acosta, J., 86
Adam, 54, 176, 182–5, 188–91, 203–4, 206, 211–12, 239, 327
aggression, 109, 111, 113, 115, 121, 307
annexation, 112, 114–81
Akzin, B., 77
Althusser, L., 336
America, 24, 29, 34, 85 ff., 98, 117, 123, 151 ff., 155, 213, 248, 335
anarchy, 20, 73, 105, 125, 127, 178, 255, 258 f., 314
appropriation, 18, 52, 180 f., 188–208; limits to, 142–53, 154, 158, 170, 173, 181, 205, 208, 260, see also, property
Aquinas, St. Thomas, 69–70, 116, 196, 235, 258, 316
arbitrary power, arbitrary rule, see power, arbitrary
Arendt, H., 111, 214, 321
Aristotle, 52, 88, 187, 216, 218, 369
Aronson, J., 45
assemblies, elected, 77, 81, 329–35, 340 f., 354; see also, Parliament
authoritarianism, 19, 21, 24 f., 46, 78, 210, 267, 293, 351–72
authority, 67, 70, 93, 110, 125, 130–5, 176, 208 ff., 221, 239–50, 261, 316 f., 327, 335, 352 f.; and power, 131, 133–4, 135, 259; delegated, 103–4, 128, 224, 299–300; magisterial, 96, 101; of government, 72, 128, 132, 142, 352 f.; parental, 59; paternal, 59, 185, 210–20, 224, 229, 231–2, 238–40, 246, 261, 327; political, 18, 27, 49, 80, 92, 133, 209–37, 246, 257, 259; royal, 214, 234, 240–56, 261, 327, 365 f.
Avineri, S., 163

Barclay, W., 234, 254, 262, 316
Barker, E., 83, 88, 181, 283 f., 311, 324 f.
barter, 85, 97, 151, 156
Bastide, C., 85, 283, 311, 322
Bay, C., 29
Beloff, M., 338
Berlin, I., 39, 55, 168, 292

Bible, the, 34, 54, 56–62, 63, 87, 100, 189, 203–6, 210, 220, 233, 240, 257
Board of Trade, 116, 118, 344
Bode, I., 64
Bodin, J., 110, 213, 220, 247, 325 ff.
Bosanquet, B., 170
Bourne, H. R. F., 45, 63, 116, 210, 276, 343
Boyle, R., 59
Bracton, H. de, 234, 255
Brogan, A. P., 46, 54
Brown, K. C., 47
Bryce, J., 326
Buchanan, J. M., 76

Cabet, E., 163
capacities, unequal, 20, 45, 50 ff., 62, 137, 144, 164, 171, 259, 293
capital, 174, 177 f.; see also, capitalism
capital punishment, 56–7, 63 f., 213–4
capitalism, 141–4, 259
Carolina, Fundamental Constitutions of, 116, 117–8, 276–7, 287–90
Cassinelli, W., 300 f.
Catlin, G. E. C., 225
charity, 174–6, 178
Cherno, M., 142, 146
Christianity, 34, 48, 60, 63 f., 116 f., 171, 181 f., 191, 197, 211, 217, 258
citizenship, 281–2, 291–3
'civic society', 141, 171, 179; see also, property relations
civil disobedience, 365–7
civil government, 102 ff., 244, 246, 344
civil society, 56, 62, 92, 96 f., 103, 107, 125, 169, 244, 246, 329; see also, political society
civil war, 35, 107, 124, 313, 320, see also, revolution
Clark, G., 111
class, social, 37, 99, 164, 179, 292
collectivism, 67, 76–7, 78, 278
colonialism, colony, 19, 114–24, 134, 176 259, 276–7, 287
Common Law, 233–6, 262, 358
commons, manorial, 98, 160, 202–3; universal, 188–90, 201, 206
commonwealth, 36, 71, 73, 84, 86 f., 104, 122, 125, 128, 166, 226–7, 236, 238, 240, 247, 250, 270, 280–1, 291, 304, 318, 320,

commonwealth—*continued*
332 ff., 341, 346, 348, 365, 370; definitions of, 87, 289
communism, 29, 35, 182, 200, 202 f.
community of things (*communio rerum*), 193, 196; natural community, 197; negative, 181–7, 190; positive, 180–3, 193, 199; rejected by Locke, 191, 198 f., 205
compact, 18, 46, 67, 86, 98, 111, 122, 154, 159 f., 162, 185, 194, 202, 219, 221–32, 245, 261, 269, 271, 276, 322
conquest, foreign, 102–3, 109–24, 125, 240, 252, 259, 273 f., 279, 305, 318
consent, 27, 40, 47, 64, 67–70, 71, 73, 82, 84, 87, 97, 106, 124, 130, 133, 159–65, 166 f., 180 ff., 187 f., 190 f., 193 f., 197, 199 f., 201 ff., 208, 214, 220 f., 223–32, 244–53, 257, 259–63, 280, 282 ff., 294 f., 297 ff., 308, 318, 355, 362, 367, 369; collective, 75–81, 293; express, 223, 226, 268–72, 275, 277 ff., 282 f., 290, 301, 329; function of freedom, 163–5; in property relations, 160–2; individual, 175–81, 267 ff., tacit, 68, 120, 129, 159, 224–5, 232, 239, 243, 249, 253, 263, 268–70, 275, 277 f., 281–3, 290, 297–301, 303, 351, 356; universal, 68, 276, 304
conservatism, 17, 209, 237, 367, 369
constitution, 21, 25, 136, 233, 235, 263, 312 f., 320, 322 ff., 328–9, 342, 351, 353 f., 362–5, 371–2; changes in, 318, 363; mixed, 243, 331–9, 341, 358, 362, 364, 369
constitutions, definition of, 136, 235–6
contractualism, 210, 233, 267, 293
Cousin, V., 45
Cowling, M., 24
Cox, R., 31 f., 35, 46, 53 ff., 60, 74, 83, 94 f., 100, 122 f., 130, 137, 141, 147 f., 225, 231, 249, 283, 304, 308, 325, 327, 339
Cranston, M., 24, 31, 49, 61, 116, 130, 210, 283, 288
Cropsey, J., 46, 141
Culverwell, 61
Cumberland, R., 102, 221

Dahl, R. A., 28, 285, 300, 311, 323
death penalty, 56–7, 63 f., 213–4
democracy, 19–20, 21–5, 77 ff., 87, 128, 246, 250, 255, 259, 283–93, 294, 301 f.,

323, 330, 346, 363, 372; distinguished from liberalism, 19–20, 22–3, 24–5
despotism, 132–3, 219, 250, 262, 307
Dicey, A. V., 326
dissent, 67, 79, 129, 135, 232, 239, 253, 258, 268, 274 f., 279, 282, 290, 292, 297–300, 303, 323, 351, 356
duty, 49 f., 65 f., 76, 79 f., 172, 175, 269 ff., 278, 282 f., 291

Easton, D., 30, 134, 137
economics, 72, 97, 138, 141, 145, 163–5, 171–9, 208, 241, 292, 369
Eisenmann, C., 336
elections, 285–93, 294, 297, 300 f., 323, 329, 340, 348, 356; *see also*, suffrage
electoral reform, 339, 343–9, 351, 354–5, 360
elitism, 18, 20, 62, 293
emigration, 272–75, 277, 278–82, 292, 319
Engels, F., 18–19, 163
equality, 50–4, 64, 80, 83, 87, 95, 144–5, 149 f., 153 ff., 165, 171–2, 179, 197, 241, 255, 257, 260, 285, 287, 303
esotericism, 33–6, 58, 60, 92, 94, 144, 313
Essays on the Law of Nature, 49, 67, 148, 152, 177, 195, 206
Essay concerning Human Understanding, 49, 82, 137, 206 f., 236, 257
ethics, 28–31, 46–9, 55 f., 67, 79 f., 194–8, 207, 231, 257; *see also*, morality
Exclusionist controversy, 36, 312–3, 364
executive, the, 38, 125, 131, 286, 324–49, 365 f., 372
executive, chief, *see*, prince
extra legal practice, 21 f., 24, 70, 308, 310, 339, 341, 351, 354, 367, 371

family life, 72, 88 f., 97–8, 150, 160–1, 184–5, 196, 208–24, 226, 238–40, 251, 261
Fetscher, I., 85 f., 102, 221
Filmer, Sir R., 39, 60, 75, 87, 101, 131, 176, 180, 182 f., 187–91, 195–8, 205–6, 208 ff., 217 f., 220, 223, 226, 230, 233, 236–7, 239, 250–6, 262, 289, 297 f., 326–7, 367, 371
First Treatise, 188, 203–5, 221, 230, 289, 327; *see also*, *Two Treatises*
force, 92, 102, 111, 123, 130 f., 133–6, 173, 175, 258 f., 305, 307, 316–7, 322–3, 363, 365, 369

foreign relations, 114, 122–3, 137, 259, 307, 360, 365
franchise, reform of, 339, 343–9, 351, 354–5, 360
freedom, *see*, liberty
French Revolution, 22, 322, 371
Friedrich, C. J., 133 f., 137, 284 f., 362, 371
Fundamental Constitutions of Carolina, 116, 117–8, 276–7, 287–90
Furley, O. W., 287

Galbraith, J. K., 174
'garantism', 371
Gauthier, D. P., 112–3, 270
Geertz, C., 121
Gierke, O., 88, 181, 284, 311
God, 54, 56–62, 64 f., 89, 148, 152, 174 ff., 183, 188 f., 191, 196, 201, 203–6, 211–2, 221 f., 229, 251, 314, 368; laws of, 15, 18, 60, 233, 368; will of, 59, 61 f., 222, 321; word of, 58
Goldwin, R. A., 32, 46, 55 f., 63, 92, 94, 100, 128, 130, 141, 145, 147 f., 158, 190, 244, 251, 284, 303 f., 316, 334, 339
Gore, C., 142, 146, 151, 164 f.
Gough, J. W., 31 f., 45, 67, 75, 83, 97, 122, 142, 170, 223, 225, 268, 275, 283 f., 287, 302, 305, 311, 325 ff., 336 f., 339, 346, 357
government, absence of, 82, 86, 89, 101, 105 f., 107–8, 124, 127, 259; authority of, 72, 128, 132, 142, 352 f.; by consent, 39, 64, 75, 77, 110, 112–3, 166, 187, 197, 285, 297–300, 305; civil, 102 ff., 244, 246, 344; dissolution of, 106, 107–14, 120, 123, 124–9, 254, 259, 278–9, 297 f., 308, 339, 347–8, 353–4, 357, 366; forms of, 87, 210, 228 ff., 236, 240 ff., 250 ff., 296 ff., 331–9, 341, 358, 362, 369; 'minimal' or 'negative', 17–21, 71, 208; origins of, 71–2, 82–106, 110, 151, 208, 209–37, 238 ff., 261, 341
Green, T. H., 17, 47–8, 192, 302–3, 320, 325
Griewank, K., 321 f.
Grotius, H., 61, 110 f., 116, 180–200, 206, 370
Grün, K., 163

Harrington, J., 174, 287
hedonism, 34, 36, 48, 58, 62 f., 143, 296

Hegel, G. F. W. 17, 27, 141, 168–71, 176, 179, 239, 283
Hess, M., 163
Hinsley, F. H., 111, 116
history, 17 f., 23, 25, 40, 61, 75, 83, 85, 97, 110, 138, 147, 200, 208–10, 226 f., 230–3, 235 ff., 256, 260, 262, 280, 322, 328, 339
Hobbes, T., 24, 34, 45 ff., 49, 63 f., 66 f., 70, 75, 82, 84 f., 91, 94, 100 ff., 110, 130, 163, 171, 187, 191, 198, 207–8, 212, 254, 256 ff., 267, 295, 306, 325 ff., 367 ff.
Hobhouse, L. T., 142, 144, 165
Hooker, R., 65, 88 f., 216 f., 221, 228, 234, 255
Hume, D., 193 f.

Incorporation by consent, 84–5, 88, 98, 165, 209 f., 219–32, 270, 275 ff., 282, 292, 297, 302, 317, 358
individual, liberty of, 17 f., 21 ff., 27, 53–4, 64, 73, 77–8, 83–5, 91–2, 95, 105, 118–9, 121, 123, 126 f., 132, 135, 162–70, 177, 181, 195, 198–9, 202, 207, 210, 217, 227, 234–5, 284–5, 293, 336, 357, 367, 369; rights of, 18, 47, 60, 63, 66, 69, 74–80, 141, 172 ff., 197, 202, 234, 258 ff., 267, 282, 284, 293, 296
industry, personal, 52, 145, 158 f., 175, 177, 207, 242, 367
inequality, 50, 52, 62, 99, 142, 144, 150, 153 ff., 158, 164, 172, 179, 257, 280, 294
inheritance, 68, 146, 150, 164, 204, 215–6, 268, 270–5, 278, 281, 290, 292
injustice, 206–7
Israel, 200, 221

James I, 250 ff., 262
Jouvenel, B. de, 22, 30
justice, 29, 48, 65, 72 f., 95, 101, 111, 123, 142, 145–6, 172, 174 f., 198, 207–8, 235, 260, 306, 310, 360, 369

Kant, E., 192
Kaplan, A., 26, 137, 293
Kelsen, H., 285
Kendall, W., 20, 31, 45, 65, 67, 73, 75 ff., 83, 142, 146, 188, 212, 223, 225, 244, 247, 277 ff., 284 f., 298, 302 ff., 309, 311, 339, 346
King, Lord Peter, 63, 210

kingship, *see*, monarchy
Krieger, L., 196, 218

labour, 68, 98, 144 ff., 149 f., 153 f., 159, 160–5, 180, 189, 191–203, 259 f., 273
laissez-faire policy, 141, 174, 179, 260
Lamprecht, S. P., 45, 49, 59 ff., 63, 67, 72, 83, 87, 100, 107, 141, 166, 210, 224, 284, 311, 314, 324 f., 339
land, 97–8, 112, 114, 117–8, 120, 144, 146, 148, 150–3, 154, 157 f., 174, 176, 186, 199–203, 269–70, 287
Larkin, P., 142, 145, 165, 170, 173 ff., 192
Laski, H., 283 f., 324, 339
Laslett, P., 25, 31 f., 34, 36, 39, 49, 54, 61, 79, 83, 87, 90, 108, 110, 116, 118, 122, 136, 142, 154, 160 ff., 165, 172, 178, 188, 191, 195, 202 f., 207, 209, 213, 217, 220, 222 f., 226, 229 f., 233, 235 f., 244, 249, 251, 255, 276, 283, 302, 305, 314 f., 325, 336, 341, 344 f., 352, 355, 357 f., 073
Lasswell, H. D., 26, 137, 293
law, 53, 73–5, 105, 159, 165, 167–71, 175, 178, 202 ff., 234–6, 248–9, 252, 276, 284, 304, 333, 346–7, 364 ff., 369, 372; and freedom, 167–70, 285; *see also*, natural law
legislation, 71, 129, 158 f., 173, 214, 235, 329, 334, 347, 357, 359 ff., 362, 365, 370, 372
legislature, the, 38, 69 f., 108, 124 ff., 129, 131, 177 ff., 246, 286, 295, 313, 323–49, 351–61, 365, 369, 372
Lenin, V. I., 18, 200
Leyden, W. von, 31, 45 f., 49, 61, 63, 207, 210
liberalism, 17–26, 32, 45, 72, 116, 141, 144, 165, 171, 181, 198–203, 208, 219, 222, 232, 260, 262, 267, 367, 369, 371–2; and conservatism, 210, 237, 367, 369; and democracy, 19–20, 22–3, 25, 322; and socialism, 198–203, 260
liberty, 17 f., 21 ff., 27, 53–4, 64, 73, 77–8, 83–5, 91–2, 95, 105, 118–9, 121, 123, 126 f., 132, 135, 162–70, 177, 181, 194 f, 198–9, 202, 207, 210, 217, 227, 231, 234–5, 239, 242, 249, 252–3, 255, 260, 272, 274, 278, 280, 284–5, 295, 336, 357, 367, 369; and law, 167–70, 285
life and death, power over, 51, 213, 217, 246
Lindsay, A. D., 22, 207
Lipset, S. M., 20, 29, 93

Loewenstein, K., 371
Luethy, H., 142

Machiavelli, N., 46 f., 236, 239
McIlwain, C. H., 234
Macpherson, C. B., 32 f., 37, 51 f., 55, 78, 94–5, 96–9, 141 ff., 145 f., 153, 158 ff., 166, 170, 173, 177, 188, 200, 283, 288, 290 ff., 296
McShea, R. J., 34
Madison, J., 311, 335, 338
majority, the, 18 f., 40, 47, 53–6, 58, 75, 77–80, 96, 120, 125, 129 f., 165, 172, 178, 186, 223 f., 244, 246 f., 257, 268, 283–93, 294–312, 314, 320, 322, 330, 353, 371
Mannheim, K., 37
marriage, 160, 196, 221
Marx, K., 18–19, 52 f., 163, 190 f., 200
Marxism, 30, 37, 52, 142, 163 f., 169, 177
master-servant relationship, 160–4, 260
Michels, R., 19–20, 21
might, and right, 119, 129–38, 259, 303, 305 f., 320
metapolitics, 34, 40, 75, 138, 256, 259, 262
Mill, J. S., 20, 47, 146, 311, 372
minorities, 18, 58, 75, 77–80, 96, 142, 177 f., 253, 296–7, 300, 302, 306, 309–10, 323
monarchy, 58, 88, 117, 211, 224, 233, 238–63, 289, 366 f., 369; absolute, 101, 103–5, 110, 152, 210, 214, 217, 220, 237, 242–56, 262, 324, 329, 365, 368; elective, 87, 229, 253, 333; not divinely ordained, 210, 243, 255, 262, 367; patriarchal, 209, 221 f., 227–31, 237 f., 245, 256, 261 f., 328, 341
money, 68, 97, 115–7, 142–3, 144, 153–9, 161, 163, 166, 172–4, 191, 259, 280
Monson, C. H., 68, 142, 170, 283
Montesquieu, Charles de Secondat, baron de, 239, 298, 324, 326, 331, 335–8
morality, 71 f., 86, 109 ff., 117, 123, 133 f., 147, 157 f., 165, 170–2, 177, 185, 194 f., 206, 257, 260 f., 267, 304–5, 306, 310, 321, 371, *see also* ethics
More, Sir Thomas, 114, 143, 187
Moulds, H., 45

natural law, 18, 23, 45–81, 83 f., 89, 121–3, 129 f., 135 ff., 142 ff., 158, 165, 167, 171, 181, 194–8, 206, 223, 235, 244, 256–9, 287, 304–5, 316 f., 350, 361, 368,

natural law—*continued*
371; applicability of, 66–75, 80–1, 82, 88, 122, 257; knowability of, 49–56, 70, 75, 82, 88, 94, 257, 294
natural rights, 51 f., 65 ff., 83, 160, 165 ff., 181, 189, 193, 195, 202, 215, 234, 258 ff., 269 ff., 282
nature, state of, 50 f., 71 f., 74, 81, 82–106, 107 f., 124, 126 ff., 135, 141, 160, 169, 207, 223, 226, 232, 249, 258, 368; and state of war, 81, 86, 91–3, 100–3, 128–9, 141, 258 f.
Neumann, F., 19
Newton, I. 178
Niebuhr, R., 67

obligation, 49 f., 80, 172; *see also*, duty
Ogg, D., 235, 344, 355
oligarchy, 19, 58, 330
Oppenheim, F. E., 167

Parliament, 32, 340–3, 352–6, 361 f; *see also*, assemblies, elected
Parry, G., 49, 172, 175, 177, 209, 211
Parsons, T., 137
Partridge, P. H., 323
paternalism, 40, 59, 88, 184–5, 208–20, 222–6, 229, 231 f., 237–40, 246, 251, 255, 261, 275, 327
patriarchalism, 40, 160, 209–23, 226–31, 237 f., 245, 256, 261 f., 327 f., 339, 341
peace, 99 f., 107, 122 f., 214, 259
Pitkin, H., 225, 296
Plamenatz, J. P., 32, 77, 88, 142, 146 f., 194, 201 f., 247, 268, 271, 274 f., 283, 285, 296, 298 ff., 325, 329, 336 f.
Plato, 46 f., 187
Plucknett, E. T., 234
Pocock, J. G. A., 174
Polanyi, M., 230
Polin, R., 31, 36 f., 45, 49, 60, 63, 66, 72, 75 f., 87 f., 90, 93, 99, 107, 119, 122, 130, 137, 141, 145 f., 148, 156, 161 f., 164, 167, 169 f., 173, 175, 188, 192, 221 f., 275, 278, 283, 286, 302, 311, 314, 316, 320, 324 f., 336, 351
political philosophy, 23, 26–31, 36–9, 54, 58, 99, 232, 258, 262
political society, 36, 74 f., 81–106, 107–8, 126, 128 f., 138, 159, 167 f., 171, 203 f., 209–37, 244 f., 259, 261, 263, 267, 269 ff., 274, 279 f., 284, 297, 309
Pollock, F., 83, 141, 209, 336

Popper, K., 76
power, 68, 84, 106, 112, 130–8, 175 f., 223, 247 ff., 270, 304, 323 f.; absolute, 51, 64, 111, 126, 131 f., 241, 245, 248–50, 262, 306; abuse of, 72, 131, 324, 341; and authority, 131, 133–4, 135, 259; arbitrary, 51, 106, 108 f., 121, 123, 125 ff., 131–3, 141, 242–50, 262, 285, 305 f., 315 f., 318, 354 ff., 368, 371; balance of, 80, 262–3, 328–35, 344, 366, 369; executive, 104, 244, 250, 262; legislative, 104, 118, 167, 179, 244, 250, 262; over life and death, 50, 213, 217, 246; parental, 210–2; paternal, 210–229, 270; separation of, 80, 262, 331, 334, 336–8, 344
prerogative, 20, 32, 234, 262, 319, 333, 339–49, 351, 353–66
primogeniture, Locke's objection to, 60, 270
princes, rule of, 69, 72, 80–1, 85–7, 101, 105 ff., 124, 126, 128 f., 136 f., 159, 177, 179, 208, 216–8, 229, 240–63, 295, 307, 309 ff., 319, 323, 325–7, 335–7, 339, 351–9, 362–70, 372; *see also*, monarchy
property, accumulation of, 18, 52, 78, 97–8, 142–53, 154, 158, 170, 173, 180 f., 188–208, 260; community of, 180–208; and membership of political society, 281–2, 290, 291–3; inseparable from political rights and duties, 271–5, 281–2; protection of, the chief end of government, 68, 74, 96, 166, 170, 246
property relations, 138, 141–79, 259–61
property rights, 18, 51–2, 68, 118, 166, 234, 260, 269, 272, 291, 357
Pufendorf, S., 85 f., 180–99, 218, 223, 370
punishment, 50, 57, 63 f., 95–6, 101, 104, 111, 113, 135, 168, 215, 305; capital, 56–7, 63 f., 213 f.

Ranney, A., 285
Rashdall, H., 146, 151, 164
reason, 17 f., 23, 45, 47 f., 50, 53–62, 66 f., 74, 76, 100, 134, 148, 163, 176–7, 189, 203, 209 ff., 228, 231 ff., 237, 257–8, 259, 272, 304, 307, 322, 328, 339
Reasonableness of Christianity, The, 55, 58, 173
rebellion, 136, 316–7; *see also*, revolution
religion, 33 f., 48, 55, 60 f., 63 f., 116 f., 171, 181 f., 191, 197, 211, 213, 217, 233, 248, 258

representation, 178, 285, 323, 339 f., 356 f., 361, 369 ff.
residents, 269–71
revolution, revolt, 18, 24, 35 f., 50, 55, 63 f., 70, 81 f., 100 f., 108–9, 113 f., 118, 123, 127–9, 135–7, 141, 172 f., 178 f., 197, 213, 232, 239, 245, 249, 253 ff., 262 f., 267, 276 f., 279, 282 ff., 286, 290, 293–323, 333, 343, 346, 351, 353 f., 358 f., 364 ff., 371; workers', 173
Richter, M., 192
right, and might, 119, 129–38, 259, 303, 305 f., 320
Rogow, A. A., 20
Rosenstock, E., 317, 321
Rotenstreich, N., 47, 237
Rothman, S., 34
Rousseau, J. J., 22, 76, 78, 86, 101 f., 107, 171, 183, 235, 239, 244
Rowen, H. H., 352
Ruggiero, G. de, 21, 24
Runciman, W. G., 26, 39, 300

Sartori, G., 19, 28, 371
Schlatter, R., 142, 145, 166, 193
Schmidt, H., 192
Schmitt, C., 362
Schulz, I., 116
Schumpeter, J. A., 19, 323
Scripture, see Bible
Second Treatise, 24, 49, 51, 54, 68, 89, 94 ff., 103, 106 f., 118, 131, 158, 173 f., 188, 203–5, 210, 221, 271, 276, 282, 287 ff., 312, 320, 327, 354
security, 65, 202, 369
Selden, J., 206
self-defence, 89, 101, 107, 111, 114
self-determination, national, 113, 120
self-preservation, 36, 46, 48 f., 58, 62–5, 70, 89, 143, 204, 257
Shaftesbury, Earl of, 36, 45, 174, 178, 209, 286, 343
Shils, E., 323
Simon, W., 45, 76, 99, 236
Singh, R., 45, 325 f.
slavery, 116–22, 131–2, 134, 160 f., 259
Smyrniades, E., 283, 302, 311, 316, 324, 339
socialism, 198–203, 260
society, dissolution of, 107–14, 123–4, 259, 306, 308
Some Considerations . . . , 172 ff., 178
Spitz, D., 300

spoilage, prohibition of, 147, 149–53, 156–8
Staël, Mme. de, 23, 219
Stephen, J. F., 339, 344
Stephen, L., 45 f., 67, 87, 141, 209, 224 f., 322
Strauss, L., 32, 33–5, 45 f., 48 f., 55 ff., 60 ff., 74, 78, 83, 87, 94, 100, 124, 127, 130, 141 ff., 145 ff., 153, 167, 211, 296, 324, 339
succession, right of, 229–30, 241, 313–4
'sufficiency clause', 147, 153, 156, 159, 205, 259
suffrage, restricted, 18, 78 f., 177, 268, 276, 283, 285–93, 297, 301, 308, 329; universal, 19, 78 f., 283–93, 311; see also, franchise, reform of

Talmon, J. L., 22 f.
Tawney, R. H., 142–3
Taylor, O. H., 142–3
taxation, 166, 179, 247, 285–6, 362
totalitarianism, 22, 25, 77
trust, 133, 357–9
Tullock, G., 76
Two Treatises of Government, 32, 34, 36, 39 f., 49, 58, 75, 100, 109 f., 121, 130, 137, 148, 152, 177, 195, 206 f., 209–10, 231, 233, 236, 257, 280, 296, 313 f., 322, 327, 352
tyranny, 64, 69, 75, 79, 126, 250–4, 259, 295, 311
Tyrrell, J., 45, 191, 213, 223

umpirage, the people's, 107–8, 294, 308, 368
usurpation, 252–4, 256, 262
utilitarianism, 46–8, 143

Vaughan, C. E., 45, 66 f., 72, 75, 78, 87, 93, 97, 108, 119, 141 f., 166, 209, 226, 269, 278, 283 f., 302, 308, 311, 316, 322, 325, 336, 339, 358
Vile, M. J. C., 335
voluntariness, 221 f.

wage-labour, 145, 161–5, 174, 178, 201
Waldman, M., 225, 275
war, 64, 81, 86, 91–3, 95, 99–103, 106 f., 111 ff., 126 ff., 141, 258–9, 305, 316, 341, 360; see also conquest, foreign
waste, 114–5, 119, 147, 149, 151
Watkins, F., 21

Weber, M., 30, 142, 214, 368
Wheare, K. C., 335
Whigs, 33, 233–4, 287, 333, 343–4, 352, 355, 364 f.
Wolin, S. S., 17, 19 f., 24, 54, 90, 100, 128, 141, 148, 169, 175, 225, 269, 284

women, 211–4
Wormuth, F. D., 358

Yolton, J. W., 46 f., 49, 54, 56, 60 f., 99, 206